Workers' Compensation Law

DELMAR CENGAGE Learning

Options.
Over 300 products in every area of the law: textbooks, online courses, CD-ROMs, reference books, companion websites, and more – helping you succeed in the classroom and on the job.

Support.
We offer unparalleled, practical support: robust instructor and student supplements to ensure the best learning experience, custom publishing to meet your unique needs, and other benefits such as Delmar Cengage Learning's Student Achievement Award. And our sales representatives are always ready to provide you with dependable service.

Feedback.
As always, we want to hear from you! Your feedback is our best resource for improving the quality of our products. Contact your sales representative or write us at the address below if you have any comments about our materials or if you have a product proposal.

Accounting and Financials for the Law Office • Administrative Law • Alternative Dispute Resolution • Bankruptcy • Business Organizations/Corporations • Careers and Employment • Civil Litigation and Procedure • CLA Exam Preparation • Computer Applications in the Law Office • Constitutional Law • Contract Law • Court Reporting • Criminal Law and Procedure • Document Preparation • Elder Law • Employment Law • Environmental Law • Ethics • Evidence Law • Family Law • Health Care Law • Immigration Law • Intellectual Property • Internships • Interviewing and Investigation • Introduction to Law • Introduction to Paralegalism • Juvenile Law • Law Office Management • Law Office Procedures • Legal Nurse Consulting • Legal Research, Writing, and Analysis • Legal Terminology • Legal Transcription • Media and Entertainment Law • Medical Malpractice Law • Product Liability • Real Estate Law • Reference Materials • Social Security • Sports Law • Torts and Personal Injury Law • Wills, Trusts, and Estate Administration • Workers' Compensation Law

DELMAR CENGAGE Learning
5 Maxwell Drive
Clifton Park, New York 12065-2919

For additional information, find us online at:
www.cengage.com/delmar

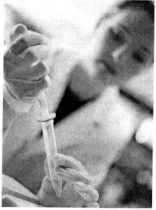

Workers' Compensation Law

by Neal R. Bevans

DELMAR CENGAGE Learning

Australia • Brazil • Japan • Korea • Mexico • Singapore • Spain • United Kingdom • United States

Workers' Compensation Law
Neal R. Bevans

Vice President, Career and Professional
Editorial: Dave Garza

Director of Learning Solutions: Sandy Clark

Acquisitions Editor: Shelley Esposito

Managing Editor: Larry Main

Product Manager: Anne Orgren

Editorial Assistant: Melissa Zaza

Vice President, Career and Professional
Marketing: Jennifer McAvey

Marketing Director: Deborah S. Yarnell

Marketing Manager: Erin Brennan

Marketing Coordinator: Jonathan Sheehan

Production Director: Wendy Troeger

Production Manager: Mark Bernard

Senior Content Project Manager:
Betty L. Dickson

Senior Art Director: Joy Kocsis

Senior Director of Product Management
for Career, Professional, and Languages:
Tom Smith

Production Technology Analyst:
Thomas Stover

© 2009 Delmar, Cengage Learning

ALL RIGHTS RESERVED. No part of this work covered by the copyright herein may be reproduced, transmitted, stored or used in any form or by any means graphic, electronic, or mechanical, including but not limited to photocopying, recording, scanning, digitizing, taping, Web distribution, information networks, or information storage and retrieval systems, except as permitted under Section 107 or 108 of the 1976 United States Copyright Act, without the prior written permission of the publisher.

For product information and technology assistance, contact us at
Cengage Learning Customer & Sales Support, 1-800-354-9706
For permission to use material from this text or product,
submit all requests online at www.cengage.com/permissions
Further permissions questions can be emailed to
permissionrequest@cengage.com

Library of Congress Control Number: 2008929276

ISBN-13: 978-1-4180-1369-1

ISBN-10: 1-4180-1369-2

Delmar
Executive Woods
5 Maxwell Drive
Clifton Park, NY 12065
USA

Cengage Learning is a leading provider of customized learning solutions with office locations around the globe, including Singapore, the United Kingdom, Australia, Mexico, Brazil, and Japan. Locate your local office at **www.cengage.com/global**

Cengage Learning products are represented in Canada by Nelson Education, Ltd.

To learn more about Delmar, visit **www.cengage.com/delmar**

Purchase any of our products at your local bookstore or at our preferred online store **www.cengagebrain.com**

Notice to the Reader
Publisher does not warrant or guarantee any of the products described herein or perform any independent analysis in connection with any of the product information contained herein. Publisher does not assume, and expressly disclaims, any obligation to obtain and include information other than that provided to it by the manufacturer. The reader is expressly warned to consider and adopt all safety precautions that might be indicated by the activities described herein and to avoid all potential hazards. By following the instructions contained herein, the reader willingly assumes all risks in connection with such instructions. The publisher makes no representations or warranties of any kind, including but not limited to, the warranties of fitness for particular purpose or merchantability, nor are any such representations implied with respect to the material set forth herein, and the publisher takes no responsibility with respect to such material. The publisher shall not be liable for any special, consequential, or exemplary damages resulting, in whole or part, from the readers' use of, or reliance upon, this material.

Printed in the United States of America
2 3 4 5 6   20 19 18 17 16

For my niece and nephew: Katie and Ben Burnett

Contents

PREFACE XV
ACKNOWLEDGMENTS XX

CHAPTER 1 Introduction to Workers' Compensation 1

INTRODUCTION: WHAT IS WORKERS' COMPENSATION? 1
   The Basic Premise of Workers' Compensation 3
   A Short History of Workers' Compensation 4
   Exclusiveness of Remedy 5
   Do Workers' Compensation Statutes Violate the U.S. Constitution? 5

DETERMINING WHO IS COVERED BY WORKERS' COMPENSATION STATUTES 6
   Who Is Covered Under Workers' Compensation? 7
   Persons Who Are Not Covered Under Workers' Compensation 8

WORKERS' COMPENSATION BENEFITS 8
   Medical Expenses 9
   Income During Injury/Illness 9
   Death Benefits 10
   Burial benefits 10
   Determining the Amount of Benefits 10
   Special Protections for Firefighters and Law Enforcement 14
   Denying Benefits for Claims of Fraud 14

CHAPTER 2 Federal Workers' Compensation and Tort Law in Workers' Compensation   24

INTRODUCTION TO FEDERAL PROGRAMS   24
COMMON-LAW INFLUENCES ON WORKERS' COMPENSATION   25
    Negligence   25
       Duty   25
          Assumption of the Risk   26
    Product Liability   26
    Intentional Torts   28
       Injuries Caused by Coworkers   29
FEDERAL WORKERS' COMPENSATION   31
    Federal Employees' Compensation Act   31
       The Federal Workers' Compensation System   32
       A Short History Lesson on Federal Workers' Compensation   32
       Qualifying Under FECA   33
       Exceptions to Federal Workers' Compensation   34
    Federal Workers' Compensation Benefits   35
       Benefits Under the Federal System   35
          Continuation of Pay (COP)   35
    Filing a Federal Workers' Compensation Claim   37
    Criminal Sanctions Under FECA   41
OTHER FEDERAL PROGRAMS THAT PROVIDE COVERAGE FOR EMPLOYEES   41
    Federal Black Lung Program   43
    Social Security   43
       History of Social Security   43
       Social Security Disability Insurance (SSDI)   49
       Supplemental Security Income (SSI)   49
    Medicare and Medicaid   49
       What Is Medicare?   49
       What Is Medicaid?   52
          Qualifying for Medicaid   52
       Comparing Medicare and Medicaid   52

Coordinating Benefits on the State
and Federal Level 54
  Fraud 54
Becoming an Advocate for Others in Social Security
and Medicare Hearings 55
  Compensation 56
The Defense Base Act 56
  Worker Benefits Under DBA 57
    Disability Payments 57
    Medical Benefits 57
    Death Benefits 57
  Who Is Covered Under DBA? 57

CHAPTER 3 Employers and Employees Under Workers' Compensation — 69

INTRODUCTION TO EMPLOYERS AND EMPLOYEES 69

EMPLOYERS AND EMPLOYEES UNDER THE WORKERS' COMPENSATION SYSTEM 70
  Employers Under Workers' Compensation 70
    Minimum Number of Employees 70
    Multiple Employers 71
      Court Doctrines that Determine Employer Status Under Workers' Compensation 72
    Employers Subject to the Workers' Compensation Statute 73
      Partnerships 74
      Statutory Employers 74
        Determining Statutory Employer/Employee Status 77
      Charities and Nonprofit Organizations 77
    Employers Who Wrongfully Deny Workers' Compensation Coverage 79
      What Is Casual Employment? 81

EMPLOYEES UNDER WORKERS' COMPENSATION 83
  Regular Employees 83
  Employees Who Do Not Qualify for Workers' Compensation 83
  Compensation 84
  Domestic Workers 84

Odd Jobs   84
Professional Athletes   84
Subcontractors   85
Independent Contractors   85
   Determining Independent Contractor Status   86
New Restrictions on Employers Under Workers' Compensation   88
  Self-Insurers   89
  Proof of Workers' Compensation Coverage   89

CHAPTER 4 Injuries Under Workers' Compensation   101

INTRODUCTION TO INJURIES   101

DEFINING INJURIES UNDER WORKERS' COMPENSATION   102
  Injuries "Arising out of" and "In the course of" Employment   104
    Defining "Arising out of"   104
    Defining "In the course of"   106

TYPES OF INJURIES UNDER WORKERS' COMPENSATION   107
  Travel to and from Work   109
    Frolic   110
    Detour   110
    Dual Purpose Trips   111
  Horseplay   112
  Psychological Injuries   112
  Acts of God or Nature   113
  Assault   114
  Preexisting Injuries   114
    Subsequent Injury   114
  Suicide   115
  Intoxication   116
  Occupational Diseases   116
    Defining Occupational Diseases   117
  Activities Not Strictly Related to Work   117
    Personal Comfort Doctrine   118
    Emergencies   119

CHAPTER 5 Benefits Under Workers' Compensation — 138

INTRODUCTION   138
MEDICAL BENEFITS   139
   Waiving Medical Benefits   140
   Physical Rehabilitation   141
   Transportation   141
   Non-Standard Injuries or Illnesses   141
   Preexisting Injuries or Illnesses   141
   The "Healing Period"   142
DISABILITY PAYMENTS   143
   Temporary Partial Disability   143
   Temporary Total Disability   143
      Differentiating Between Temporary and Permanent   145
   Permanent Partial Disability   145
      Defining Partial Disability   146
   Permanent Total Disability   150
   Lump Sum Disability Payments   151
   Awards for Pain and Suffering   151
   Earning Capacity   152
   Awards for Multiple Injuries   153
   Disfigurement   153
   Preexisting Conditions   153
VOCATIONAL REHABILITATION AND JOB PLACEMENT SERVICES   155
   Job Placement Services   156
DEATH BENEFITS   156
DENIAL OR TERMINATION OF BENEFITS   157
   False Representations by the Employee   158
   Refusing Medical Treatment   159
   Illegal Aliens, Immigration Status   160
CASE MANAGEMENT ISSUES IN WORKERS' COMPENSATION   160
   Case Manager   160
CATASTROPHIC CLAIMS   162
   What Qualifies as a Catastrophic Claim?   163

CHAPTER 6 The Workers' Compensation System 173

INTRODUCTION TO THE WORKERS'
COMPENSATION SYSTEM 173
   Benefit Disputes 174
FILING A CLAIM 174
   Statutes of Limitation 177
   Notice of Hearing 177
   Filing Forms 178
PREPARING FOR THE HEARING 180
   Discovery in Workers' Compensation
     Hearings 180
   Types of Discovery 184
     Depositions 184
       Video Depositions 184
     Interrogatories 185
     Request for Production of Medical Records 185
     Request for Independent Medical Examination 185
   Refusal to Abide by Discovery 186
   Reviewing the Workers' Compensation File 186
     Adding Documents to the File 187
WORKERS' COMPENSATION HEARINGS 187
   Benefit Review Conference 187
   Arbitration Hearings 189
   Hearings 194
     Location of the Hearing 194
     Hearing Date 194
     Canceling the Hearing 194
   Representation at the Hearing 194
     Compensating Attorneys 195
   Evidentiary Rules 197
ADMINISTRATIVE LAW JUDGES 198
   Powers of the ALJ 198
   Communicating with Administrative Law Judges 199
   Requesting a Different Judge 199
   Administrative Law Judge's Role at the
     Hearing 199

CONDUCTING THE HEARING 200
   Witnesses 200
      Subpoenas 200
      Direct Examination 201
      Cross Examination 202
      Rule of Sequestration 202
      Refusal to Testify 202
INITIAL AND FURTHER HEARINGS 203
   Recording the Hearing 203
   Concluding the Hearing 203
   Settling Workers' Compensation Cases 203

CHAPTER 7 Workers' Compensation Insurance   211

INTRODUCTION TO INSURANCE 211
WORKERS' COMPENSATION INSURANCE 213
   Multiple Workers' Compensation Insurance Policies 216
   The Requirement to Provide Insurance 216
      Enrollment in a State-Based Insurance Program 217
      Purchasing Private Insurance 218
      Self-Insurance 218
      Requirement to Invest Funds Collected 218
STATE REGULATION OF WORKERS' COMPENSATION INSURANCE 221
   Rates 221
   Premiums 222
      Calculating Premiums 222
      Risk Exposure 222
   Classifications 222
   Refusal to Pay Benefits 222
   Verifying Coverage 224
   Penalties for Failing to Maintain Workers' Compensation Coverage 224
PRACTICAL APPLICATIONS OF INSURANCE COVERAGE 225
   Policy Ambiguities 225
      Font Sizes 226
      Exclusions 226

Documentation to Be Submitted to the Workers' Compensation Board 226
Duty to Defend 227
   Declaratory Judgments 228

CHAPTER Appealing a Workers' Compensation Award   242

INTRODUCTION 242
SETTLEMENT IN WORKERS' COMPENSATION CLAIMS 243
  Compromise and Release 246
    Factors to Consider Before Attempting to Settle 247
    Evaluation of Claims for Settlement Purposes 250
  Creating a C&R Settlement 251
THE WORKERS' COMPENSATION BOARD 251
  Petition for Reconsideration 251
    Deadlines 252
THE WORKERS' COMPENSATION APPEALS BOARD 254
  Procedure at the Workers' Compensation Appeals Board 254
    Actions by the Appeals Board 258
THE STATE COURT OF APPEALS 258
  The Organization of Court Systems in the United States 258
  Courts of Appeal 259
    Terminology in Appellate Courts 260
  The State Supreme Court 260
    Certiorari 261
      Grounds for Granting Cert 261
  The Federal Appellate Court System 261
  The U.S. Supreme Court 262
BRINGING AN APPEAL 263
  Notice of Appeal 263
  Appellate Briefs 263
    Contents of an Appellate Brief 263
      Title Page 264
      Statement of Facts 264
      Enumerations of Error 264
      Argument 264
      Conclusion 264

POWERS OF APPELLATE COURTS 265
  Affirming a Decision 265
  Reversing a Decision 265
  Modifying a Decision 265
  Remanding a Case 266

CHAPTER **Medical Utilization Issues in Workers' Compensation** 276

INTRODUCTION 276
PRE-EMPLOYMENT SCREENING 277
EMPLOYER INITIATIVES TO DECREASE ON-THE-JOB INJURIES 278
  Near Miss Reports 278
  Enhanced Safety Training 279
MEDICAL UTILIZATION ISSUES 279
  Tracking Medical Costs 279
  Income-Based Disparities 280
PROPOSALS TO CHANGE THE WORKERS' COMPENSATION SYSTEM 280
  Medical Fee Schedules 281
  Evidence-Based Medicine 282
  Training Physicians in Disability Ratings 282
  Generic Drug Initiatives 283
  New and Better Training Programs for Claims Handlers 283
  Revised Sanctions and Fines Under the Workers' Compensation System 283
  Streamlined Grievance Procedures 292
  Better Fraud Detection 292

APPENDIX A – State-by-State Listing of Workers' Compensation Web Sites 303
GLOSSARY 305
INDEX 309

Preface

Workers' compensation law is one of the most important specialties in modern legal practice. Chances are high that anyone who is employed will, at some time, receive an injury, suffer an illness, or incur some occupational disease that will mean filing and perhaps adjudicating a workers' compensation claim. Many paralegals find themselves interviewing for and eventually working at firms that specialize in this area of the law. These are all good reasons for a text focusing on workers' compensation law. This book was written with the needs of paralegal students in mind. It introduces students to the basic foundations of the workers' compensation system and then builds toward more complicated issues.

FEATURES OF THE TEXT

The text has numerous features that take advantage of the various learning styles that students employ and/or find most comfortable. Based on the recognition that students who apply their newly acquired knowledge often retain it much better than those who do not, this text requires students to apply the knowledge that they have gained. Each chapter has practical examples of workers' compensation in action and also relies heavily on the abundant information to be found on the Internet.

- Each chapter analyzes important aspects of workers' compensation law, including exclusiveness of remedy, rights, duties and responsibilities of the parties, the participants, and the important role played by attorneys and paralegals in filing, pursuing, and settling workers' compensation claims.
- Significant cases are excerpted and explored in great detail.

- Web sites for further research and/or discussion are provided at the end of each chapter.
- Chapter discussions are geared toward a real-world understanding of the workers' compensation system and demystifying what can often be a complex area of the law.
- Numerous scenarios and practical examples are offered to bring home the issues discussed in each chapter.
- Practical assignments are given, based on real-world problems faced by employers, injured workers, paralegals, and attorneys, among others.
- Sidebars are presented in each chapter addressing a wide variety of issues.
- The end-of-chapter exercises, hands-on assignments, and practical applications emphasize the theoretical concepts presented in the text.
- The material is also topical, including discussions about ethical concerns for legal professionals, with extensive emphasis on the role of the paralegal specializing in a workers' compensation practice.

KEY FEATURES OF EACH CHAPTER

Each chapter has numerous features designed to assist the student in achieving a thorough understanding of workers' compensation law, including:

- *Learning objectives are stated at the beginning of each chapter.*
  The learning objectives for the chapter are stated clearly and succinctly at the beginning of each chapter. These learning objectives help the student and the instructor focus on the critical issues for each chapter and provide the student with a method for evaluating the student's mastery of the material.
- *Terms and legal vocabulary are defined immediately for the student.*
  The first time a key word or legal term is mentioned in the text, a definition of it appears in the margin. This helps students grasp the meaning without breaking into the flow of the reading by having to turn to the glossary.
- *Exhibits and tables are offered to illustrate crucial points and are designed to capitalize on different student learning styles.*
  The author provides numerous exhibits and tables to develop certain points from the material. This feature takes advantage of the different learning styles among students, allowing those geared to a more visual learning style the opportunity to absorb the material appropriately.

- ***Numerous examples are provided to help students develop their understanding of the material.***
  The author uses examples and scenarios to emphasize particular issues raised in the text. These examples and scenarios also provide a jumping off point for classroom discussion.
- ***Case law that explores topics raised in the chapter.***
  Each chapter contains an appellate case, edited for length and focused on specific issues, taken from various state jurisdictions. The chapter case excerpts are all adapted from WESTLAW and are reprinted with permission. These cases emphasize and reinforce concepts raised in the chapter. The author also includes a question section at the end of each case that is directed to specific issues in the case.
- ***Numerous sidebars accompany the chapters.***
  Each chapter also contains numerous sidebars. These explore aspects of the text in greater detail, explaining numerous facets of workers' compensation law.
- ***End-of-chapter questions, activities, and assignments are provided to increase student comprehension and retention of the concepts presented in the chapter.***
  End-of-chapter exercises include review questions, practical applications of theoretical concepts, and additional material to assist the student in continuing to apply the concepts presented in the chapter.
- ***Ethics block to encourage student awareness of real-life issues.***
  Ethics is crucial for any legal professional. Each chapter explores an important ethical question and explains the relevance of ethical systems for the day-to-day practice of law.
- ***Web sites for further research and/or discussion are included throughout the text.***
  Each chapter contains Web references related to the forms and examples provided in that chapter. Students are provided with the links to assist them with exercises, examples, and figures provided in each chapter. These exercises help students reach a better understanding of the concepts discussed in the chapter and how these concepts apply to real-world applications.
- ***State Workers' Compensation Web sites are provided in Appendix A.***
  The author provides a complete set of state workers' compensation Web sites for all 50 states, as well as for the federal workers' compensation system and additional U.S. territories in the appendix. This aids students in applying the general materials in the text to their specific state law.

- *Glossary containing definitions of all terms used in the text is located at the end of the textbook.*
  All of the terms and phrases defined throughout the text are also provided in a handy glossary.

PEDAGOGY

Because workers' compensation law depends so heavily on administrative rules and regulations, it is especially important to have a text that presents the concepts in clearly written passages that relate workers' compensation concepts to real-world examples. The author builds on preliminary information to expand the student's understanding of the workers' compensation system and other vitally important concepts. The text follows a logical pattern, developing underlying concepts, then moving toward rights and duties of employers and employees, then to the adjudication of a workers' compensation claim, and concluding with an examination of settlement and appellate issues raised in such cases. In order to maximize the learning experience, the author also relies on charts, tables, diagrams, forms, and exhibits to emphasize particular points throughout the text. At the conclusion of each chapter, the author presents practical, hands-on assignments and discussion questions that help to engage students in many of the issues and concepts developed in the chapters. The author establishes a balance of theoretical discussion with real-world examples, and legal concepts with practical examples.

NON-GENDER-SPECIFIC LANGUAGE

In recognition of the impact of gender-specific language, the author has adopted the following convention in the text: Wherever possible, the author has refrained from using "he" and instead has adopted other terms to negate gender specific concepts.

SUPPLEMENTS

Printed Instructor's Manual

The author has developed an instructor's manual to accompany the text. Recognizing the needs of instructors for multiple resources, the author has provided the following features:

- *Suggested syllabi and lesson plans*
- *Annotated outlines for each chapter*

- *Answers to all end-of-chapter questions*
- *Test bank*

    The test bank includes a variety of test questions, including:

    - Essay questions (5 per chapter)
    - Short Answer (10 per chapter)
    - Multiple Choice (25 per chapter)
    - True-False (10 per chapter)

ONLINE INSTRUCTOR'S MANUAL

The online instructor's manual makes available PowerPoint® slides for each chapter and an electronic version of the Instructor's Manual.

ONLINE COMPANION FOR STUDENTS

The Online Companion™ provides students with additional support materials. The Online Companion™ can be found at <http://www.paralegal.delmar.cengage.com> in the Online Companion™ section of the Web site.

ONLINE STUDY GUIDE

The Online Study Guide contains key terms, review questions, and case studies.

WEB PAGE

Come visit our Web site at <http://www.paralegal.delmar.cengage.com> where you will find valuable information such as hot links and sample materials to download, as well as other Delmar, Cengage Learning products.

Acknowledgments

The author would like to thank the following people for their assistance in creating this book:

Deborah Bevans, Diane Colwyn, Shelley Esposito, Lisa McHugh, Darlene Burgess, Steve Willis, and Alicia Parks.

REVIEWERS

Henry H. Arnold, III,
Aiken Technical College

Les Ennis,
Samford University

William R. Foman,
South University

Brian J. Halsey,
Pierce College

Shepard A. Jacobson,
Fullerton College

Elizabeth Mann,
Greenville Technical College

George Waldron,
Quinnipiac University

Lorrie Callison Watson,
Orangeburg–Calhoun Technical College

Mitzi Wortman,
San Francisco State University

Introduction to Workers' Compensation

CHAPTER 1

CHAPTER OBJECTIVES

At the completion of this chapter, you should be able to:

- Explain the purpose of Workers' Compensation
- Describe who is—and who is not—covered by workers' compensation statutes
- Define "exclusiveness of remedy"
- Describe the types of benefits available to injured employees
- Explain the historical development of workers' compensation

INTRODUCTION: WHAT IS WORKERS' COMPENSATION?

Workers' compensation is a form of insurance that guarantees compensation to injured workers for medical expenses, rehabilitation, and weekly wages until the employee has recovered sufficiently to return to work. Under workers' compensation, an employee waives his or her right to bring an independent action for a work-related injury. Employers, who fund the Workers' Compensation system, cannot be sued in civil court for workers' injuries. Essentially, both parties give up something of value in exchange for greater security. Employees give up rights to bring independent suits in exchange for more or less guaranteed awards

Workers' compensation
A system created in the early twentieth century to provide minimal medical coverage and benefits for injured workers.

for injuries. Employers pay into a system that is more liberal in making awards to injured employees than the civil system, but receive the assurance that they will not be hit with large jury awards from civil cases.

Checklist

A client has come to our office with a complaint about a knee injury that she says she received on the job. What do we need to know from this client? Here is a partial list of necessary information, along with references to various state agencies that provide additional information on the questions.

1. Was she employed at the time of her injury?

    Ask the employee to detail not only what company she was working for, but what her duties were and who actually paid her salary.

2. What should we do if the employee doesn't speak English?

    An administrative law judge will hire an interpreter for the hearing, but you may need to arrange for an interpreter in order to interview her.
    http://www.ica.state.az.us/faqs/alj/Hearings_English.html

3. What precisely happened at the time of her injury?

    Here you must focus on the details: who, what, when, where, and how the injury occurred. http://www.maine.gov/wcb/departments/Claims/claimsindex.htm

4. Did the employee report her injury to her employer?

    Employer must be notified of an injury within 30 days of the occurrence.
    http://www.wcb.state.ny.us/content/main/onthejob/OnTheJobInjury.jsp

5. If the employee notified her employer of her injury, did the employer agree to file a workers' compensation claim?

    A claim must be filed via the "employer's workers' compensation insurance carrier" if the employer refused to file a claim on the employee's behalf.
    http://www.state.sd.us/applications/LD01DOL/frameset.asp?navid=&filtertype=1

6. If the injury required medical attention, did a "designated ... medical provider" perform the treatment?

    Employee may be liable for medical costs where he/she fails to obtain treatment from a medical provider elected by the employer. http://www.coworkforce.com/dwc/FAQs/InjuredWorkerFAQs.asp

7. What is the total amount of earnings received by the employee; and, can she provide source documents to support those earnings?

The workers' compensation insurer must be provided with a report of all wages, included wages received from a source other than the employer who has/will file a claim. *http://www.dli.state.pa.us/landi/cwp/view.asp?A=138&Q=61519*

8. Is she scheduled to undergo an independent medical examination?

An employee must undergo an IME, either scheduled by the employer or the employer's workers' compensation insurer. *http://www.gencourt.state.nh.us/rules/lab500.html*

The Basic Premise of Workers' Compensation

The basic premise behind workers' compensation is that an injured worker will receive a specified monetary award for a particular injury. Under workers' compensation, employees and employers do not have to waste time and resources pursuing personal injury actions. Instead, both parties are assured of, to a reasonable degree of certainty, exactly what an injured employee will receive in the event of a job-related injury. However, that simple idea has spawned an entire industry of lawyers, doctors, insurance companies, and an entire branch of law devoted to adjudicating these claims.

The critical component of the workers' compensation system is that it is a "no-fault" arrangement. Employers agree to pay all bills associated with an on-the-job injury and employees agree not to bring independent civil suits against employers for their injuries. In the 1920s, many states amended their workers' compensation rules to include not only work-related injuries, but also on-the-job illnesses, such as black lung disease, suffered by coal miners. These days, on-the-job illnesses and injuries can include a wide variety of complaints from broken bones to carpal tunnel syndrome.

Employees do not pay into the workers' compensation system; employers do. Most employers have insurance carriers who handle actual payments to injured workers. Payment amounts are determined by preset formulas, with so much money allotted for an injured hand, foot, spine, and so on. When there is a dispute between employers and employees, or insurance carriers and employees, the case is referred to a **Workers' Compensation Board** that is empowered to make binding decisions on amounts. Workers' Compensation Boards do not make determinations of liability or fault. Instead, they decide if the employee should receive compensation. The Workers' Compensation Board is part of the state government. This board has the right to reinstate or modify the original benefits. The board's decision comes at the conclusion of a hearing that resembles the trial of a civil case. In a later chapter, we will address the similarities, and important differences, between workers' compensation hearings and other types of civil actions.

> **SIDEBAR**
>
> Workers' compensation works like insurance: the employer pays into a fund and an injured employee is compensated from this fund.

Workers' Compensation Board
The governmental unit responsible for administering the workers' compensation system.

A Short History of Workers' Compensation

Workers' compensation movements began in the early part of the twentieth century as a direct response to the Industrial Revolution and the problems that it spawned. Prior to the creation of workers' compensation statutes, an injured worker's only recourse was to sue the company for his medical bills and lost wages. The state of tort law at the time heavily favored employers and the result was that an injured employee would often receive nothing for an on-the-job injury.

Prior to the enactment of workers' compensation statutes, the law took a harsh view of employee injuries. Courts ruled that the employee had assumed the risk of any injury by accepting employment. See Exhibit 1-1. The law on workers' compensation underwent dramatic changes in the second decade of the twentieth century. Many workers' compensation statutes were enacted in 1913 and 1914 and were heavily influenced by European systems that took a more advanced view of the topic. Under the European system, workers who were injured on the job were compensated out of a fund created and maintained by employers.

Before the enactment of workers' compensation statutes, employers could raise any of several defenses to paying any compensation to an injured employee. These defenses included:

- Assumption of the risk (that the employee had assumed the risk by accepting employment)

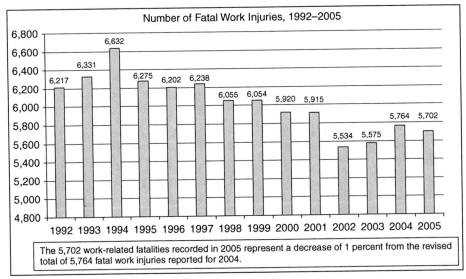

EXHIBIT 1-1 Number of Fatal Work Injuries, 1992–2005. *Bureau of Labor Statistics.*
Note: Data from 2001 exclude fatalities resulting from the September 11 terrorist attacks.
Source: U.S. Department of Labor, Bureau of Labor Statistics, Census of Fatal Occupational Injuries, 2005.

- Negligence of the employee (that the employee's own negligence caused the injury and therefore the employer was not liable)
- Intentional actions by third parties (that some person, other than the employer, had caused the employee's injuries, thus relieving the employer of liability)

Exclusiveness of Remedy

Workers' compensation is often referred to as an **exclusive remedy**, meaning that the workers' compensation system is the only forum through which the parties can work out their differences. Normally, a person who is injured by the negligence of another has the right to bring a personal injury action against the person who caused the injury. Personal injury cases are some of the most common lawsuits in the United States today. However, workers' compensation statutes specifically bar employees from bringing these actions. Instead, they must bring their claim through the workers' compensation system or not at all. When these statutes were originally enacted, several important questions had to be answered, such as whether Workers' Compensation deprives workers of important constitutional rights.

Exclusive remedy
The only legal remedy available to the parties.

Do Workers' Compensation Statutes Violate the U.S. Constitution?

In reviewing workers' compensation statutes, an important question often arises: Do these statutes take away some employees' constitutional rights? For instance, if the statute requires employees to submit their claims to the Workers' Compensation Board and bars them from bringing civil suits, is that an unconstitutional infringement of a citizen's rights? In the United States people are guaranteed access to the courts. When the states adopted workers' compensation statutes, many amended their constitution to address this question of surrendering important constitutional rights. Courts have also ruled that, although the exclusivity arrangement of workers' compensation statutes does abridge an important right, the new rights conferred by the statutes outweigh the rights lost. (For an explanation of this outlook, see this chapter's Case Excerpt.)

Workers' compensation statutes are a balancing act: They both confer rights and remove others. Employees who have claims against employers can submit their claims to an administrative law judge in a system that is far more liberal than the regular court system. In exchange for that benefit, they give up an important right—the power to sue the employer over the injury. Personal

> **SIDEBAR**
>
> Courts have ruled that the exclusivity provision of workers' compensation statutes is not unconstitutional.

> **SIDEBAR**
>
> Other challenges to workers' compensation statutes include due process claims. Employees have claimed that workers' compensation statutes have denied due process rights guaranteed under the Fifth and Fourteenth Amendments to the U.S. Constitution. Courts have ruled that denied this claim.[1]

injury cases are brought everyday in the United States, but not by employees who are covered by workers' compensation statutes. Those employees must go through the workers' compensation system. They cannot opt to forego their benefits under workers' compensation in order to bring a civil suit; they are stuck with the workers' compensation system for almost all injuries.

DETERMINING WHO IS COVERED BY WORKERS' COMPENSATION STATUTES

Employees who are covered by workers' compensation statutes surrender their right to sue the employer in exchange for guaranteed payments for medical bills and lost wages. However, not all employee injuries fall within the jurisdiction of the workers' compensation system. Some injuries are excluded from coverage, meaning that the employee and employer can bring suit in a civil court. These exceptions include:

- Injuries brought about by the employee's voluntary intoxication
- Injuries brought about by the employee's willful intent
- Injuries brought about by the intentional action of the employer

An employer may also not be covered by the workers' compensation system when the employer fails to acquire workers' compensation insurance. Such failure places the issues outside the workers' compensation system and permits the employee to bring a civil suit against the employer.

Checklist

A new business owner needs help determining if he will need to purchase insurance for his company. What clarifications must be gathered in order to decide whether he is required to purchase worker's compensation insurance or not?

1. What type of business form is the business? Is it a corporation? A sole proprietorship?

    A sole proprietorship may opt out of purchasing worker's compensation insurance as long as the business owner has no employees. All other business entities are required to carry either worker's compensation insurance or, if able to meet qualifications, individual self-insurance. http://www.dir.ca.gov/dwc/faqs.html

2. What type of industry is the company in?

    Where the statute requires companies employing one or more workers to carry worker's compensation insurance, in the industry of farming that coverage is not mandatory, only optional. http://delawareworks.com/industrialaffairs/services/WorkersCompInfo.shtml#covered

3. Will any of the employees be paid strictly on a commission basis?

   The insurance policy does not provide protection for workers who are not compensated by the business owner in relation to the hours they work, but are instead paid an amount determined by their sales. http://www.rilin.state.ri.us/Statutes/TITLE28/29-29/28-29-7.1.HTM

4. Does the sole proprietor also want workers' compensation for himself?

   Owners/partners will be covered by worker's compensation when they specifically incorporate their names into the application. If they fail to do so, they will not be covered because owners and partners do not fall under the definition of employee. http://www.iowaworkforce.org/wc/faq.htm#eligible

5. At any given time, will the business hire a subcontractor and/or consultant?

   If subcontractors/consultants have purchased their own worker's compensation insurance, a business owner/contractor will not have to include them in the company's policy. http://sbwc.georgia.gov/00/article/0,2086,11394008_11400533_13292004,00.html

6. Will any of his employees be working under the classification of part time?

   Part-time employees must be covered by worker's compensation insurance if their work is ongoing. http://wcbnec03.wcb.state.in.us/faq.asp

7. What is the net worth of the company?

   An employer is required to have at least a 5 million dollar value on the company's net worth in order to be granted permission to bypass the required worker's compensation insurance. However, it is then be mandatory for the employer to purchase individual self-insurance. http://dir.alabama.gov/wc/insurance.aspx#indivself

8. At any time, will the business owner allow subordinates to be employed by his employees?

   A business owner will be held liable for "all helpers and assistants ... if employed with the knowledge ... of the employer." Therefore, they must be covered by the company's worker's compensation insurance. http://www3.state.id.us/cgi-bin/newidst?sctid=720020004.K

Who Is Covered Under Workers' Compensation?

The question of coverage under workers' compensation is an important one. If an employee is covered, it means that he or she will probably receive some kind of medical treatment, payment of medical bills, and payment of a percentage of weekly income. If the employee is not covered by workers' compensation, then the employee must sue the employer for these benefits. There is often a huge disparity between the financial resources of employees and those of employers. The chances of an individual prevailing over a large, multinational corporation are slim. State workers' compensation statutes provide that the following employees are covered under workers' compensation:

- Employees who are employed by for-profit businesses
- Employees who work for counties and towns and work in "hazardous" areas
- Most public school teachers, with some important exceptions
- Employees who work 40 or more hours per week
- Seasonal or agricultural workers who earn $1,200 or more
- Any other employee deemed covered by the state Board of Workers' Compensation

Persons Who Are Not Covered Under Workers' Compensation

Just as important as the question of who is covered under workers' compensation statutes is the question of who is not. State boards have ruled that the following individuals do not fall under the protection of workers' compensation:

- Members of the clergy
- Teachers at religious institutions
- Members of the merchant marines and other sea-going professions
- Railroad workers
- Federal employees
- Casual laborers
- Employees of foreign governments
- Sole proprietors and other small business owners

WORKERS' COMPENSATION BENEFITS

Once the question of who is covered by workers' compensation benefits is answered, the next question concerns exactly what these benefits are. Workers' compensation benefits include:

- Medical expenses
- Income during the injury/illness

National and Florida Rates of Permanent Total (PT) Disability

Policy Period	Florida's PT Rate per 100,000 Workers	National PT Rate per 100,000 Workers*	Florida's Ranking**
10/88–9/89	67	N/A	1
10/89–9/90	52	N/A	1
10/90–9/91	22	7	5
10/91–9/92	18	5	3
10/92–9/93	9	4	4
10/93–9/94	16	5	2
10/94–9/95	23	7	1
10/95–9/96	27	7	2

*Excludes California, Delaware, Massachusetts, Minnesota, New York, Pennsylvania, and Texas.
**Includes all states.
Source: National Council on Compensation Insurance's Annual Statistical Bulletins, 1993–2000.

EXHIBIT 1-2

Florida Permanent Total Supplemental Benefits in Workers' Compensation Cases, 1995–2006.

- Death benefits
- Burial benefits

Medical Expenses

The **medical expense** benefit provided under workers' compensation pays the total cost of the medical bills that flow from treating the injury or illness. Most workers' compensation statutes provide that all medical expenses reasonable and necessary to the employee's recovery must be paid.

▪ **Medical expense**
Payment for treatment received by an injured worker for a covered accident or illness.

Income During Injury/Illness

Workers' compensation also provides for payments to an injured employee during the period that he or she is unable to work because of a work-related injury or illness. These payments are usually a percentage of the employee's total income. As we will see in later chapters, the amount that an employee actually receives varies according to several factors, including the extent of the employee's injuries, whether the employee's impairment is permanent or temporary, and whether the employee can return to work. For instance, many states have schemes that allow an employee to receive 70 percent of his or her income as a temporary **income benefit**. In later chapters, we will also examine the issue of supplemental income benefits. See Exhibit 1-2.

▪ **Income benefit**
Payments made to an injured worker to provide some percentage of income during the worker's rehabilitation or permanent injury period.

Death Benefits

Death benefits under workers' compensation pay family members for some of the income lost because of an employee's death. Only certain family members are qualified to receive death benefits. These include spouses, dependent children, and/or grandchildren. See Exhibit 1-3 and Exhibit 1-5.

Death benefit
Payment to a deceased worker's family.

Burial Benefits

Workers' compensation also provides some costs that can be applied to an employee's burial expenses. For example, many states provide a maximum $6,000 benefit for an employee's funeral expenses under the **burial benefit** provisions of a workers' compensation insurance plan. See Exhibit 1-4.

Burial benefit
Payment for a portion of an injured worker's burial costs.

Determining the Amount of Benefits

One of the responsibilities of a state Board of Workers' Compensation is to determine the extent of the employee's injuries. For instance, if the employee is found to be temporarily totally disabled, the employee will receive two-thirds of the employee's weekly wage for as long as the disability remains. See Exhibit 1-4.

As part of the process, the injured employee must submit to an independent medical examination by medical professionals hired by the employer. The board will also hold a hearing to determine what benefits, if any, should be awarded to the employee. Following a hearing, the employee can contest the administrative law judge's decision by requesting a review. If the employee is still not satisfied, he or she can file an appeal to the Appellate Division of the Workers' Compensation Board.

As we will see in Chapter 6, workers' compensation hearings are not conducted in the same way, or with the same formalities, as are civil jury trials. In fact, workers' compensation hearings are informal, have no juries, and are frequently held in office buildings instead of courthouses.

INSIDER'S VIEWPOINT: Workers' Compensation Hearings

"Workers' compensation hearings are very informal," according to Norma Schvaneveldt, who has spent the last 17 years working as a paralegal in all varieties of litigation from personal injury to workers compensation and Social Security hearings. "Unlike personal injury, where you have lots of court hearings and full blown trials, workers'

STATE OF CALIFORNIA
DEPARTMENT OF INDUSTRIAL RELATIONS
DIVISION OF WORKERS' COMPENSATION

FORWARD TO

P.O. BOX 422400
SAN FRANCISCO CA 94142

NOTICE OF EMPLOYEE DEATH

EACH EMPLOYER SHALL NOTIFY THE ADMINISTRATIVE DIRECTOR OF THE DEATH OF EVERY EMPLOYEE REGARDLESS OF THE CAUSE OF DEATH EXCEPT WHERE THE EMPLOYER HAS ACTUAL KNOWLEDGE OR NOTICE THAT THE DECEASED EMPLOYEE LEFT A SURVIVING MINOR CHILD (TITLE 8, CHAPTER 4.5, SECTION 9900).

DECEASED EMPLOYEE:

NAME: _____ AGE: _____ SOCIAL SECURITY NUMBER: _____

LAST KNOWN ADDRESS: _____

NAME, RELATIONSHIP AND LAST KNOWN ADDRESS OF NEXT OF KIN: _____

JOB TITLE AND NATURE OF DUTIES: _____

DATE, TIME AND PLACE OF ACCIDENT: _____

DATE, TIME AND PLACE OF DEATH: _____

CIRCUMSTANCES OF DEATH (DESCRIBE FULLY THE EVENTS WHICH RESULTED IN DEATH. TELL WHAT HAPPENED. USE ADDITIONAL SHEET IF NECESSARY):

CAUSE OF DEATH (ATTACH COPY OF DEATH CERTIFICATE OR CORONER'S REPORT):

HAVE ANY WORKERS' COMPENSATION DEATH BENEFITS BEEN PROVIDED IN CONNECTION WITH THIS DEATH? ____YES ____NO
IF YES, TO WHOM: _____

ATTACH A COPY OF THE FORM 5020, "EMPLOYER'S REPORT OF OCCUPATIONAL INJURY OR ILLNESS," IF ONE WAS FILED.

PLEASE NOTE:

IF THE DEATH IS WORK-RELATED, THE EMPLOYER ALSO IS REQUIRED TO REPORT THE DEATH TO HIS OR HER WORKERS' COMPENSATION INSURANCE CARRIER AND TO THE NEAREST OFFICE OF THE DIVISION OF INDUSTRIAL SAFETY IMMEDIATELY BY TELEPHONE OR TELEGRAPH. AN EMPLOYER'S REPORT OF OCCUPATIONAL INJURY OR ILLNESS SHOULD ALSO BE FILED WITH THE WORKERS' COMPENSATION INSURANCE CARRIER.

( ) INSURED   ( ) SELF-INSURED   ( ) LEGALLY UNINSURED

EMPLOYER: _____

INSURANCE CARRIER
OR ADJUSTING AGENT: _____

STREET: _____

STREET: _____

CITY/STATE: _____ ZIP: _____

CITY/STATE: _____ ZIP: _____

TELEPHONE: _____
(INCLUDE AREA CODE)

TELEPHONE: _____
(INCLUDE AREA CODE)

BY: _____

TITLE: _____

DATE: _____

DIA 510 (REV. 9/84)

EXHIBIT 1-3 Notice of Employee Death (California). *Reprinted courtesy of the California Chamber of Commerce.*

Texas Department Of Insurance
Division of Workers' Compensation
Records Processing
7551 Metro Center Dr. Ste.100 • MS-94
Austin, TX 78744-1609
(800) 252-7031 (512) 804-4378 fax www.tdi.state.tx.us

DWC Claim#
Carrier Claim#

← Send the completed form to this address.

Notice of Fatal Injury or Occupational Disease and Claim for Compensation for Death Benefits (DWC Form-042)

• Beneficiaries of an employee who died from an on-the-job injury or occupational disease must file this form with the Texas Department of Insurance, Division of Workers' Compensation (Division) **no later than one year** after the employee's death to protect your claim for entitlement to death benefits.
• If you do not know the answer to a question on this form, please reply "unknown."

I. DECEASED EMPLOYEE INFORMATION

Name (First, Middle, Last)	**Social Security Number**	**Date of birth** (mm / dd / yyyy)
Address at time of death (street, city/town, state, zip code, county, country)		
Race / Ethnicity ☐ White, not of Hispanic Origin ☐ Black, not of Hispanic Origin ☐ Hispanic ☐ Asian or Pacific Islander		
Did the employee speak English? ☐ Yes ☐ No If no, specify language		
Marital status ☐ Married ☐ Widowed ☐ Separated ☐ Single ☐ Divorced	**Sex** ☐ Male ☐ Female	

II. INJURY INFORMATION

Death occurred as a result of an ☐ injury ☐ occupational disease	**Date of injury** (mm / dd / yyyy)	**First work day missed** (mm / dd / yyyy)
Date of Hire (mm / dd / yyyy)	**Occupation at time of injury**	
Time of injury	**Body part affected**	
Describe cause of injury or occupational disease, including how it is work related		
Witness(es) to the injury		
If accident occurred outside of Texas, on what date did the employee leave Texas? (mm/dd/yyyy)		
Where injury/accident occurred **County**	**State**	**Country**
Date of death (mm/dd/yyyy)	**Cause of death**	
If death was the result of an occupational disease: **1. On what date was the employee last exposed to the cause of the occupational disease?** (mm / dd / yyyy) **2. Explain how the disease was related to the employment.**		

III. EMPLOYER INFORMATION (at the time of the injury)

Employer name	**Employer address** (street, city/town, state, zip code, county, country)
Employer phone number	**Supervisor name** (First, Last)

IV. DOCTOR INFORMATION

Name of treating doctor	**Phone number**
Address (street, city/town, state, zip code)	

DWC042 Rev. 03/07 Page 1 of 2

EXHIBIT 1-4 Notice of Fatal Injury or Occupational Disease and Claim for Compensation for Death Benefits (Texas). *Reprinted courtesy of the Texas Department of Information, Workers' Compensation.*

compensation hearings are less formal. Without juries and other courtroom hearings, it really cuts down on what you have to do. When you have a hearing before an administrative law judge, it's not anywhere near as intense as a trial.

EXHIBIT 1-5 Annual Death Benefits Questionnaire (Ohio). *Reprinted courtesy of the Ohio Bureau of Workers' Compensation.*

"The other nice thing about administrative law hearings is that they take advantage of technology. It's almost unheard of to do a telephone conference in the middle of a trial, but you do it all the time in workers' compensation hearings."

Special Protections for Firefighters and Law Enforcement

Included in the benefits awarded to workers are provisions specifically designed to single out certain classes of employees. Firefighters and law enforcement officers, for example, often have a specific statutory protection when it comes to defining "accident" or "injury." In these cases, a statute will require an administrative law judge or Workers' Compensation Appeals Board to presume that any heart or lung disease is caused by working conditions. Most other employees do not receive this special legal presumption (see Exhibit 1-6). The practical effect of such a presumption is to force the employer to prove that the law enforcement officer's heart disease *was not* caused by the job, instead of the other way around. Disproving that presumption may be impossible and creates a powerful protection for firefighters and law enforcement officers. The reasons for creating this special category are plain: Legislators in many states want to offer greater protections for these individuals. It is a small way to offset the detractions of these professions. Firefighters and police officers receive relatively low pay for constantly working under extremely dangerous job conditions.[2] See Exhibit 1-6.

Denying Benefits for Claims of Fraud

All of the benefits discussed so far can be denied in cases where an employee engages in fraud. Examples of fraud are almost too numerous to mention, but can be broken down into major categories. An employee might, for example, make multiple claims on the same injured body part. In other cases, an employee might simply fake an injury or file a claim for an injury that was not work-related. In any of these situations, should the board

EXHIBIT 1-6
Defining "Accident" or "Illness" to Create Presumption in Favor of Firefighters and Law Enforcement Officers.

> Provided, any condition or impairment of health of a full-time paid fireman or law enforcement officer caused by lung or respiratory disease, hypertension, or heart disease resulting in total or partial disability or death shall be presumed to have been suffered in the line of duty and shall not be attributed to any disease existing prior to such total or partial disability or death unless the contrary be shown by competent evidence, provided, further, that such full-time paid fireman or law enforcement officer shall have completed two years of continuous service and have successfully passed a physical examination which examination fails to reveal any evidence of such condition.

> **EXAMPLE 1-1**
>
> Tommy is working as a truck driver and has filed a claim for injuries. Earlier this year, he claims that he stood up while working on a transmission and struck the left side of his neck. When he was taken to the hospital, he reported that the injury was to the right side of his neck. Over the next several weeks, he made conflicting reports about which side of his neck was injured. Later, the attorney representing the employer discovered that Tommy had had a previous neck injury while working for a different employer, but had not revealed that information when the hospital took his medical history. (He also failed to list that information on his employment application, raising some issues we will discuss in a later chapter.) Tommy had surgery on his neck and the physician determined that he has an 80 percent disability ratin. The employer settled with Tommy, accepting that the injury was work related. The court must now consider whether or not to revoke the settlement. What should the court do?

become aware of the fraud, the employee's settlement can be revoked. Of course, any allegation of fraud must be proven and that can present practical problems. For instance, suppose that the claimant's version differs from that of a witness. How does the court decide which party to believe? What if there is medical testimony supporting the claim, but no proof that the injury occurred on the job? In these cases, the judge must evaluate the credibility of the witnesses, including the worker, and make an independent judgment about the most credible version of the facts. As a general rule, appellate courts will not overturn a judge's on-the-spot evaluation unless it is clearly wrong or runs counter to legal principles. Consider Example 1-1.

Checklist

1. What is the total cost of the medical treatment the injured worker has received?

   All medical costs will be covered by worker's compensation benefits as long as the treatment received is "reasonable and necessary". *http://www.idahosif.org/injured_worker/medical_benefits.aspx*

2. Will the injured worker require additional medical treatment, such as physical therapy or another form of rehabilitation?

   Vocational rehabilitation is available for those injured workers who still experience some physical constraints despite the fact that they have recovered from their work-related injury. *http://www.labor.ky.gov/workersclaims/medicalservices/rehabilitationretraining/*

3. After being broken down into per week amounts, what was the total (weekly) income the injured worker was receiving at the time the injury occurred?

    Worker's compensation benefit checks cover two-thirds of the employee's "average weekly income." The average weekly income is determined by calculating the mean of 13 previous weekly checks, excluding the week the injury occurred. *http://www.fldfs.com/WC/faq/faqwrkrs.html#11*

4. Has the employer's medical provider stated that the worker must remain off-duty for a period longer than 7 days?

    Temporary total disability will be granted to the employee, covering up to 2 years after the injury. *http://www.doli.state.mn.us/guide.html#What%20monetary%20benefits%20are%20available?*

5. Does his case allow for suit to be brought against the manufacturer of the ladder?

    Yes. If the ladder can be proven defective, the employee may bring suit against the third party corporation in addition to receiving worker's compensation benefits from his/her employer. *http://data.opi.state.mt.us/bills/mca/39/71/39-71-412.htm*

6. Does the construction worker have a second job, which he is also unable to attend?

    An employee may be eligible to receive "concurrent employment benefits" if both employers report the employee's wages over the past year. *http://hawaii.gov/labor/dcd/faq.shtml*

7. Did the medical provider determine if the employee is able to return to work while still recovering from his injury?

    If so, an employer is required to "develop a temporary work opportunity for the injured employee." *http://www.labor.state.nh.us/injured_worker_temporary_duty.asp?ptype=*

8. Did the construction worker refuse to follow any of the safety procedures required in the company's employment policy, which could have prevented the injury from occurring?

    Worker's compensation benefits will be reduced 25–50 percent if the employee is found to have ignored safety procedural requirements dictated by the employer. *http://www.dolir.missouri.gov/wc/faq_employers.htm#faq12*

CASE EXCERPT

DO WORKERS' COMPENSATION STATUTES TAKE AWAY IMPORTANT CONSTITUTIONAL PROTECTIONS?

Abbott v. Gould, Inc., 232 Neb. 907, 443 N.W.2d 591 (1989)

CAPORALE, Justice.

In these consolidated appeals the plaintiffs-appellants, a number of former employees and personal representatives of certain former employees of defendant-appellee, Gould, Inc., seek to recover damages allegedly caused by the employer's conduct and that of its contract physician, defendant Robert J. Fitzgibbons, Sr., M.D. Gould demurred in part on the ground that the district court lacks subject matter jurisdiction. That court sustained Gould's demurrers and dismissed the actions as against it, which dismissal the plaintiffs assign as error. We affirm.

Pursuant to the district court's novel "Standing Order," the propriety of which does not now concern us, the various plaintiffs filed a "Master Long Form Petition," setting forth common allegations of fact. In addition, each plaintiff filed a "Short Form Petition," setting forth allegations of fact unique to each.

So far as is relevant to these appeals, the petitions allege that at the relevant times, Gould operated a secondary lead smelting and refining plant; that Gould knowingly misrepresented to its employees that their work environment was reasonably safe and that the clothing and devices provided them and safety precautions taken would protect them from harm; that, in fact, Gould intentionally subjected its employees to contact with and ingestion of various airborne particles and fumes known to Gould to be injurious to human health; that Gould exacerbated the work hazards by intentionally failing to provide adequate safeguards at the worksite and by intentionally refusing to disclose the true hazardous character of the work environment; that in an attempt to cover up the effects of the toxic exposures, Gould falsely and intentionally misrepresented that certain drugs and medications would prevent the harmful effects of whatever substances might be present in the work environment; that, as intended by Gould, its employees relied upon the misrepresentations and were thereby caused to ingest, without their informed consent, certain drugs and medications which independently caused them additional injury; and that Gould accomplished the foregoing in conspiracy with its contract physician.

The Nebraska Workers' Compensation Court has exclusive jurisdiction in actions arising under the Workers' Compensation Act. Neb.Rev.Stat. § 48–101 (Reissue 1988)

Continued

provides, so far as pertinent to our inquiry, for workers' compensation benefits when an employee suffers personal injury caused by an occupational disease which arises out of and in the course of his or her employment.

An occupational disease must be a natural incident of a particular occupation and must attach to that occupation a hazard which distinguishes it from the usual run of occupations and which is in excess of that attending employment in general.

Plaintiffs argue, in effect, that Gould's acts elevated the hazards to which they were exposed to a point well beyond that "natural[ly] incident" to the occupation of lead smelting and that their injuries thus are not within the comprehension of "occupational disease" as that term is used in the Workers' Compensation Act.

In *Marlow v. Maple Manor Apartments*, 193 Neb. 654, 659, 228 N.W.2d 303, 306 (1975), this court held that the Workers' Compensation Act is intended to cover only claims arising out of and in the course of the employment. The operative fact is one of coverage, not of election to file a claim for compensation. If coverage exists, even though for some reason compensation may not be payable, the [Workers'] Compensation Act is exclusive.

The Workers' Compensation Act provides the exclusive remedy by the employee against the employer for any injury arising out of and in the course of the employment. This is the basis on which the rights of employers and employees are put in balance. The employer, by having liability imposed on him without fault, receives in return relief from tort actions.

This court has never before faced the precise question presented in this appeal: whether allegations that an employer intentionally concealed the dangers inherent in the work environment, intentionally inflicted injury resulting in occupational disease, and intentionally concealed the true nature and effect of the disease fall within or without the Workers' Compensation Act.

It is not uncommon for an employer to "put his mind" to the existence of a danger to an employee and nevertheless fail to take corrective action. In many of these cases, the employer does not warn the employee of the risk. Such conduct may be characterized as intentional or even deceitful. Yet if an action at law were allowed as a remedy, many cases cognizable under workers' compensation would also be prosecuted outside that system. The focus of the inquiry in a case involving work-related injury would often be not whether the injury arose out of and in the course of employment, but the state of knowledge of the employer and the employee regarding the dangerous condition which caused the injury. Such a result would undermine the underlying premise upon which the workers' compensation system is based. That system balances the advantage to the employer of immunity from liability at law

Continued

against the detriment of relatively swift and certain compensation payments. Conversely, while the employee receives expeditious compensation, he surrenders his right to a potentially larger recovery in a common law action for the negligence or willful misconduct of his employer. This balance would be significantly disturbed if we were to hold, as plaintiff urges, that any misconduct of an employer which may be characterized as intentional warrants an action at law for damages.

In the present case, plaintiff alleges that defendant fraudulently concealed from him, and from doctors retained to treat him, as well as from the state, that he was suffering from a disease caused by ingestion of asbestos, thereby preventing him from receiving treatment for the disease and inducing him to continue to work under hazardous conditions. These allegations are sufficient to state a cause of action for aggravation of the disease, as distinct from the hazards of the employment which caused him to contract the disease.

The primary object of compensation acts was to do away with the inadequacies and defects of the common-law remedies, to destroy the common-law defenses, and, in the employments affected, to give compensation, regardless of the fault of the employer.

An employer could not, of course, be protected by the provisions of the compensation act where he intentionally inflicts an injury upon an employee. Such an injury could hardly be said to be one which would be incidental to the employment, or one which would arise from the operation of the employer's business.

To ask us to read the compensation act of this jurisdiction in such a way as to require employers not only to provide workers' compensation benefits but also to defend and respond in damages to employee tort actions is to invite us to subvert the very purpose of the whole workers' compensation scheme.

We thus hold that the allegations of the plaintiffs against Gould fall within the ambit of this state's Workers' Compensation Act and that the district court is therefore without subject matter jurisdiction in regard to those allegations.

Remaining to be considered is plaintiffs' contention that to so construe the act is to subject them to involuntary servitude in violation of U.S. Const. amend. XIII and Neb. Const. art. I, § 2, and to deprive them as well of due process by denying them a remedy by due course of law for their injuries, in violation of U.S. Const. amend. XIV and Neb. Const. art. I, §§ 3 and 13.

Plaintiffs' involuntary servitude argument under the federal Constitution is foreclosed by the holding in *U.S. v. Kozminski*, 487 U.S. 931, 108 S.Ct. 2751, 101 L.Ed.2d 788 (1988), to the effect that the conduct proscribed by the 13th amendment is limited to the use or threat of physical force or legal coercion to extract labor from

Continued

an unwilling worker. Thus, the deceit, howsoever intentional, alleged here does not constitute involuntary servitude within the meaning of that amendment. We find nothing in Neb. Const. art. I, § 2, which requires different treatment than does the Constitution of our nation.

Plaintiffs' remaining constitutional arguments are resolved by noting that they have a remedy under the Workers' Compensation Act for all personal injuries proved to have been caused by an occupational disease arising out of and in the course of their employment with Gould, including both the initial effects caused by the work environment and any subsequent exacerbations of the same.

AFFIRMED.

Case Questions:

1. According to the court, what improper activities did the employer carry out in this case?
2. Is it significant to the decision that Gould intentionally exposed its employees to dangerous airborne elements?
3. How does this court explain the exclusive remedy provided by workers' compensation?
4. How do intentional acts by employers affect workers' compensation coverage?
5. Explain the plaintiff's "involuntary servitude" argument.

ETHICAL CONSIDERATION:

Avoiding Fraudulent Workers' Compensation Claims

Studies have shown that nearly 25 percent of workers' compensation claims involve some form of fraud. Fraudulent insurance claims account for 10–20 percent of the average premium. Arrests and prosecutions for insurance fraud have increased dramatically over the past 3 years and cost the economy over $80 billion a year.[3] All of these factors point to a disturbing reality: If you work for a workers' compensation firm for any length of time, some of your clients will engage in insurance fraud.

Defrauding an insurance company appears to be one of the so-called "victimless crimes." After all, who is going to feel sorry for a large corporation? Employees may sometimes feel that they are entitled to some award for all of the hard work they have put in over the years. Financial pressures may also drive an employee to exaggerate an injury to increase an award. How can you spot insurance fraud? Here are some telltale signs:

- The employee continually inflates, exaggerates, or overstates his or her losses.
- The amount of loss seems to be out of line with the visual injuries.
- The employee has had numerous other claims with other insurance companies.

One of the best ways to combat insurance fraud is by documenting the facts. Employers should insist on proper documentation of every claim. No matter what injury the employee claims he has suffered, there should be documentation supporting it. This is a good idea in all cases. Injured employees should also keep track of medical bills and other out-of-pocket expenses. This information will help when the employee prepares to settle the case. It will also help in case there is any question of a fraudulent claim.

CHAPTER SUMMARY

Workers' compensation is a statutory system created to protect employees and to provide a mechanism for compensating them. Employees who are injured on the job are entitled to monetary compensation for lost wages, medical bills, and rehabilitation. In exchange for these payments, the employee surrenders the right to bring a separate civil action against the employer. Employers, or employers' insurance carriers, pay a worker's claims. Workers' compensation statutes insulate employers from liability claims in civil suits, thus avoiding the possibility of a large jury award on the employee's behalf. However, with this advantage come several disadvantages: the rules regarding employee awards are more liberal. Employees are free to contest the denial of benefits or the amount of the employer award. Workers' compensation is an exclusive remedy, meaning that employees and employers are barred from other civil actions and must contest the issues through the Workers' Compensation Board. Monetary benefits under workers' compensation include medical bills, rehabilitation costs, partial reimbursement for lost wages, death benefits, and burial benefits.

KEY TERMS

Burial benefit
Death benefit
Exclusive remedy
Income benefit

Medical expenses
Workers' compensation
Workers' Compensation Boards

REVIEW QUESTIONS

1. Explain the basic arrangement in a workers' compensation scheme.
2. What is meant by "exclusive remedy" as that term applies to workers' compensation?
3. Do workers compensation statutes deprive employees of important constitutional rights? Explain your answer.
4. What types of monetary benefits are available to injured employees under workers' compensation statutes?
5. When did workers' compensation statutes originate in the United States?
6. Why was there a need for workers' compensation statutes in the United States?
7. What was the state of law for injured employees prior to the creation of workers' compensation statutes?
8. Who is responsible for paying into the workers' compensation fund from which employees draw their compensation?
9. What is a burial benefit?
10. What is the function of a Workers' Compensation Board?
11. Prior to the enactment of workers' compensation statutes, what defenses would employers use in order to avoid paying for employee injuries?
12. What types of employees are covered by workers' compensation statutes?
13. What types of workers are not covered by workers' compensation statutes?
14. What is the income benefit under workers' compensation?
15. Explain the significance of this chapter's Case Excerpt.

QUESTIONS FOR REFLECTION

Is there still a need for workers' compensation statutes? Has the state of law progressed to a point where employees and employers could easily be absorbed into the civil law system?

WEB SITES

Legal Information Institute
http://www.law.cornell.edu/topics/workers_compensation.html

New York State Workers' Compensation Board
http://www.wcb.state.ny.us/

Texas Workers' Compensation Commission
http://www.twcc.state.tx.us/

PRACTICAL APPLICATIONS

Locate your state's workers' compensation web site. What information is available on this site? Does the site provide forms and other information on workers' compensation hearings?

END NOTES

1. *Abbott v. Gould, Inc.*, 232 Neb. 907, 443 N.W.2d 591 (1989).
2. *Sunderland v. North Dakota Workmen's Compensation Bureau*, 370 N.W.2d 549 (N.D., 1985).
3. Insurance Research Council, 2001.

Online Companion™
For additional resources, please go to
http://www.paralegal.delmar.cengage.com

Federal Workers' Compensation and Tort Law in Workers' Compensation

CHAPTER 2

■ CHAPTER OBJECTIVES

At the completion of this chapter, you should be able to:

- Explain the common law influences and limitations on workers' compensation
- Describe the exceptions to the rule that employees cannot bring civil actions for on the job injuries
- Demonstrate your understanding of the federal workers' compensation system
- Describe other important federal programs that provide benefits
- Explain the benefit structure under federal workers' compensation

INTRODUCTION TO FEDERAL PROGRAMS

In this chapter, we will examine the various federal programs that protect employees and also summarize the benefits that each provides. Federal programs, such as the Federal Employees' Compensation Act (FECA), the Black Lung Program, and the Defense Base Act all provide benefits to employees who work in various capacities for the federal government. Before we examine the specifics of those programs, we must first review the options available to employees before these Acts were created.

COMMON-LAW INFLUENCES ON WORKERS' COMPENSATION

In the first chapter, we saw that workers' compensation systems developed as a direct response to the fact that injured workers usually had no legal recourse for on-the-job injuries. In this chapter, we will examine the legal venues available to injured workers prior to the enactment of state and federal workers' compensation systems. We will begin our discussion with negligence law.

Negligence

The law of negligence has been a vital area of law for many years. In fact, negligence lawsuits are some of the most common in the United States. If you consider the frequency with which persons injured in car wrecks sue one another, you can easily understand why there are so many cases involving negligence issues. However, this area of law, which provides such a powerful remedy for victims in medical malpractice and personal injury cases, fails dismally when it is applied to workers' compensation cases. Why should that be so?

The basic elements of a negligence suit are famously brief. They consist of four elements: Duty, Breach, Causation, and Damages. When a plaintiff can establish these four elements, he or she has proven the case for the plaintiff. However, each element builds on the previous one. If the defendant is unable to prove the first element, he or she cannot move on to the next. How do these four elements apply in typical employment situations?

Duty

A plaintiff in a negligence suit must establish that the defendant owed him or her a duty. In car wreck cases, this is extremely easy to do. All automobile drivers owe other drivers and pedestrians the duty to act with vigilance and ordinary care. No one would dispute the fact that a defendant driver must keep a sharp lookout for others and take actions to avoid causing a wreck. A driver must stop for traffic lights, obey traffic signs, and take other actions to protect not only the driver, but also other motorists. Does this element apply in employment situations?

At first blush, the answer seems to be yes. Surely an employer has the duty to maintain a clean and safe working environment? However, the answer isn't as clear as we would like for it to be. Certainly with federal agencies (such as OSHA) and legislation requiring safe working environment, we know that modern employers must maintain a safe environment for their employees. But was this true in the early 1900s? What about the 1800s? Remember, this was the time before the creation of workers' compensation systems. When an employee was injured on the job prior to the enactment of workers' compensation, he or she could bring a negligence action, but could the injured employer prove the four elements of a negligence action?

In proving duty, the worker would have to establish that the employer had a legally-recognized responsibility to provide safe working conditions. The employee might have a hard time doing that, especially when the employer could interpose the defense of "assumption of the risk."

Assumption of the Risk

A defense of **assumption of the risk** is one that a defendant can raise to show he or she did not violate a duty to the plaintiff because the plaintiff was fully aware of the dangers inherent in carrying out an activity and voluntarily chose to expose him- or herself to them. When a defendant can prove assumption of the risk, then a court is authorized to dismiss a negligence case. Assumption of the risk was an easy defense for an employer to use against employees. After all, the employee worked on the premises and was well aware of the dangers involved. The employee was faced with a simple choice: continue working and assume the risks of an accident, or quit and go to work somewhere else.

When assumption of the risk was applied to a negligence action by an employee against an employee, courts frequently ruled against the employee. The court's ruling was usually based on the fact that the employee was unable to establish the first element in a negligence action, and therefore the plaintiff's entire case must fail.

Because of the problems inherent in bringing a negligence case, some injured employees sought redress under other legal theories, such as product liability lawsuits.

Product Liability

When an injured worker brings a case under the theory of **product liability**, he or she is using a relatively recent legal innovation. A lawyer from the early 1900s would not have recognized the term. The area of product liability really came into vogue during the middle of the twentieth century. Product liability as a legal premise has some distinct advantages over suing under negligence theory. For one thing, the case is not based on the employer committing any negligence. Instead, the case rests on the fact that a defective product injured a person.

Assumption of the risk
A defense in negligence cases that shows that the plaintiff was aware of the dangers inherent in a specific activity and chose to carry out the action in full knowledge of these dangers.

Product liability
A legal theory for a cause of action against a manufacturer or seller of a product that causes injury to a person; liability is not based on fault.

Product liability assesses liability against a manufacturer, seller, or wholesaler for placing a dangerous or defective product on the market that causes injury or damage. The interesting thing about product liability cases is that it is not a legal defense for the manufacturer to prove that it did nothing wrong. In fact, a manufacturer can be liable even when the plaintiff cannot show that there was anything wrong with the way that the product was designed. The only thing that a plaintiff has to show is that the product caused an injury.

How would a product liability case apply to a workers' compensation action? If a worker is on the job and is injured by a product, he or she may bring an action against the manufacturer of the product that caused the injury. However, the obvious disadvantage of only being able to rely on product liability for injured workers is that not all injuries are the result of defective equipment. In order to be victorious in a product liability suit, an injured employee must prove the following:

- That a product caused an injury
- That the injury was foreseeable
- That the product was placed into the stream of commerce and was therefore available to consumers

Proof of the first element in a product liability case is relatively simple. If the injured employee can show that a product was defective, he or she can establish the first step. However, the product must actually be defective. If the employee's injury is not related to a malfunction, the rest of the elements in the case are irrelevant. Without proof that the product caused the injury, the case does not proceed to the other steps. Consider Example 2-1.

Once the injured employee has met the first hurdle of proving that the defective product caused the injury, the remaining elements are relatively easy to establish. A foreseeable injury is one that a reasonable person could infer would happen from the use of the product. The third element, that the product was placed into the stream of commerce, is the requirement that the

EXAMPLE 2-1

Harper is at work one day and she slips on a wet floor. She wants to bring a product liability suit against the manufacturer of the mop used by another employee, who failed to properly clean up the mess. Can she prove the first element in a product liability suit?

Answer: No. When a product performs and does not cause an injury, there is no basis for a product liability suit. The fact that another employee did not use it correctly does not give the injured worker a product liability action.

product was actually intended to be sold and used by others. This justifies a claim that the product manufacturer should be liable for any injuries it causes.

The modern approach in workers' compensation cases is to bar the injured worker from bringing any action against the employer. Instead, the workers' compensation system is a "no fault" scheme. It does not assess blame for either the employee's or the employer's actions. Under that system, a worker waives his or her right to bring a separate civil action against the employer for any injuries sustained on the job. However, because a product liability suit is not an action against the employer, modern workers' compensation law allows the employee to bring two actions: one through the workers' compensation system and the other based on product liability—assuming that the employee's injuries were caused by a defective product. Workers' compensation was never intended to replace general tort law; it was only designed to protect employees. If a product injures the employee, the employer will pay the claim as it would for any other workers' compensation claim, and the injured employee can still bring a suit against the manufacturer. As such, product liability suits are an exception to the general rule that an employee cannot sue based on work-related injuries. There is one other area that also falls into this exception: intentional torts.

Intentional Torts

Tort

A wrong for which the law provides a remedy.

A **tort** is an injury for which the law provides a remedy. There are lots of things that happen to individuals for which the law does not provide any redress. Consider Example 2-2.

You will notice that, in Example 2-2, as long as the man at the party did not engage in physical violence, Ron had no potential legal action against him. The situation changes completely, however, if the man strikes Ron. A person commits an intentional tort when he or she deliberately injures another person. Examples of intentional torts include assault and battery. Assault is the

> ### EXAMPLE 2-2
>
> Ron is at a party and a man comes up to him and says, "You are a jerk." Does Ron have a potential lawsuit against the man?
>
> *Answer:* No. Unless the man engages in some action, such as physical violence or threats, there is really nothing that Ron can do through the legal system to take action against the man. This is one of those things that we must all put up with.

apprehension of physical injury, and battery is the infliction of physical injury. A person who has been physically accosted has the right to bring a civil suit against the attacker. One of the things that often confuses the issue in such cases is that punching someone in the nose may also be a criminal violation. Unfortunately, the actions are referred to by the same name—battery. Therefore, there can be a crime of battery and a civil action for battery. When a person is punched in the nose, he or she can bring a civil suit against the person and also request the police to charge the person with a crime. This dual nature comes into play in workers' compensation cases, as well. Consider Example 2-3.

Injuries Caused by Coworkers

"Coworker injury" falls outside the normal prohibitions found in workers' compensation cases. The basic premise of workers' compensation is that an employee surrenders his or her rights to sue the employer for on-the-job injuries. However, there is no legal bar to an injured employee who wants to sue a coworker for an injury. The workers' compensation system was never designed to strip people of their rights to sue for other actions; it only acts as a bar against employee-employer civil suits. What happens in situations where the person who commits an intentional tort is a member of management? Does that give the injured employee the right to sue the employer? Or, does the workers' compensation system prevent the employee from suing his supervisor in addition to filing a workers' compensation action?

The answer, in most jurisdictions, is relatively simple. It does not matter if the person who committed the intentional tort was a fellow employee or a member of management. The employee can bring a separate civil action against the individual, but is not permitted to sue the company. There are some exceptions to this rule that we will explore in later chapters.

EXAMPLE 2-3

Ron is at work. Another employee comes up to him and says, "You are a jerk," and punches Ron in the nose. Can Ron bring a workers' compensation case for his injuries, as well as a civil action against the other employee?

Answer: Yes. Employees under the workers' compensation system have waived their potential lawsuits against employers, not other employees. In this case, Ron is free to request benefits under workers' compensation for his injured nose and to file a civil action against the other employee for hitting him. The case might also become a criminal prosecution if the police decide to charge the man with criminal battery.

Checklist

A man was gunned down at work while closing out accounting books in the company's vault. The incident occurred at a time when the premises were closed to the public. His wife is seeking redress. What do we need to know in order for her to receive the maximum damages/compensation for the loss of her husband?

1. Did he meet employee requirements in order to receive worker's compensation benefits?

    If yes, the family of the deceased employee may receive payment for no more than $5000. *http://www.state.sd.us/dol/dlm/workr-qa.htm*

2. Was her husband the sole financial provider for the family?

    As a surviving spouse, she will receive compensation for the remainder of her life, or in the form of lump sum (value of 2 years' worth of payments) if she remarries. Her children will also receive compensation until they reach the age of 18. *http://www.iowaworkforce.org/wc/faq.htm#?*

3. Does the company currently have a worker's compensation insurance policy?

    Employers, who are required under the statute to carry worker's compensation insurance and who fail to purchase such policy, can be held liable for an employee's death. Beneficiaries of the deceased employee will not be barred from seeking compensation by way of a civil suit. *http://www.lrc.state.ky.us/KRS/342-00/690.PDF*

4. Are there security systems in use for the premises? If so, were they in operation at the time of the incident?

    If yes, the employer will be protected as long as there was no prior knowledge of defect. *http://sbwc.georgia.gov/00/article/0,2086,11394008_11400533_13292004,00.html*

5. Has the employer found any defect with the sounding alarm, surveillance cameras, or other parts of the security system following the incident?

    If yes, she may file suit against the manufacturer and/or installer of the security system if they are found to have shared in the liability of his death. *http://landru.leg.state.or.us/ors/656.html*

6. While working in the vault, did her husband secure the entrance? If so, has the employer found any defect with the lock for the vault door following the incident?

    If yes, she may file suit against the manufacturer of the vault door if it is found to have shared in the liability of his death. *http://janus.state.me.us/legis/statutes/39-A/title39-Asec107.html*

7. If no defect was found with the lock for the vault door, is there any evidence showing the disclosure of the lock's combination by a co-employee to the shooter?

If yes, she may file suit against the co-employee if he or she is found to have shared in the liability of his death. *http://data.opi.state.mt.us/bills/mca/39/71/39-71-414.htm*

8. Has a criminal case been set into play against the shooter? If so, is the evidence plentiful enough to meet the civil "preponderance of the evidence" requirement?

If yes, she may file suit against the shooter if he or she is found to have shared in the liability of his death. *http://www.scfaz.com/publish/article_626.shtml*

FEDERAL WORKERS' COMPENSATION

In Chapter 1, we discussed the general characteristics of the state-based workers' compensation systems. We saw that each state had a slightly different system, based in part on previously existing laws and the model workers' compensation codes available. Here, we will examine the elements of the federal workers' compensation system, which has features that differ sharply from the state-based systems.

Federal Employees' Compensation Act

The chance of a workers' compensation claim involving a federal employee is pretty high. After all, the federal government is one of the largest employers in our nation. Federal workers include everyone from nurses at federal institutions, to teachers and air traffic controllers, just to name a few. In fact, the most recent data puts the total number of federal employees somewhere between 3.8 and 4.1 million. See Exhibit 2-1.

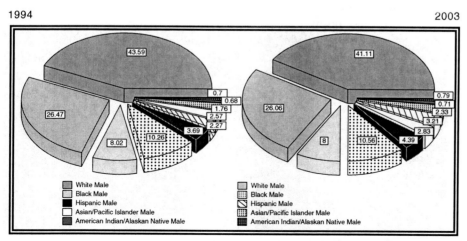

EXHIBIT 2-1 Federal Workers as of 2004.

The Federal Workers' Compensation System

The federal workers' compensation system was created under the authority of the Federal Employees' Compensation Act, otherwise known as FECA. This Act provides compensation to civilian employees who work in the federal government. The federal system has always been more liberally construed than most states' workers compensation systems. There are several reasons for this. For one thing, the federal system must cover a much broader group of people than the typical state system. The federal government employs people in every state, territory, and U.S. possession at all levels of government.

There are important differences between the federal system and the state systems. Under FECA, employees who are injured on-the-job are entitled to payments not only for medical and surgical costs, but also for rehabilitation and other costs. FECA is administered through the U.S. Department of Labor, Office of Workers' Compensation Programs. See Exhibit 2-2. There are 12 of these offices scattered around the country.

A Short History Lesson on Federal Workers' Compensation

The federal workers' compensation law was created in 1916, predating the creation of workers' compensation systems in many of the states. The federal workers' compensation program is not only older than most states programs; it is also more liberal. The early 1900s was a time all of social unrest; many workers were complaining about conditions and the federal government was beginning to pay greater attention to business practices by major corporations. It was at this time that the federal government started investigating and breaking up business monopolies and taking away some of the monopolies held by the so-called "robber barons." These individuals ran the largest corporations the world had ever seen up to that point. The historical roots of the federal workers' compensation system help explain why the federal program is so different from many of the versions created by the states. The federal workers' compensation system was created as a direct result of rapid changes in society during an era of burgeoning social rights and the recognition that workers were being exploited. By the 1930s and 1940s, when some states

EXHIBIT 2-2
FECA Coverage.[1]

> FECA covers most civilian federal employees, Peace Corp and VISTA volunteers, federal petit or grand jurors, volunteer members of the Civil Air Patrol, Reserve Officer Training Corps Cadets, Job Corps and Youth Conservation Corps enrollees and in certain cases, nonfederal law enforcement officers under certain circumstances involving crimes against the United States.

were creating their own version of the workers' compensation system, the pendulum had swung the other way, and the workers' compensation systems created by the states were much more conservative in their approach.

Qualifying Under FECA

How does a person qualify as an employee to be covered by FECA? The definition section for FECA is found in 5 U.S.C.A. § 8101. Among the definitions is one that explains what makes a person an employee under the federal law, and thus covered under FECA.

Under federal law, a person qualifies for federal workers' compensation benefits when the person:

- Works for any branch of the federal government
- Works for the District of Columbia government

That definition is straightforward. If a person works in any branch of the federal government, in any capacity, then he or she is covered by FECA. It does not matter that the person is a seasonal worker, a temporary worker, or a part time worker. However, there are some exceptions.

Checklist

While wearing a testing device, an aerospace technician was electrocuted. She is currently hospitalized; therefore, a family member is seeking clarification as to what needs to be done in order to receive help, and also what relief is available.

1. Was she an apprentice for the agency?

    When determining the amount of compensation a qualified injured worker will receive, the existence of potential increases in earnings, had the worker not been injured, will be taken into consideration as long as the worker was "employed in a learner's capacity at the time [the] injury [occurred]." *http://wyomcases.courts.state. wy.us/applications/oscn/DeliverDocument.asp?CiteID=185437*

2. Did an approved medical provider find her disability to be provisional?

    For an injured worker to begin receiving compensation under the FECA, the temporary disability must remain as such for more than 2 weeks. *http://www.dol.gov/esa/regs/ compliance/owcp/laws/8117.htm*

3. Has an approved medical provider diagnosed her with partial or total disability?

    Once potential increases in earnings for the worker have been determined, the earnings earned in 1 month, at the time of injury, will be subtracted from the estimated potential. The injured worker will receive "66 2/3 percent

of the difference" (a.k.a. "basic compensation for partial disability").
http://www.nmd.state.ne.us/HRO/documents/ca-550.pdf
An injured worker will receive compensation in the amount of "66 2/3 percent" of the income earned each month (a.k.a. "basic compensation for total disability"). *http://www.rnet.state.gov/forms/Death_Disability_Benefits_Iraq_ Afghanistan.pdf*

4. As a result of the electrocution, is she now blinded, paralyzed, and/or in need of constant care?

    An injured worker can receive up to $1,500 per month, in addition to his/her basic compensation. *http://www.dol.gov/esa/regs/compliance/owcp/laws/8111.htm*

5. Is there anyone who qualifies as her dependant(s)?

    If an injured worker has at least one qualified dependant, the compensation for both partial and total disability will be increased by "8 1/3 percent." *http://www.usda.gov/da/shmd/20cfr810.pdf*

6. Does liability for her injury extend to parties other than the U.S. agency she is employed by?

    The FECA requires that an injured worker, or his or her representative, file for suit against all other parties, which can be found to share in the liability of the injury. After receiving a monetary reward, the injured worker, or his or her representative, must reimburse the "Employees' Compensation Fund." Any injured worker who refuses to seek additional compensation from other liable parties will not be entitled to receive compensation from the FECA. *http://www.usdoj.gov/osg/briefs/1983/sg830153.txt*

7. Will the need of vocational rehabilitation arise?

    An injured worker, having no dependants, will receive compensation in the amount of "66 2/3 percent" of the income earned each month, minus any income earned under a different employer. Having at least one dependant will result in an "8 1/3 percent" increase, totaling 75 percent. *http://www.calguard.ca.gov/CAHR/pubs/FPR/CNGFPH_810.pdf*

8. Is she receiving payments from her employer in the form of either annual leave or sick leave?

    If an injured worker chooses to receive annual leave or sick leave, compensation under the FECA will begin only in the event that such payments have stopped. *http://www.hhs.gov/dab/decisions/cr-324.htm*

Exceptions to Federal Workers' Compensation

Although FECA applies to all federal employees, there are exceptions. The courts take the following approach when determining coverage: A person is assumed to be covered under FECA unless proven to be covered under some other federal statute. As a result, federal courts take a liberal approach to defining employee status, ensuring that individual workers do not fall between the cracks, by taking the approach that all employees are covered unless proven otherwise. We will discuss other federal programs that provide coverage later in this chapter.

Federal Workers' Compensation Benefits

In Chapter 1, we introduced the topic of the benefits paid to claimants and showed how these payments varied according to classification as temporary or permanent disability and also on the basis of temporary partial disability and temporary total disability. The federal system sidesteps these classifications. Federal benefits are paid at a rate of two-thirds of the employee's normal salary, unless the employee falls into the category of traumatic injury. In that case, he or she will receive full payments for at least 45 days, followed by a payment of two-thirds of the salary for the rest of his or her illness.

Benefits Under the Federal System

COP refers to **continuation of pay** during an injured employee's recuperation from illness. This is the federal version of temporary and permanent benefits available under various state systems. Under the federal system an employee is entitled to receive his or her regular pay for 45 days because of disability or medical treatment. Federal employees who develop occupational illnesses, such as carpal tunnel syndrome or repetitive stress injuries, are not entitled to receive COP. They are covered in different ways. The advantage of COP is that, instead of receiving reduced payments, the federal employee receives full pay.

Continuation of pay
The name for the workers' compensation benefit available to employees under the Federal Employees' Compensation Act.

Continuation of Pay (COP)

COP payments can be stopped if the employer can prove that the employee's injuries are a result of occupational illness, such as repetitive stress syndrome, as opposed to a dramatic injury like a skull fracture from a falling box. The employer can also stop COP payments if the employer can prove that the employee is not a citizen of the United States. See Exhibit 2-3.

When a company challenges continuation of pay, it controverts the payments. The determination of whether the payments should continue lies with the administrative board that oversees the FECA system. When an employee receives COP, the employer must continue the employee's regular pay unless it controverts COP for any of the following reasons:

- The injured employee's disability is due to an occupational disease or illness
- The employee decides to continue working without receiving COP
- The employee is not a citizen of the United States

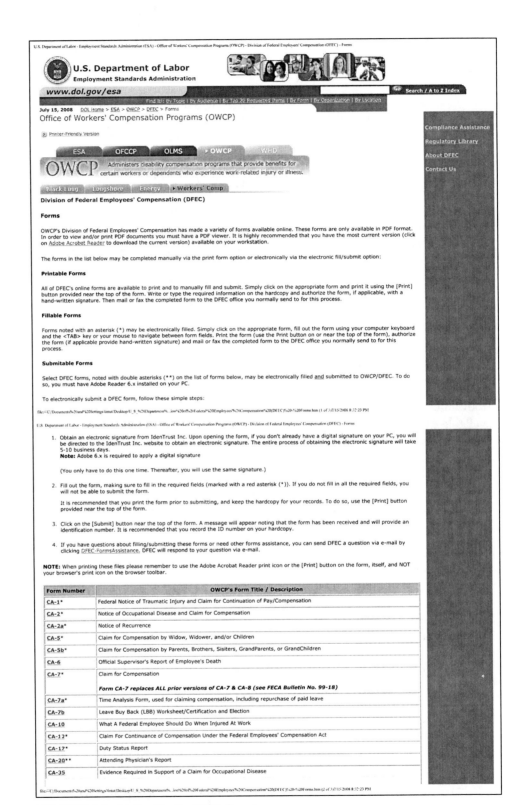

EXHIBIT 2-3 Online Site for FECA Forms.
FECA forms can be accessed at: http://www.dol.gov/esa/regs/compliance/owcp/forms.htm.

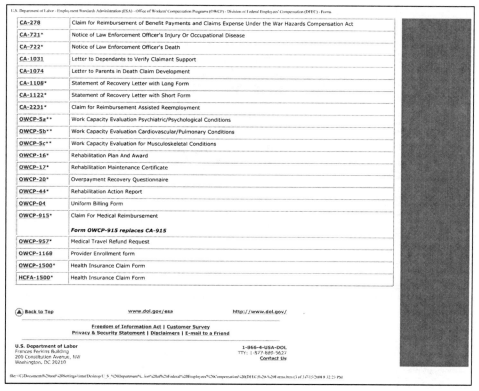

EXHIBIT 2-3 *(Continued)*

- The employee's injury occurred off the employer's premises
- The employee caused the injury him- or herself
- The employee was injured while using illegal drugs or narcotics

Filing a Federal Workers' Compensation Claim

There are several basic elements that an injured worker must prove before filing a claim under FECA. See Exhibit 2-4. For instance, the employee has to show the following:

- That he or she qualified as an employee as that term is defined under federal law
- That he or she was performing job duties at the time of the injury
- That the medical condition was a direct result of the injury sustained on-the-job

Although we will discuss filing claims under both federal and state workers' compensation systems in Chapter 6, a brief word about federal

IMPORTANT: READ CAREFULLY THE INSTRUCTIONS ON THE OTHER SIDE OF THIS FORM BEFORE ANSWERING THE QUESTIONS BELOW

I HEREBY APPLY FOR CONTINUANCE OF COMPENSATION BENEFITS AWARDED TO ME (OR TO THE CLAIMANT ON WHOSE BEHALF I AM NOW ACTING) BY THE OFFICE OF WORKERS' COMPENSATION (OWCP) ON ACCOUNT OF THE DEATH OF:

A. Name of Deceased Employee	Employee's Federal Retirement Plan ☐ CSRS ☐ FERS ☐ Other	OWCP File No.

THIS BLOCK TO BE COMPLETED BY WIDOW/WIDOWER RECEIVING COMPENSATION

B. 1. Have You Married since the Death of Above Named Employee? ☐ Yes ☐ No (If "Yes" complete 10)

2. Do You Receive a Pension or Allowance from any other Federal Agency such as the Veterans' Administration, Social Security Administration or the Civil Service Commission on Account of the Death of this Employee? ☐ Yes ☐ No (If "Yes" complete 11)

THIS BLOCK TO BE COMPLETED BY ANY PERSON RECEIVING COMPENSATION ON BEHALF OF CHILD GRANDCHILD, OR DEPENDENT INCAPABLE OF SELF-SUPPORT

C. 3. Have any Dependents You Claim Compensation for Married Since the Death of the Above Named Employee? ☐ Yes ☐ No (If "Yes" complete 10)

4. Do Any Dependents You Claim Compensation for Receive a Pension or Allowance from Any Other Federal Agency Such as the Veterans' Administration, Social Security Administration, or the Civil Service Commission on Account of the Death of this Employee? ☐ Yes ☐ No (If "Yes" complete 11)

5. Give the Following Information for Each Person You Receive Compensation For:

NAME	AGE	IS PERSON IN YOUR CUSTODY? (Yes or No)	NAME, ADDRESS, AND RELATIONSHIP OF PERSON(S) HAVING CUSTODY IF NOT IN YOUR CUSTODY

THIS BLOCK IS TO BE COMPLETED BY PARENT, GRANDPARENT, OR DEPENDENT PHYSICALLY INCAPABLE OF SELF-SUPPORT

D. 6. Have You Married Since the Death of the Above Named Employee'? ☐ Yes ☐ No (If "Yes" complete 10)

7. Do You Receive a Pension or Allowance from any other Federal Agency such as the Veterans' Administration or the Civil Service Commission on Account of the Death of this Employee? ☐ Yes ☐ No (If "Yes" complete 11)

8. Are You Capable of Self-Support? ☐ Yes ☐ No

9. Have You Been Employed Since Filing Your Last Claim Form? ☐ Yes ☐ No (If "Yes" complete 12)

ADDITIONAL INFORMATION: THIS BLOCK TO BE COMPLETED ONLY WHEN AN ANSWER TO 1, 2, 3, 4, 5, 6, 7, or 9 IS "YES."

E.	(Space for Answers to questions 10, 11, and 12)
10. When and Where was the Marriage Performed and What was the Change in Name, If Any?	
11. What Agency is Paying the Benefits and For What Reason Are They Being Paid?	
12. State the Name of Your Employer, Nature of Employment, Dates Employed, and Amount Earned.	

CLAIMANT'S CERTIFICATION - TO BE COMPLETED IN ALL INSTANCES

F. I DECLARE UNDER THE PENALTIES OF PERJURY THAT THE INFORMATION CONTAINED ON THIS FORM IS TRUE AND CORRECT AND THAT I WILL IMMEDIATELY NOTIFY THE OFFICE OF WORKERS' COMPENSATION PROGRAMS OF ANY CHANGES IN STATUS.

Signature of Claimant (or guardian)	Date (month, day, year)
Address of Claimant (or guardian)	Telephone Where You Can Be Reached
Signature of Witness and Date Witnessed if Claimant Signs by Mark (X)	

Form CA-12

EXHIBIT 2-4 Claim for Continuance of Compensation Under the Federal Employees' Compensation Act.

claims forms is also appropriate here. Under FECA, the injured employee must file a complete and written report (known as a form CA-1 or CA-2) detailing the injury, and give it to the supervisor. See Exhibit 2-5. This form sets out the following information:

Federal Employee's Notice of Traumatic Injury and Claim for Continuation of Pay/Compensation

Reset | Print

U.S. Department of Labor
Employment Standards Administration
Office of Workers' Compensation Programs

Employee: Please complete all boxes 1 - 15 below. Do not complete shaded areas.
Witness: Complete bottom section 16.
Employing Agency (Supervisor or Compensation Specialist): Complete shaded boxes a, b, and c.

Employee Data

1. Name of employee (Last, First, Middle)
2. Social Security Number
3. Date of birth Mo. Day Yr.
4. Sex ☐ Male ☐ Female
5. Home telephone
6. Grade as of date of injury Level ☐ Step ☐
7. Employee's home mailing address (Include city, state, and ZIP code)
8. Dependents ☐ Wife, Husband ☐ Children under 18 years ☐ Other

Description of Injury

9. Place where injury occurred (e.g. 2nd floor, Main Post Office Bldg., 12th & Pine)
10. Date injury occurred Mo. Day Yr. Time ☐ a.m. ☐ p.m.
11. Date of this notice Mo. Day Yr.
12. Employee's occupation
13. Cause of injury (Describe what happened and why)

a. Occupation code

14. Nature of injury (Identify both the injury and the part of body, e.g., fracture of left leg)

b. Type code c. Source code

OWCP Use - NOI Code

Employee Signature

15. I certify, under penalty of law, that the injury described above was sustained in performance of duty as an employee of the United States Government and that it was not caused by my willful misconduct, intent to injure myself or another person, nor by my intoxication. I hereby claim medical treatment, if needed, and the following, as checked below, while disabled for work:

☐ a. Continuation of regular pay (COP) not to exceed 45 days and compensation for wage loss if disability for work continues beyond 45 days. If my claim is denied, I understand that the continuation of my regular pay shall be charged to sick or annual leave, or be deemed an overpayment within the meaning of 5 USC 5584.

☐ b. Sick and/or Annual Leave

I hereby authorize any physician or hospital (or any other person, institution, corporation, or government agency) to furnish any desired information to the U.S. Department of Labor, Office of Workers' Compensation Programs (or to its official representative). This authorization also permits any official representative of the Office to examine and to copy any records concerning me.

Signature of employee or person acting on his/her behalf __________ **Date** ______

Any person who knowingly makes any false statement, misrepresentation, concealment of fact or any other act of fraud to obtain compensation as provided by the FECA or who knowingly accepts compensation to which that person is not entitled is subject to civil or administrative remedies as well as felony criminal prosecution and may, under appropriate criminal provisions, be punished by a fine or imprisonment or both.

Have your supervisor complete the receipt attached to this form and return it to you for your records.

Witness Statement

16. Statement of witness (Describe what you saw, heard, or know about this injury)

Name of witness | Signature of witness | Date signed

Address | City | State | ZIP Code

Form CA-1
Rev. Apr. 1999

EXHIBIT 2-5 Form CA-1.

Official Supervisor's Report: Please complete information requested below:

Supervisor's Report

17. Agency name and address of reporting office (include city, state, and zip code) — OWCP Agency Code — OSHA Site Code — ZIP Code

18. Employee's duty station (Street address and ZIP code)

19. Employee's retirement coverage — CSRS — FERS — Other, (identify)

20. Regular work hours From: ___ a.m./p.m. To: ___ a.m./p.m.

21. Regular work schedule — Sun. Mon. Tues. Wed. Thurs. Fri. Sat.

22. Date of Injury — Mo. Day Yr.

23. Date notice received — Mo. Day Yr.

24. Date stopped work — Mo. Day Yr. — Time: a.m./p.m.

25. Date pay stopped — Mo. Day Yr.

26. Date 45 day period began — Mo. Day Yr.

27. Date returned to work — Mo. Day Yr. — Time: a.m./p.m.

28. Was employee injured in performance of duty? Yes □ No □ (If "No," explain)

29. Was injury caused by employee's willful misconduct, intoxication, or intent to injure self or another? Yes □ (If "Yes," explain) No □

30. Was injury caused by third party? Yes □ No □ (If "No," go to item 32.)

31. Name and address of third party (Include city, state, and ZIP code)

32. Name and address of physician first providing medical care (Include city, state, ZIP code)

33. First date medical care received — Mo. Day Yr.

34. Do medical reports show employee is disabled for work? Yes □ No □

35. Does your knowledge of the facts about this injury agree with statements of the employee and/or witnesses? Yes □ No □ (If "No," explain)

36. If the employing agency controverts continuation of pay, state the reason in detail.

37. Pay rate when employee stopped work $ _____ Per _____

Signature of Supervisor and Filing Instructions

38. A supervisor who knowingly certifies to any false statement, misrepresentation, concealment of fact, etc., in respect of this claim may also be subject to appropriate felony criminal prosecution.

I certify that the information given above and that furnished by the employee on the reverse of this form is true to the best of my knowledge with the following exception:

Name of supervisor (Type or print)

Signature of supervisor — Date

Supervisor's Title — Office phone

39. Filing instructions
   □ No lost time and no medical expense: Place this form in employee's medical folder (SF-66-D)
   □ No lost time, medical expense incurred or expected: forward this form to OWCP
   □ Lost time covered by leave, LWOP, or COP: forward this form to OWCP
   □ First Aid Injury

Form CA-1
Rev. Apr. 1999

EXHIBIT 2-5 *(Continued)*

> Whoever, being an officer or employee of the United States charged with the responsibility for making the reports of the immediate superior specified by section 8120 of title 5, willfully fails, neglects, or refuses to make any of the reports, or knowingly files a false report, or induces, compels, or directs an injured employee to forego filing of any claim for compensation or other benefits provided under subchapter I of chapter 81 of title 5 or any extension or application thereof, or willfully retains any notice, report, claim, or paper which is required to be filed under that subchapter or any extension or application thereof, or regulations prescribed thereunder, shall be fined under this title or imprisoned not more than one year, or both.

EXHIBIT 2-6

Criminal Sanctions Under FECA.

- The claim was filed within the time limits set by the FECA
- The injured or deceased person qualified as an "employee" under FECA
- The employee developed a medical condition
- The employee was carrying out his or her job duties when the injury occurred
- The medical condition was directly caused by the injury

Once a worker meets these basic elements, he or she is entitled to receive continuation of pay for 45 days or until the employer controverts the payments.

Criminal Sanctions Under FECA

Under FECA an employer can be criminally punished for failing to provide medical attention to injured employees. The criminal provisions of FECA are set out in 18 U.S.C. §1922. See Exhibit 2-6.

Under this statute, an employer can be prosecuted in federal court for a criminal action and can be fined and imprisoned for up to year, per incident.

OTHER FEDERAL PROGRAMS THAT PROVIDE COVERAGE FOR EMPLOYEES

There are many other federal programs designed to provide benefits to specific categories of employees. For instance, the Longshore and Harbor Workers' Compensation Act of 1927 was created a few years after the Federal Workers' Compensation Act to provide benefits for an entire group of employees who did not fall under the jurisdiction of the federal act. See Exhibit 2-7. Under this Act, workers who are injured or killed working on piers, loading docks, or terminals are compensated in much the same way as employees under the FECA system.

Notice of Employee's Injury or Death
Longshore and Harbor Workers' Compensation Act,
As Extended (See instructions on reverse)

U.S. Department of Labor
Employment Standards Administration
Office of Workers' Compensation Programs

This form should be furnished by the employer to any employee covered by the Longshore and Harbor Workers' Compensation Act or a related law who reports an occupational injury or illness to his/her employer.
This form is used to provide written notice of an injury or death. Notice is required to obtain a benefit (20 CFR 702.212). The information will be used to determine entitlement to benefits. Persons are not required to respond to this collection of information unless it displays a currently valid OMB control number.

OMB No. 1215-0160

Print Reset

1. Employee's Name (Last, first, middle)
Last Name First Name M.I.

2. Home Mailing Address (Number, street, city, state, ZIP code)
line 1: city:
line 2: st: zip:
country:

3. Date of Birth (Month, day, year)

4. Sex
☐ Male
☐ Female

5. Social Security Number (Required by Law)

6. Home Telephone
Area Code + Number

7. Name and Address of Employer (Number, street, city, state, ZIP code)
name:
line 1: city:
line 2: st: zip:
country:

8. Employee's Job Title

9. Date of Injury (Month, day, year)

10. Hour of Injury

11. Place Where Injury Occurred

12. Name of Supervisor at Time of Injury

13. Did Employee Stop Work Due to Injury? ☐ Yes ☐ No

14. If Yes, Date Stopped

15. Cause of Injury (Explain in what way the injury or occupational illness was caused by employment)

16. Effects of Injury (Indicate parts of body affected or if death occurred)

NOTE: **If reporting injury, employee signs Item 17; if reporting death, claimant or representative signs Item 18**

17. I am requesting the employer named in item 7 to provide me appropriate compensation and medical care for my injury, and I hereby make claim for all benefits to which I may be entitled under the Longshore and Harbor Workers' Compensation Act, or a related law.

Signature of Employee Date
Print Name

18. Request is hereby made to the employer named in Item 7 to provide appropriate death benefits to the survivors of the employee named in Item 1, and a claim is hereby made for those death benefits to which these survivors may be entitled under the Longshore and Harbor Workers' Compensation Act, or a related law.

Signature of Compensation Claimant or Representative of Claimant Date
Print Name

19. This notice is being personally delivered, or mailed, to the employer named in Item 7 (or his/her representative) and a copy is being sent to the District Director of the Office of Workers' Compensation Programs by the party named in either Item 17 or 18 on this date.

Date

IMPORTANT NOTICE

Section 31 (a)(1) of the Longshore and Harbor Workers' Compensation Act , 33 U.S.C. 931 (a)(1), provides as follows: Any claimant or representative of a claimant who knowingly and willfully makes a false statement or representation for the purpose of obtaining a benefit or payment under this Act shall be guilty of a felony, and on conviction thereof shall be punished by a fine not to exceed $10,000, by imprisonment not to exceed five years, or by both.

Form LS-201
Rev. Jan 1999

EXHIBIT 2-7 Notice of Employee's Injury or Death (Longshore and Harbor Workers' Compensation Act).

There are many other federal programs that also provide some type of benefits to specific groups. For instance, the Black Lung Benefits Reform Act of 1977 provides coverage for coal miners. There is also the Division of Energy Employees' Occupational Illness Compensation Act, which provides benefits to employees of the Department of Energy. These are the people who may have been exposed to radiation or other substances while working on DOE projects around the country. There is also a program to protect workers on military bases outside the United States. We will address each of these in turn.

Federal Black Lung Program

The Federal Black Lung Program is administered through the Department of Labor. Under this benefit system, coal miners who have contracted pneumoconiosis (black lung disease) are provided with monthly payments for both income and medical needs. It also provides financial assistance to members of the miner's family. See Exhibits 2-8 and 2-9.

Social Security

In addition to federal programs designed to provide benefits to specific groups such as longshoremen and coal miners, there are several federal programs that provide benefits to individuals who have been injured on the job. The largest is the Social Security Administration.

In this section, we will explain the basic arrangement of Social Security, explain the benefits available, and explain how these benefits interact with an injured worker's payments under the workers' compensation system. But first, we will address the issue of how Social Security came into existence.

History of Social Security

The national Social Security program came into existence in 1935 as part of Franklin Roosevelt's New Deal. His plan was to offer a financial safety net for people who had grown too old to work. Before this plan, individuals who had worked their entire lives faced the prospect of having to live on the generosity of family members or religious organizations or find some way to earn enough money to live by other means. The program was, and continues to be, very popular. We all know that part of our paychecks go into the Supplemental Security Income (SSI) fund. Social Security is significant in any discussion about workers' compensation. This is not because payments are made to individuals over a certain age. There is another part to Social Security that figures prominently in workers' compensation cases.

U.S. DEPARTMENT OF LABOR, ESA
Office of Workers' Compensation Programs
Division of Coal Mine Workers' Compensation

BLACK LUNG BENEFITS IDENTIFICATION CARD

John Doe

Effective Date: 01/31/02
Expiration Date: Lifetime

No Deductible / No Co-Pay

1. This card is the property of the U.S. Government and its counterfeiting, alteration or misuse is a violation of Section 499, Title 18, U.S. Code.
2. Carry this card with you at all times and show it to your doctor, clinic or hospital when you are in need of medical services for your lung condition.
3. The U.S. Department of Labor will pay for medical treatment that is authorized under the Black Lung Act. Call 1-800-638-7072 for specific details.
4. All bills should be submitted to the DOL Black Lung Program, P.O. Box 8302, London, KY 40742-8302.
5. If found, drop in mailbox. Postmaster, postage guaranteed. Return to: DOL Black Lung Program, P.O. Box 8302, London KY 40742-8302.
6. When using the DOL OWCP bill payment website (http://owcp.dol.acs-inc.com/) to request an authorization for medical services or to verify eligibility, your doctor must use the following Card ID Number: 1234567830. Claimants can also use this Card ID Number to access the DOL OWCP bill payment website.

MISUSE OF CARD IS PUNISHABLE BY LAW

EXHIBIT 2-8 Black Lung Benefits Identification Card.

In addition to providing a measure of financial security to people who have retired, the Social Security Administration also provides disability insurance (SSDI) for people who can no longer work. That places it squarely into any issue dealing with workers' compensation. If the Social Security Administration determines that a person has been injured and is permanently unable to return to work, he or she will receive regular payments, referred to as supplementals, for the rest of his or her life. As far as

Miner's Claim For Benefits Under The Black Lung Benefits Act

U.S. Department of Labor
Employment Standards Administration
Office of Workers' Compensation Programs

Reset | Print

I hereby claim all benefits which may be payable to me under the Black Lung Benefits Act. I also hereby apply on behalf of my family for any benefits that may be payable under the Act.

OMB No. 1215-0052
Expires: 08-31-08

IMPORTANT: No benefits may be paid under the Black Lung Benefits Act, unless a completed application form has been received. However, disclosure of your Social Security Number is voluntary; the failure to disclose such number will not result in the denial of any right, benefit or privilege to which an individual may be entitled. Collection of the information on this form is authorized by law (30 U.S.C. 901, et. seq.). This information is required to obtain a benefit.

(FOR DOL USE)

1. Miner's full name (First, middle, last)
   First Name M.I. Last Name

2. Miner's Social Security Number

3. Miner's date of birth (Month, day, year)

4. Highest grade miner completed in school

5. Have you (or someone on your behalf) ever filed a claim for Federal Black Lung benefits before?
   ☐ Yes ☐ No

6. Decision made (If more than one claim filed, identify and show disposition of each in item 18, "Remarks")
   ☐ Allowed ☐ Denied
   ☐ Withdrawn ☐ Pending

7. Are you still working in or around coal mines? ☐ Yes If "yes," answer only c.
   ☐ No If "no," answer a-c.

a. When did you stop working in or around coal mines or a coal preparation facility in the extraction, transportation or preparation of coal, or in coal mine construction or maintenance in or around a coal mine?

b. Why did you stop working in or around coal mines or in a coal preparation facility in the extraction, transportation or preparation of coal, or in coal mine construction or maintenance in or around a coal mine?

c. Have you ever been transferred from your regular coal mine job to lighter duty?
   ☐ Yes ☐ No
   if "yes," provide date and reasons why you were transferred. Use space in item 18, "Remarks".

8. How many years have you worked in or around coal mines, or in a coal preparation facility in the extraction or preparation of coal, or worked in coal mine construction or transportation in or around a coal mine?______ To the best of your knowledge list your complete coal mine Employment History on Form CM-91 1 a.

NOTE: If available evidence is not sufficient to arrive at a determination, you may be requested to have an independent medical examination at no expense to you. Should the Department of Labor obtain information useful to your physician for treatment, such information may be furnished to that physician.

9. Describe briefly any disability you believe you have due to pneumoconiosis (Black Lung) or other respiratory or pulmonary disease resulting from coal mine employment. Specifically, what aspect(s) of your regular job in the coal mines are you physically unable to perform as a result of your disability?

Form CM-911
Rev. Sept. 1998

EXHIBIT 2-9 Miner's Application for Benefits Under the Black Lung Benefits Act.

NOTE: The amount of any state or Federal Workers' Compensation/Occupational Disease benefits you are receiving based on your disability due to coal workers' pneumoconiosis will be subtracted from your benefits under Part C of the Black Lung Benefits Act.

10. Have you filed a workers' compensation claim under any state or Federal law on account of your disability, due to coal workers' pneumoconiosis?
    ☐ Yes ☐ No (if "yes," complete items a through j).

a. With what State or Federal agency was the claim filed?

b. Approximate date of filing:

c. Claim No. (if known):

d. Decision made
   ☐ Allowed ☐ Denied ☐ Pending

e. Employer against whom Workers' Compensation Claim was filed?

f. Amount of payment:
   Weekly: $ _____ per week
   Other: $ _____ per _____

g. Date payment began:

Date payment ended:

h. Did you pay any attorney's fees or legal fees in securing your workers' compensation award?
   ☐ Yes ☐ No

i. If you have received a lump-sum payment based on you compensation claim, please indicate the following:
   Period covered (fill in below):   Amount: $ _____
   From: _____   To: _____

j. Do you receive any medical treatment benefits as part of your Workers' Compensation benefits?   ☐ Yes ☐ No

NOTE- The amount of your earnings, either as an employee or from self-employment, will help us to determine the correct amount of black lung benefits to which you may be entitled. This information is required by the 1981 Amendment to the Black Lung Benefits Act.

11 a. Enter the names and addresses of all persons, companies, or government agencies for which you worked during the previous calendar year. If self-employed, so indicate.

Name and Address of Employer	Work Began Month, Year	Work Ended Month, Year	Approximate Earnings
city: _____ state: _____ zip: _____			

b. How much do you expect your total earnings to be this year? (Count all of your earnings beginning with the first of the year and all expected earnings through the end of this year.) $ _____

12. Are you married now? ☐ Yes ☐ No (if "Yes" Complete items a-f.)
    (if "No" go to item 13).

a. Date of marriage

b. Your spouse's first and maiden name (Print)
   First Name _____ Maiden Name _____
   SSN: _____

c. Spouse's birth date

d. **Do you and your spouse live together?**
   ☐ Yes ☐ No (If "no", answer items e and f)

e. Are you under a court order to make support payments to your spouse?
   ☐ Yes ☐ No (if "yes", attach a copy of the order)

f. Do you make regular support payments to your spouse?
   ☐ Yes ☐ No (if "yes", indicate amount)
   $ _____ per _____ (week, month, other)

13. Were you previously married? ☐ Yes ☐ No (if "yes" answer a through f)

a. Full Name of your previous spouse:
   First Name _____ M.I. _____ Last Name _____

b. Date married (Month, day, year)

c. Place married (City & State)

d. How marriage ended: (death, divorce)

e. Date marriage ended:

f. Place marriage ended (City, State)

If prior marriage ended by divorce and you were married for 10 years before the divorce action, answer questions 14 and 15.

14. Are you under a court order to make support payments to a divorced spouse?
    ☐ Yes ☐ No (if "yes", attach a copy of the orders)

15. Do you make substantial contributions to a divorced spouse?
    ☐ Yes ☐ No (if "yes", indicate amount)
    $ _____ per _____ (week, month, other)

EXHIBIT 2-9 *(Continued)*

EXHIBIT 2-9 *(Continued)*

the Social Security Administration is concerned, a person is unable to return to work when he or she cannot find gainful employment because of a specific medical or psychiatric disability. This definition is different from the one developed for state or federal workers' compensation programs.

EXHIBIT 2-9 *(Continued)*

In order to qualify for benefits from the SSA, it must be determined that a person is suffering from a disability that will keep him or her from working for more than 12 months. That is one reason why an injured worker can receive both workers' compensation payments and SSI payments at the same time. They have different standards for determining when a person is entitled to receive benefits.

The Social Security Administration is a vast bureaucracy and easily one of the largest in the federal government. It has offices across the entire nation, including Alaska, Hawaii, and U.S. territories.

Social Security Disability Insurance (SSDI)

SSDI is a federal "insurance program" for people who are unable to work because of a disability. Like other insurance, individuals only receive benefits if they have paid into the system. According to the Social Security Administration, a person must have made payments into the system before he or she even qualifies for benefits. After that, SSA has its own formula for determining how much coverage a person is entitled to receive based on work history.

Supplemental Security Income (SSI)

SSI is a different program from SSDI. Both are funded by tax dollars, but SSI refers to the payments that retired persons, disabled persons, and others receive. SSDI, on the other hand, refers to the payments made to people who are unable to work for 12 months, regardless of their age or disability.

Medicare and Medicaid

In addition to Social Security, there are two other programs that are vitally important for injured workers and may provide benefits in addition to those that the worker receives through state or federal workers' compensation systems. These two programs are Medicare and Medicaid.

1965 was an important year for the creation of federal programs designed to provide benefits to individuals who needed assistance with medical care. That was the year that both Medicare and Medicaid were enacted.

What Is Medicare?

Medicare is a national insurance program for particular groups of people, including:

- Individuals who are 65 years of age or older
- Individuals with disabilities
- Individuals who suffer from kidney failure

Anyone who falls into these categories is automatically covered and will receive medical attention and, more importantly, have their medical bills paid by the U.S. government. Members are issued identifying cards and must complete extensive forms, but if they are covered under the program, they will receive medical treatment. Medicaid, on the other hand, is designed to cover different needs. See Exhibit 2-10.

EXHIBIT 2-10 Patient's Request for Medical Payment (Medicare/Medicaid).

HOW TO FILL OUT THIS MEDICARE FORM

Medicare will pay you directly when you complete this form and attach an itemized bill from your doctor or supplier. Your bill does not have to be paid before you submit this claim for payment, but you MUST attach an itemized bill in order for Medicare to process this claim. Mail your completed claim form to the Medicare Carrier responsible for processing your claim. If you do not know the address of your carrier, call 1-800-MEDICARE (1-800-633-4227).

FOLLOW THESE INSTRUCTIONS CAREFULLY:

A. Completion of this form.

Block 1.   Print your name shown on your Medicare Card (Last Name, First Name, Middle Name).

Block 2.   Print your Health Insurance Claim Number including the letter at the end **exactly** as it is shown on your Medicare card. Check the appropriate box for the patient's sex.

Block 3.   Furnish your mailing address and include your telephone number in Block 3b.

Block 4.   Describe the illness or injury for which you received treatment. Check the appropriate box in Blocks 4b and 4c.

Block 5a. Complete this Block if you are age 65 or older and enrolled in a health insurance plan where you are currently working.

Block 5b. Complete this Block if you are age 65 or older and enrolled in a health insurance plan where your spouse is currently working.

Block 5c. Complete this Block if you have any medical coverage other than Medicare. Be sure to provide the Policy or Medical Assistance Number. You may check the box provided if you do not wish payment information from this claim released to your other insurer.

Block 6.   Be sure to sign your name. If you cannot write your name, make an (X) mark. Then have a witness sign his or her name and address in **Block 6** too.

If you are completing this form for another Medicare patient you should write (By) and sign your name and address in **Block 6**. You also should show your relationship to the patient and briefly explain why the patient cannot sign.

Block 6b. Print the date you completed this form.

B. Each itemized bill MUST show all of the following information:

- Date of each service

- Place of each service
  - Doctor's Office
  - Nursing Home
  - Independent Laboratory
  - Patient's Home
  - Outpatient Hospital
  - Inpatient Hospital

- Description of each surgical or medical service or supply furnished.

- Charge for EACH service.

- Doctor's or supplier's name and address. Many times a bill will show the names of several doctors or suppliers. IT IS VERY IMPORTANT THE ONE WHO TREATED YOU BE IDENTIFIED. Simply circle his/her name on the bill.

- It is helpful if the diagnosis is also shown on the physician's bill. If not, be sure you have completed **Block 4** of this form.

- Mark out any services on the bill(s) you are attaching for which you have already filed a Medicare claim.

- If the patient is deceased, please contact your Social Security office for instructions on how to file a claim.

- Attach an Explanation of Medicare Benefits notice from the other insurer if you are also requesting Medicare payment.

COLLECTION AND USE OF MEDICARE INFORMATION

We are authorized by the Centers for Medicare & Medicaid Services to ask you for information needed in the administration of the Medicare program. Authority to collect information is in section 205(a), 1872 and 1875 of the Social Security Act, as amended.

The information we obtain to complete your Medicare claim is used to identify you and to determine your eligibility. It is also used to decide if the services and supplies you received are covered by Medicare and to insure that proper payment is made.

The information may also be given to other providers of services, carriers, intermediaries, medical review boards, and other organizations as necessary to administer the Medicare program. For example, it may be necessary to disclose information to a hospital or doctor about the Medicare benefits you have used.

With one exception, which is discussed below, there are no penalties under Social Security law for refusing to supply information. However, failure to furnish information regarding the medical services rendered or the amount charged would prevent payment of the claim. Failure to furnish any other information, such as name or claim number, would delay payment of the claim.

It is mandatory that you tell us if you are being treated for a work related injury so we can determine whether worker's compensation will pay for the treatment. Section 1877(a)(3) of the Social Security Act provides criminal penalties for withholding this information.

According to the Paperwork Reduction Act of 1995, no persons are required to respond to a collection of information unless it displays a valid OMB control number. The valid OMB control number for this information collection is 0938-0008. The time required to complete this information collection is estimated to average 16 minutes per response, including the time to review instructions, searching existing data resources, gather the data needed, and complete and review the information collection. If you have any comments concerning the accuracy of the time estimate(s) or suggestions for improving this form, please write to: CMS, Attn: PRA Reports Clearance Officer, 7500 Security Boulevard, Baltimore, Maryland 21244-1850.

DO NOT MAIL COMPLETED CLAIM FORMS TO THIS ADDRESS.

EXHIBIT 2-10   (Continued)

What Is Medicaid?

There is always a strong inclination to think of Medicaid as a part of Medicare. In fact, they are very different programs. Medicaid is run by the various states and, as a result, the rules about who qualifies and how they receive Medicaid benefits depend primarily on the state. Because of this variance, we will keep our discussion general. Medicaid was designed to provide medical care to the nation's poor. It is, by far, the biggest medical program in the United States.

Qualifying for Medicaid

Exactly who does and who does not qualify for Medicaid can be a tricky question. There are 25 different eligibility categories that include income, age, and a few other factors. However, there are five main categories of eligibility. The following people are eligible for Medicaid assistance:

- Pregnant women
- Children
- Adults who meet income limits and have dependent children
- Persons with specific disabilities
- Persons age 65 and older

Comparing Medicare and Medicaid

Remember, one of the biggest mistakes that people make is thinking that Medicare and Medicaid are the same thing or at least flip sides of the same coin. They are not. In fact, they are very different and the only reason that they are usually discussed at the same time is that they focus on the same thing: medical care for a specific group of people. If a person qualifies for Medicaid, he or she might qualify for Medicare, and vice versa. Technically, a person could also receive benefits or coverage under Medicaid, Medicare, Social Security Disability Insurance, and Workers' Compensation all at the same time. Of course, these systems were never designed to act as windfalls for individuals. There are programs that attempt to monitor an individual's benefits under all of these systems and to adjust benefits accordingly.

Checklist

An oil mining engineer was injured while working in Iraq. His private health insurer denied him coverage. What other avenues are available for him to receive some form of compensation?

1. What type of disability has he been diagnosed with?

   Coverage by Social Security Disability Insurance (SSDI) is only granted to an employee if the disability resulting from an injury is classified as "total disability." http://www.ssa.gov/dibplan/index.htm

2. Does the liquidated value of his personal estate satisfy the "limited resources" requirement?

   A disabled individual may receive Supplemental Security Income if both of his or her "income" and "resources" can be defined as "limited." http://www.ssa.gov/ssi/text-eligibility-ussi.htm

3. What is his age?

   Anyone U.S. citizen younger than 65 may be eligible for Medicare as long as the type of disability is met with approval. http://www.medicare.gov/MedicareEligibility/Home.asp?dest=NAV|Home|GeneralEnrollment#TabTop

4. Is he able to afford the medical bills?

   If an individual lacks the means to afford payment of medical expenses and is receiving Supplemental Security Income, he or she may qualify for Medicaid. http://www.health.state.ny.us/health_care/medicaid/#qualify

5. Is his employer carrying out a project in contract with the United States?

   If an employee is injured under an employer in contract with the United States, he or she will be eligible to receive compensation under the Defense Base Act (DBA). http://www.dol.gov/esa/owcp/dlhwc/DBAFaqs.htm

6. What classification of disability does his injury fall under?

   If an injured worker qualifies to receive compensation under the DBA, and his or her disability has been classified as "total disability," he or she will receive no greater than "$1114.44 per week." http://www.export.gov/Iraq/bus_climate/dba.html

7. Has his injury been deemed a "permanent total disability?"

   If an injured worker qualifies to receive compensation under the DBA, and his or her disability has been deemed a "permanent total disability," he or she will receive compensation for as long as he or she is living. http://www.dol.gov/esa/owcp/dlhwc/BenefitsundertheDBA(handout).pdf

8. Is he a U.S. citizen?

   If an injured worker is not a U.S. citizen and qualifies to receive compensation under the DBA, he or she will receive compensation in the form of one "lump sum ... representing half of the present value of future compensation." http://www.defensebaseact.com/defensebaseactlaw.asp

Coordinating Benefits on the State and Federal Level

Centers for Medicare & Medicaid Services is a federal agency, usually referred to by its initials, "CMS," that is responsible for coordinating the benefits that a person can receive under state and federal programs. The idea behind CMS is simple: It is supposed to make sure that an injured person receives his or her fair share of compensation, but does not get double or triple awards for the same injury. To that end, CMS requires applicants to submit information about all of their other sources of compensation, from insurance to workers' compensation.

As of May 1, 2004, the connection between federal benefits and state-based workers' compensation became even more important. The Workers' Compensation Medicare Set-aside Arrangement (WCMSA) took effect on that date. Under this legislation, federal agencies must coordinate and adjust payments to injured employees by taking into account how much they are receiving through workers' compensation payments. The amount of federal benefits decreases in direct relation to the amount that a person receives through workers' compensation. Consider Example 2-4.

CMS works with local, state, and federal agencies to make sure that individuals are receiving their fair share of benefits. This means that a person who is on workers' compensation must file appropriate paperwork with Medicare, Medicaid, and Social Security. Of course, there is a natural tendency among injured individuals to try to receive as many benefits as possible. However, when a person receives more than his or her fair share of benefits dire consequences can result, including possible criminal action for Medicaid fraud.

Fraud

Medicare, Medicaid, and the Social Security Administration all have criminal enforcement provisions that allow them to bring criminal actions against persons who have defrauded the federal government. Interestingly enough, most people don't realize that federal and state agencies have the right not only to seek criminal charges against a "double-dipper," but also the right to sue that person in a civil action. In the criminal case, the government will arrest an individual and charge him with a crime. That person is facing jail time, fine, and restitution. The restitution consists not only of the total amount of unearned benefits, but also of the cost of the investigation to figure it all out. The government also has the right to sue the same individual.

A civil suit will not result in jail time, but it can result in a verdict and monetary judgment against a person. That judgment can be assessed against a person's assets. The government can ask the court for permission to seize property to satisfy the judgment and then auction it off for what the person owes.

> **EXAMPLE 2-4**
>
> Mel receives a check from the Social Security Administration for $5,000. He has no idea why he received it and knows that he has no case pending before any federal agency. However, he cashes the check—figuring that if they sent it to him, it's his to do with as he sees fit? Is he right?
>
> *Answer:* No. If a person receives benefits that he or she is not entitled to receive, or receives them without admitting that other benefits are also being paid, the government has the right to bring a fraud action.

In recent years, the government has not only prosecuted individuals for Medicare, Medicaid, and Social Security fraud, but also the private companies that allowed them to carry out their schemes. In some cases, medical offices were billing for persons who never appeared for appointments, or charging for services that were never provided. In some cases, company officials have been sentenced to multiple-year sentences and hefty fines for carrying out such schemes.

Becoming an Advocate for Others in Social Security and Medicare Hearings

One of the interesting aspects to Social Security, Medicaid, and Medicare benefits is that when individuals are denied coverage, they can hire a nonlawyer to represent them at hearings. Paralegals and other nonlawyers routinely represent clients at such hearings.

How is it that a paralegal can represent clients and conduct hearings? The Social Security Administration and the Medicaid Administration allow nonattorneys to represent clients in their hearings. SSA allows persons to hire "an attorney or any other qualified person" to represent them at a hearing. Among the "qualified persons" are paralegals. They can represent clients, conduct direct and cross-examinations, and argue the client's position to an administrative law judge—all for a fee. Many paralegals find this to be extremely challenging work. In some situations, law firms turn the entire case over to the paralegal to handle from beginning to end.

The case often begins when a person is denied benefits. A paralegal representative can set up a client screening and do an in-depth interview. The paralegal can go over the client's work history, medical problems, and education. Paralegals can prepare pleadings in such cases and conduct the entire case. See Exhibit 2-11.

EXHIBIT 2-11

Five Tips for SSI or Medicaid Hearings.

1. Notify the board as soon as possible that you are the claimant's representative. If the agency requires a specific form for notification, make sure that you use it.
2. If you wish to be treated like a professional, act like one. Start with your appearance. Dress like a legal professional who is representing clients. First impressions are as important in administrative hearings as they are in every other aspect of life.
3. You should be cordial to the opposing side, whether you win or lose. This also projects an air of professionalism and might win you more business. Sometimes the opposition will recommend you to a person who has a claim.
4. Always explain the process to your client, especially the length of time involved in getting a decision. It may take 60 days to request a hearing after a denial and then as long as 6 months to actually have one. It could be 30 months before you get a ruling. Remember that although you may have done this a hundred times before, this is your client's first time. Always give your client the time and attention that he or she deserves.
5. Be prepared. When you represent a client at a hearing, you are allowed to cross-examine witnesses. As is true in any court hearing, good cross-examination has more to do with preparation than performance. The secret to effective use of cross-examination is to know the case better than anyone else in the room.

Compensation

Nonlawyers are permitted to charge fees. However, the government must approve these fees. In Social Security hearings, the fee is 25 percent of the past due benefits or $5,300, whichever is less. In order to be paid by the Social Security administration, representatives must also file a petition with that agency.

The Defense Base Act

The Defense Base Act (DBA) was created in 1941 as a way to supplement coverage for workers on military bases outside the United States and its territories. Virtually all government programs that are carried on outside the United States fall under the jurisdiction of the DBA. In many ways, the DBA resembles the provisions of the Longshore and Harbor Workers' Compensation Act, but it applies them to nonmilitary workers on bases around the world. Every contract falling under the auspices of the Defense Base Act must contain provisions that require contractors (and subcontractors) to provide compensation and benefits for injured workers and that the provisions for employee benefits will remain in effect for the full term of the contract.[2]

Worker Benefits Under DBA

The Defense Base Act provides a broad umbrella of benefits to workers, including:

- Disability payments
- Medical payments
- Death benefits

Disability Payments

When calculating total disability, an injured worker can receive up to two-thirds of his or her average weekly earnings, or $1,030.78, whatever is less.

Medical Benefits

Injured employees may receive medical treatment from their own medical providers and may choose their own providers if they do not already have a medical provider.

Death Benefits

Death benefits provide for one-half of the employee's wages to the surviving spouse; a different formula is applied when there are surviving children and a spouse. These death benefits are provided and are even adjusted for cost of living increases.

Who Is Covered Under DBA?

The Defense Base Act provides that coverage must be extended to all of the following:

- Employees working on military bases located outside the territorial limits of the United States
- Employees carrying out U.S. government-funded public works outside the United States
- Employees carrying out public works with a foreign government where such works have been designated necessary to the national security of the United States
- Employees providing services funded by the United States that fall outside the normal activities for regular military employees
- Subcontractors of any of the above

> ### CASE EXCERPT
>
> #### DUE PROCESS AND WORKERS' COMPENSATION
> *Stuto v. Fleishman*[3]
>
> WALKER, Circuit Judge:
>
> Plaintiff-appellant Michael J. Stuto appeals from the judgment entered December 2, 1997, by the United States District Court for the Northern District of New York (Lawrence E. Kahn, Judge), dismissing his complaint pursuant to Fed.R.Civ.P. 12(b)(6). This judgment followed upon two orders of the district court: the first, issued by Judge Con C. Cholakis, dismissed most of Stuto's claims; Judge Lawrence E. Kahn later dismissed the balance of the complaint. Stuto's complaint alleged a Bivens-type damages claim against defendants-appellees Seymour Fleishman, Thomas Pavloski, and Kenneth Hamlett for violation of his right to due process under the Fifth Amendment, as well as claims against the United States, the United States Department of Labor, and the New York City branch of the Office of Workers' Compensation Programs ("OWCP") (collectively the "government" or "government defendants") under the Federal Tort Claims Act ("FTCA"), 28 U.S.C. §§ 1346, 2671 et seq., for misrepresentation, fraud, and negligent and intentional infliction of emotional distress arising out of the improper termination of Stuto's disability benefits under the Federal Employees' Compensation Act ("FECA"), 5 U.S.C. § 8101 et seq. Stuto appeals only from Judge Cholakis's dismissal of his due process claim and Judge Kahn's dismissal of his FTCA claim for intentional infliction of emotional distress. Because we hold that Stuto's due process rights were not violated and that he has failed to state a claim for intentional infliction of emotional distress, we affirm.
>
> BACKGROUND
>
> Stuto's complaint alleges the following facts. In September 1985, Stuto, a mailhandler employed by the United States Postal Service in Albany, New York, suffered a disabling work-related injury to his lower back that required surgery. Two months later he began receiving workers' compensation benefits pursuant to FECA. Four years later, in September 1989, Stuto was given medical clearance for limited job duty of three hours a day. Soon after starting a job repairing damaged mail, his back injury worsened and his physician, Dr. Guidarelli, declared him totally disabled. In November 1989, a Dr. Fay performed a "fitness for duty exam" for the Postal Service and determined that Stuto "would benefit from a ... Work Assessment
>
> *Continued*

Conditioning Center." Stuto attended the program, but his condition did not improve. Stuto continued to receive disability payments.

On March 18 and June 26, 1991, at the request of the Department of Labor, Stuto was examined by Drs. Fay and Kavanaugh. Both concluded that Stuto was capable of limited sedentary work. Over the next year Stuto accepted new job offers from the Postal Service, but, for reasons not stated in the complaint, he never actually entered into any of these jobs.

On May 29, 1992, Fleishman of OWCP sent a letter to Stuto advising him that OWCP had determined that a new job offer from the Postal Service was suitable for Stuto in light of the medical evidence concerning Stuto's ability to work. He gave Stuto "30 days from the receipt of this letter to either accept the job or to provide a reasonable, acceptable explanation for refusing the offer." On July 2, Stuto sent a letter to OWCP stating that he accepted the job offer but also that he had been advised by his physicians, Drs. Guidarelli and Patel, that he was totally disabled. He requested that OWCP send him to a medical referee to resolve any conflict. He also objected to several of the medical reports in his file as not having been obtained in accordance with FECA regulations.

Meanwhile, on July 1 Stuto had submitted to a "fitness for duty" exam by a Dr. Rogers, as required by the Postal Service. Dr. Rogers sent a medical report to the Postal Service on July 2, stating that in his opinion Stuto was totally disabled and incapable of working. That report allegedly was forwarded to OWCP by the Postal Service on July 7, accompanied by a memorandum from the Postal Service stating that it needed clarification regarding Stuto's current medical condition before he could report for work. Because Stuto's medical condition remained unclear, the Postal Service did not request that he report for work, and Stuto never did so.

Stuto did not receive his scheduled worker's compensation payment for July. In a telephone call on July 29, Fleishman informed Stuto's brother, Peter Stuto, that Stuto's disability benefits were "terminated because he is not working." According to Stuto's complaint, Fleishman denied that Dr. Rogers's "fitness for duty" report had been received by OWCP.

OWCP then sent Stuto an order dated August 5, declaring that his benefits had been terminated because "[i]n a statement ... dated July 2, 1992, [Stuto] accepted the job offer but then refused it based on the advice of his physician." Attached to the order was a letter explaining, inter alia, that the "decision [to terminate his benefits] was based on all evidence of record and on the assumption that all available evidence was submitted. If you disagree with the decision, you may follow any one of the courses of action outlined on the attached appeal rights."

Continued

The "appeal rights" referred to an enclosed memorandum entitled "Federal Employees' Compensation Act Appeal Rights."

According to Stuto, the individual defendants at OWCP continued to deny that they had received Dr. Rogers's report, even though Stuto's OWCP file indicates that the OWCP received the report on July 7, that its substance was communicated to the defendants several times, and that a second copy of the report was sent to OWCP on August 5. Moreover, the individual defendants refused to reconsider their decision to terminate Stuto's benefits in light of the report. In response to Stuto's complaint that he would be in a difficult financial condition if his benefits did not resume, Pavloski allegedly suggested that Stuto request another "fitness for duty exam" and tell the doctor that he could do the job. Pavloski told Stuto that he could appeal the termination, but that "his case was very weak, and if the appeal were lost, the Post Office would never offer him another job." Stuto also alleges that the individual defendants conspired to put Dr. Rogers's report into Stuto's file after the date of the termination "in an effort to sabotage Mr. Stuto's right to appeal to the Employees' Compensation Appeals Board ['ECAB']."

On August 10, 1992, Stuto filed an appeal with the ECAB for review of the decision to terminate his benefits. On November 4, 1992, the Director of the OWCP filed a motion to set aside the decision to terminate and to remand the case. He contended that OWCP had not followed proper procedures in two ways: (1) it failed to notify Stuto that the medical examination by Dr. Kavanaugh was for the purpose of resolving a conflict in the medical evidence, and therefore Dr. Kavanaugh's report could not be used to resolve the conflict, and (2) it failed to give Stuto appropriate notice prior to terminating his benefits, as required by FECA Bulletin No. 92-19. The Director stated that "[o]n remand, the Office will reinstate appellant's monetary benefits, retroactive to July 11, 1992, . . . will ensure that Dr. Kavanaugh's June 26, 1991 report is excluded from further review in appellant's claim [,] and will follow proper procedures to resolve the conflict of medical evidence." On January 11, 1993, the ECAB granted the Director's motion to remand. See In the *Matter of Michael Stuto*, No. 92-1978 (ECAB January 11, 1993).

In November of 1992, prior to the ECAB's decision to remand, Stuto filed an action in the United States District Court for the Northern District of New York alleging that the Secretary of Labor violated his rights under the Due Process Clause and FECA by improperly terminating his disability benefits. Stuto moved for a preliminary injunction reinstating his disability benefits. In response, the government agreed to reinstate his benefits retroactively, and the motion for a preliminary injunction was withdrawn. Following the ECAB's remand of the case, an

Continued

impartial medical examination determined that Stuto was totally disabled; his benefits have continued to the present day.

DISCUSSION

There can be little doubt that Stuto's disability benefits under FECA constitute a valid property interest. Stuto argues that the individual defendants intentionally, or at least negligently, deprived him of this property interest by improperly terminating his benefits. However, the negligent or intentional deprivation of property through the random and unauthorized acts of a state or federal employee does not constitute a deprivation of due process if "a meaningful post deprivation remedy for the loss is available." In her concurring opinion in *Hudson*, Justice O'Connor explained that

> Of course, a mere allegation of property deprivation does not by itself state a constitutional claim under [the Due Process] Clause. The Constitution requires the Government, if it deprives people of their property, to provide due process of law and to make just compensation for any takings. The due process requirement means that Government must provide to the [plaintiff] the remedies it promised would be available. *Hudson*, 468 U.S. at 539, 104 S.Ct. 3194 (O'Connor, J., concurring).

Here, Stuto had available to him a menu of possible post-deprivation remedies for the termination of his benefits. In fact, his appeal to the ECAB resulted in the retroactive restoration of his benefits due to the procedural irregularities that had led to termination. That Stuto "might not be able to recover under these remedies the full amount which he might receive in another action is not ... determinative of the adequacy of the administrative remedies." Accordingly, we find that Stuto has not alleged a violation of due process.

Stuto argues that the individual defendants purposefully suppressed Dr. Rogers's report and intentionally deprived him of access to FECA's post- deprivation remedies by placing the report in Stuto's file after the order to terminate had been issued so that it was not part of the record reviewed by the ECAB. Thus, Stuto contends, he was "forced to go outside the established administrative process to redress his grievances." We reject this argument.

Stuto appears to be correct that on appeal, the ECAB could consider only the evidence contained in the record at the time the termination order was issued. However, as explained in "Federal Employees' Compensation Act Appeal Rights," an appeal to the ECAB was only one of several avenues of recourse open to Stuto. He could have sought an oral hearing before an OWCP representative within 30 days

Continued

after the termination decision, where he would have had "the opportunity to present oral testimony and written evidence in further support of [his] claim." Similarly, Stuto could have sought reconsideration. The memorandum informed Stuto that

> If you have additional evidence which you believe is pertinent, you may request, in writing, that OWCP reconsider this decision. Such a request must be made within one year of the date of the decision, clearly state the grounds upon which reconsideration is being requested, and be accompanied by relevant evidence not previously submitted, such as medical reports or affidavits, or a legal argument not previously made. . . . In order to ensure that you receive an independent evaluation of the evidence, your case will be reconsidered by persons other than those who made this determination.

Under either of these two procedures, Stuto would have been allowed to submit new evidence such as Dr. Rogers's report. The fact that Stuto opted for a direct appeal, the one avenue that prevented him from submitting Dr. Rogers's report, does not lead us to conclude that he was denied due process when other avenues that would have satisfied his objectives were open to him.

Finally, to the extent Stuto's complaint alleges a facial challenge to the absence of pre-termination notice procedure, his premise is in error. As noted in the Director of OWCP's motion to remand and in the ECAB decision granting remand, FECA Bulletin 92-19, effective July 31, 1992, already required such pre-termination notice at the time Stuto's benefits were terminated. These are now apparently permanent requirements. As discussed above, the fact that Stuto did not receive the notice due to the individual defendants' failure to follow these procedures was constitutionally remedied by the availability of adequate post-deprivation review.

FTCA Claim

With respect to the FTCA claims, Stuto challenges only the dismissal of the claim for intentional infliction for emotional distress. Judge Kahn dismissed this claim on the grounds that (1) it was barred by the "discretionary functions" exception to the FTCA, 28 U.S.C. § 2680(a), and (2) the alleged conduct was not sufficiently outrageous to satisfy the requirements for intentional infliction of emotional distress under New York law. We need not decide whether Stuto's claim would be barred by any of the exceptions to the FTCA because we agree with the district court that, in any event, the conduct at issue does not meet the stringent requirements for this tort under New York law.

Under the FTCA, the government may be held liable for tortious conduct of federal agencies or employees only if a private actor would have been found liable

Continued

under the state law where the tortious conduct occurred. See 28 U.S.C. § 1346(b) (FTCA only comprises causes of action that are "in accordance with the law of the place where the act or omission occurred"). Accordingly, we look to New York state tort law to determine whether Stuto has stated a claim.

Under New York law, a claim for intentional infliction of emotional distress requires a showing of (1) extreme and outrageous conduct; (2) intent to cause, or reckless disregard of a substantial probability of causing, severe emotional distress; (3) a causal connection between the conduct and the injury; and (4) severe emotional distress. Liability has been found only where the conduct has been so outrageous in character, and so extreme in degree, as to go beyond all possible bounds of decency, and to be regarded as atrocious, and utterly intolerable in a civilized society. Thus, it has not been enough that the defendant has acted with an intent which is tortious or even criminal, or that he has intended to inflict emotional distress, or even that his conduct has been characterized by "malice," or a degree of aggravation which would entitle the plaintiff to punitive damages for another tort. Whether the conduct alleged may reasonably be regarded as so extreme and outrageous as to permit recovery is a matter for the court to determine in the first instance.

As the district court noted, several New York courts have dismissed cases involving acts of coercion and misrepresentation related to employment or disability decisions on the ground that such conduct was not extreme and outrageous. For example, in *Murphy*, 58 N.Y.2d at 293, 461 N.Y.S.2d 232, 448 N.E.2d 86, the plaintiff alleged that he was transferred and demoted for reporting fraud, coerced to leave by being told that he would never be allowed to advance, discharged and ordered to leave immediately after reporting other alleged in-house illegal conduct, and then forcibly and publicly escorted from the building by guards when he returned the next day to pick up his belongings. The Court of Appeals held that this conduct fell "far short" of the tort's "strict standard" for outrageous behavior. Id. at 303, 461 N.Y.S.2d 232, 448 N.E.2d 86; see also *Burlew v. American Mut. Ins. Co.*, 63 N.Y.2d 412, 415, 417–18, 482 N.Y.S.2d 720, 472 N.E.2d 682 (1984) (defendant's intentional five-month delay in authorizing needed surgery in connection with plaintiff's worker's compensation claim, statement to plaintiff that "You're crazy if you think we're going to support you for the rest of your life," and procurement of an affidavit from an employee stating that plaintiff's condition resulted from a pre-existing injury not sufficiently extreme or outrageous to state a claim).

Huzar v. New York, 156 Misc.2d 370, 590 N.Y.S.2d 1000 (N.Y.Ct.Cl.1992), is similar on its facts to the case at hand. There, a correction officer's disability claim was

Continued

controverted by the Department of Correctional Services as a matter of routine policy, although the Workers' Compensation Board later determined that the plaintiff was disabled. The court found that the plaintiff had failed to state a claim for intentional infliction of emotional distress, notwithstanding his allegations that he was threatened by the facility staff that I would be fired if I did not return to work, even though they knew that I had a legitimate job related disability that prevented me from working.... I was told that I would not be allowed to receive my Workers' Compensation benefits. I was told that if I continued to stay out of work, I would be taken off the payroll and lose all of my medical benefits. Calls were made to my home, demanding that I return to work, and if I was not home at the time the calls were made, my wife would be harassed with these calls, and would be questioned as to my whereabouts.

Id. at 1004

As in *Huzar*, Stuto has failed to allege any conduct that is sufficiently "extreme and outrageous" to meet the stringent New York standard as enunciated in the foregoing cases. The crux of his complaint is that OWCP officials "intentionally, recklessly, and/or negligently ignored" dispositive medical evidence, "lied to Mr. Stuto, requested that he lie during his medical examinations, and used his financial need for disability benefits as a weapon to coerce him into acceding to their invalid demands that he return to work." We agree with the district court's observation that coercion is inherent in any decision by OWCP to require a recipient of disability benefits to go to work on the basis that the medical evidence indicates that he is capable of such work. As Stuto acknowledged in his complaint, the individual defendants had before them two medical reports stating that Stuto was capable of limited sedentary work, and OWCP had determined that the job offer at the Postal Service was suitable. Moreover, their disregard of Dr. Rogers's report, while certainly improper, was not sufficiently outrageous given the fact that Stuto could have introduced this report at an oral hearing or upon reconsideration, had he requested either. Stuto points to several cases in which courts have sustained claims for intentional infliction of emotional distress. However, these cases all involved some combination of public humiliation, false accusations of criminal or heinous conduct, verbal abuse or harassment, physical threats, permanent loss of employment, or conduct contrary to public policy.

The conduct in these cases is readily distinguishable from that alleged by Stuto. The individual defendants here neither verbally abused, physically threatened, nor

Continued

publicly humiliated Stuto; they neither falsely accused him of criminal or heinous misconduct, threatened him with prosecution, nor permanently deprived him of his benefits or employment. Accordingly, we affirm the district court's dismissal of Stuto's claim under the FTCA for intentional infliction of emotional distress.

CONCLUSION

We hold that (1) Stuto failed to state a claim for denial of due process because adequate post-deprivation remedies existed to restore his benefits; and (2) Stuto failed to allege sufficiently "extreme or outrageous" conduct to state a claim under the FTCA for intentional infliction of emotional distress. The judgment of the district court dismissing Stuto's claims is affirmed.

Case Questions:

1. For whom did Stuto work?
2. What was the nature of his injury?
3. What did the Department of Labor doctors determine about Stuto's condition?
4. According to the court, are disability benefits a property right?
5. Explain the basis of Stuto's claim for intentional infliction of emotional distress.

ETHICAL CONSIDERATION:
Client Contact

An area that is rife with potential ethical issues is dealing with clients. As we will see in the next chapter, a paralegal who gives legal advice or performs certain activities might fall under the category of unauthorized practice of law. But negotiating the minefield of legal advice is only one issue that arises in daily contact with clients. Clients often request information that they are not entitled to receive, such as the issues pending in other cases or the names of the firm's other clients. The reasons behind such questions may be as simple as a need for reassurance and information rather than a desire to know confidential information. Of course, you cannot discuss client issues with different clients and you must respect the confidentiality of each client's case. If you understand that the reason behind persistent client questions is merely to seek some reassurance, you can address the issues in that client's case without discussing confidential matters in other cases.

CHAPTER SUMMARY

Workers' compensation is a system that was developed outside the normal civil actions available to an injured person. Unlike negligence cases, where an injured person must establish duty, violation of that duty, causation, and damages, workers' compensation does not assign blame. In a negligence case, an injured employee would be at a distinct disadvantage in bringing such an action against an employer. This is one reason why workers' compensation system acts as a no-fault system. Injured employees are not required to sue employers in order to receive benefits. In fact, in order to qualify for workers' compensation coverage, an employee must waive his or her rights to bring a civil action against an employer. However, this does not mean that an employee waives all rights. An employee can, for instance, bring product liability and intentional tort actions against employers or fellow coworkers who have caused injury to the employee.

The federal workers' compensation system was created in 1916 and is generally more liberal in its application than most state systems. Under the Federal Employees' Compensation Act, an injured employee is entitled to continuation of benefits equal to two thirds of his or her salary. Other federal programs, such as the Federal Black Lung Program, Social Security, Medicaid, and Medicare, all provide other benefits for people who have been injured. Most of these federal programs work in conjunction with one another and state-based workers' compensation systems in order to ensure that a person does not receive a windfall of unearned benefits.

■ KEY TERMS

Assumption of the risk
Continuation of pay

Product liability
Tort

■ REVIEW QUESTIONS

1. Explain the basic elements of the negligence action.
2. What is product liability?
3. How would an injured worker bring a product liability lawsuit?
4. Injured workers do not waive their rights to bring intentional tort actions. What does this mean?
5. Can an injured employee sue a coworker? Explain your answer.

6. When was the federal workers' compensation system created?
7. What social pressures were brought to bear in the creation of the Federal Employees' Compensation Act?
8. How does the federal workers' compensation system award temporary benefits?
9. What is continuation of pay?
10. What are examples of other federal programs that provide coverage for individuals who are injured?
11. What does it mean when an employer controverts continuation of pay?
12. What is a Form CA-1?
13. Does the Federal Employees' Compensation Act provide criminal sanctions? Explain.
14. What is the Federal Black Lung Program?
15. Explain the development of Social Security.
16. What is Social Security Disability Insurance?
17. Explain the function of Medicare.
18. How does Medicaid compare to Medicare?
19. How does a person qualify for Medicaid?
20. What agency is responsible for coordinating benefits a person receives on the state and federal level?
21. Give an example of Medicaid fraud.
22. Can paralegals represent individuals in Medicare and Medicaid hearings? Explain.
23. In this chapter's case excerpt, was the injured employee successful in his claim concerning the intentional tort of infliction of emotional distress? Why or why not?

QUESTIONS FOR REFLECTION

1. Should state systems be brought more in line with the federal approach? Why or why not?
2. Based on what you learned in Chapters 1 and 2, would a person be better off covered under a federal program or a state program? Explain your answer.

WEB SITES

California Commission on Health and Safety
http://www.dir.ca.gov/CHSWC/chswc.html

Ohio Bureau of Workers' Compensation
http://www.ohiobwc.com/

PRACTICAL APPLICATIONS

Go to the 2003 report on the Missouri State Workers' Compensation site, found at http://www.dolir.mo.gov and answer the following questions:

- When was the Missouri Workers' Compensation system enacted?
- Under Missouri law, the law requires employers with a minimum of how many employees to provide compensation benefits to employees?

END NOTES

[1] http://nt5.scbbs.com/cgi-bin/om_isapi.dll?clientID=208915801&infobase=agencyhb.nfo&jump=3–2&softpage=PL_frame#JUMPDEST_3–2.

[2] 42 U.S.C. §§ 1651(a)(4).

[3] 164 F.3d 820 (C.A.2 (N.Y.) 1999).

Online Companion™
For additional resources, please go to
http://www.paralegal.delmar.cengage.com

Employers and Employees Under Workers' Compensation

CHAPTER 3

■ CHAPTER OBJECTIVES

At the completion of this chapter, you should be able to:

- Describe the definition of employer and employee under workers' compensation
- Define "statutory employer" and "casual employee" under workers' compensation rules
- Describe the significance of classification as an independent contractor
- Explain the rule about workers' compensation coverage when there is more than one employer for a particular employee
- Demonstrate the consequences of wrongfully denying workers' compensation coverage

INTRODUCTION TO EMPLOYERS AND EMPLOYEES

In this chapter, we will examine the important issue of exactly who qualifies as **employer** and employee under the workers' compensation system. If a person does not meet the qualifications of either, then workers' compensation does not apply. That means that the "employer" doesn't have to provide workers' compensation insurance coverage and the "employee" won't receive any

Employer
An individual or company that has employees.

benefits for a work-related injury. We will begin with the definition of employer under workers' compensation and then progress to the issues surrounding employees.

EMPLOYERS AND EMPLOYEES UNDER THE WORKERS' COMPENSATION SYSTEM

It might seem to be obvious who qualifies as an employer for purposes of workers' compensation coverage, but that classification isn't always as clear as one might suppose. For instance, who is considered the employer when an employee works for multiple employers or when the employment structure consists of subsidiary companies under the umbrella of a much larger corporation? Which department is considered to be the "employer?" These questions are more than mere academic exercises. Determination of who the employer is can have a profound impact on workers' compensation issues, including insurance coverage, benefits and even, in the case of an individual classified as an independent contractor, whether there is an employer at all.

Employers Under Workers' Compensation

Each state sets its own parameters about the definition of employer. To be absolutely sure about the definition in your state, you will have to look at your own workers' compensation statute. Having said that, there are some generalizations we can make about who qualifies as an employer under almost all workers' compensation statutes. An employer is someone who hires someone else to perform regular services. The employer has the right to control the actions of the employee and, of course, the employer pays the employee's wages.

Minimum Number of Employees

In previous decades, workers' compensation statutes often provided a minimum number of employees that an employer must have had before a state workers' compensation act applied. For instance, up until the 1970s and 1980s, most states had a provision that said only employers with three or more employees fell under the jurisdiction of state workers' compensation laws. Those rules have now changed everywhere. Instead of providing a minimum number of employees, most statutes provide that all employees are covered. However, there are still some states that impose the minimum number of employees rule. In most states, though, the rule is that all employees are covered if they meet certain requirements.

In states that continue to follow the rule for a minimum number of employees before workers' compensation coverage is triggered, there are frequent complications and exceptions. For instance, how do these states address the issue of seasonal or temporary workers? In farming and agriculture, for instance, it is very common for a company to have periods where they employ many individuals and other times when there are virtually no employees. How do statutes address this situation?

Faced with the complexities of the work force, workers' compensation laws have come up with some general guidelines to help employers figure out when they must abide by workers' compensation laws and when the employer does not. For instance, an employer must provide workers' compensation benefits when the employer regularly employs more than the minimum number. In this context, "regularly" means the number of employees routinely used for a specific purpose and for a reasonable period of time. Under that definition, temporary or seasonal workers would satisfy the minimum number if they are needed for the workload at the business and that work load is something that the employer knows about. Harvesting crops, for instance, is a regular part of a farming enterprise, and those seasonal employees would be counted under the statute. If the number of employees occasionally falls below the minimum number required under workers' compensation law, it will not affect the computations. The employer must continue to provide workers' compensation coverage as long as the number met the minimum at sometime during the year.

These statutes seem to skew the coverage debate toward providing coverage for individuals as opposed to finding ways to avoid employee coverage. The principle behind workers' compensation that we have seen in several other contexts also applies here: When in doubt, make workers' compensation apply to employers and employees. See Exhibit 3-1.

Multiple Employers

What happens in a situation where a person works for one company but then is loaned out to another company? In that situation, who is the employer for purposes of workers compensation? It turns out that the answer may be both. It all depends on what rights the new employer has. If the new employer has the power to hire and fire and also pays the employee's wages, then for workers' compensation purposes this is the employer and it will be this employer's insurance company that will have to pay a workers' compensation claim. However, if it turns out that the employee is still paid by his original employer

EXHIBIT 3-1

What the Employer Should Know (Arkansas).

- Most employers in Arkansas with **three or more employees** are required by law to have workers' compensation insurance coverage for their employees.
- There are **exceptions** to the three-or-more requirement, so employers with fewer than three should check with authorities before assuming they do not fall under the workers' compensation laws. Employers in doubt may contact their agent or the commission's Information Officer, its Operations/Compliance Division, or the Legal Advisor Division.
- The insurance is purchased by the employer; no part of it should be paid for by employees or deducted from their pay.
- The coverage is provided through a workers' compensation insurance policy or by the employer receiving state approval to be self-insured for such purposes. Any other arrangement by the employer's representative may constitute fraud.
- Employers failing to comply with these laws may be subject to penalties by the state and, in addition, may lose protections afforded them by workers' compensation insurance and the laws of the state.

and his original employer retains the right to fire him or her, then the original employer is responsible for any workers compensation claim. If there is a blurring of distinction on these two points—who has the right to fire the employee and who is actually paying employee—then the employee may be able to bring a workers' compensation claim against both of them.

Court Doctrines that Determine Employer Status Under Workers' Compensation

In addition to statutory mandates that dictate who can be considered an employer under workers' compensation statutes, courts have also developed doctrines or tests that also seek to answer that question. One such test is the economic reality test. If the answers to the four questions under the economic reality test are yes, then an employer-employee relationship exists and the employer must provide workers' compensation benefits. The four elements of the economic reality test are:

1. **Does the employer control the actions of the worker?**
   This question has several lesser components, including:

   - Does the employer have control and supervision over the workers?
   - Does the employer furnish the worker's tools?
   - Does the employer determine the hours that the worker will be on the job?
   - Does the employer tell the worker what actions to perform?

The answer to just one of these questions is not dispositive on the issue of qualifying as an employer under workers' compensation statutes, but the answers do build toward a conclusion, especially when you consider the remaining questions under the economic reality test.

2. Who pays the worker's wages?

Although simply signing a paycheck is not determinative of employer status, the question is important, especially when the worker's pay includes insurance and health benefits, whether these benefits are automatically deducted from the worker's paycheck and whether one employer reimburses the other for making these payments.

3. Does the employer have the right to hire, fire, and discipline the workers?

Even if multiple employers share the rights to hire, fire, and discipline workers, a court can determine that a company falls under the purview of workers' compensation statutes. Courts can make this determination even when the rights are shared between two or more companies, or even when one company only exercises these rights indirectly, such as requiring Company A to fire a worker completing a project for Company B.

4. Does the work performed build on a common project or goal?

This final criterion examines the actual work performed and asks the simple question: Who benefits from the work performed? If the actions of the workers benefit both employers, then they are both employers for workers' compensation purposes. The question here is often phrased, "Was the work so integrally related that their common objectives [were] only realized by a combined business effort?".[1] If the answer to this question is yes, then an employer-employee relationship exists and the companies must comply with workers' compensation rules and regulations.

> **SIDEBAR**
>
> "[The economic reality] standard examines a number of criteria including control, payment of wages, hiring, firing, the maintenance of discipline, and common objective. These factors are viewed together in their entirety under a totality of the circumstances test... No one factor is controlling." *Kidder v. Miller-Davis Co.*, 455 Mich. 25, 564 N.W.2d 872 (1997).

Employers Subject to the Workers' Compensation Statute

Most states have laws, which specify exactly who qualifies as an employer. For instance, one statute provides that an "employer" is:

> Every person, firm and private corporation, including any public service corporation but excluding, however, all nonprofit charitable, fraternal, cultural, or religious corporations or associations, that have in service five (5) or more workmen or operatives regularly in the same business or in or about the same establishment under any contract of hire, express or implied.[2]

> **EXAMPLE 3-1**
>
> Mario answered an ad in the paper for Simple Scrapbooks. Diane, who owns the company, placed an ad for someone who could build display cabinets and other units for scrapbooking products that she sells from her store. Diane meets with Mario, asks him some questions about his experience and then says, "Great! I'll see you Monday at 10 a.m." Is Mario an employee?
>
> *Answer:* Yes. As far as workers' compensation laws are concerned, Mario is an employee. Even though nothing has been said about Mario's work hours or even his hourly wage, the law will classify this arrangement as an employer-employee arrangement. There is no requirement that any of these details must be in writing. Workers' compensation laws allow for a certain fluidity when it comes to defining employers and employees.

Under this definition, any company or individual that has five or more employees working in the same business or on the business premises is an employer. See Exhibits 3-2 and 3-3. Employees include anyone who is being paid for services, even when the employment agreement is only implied. Consider Example 3-1.

Partnerships

Although a partnership can certainly qualify as an employer under workers' compensation laws, that is only true when it actually has workers. The partners do not qualify as employees. One partner is not the employee of the other partner and, as a result, when there are only partners in the business, none of them are covered under workers' compensation. The same rule applies in the context of a limited partnership. In a limited partnership, there are two classes of partners: general partners and limited partners. A limited partner can contribute money or other goods to the partnership, but does not take part in the day to day operations of the company. He or she may share in profits and losses, but is not permitted to make hiring and firing decisions. Limited partners, like general partners, do not qualify under workers' compensation statutes.[3]

Statutory Employers

Statutory employer
An individual or company classified as an employer for workers' compensation purposes only.

The term **statutory employer** was created specifically to deal with situations where there is some question about employer/employee definitions. Under the definition of statutory employer, a business owner may be an employer for

EMPLOYER CERTIFICATE OF COMPLIANCE

You must submit this Certification to your workers' compensation insurer. Failure to submit this Certification as required may result in your being penalized by a fine of $500, payable to your insurer.

You must secure workers' compensation for your employees through insurance or by becoming an authorized self-insured. If you fail to provide security for workers' compensation, you must pay an additional 50% in weekly benefits to your injured workers.

If you willfully fail to provide security for workers' compensation, then you are subject to a fine of up to $10,000, imprisonment with or without hard labor for not more than 1 year, or both. If you have been previously fined and again fail to provide security for workers' compensation, then you are subject to additional penalties, including a court order to cease and desist from continuing further business operations.

You must not collect, demand, request, or accept any amount from any employee to pay or reimburse for the workers' compensation insurance premium. If you violate this provision, you may be punished with a fine of not more than $500, or imprisoned with or without hard labor for not more than one year, or both.

It is unlawful for you to willfully make, or to assist or counsel someone else to make, a false statement or representation in order to obtain or to defeat workers' compensation benefits. If you violate this provision, you may be fined up to $10,000, imprisoned with or without hard labor for up to 10 years, or both depending on the amount of benefits unlawfully obtained or defeated. In addition to these criminal penalties, you may be assessed a civil penalty of up to $5,000.

EMPLOYER CERTIFICATION

I certify that I have read this entire document and understand its contents, and that I understand I am held responsible for this information. I certify my compliance with the Louisiana Workers' Compensation Act.

Preparer Name   (PRINT)   Signature   Date

Company Name   Company Address

( )
Phone Number   Insurance Policy Number

Employee Name   Employee Social Security Number

EXHIBIT 3-2 Employer Certification of Compliance (Louisiana). *Reprinted courtesy of the Louisiana Department of Labor.*

purposes of workers' compensation laws when the owner has direct employees, borrowed employees, or even indirect employees. An indirect employee is someone who works for a contractor, who in turn works for the business owner. As you can see, the laws are geared to recognize that someone is an employer under workers' compensation in many circumstances where, in other situations, the law might not presume a traditional employer-employee relationship exists. The whole idea behind creating a classification called "statutory employer" is to make sure that as many workers as possible are covered under workers' compensation. See Exhibit 3-4.

All Indiana public and private employer-employee relationships (with a few exceptions, discussed below) are covered by the Workers' Compensation and Occupational Diseases Acts. It does not matter how many workers are employed in a business; all employees must be covered. Employees who have been injured while working and have been told that they are ineligible for worker's compensation, either because the employment is not covered by the Act or because the employer does not consider the worker to be an employee, may contact the Workers' Compensation Board for information or an attorney for advice.

(1) Executive officers elected or appointed and empowered in accordance with the charter and bylaws of a private corporation are employees under the Act and are covered. Ind. Code §22-3-6-1(b)(1).

(2) Employees working outside of the State of Indiana, whether in another state or outside of the United States, are covered by workers' compensation as long as there is an Indiana employment relationship. Ind. Code §22-3-2-20.

(3) Members of the Indiana General Assembly and Field Examiners of the State Board of Accounts are covered. Ind. Code §22-3-2-2(g).

(4) Employees of boxing, wrestling, and other ring exhibitions must be covered by workers' compensation insurance, in addition to other types of insurance. 808 IAC 2§33§1.

(5) Part-time employees are covered.

(6) Minor employees are covered. If a child under the age of seventeen (17) years is forced, required, or permitted to work in violation of Ind. Code §20-8.1-4-24 or Ind. Code §20-8.1-4-25, the Board is required to award the child employee double the compensation ordinarily payable under the Act. Ind. Code §22-3-6-1(c). Ind. Code §20-8.1-4-25 prohibits child labor in any hazardous occupation designated under the federal Fair Labor Standards Act (29 U.S.C. §§201-219), as amended. Half of an award of double compensation for child labor violations would be payable directly by the employer; the other half would be the responsibility of the employer's insurance carrier. Ind. Code §22-3-6-1(c)(2).

Payments of compensation in excess of one hundred dollars ($100) to employees under the age of eighteen (18) years must be made to a trustee or guardian, or to the parents of the employee if ordered by the Workers' Compensation Board. Ind. Code §22-3-3-28.

(7) Students participating in on-the-job training under the federal School to Work Opportunities Act (20 U.S.C. 6101 et seq.) are eligible to receive medical benefits, permanent partial impairment compensation, and in the event of death, burial compensation, and a lump sum payment of one hundred seventy-five thousand dollars ($175,000). Ind. Code §22-3-2-2.5.

EXHIBIT 3-3

Employment Relationships Covered Under Workers' Compensation (Indiana).

> (1) The nature of the business of the alleged principal;
> (2) Whether the work was specialized or non-specialized;
> (3) Whether the contract work was routine, customary, ordinary, or usual;
> (4) Whether the alleged principal customarily used his own employees to perform the work, or whether he contracted out all or most of such work;
> (5) Whether the alleged principal had the equipment and personnel capable of performing the contract work;
> (6) Whether those in similar businesses normally contract out this type of work or whether they have their own employees perform the work;
> (7) Whether the direct employer of the claimant was an independent business enterprise who insured his own workers and included that cost in the contract; and
> (8) Whether the principal was engaged in the contract work at the time of the incident.[3]

EXHIBIT 3-4
Factors that Determine Statutory Employer Status.

Determining Statutory Employer/Employee Status

The importance of the determination of employer/employee status is critical in a workers' compensation case. Given that most states provide the workers' compensation system as an exclusive remedy for injured workers, the analysis comes down to a simple determination: If the employee is covered, then he or she has no separate cause of action in tort against the employer; if the employee is not covered, then the employee has such a cause of action. Of course, this analysis centers on negligent actions. We have seen that intentional torts do not come under this analysis and may provide separate causes of action. See Exhibit 3-5. But for this discussion, we will assume that an employee has been injured on the job through negligence or some other nonintentional action. In this situation, the workers' compensation system must make a simple determination: Does the injury fall within the purview of the workers' compensation act or not? If it does, then the worker will receive benefits, but will also be barred from bringing a separate action against the employer. That is both the benefit and the detraction of the workers' compensation system. This provision also applies against fellow employees. If the injured worker has no separate cause of action for negligence against the employer, then the worker has no such action against coworkers. Consider Example 3-2.

Charities and Nonprofit Organizations

Does workers' compensation apply to charities and nonprofit organizations? Generally, no. There are some jurisdictions that specifically state in their laws that charitable organizations, like church societies and other similar

EXAMPLE 3-2

Don, James, and Hakim are working at a factory that manufactures very large steel pipes. While they are carrying a large section of pipe, James and Hakim accidentally drop it. Don is pinned by the heavy pipe against a wall and injures his back. Don files a claim for workers' compensation benefits, but then brings a separate suit against Hakim and James for negligence. Don alleges that James and Hakim worked for ABC Fluidic Design, a subcontractor employed by Don's employer, XYZ International Piping. Don alleges that since the other two worked for a different employer, he should be able to sue them for negligence, despite the exclusive remedy provisions of the workers' compensation statute. How does the court rule?

Answer: Our discussions have shown that an employer, even a statutory employer, must provide workers' compensation coverage. However, the rules don't change where a company hires one employee directly and the others through subsidiary companies. In this context, an employer is an employer and because of the provisions of state workers' compensation statutes, cannot be sued. This protection also applies to coworkers, whether they work for the same company or a subsidiary.[5]

None of the provisions of this law shall apply to the following employments unless coverage thereof is elected as provided in section 72-213, Idaho Code.

(1) Household domestic service.
(2) Casual employment.
(3) Employment of outworkers.
(4) Employment of members of an employer's family dwelling in his household.
(5) Employment of members of an employer's family not dwelling in his household if the employer is the owner of a sole proprietorship, provided the family member has filed with the commission a written declaration of his election for exemption from coverage. For the purposes of this subsection, "member of an employer's family" means a natural person or the spouse of a natural person who is related to the employer by blood, adoption or marriage within the first degree of consanguinity or a grandchild or the spouse of a grandchild.
(6) Employment as the owner of a sole proprietorship; employment of a working member of a partnership or a limited liability company; employment of an officer of a corporation who at all times during the period involved owns not less than ten percent (10%) of all of the issued and outstanding voting stock of the corporation and, if the corporation has directors, is also a director thereof.[6]

EXHIBIT 3-5

§ 72-212. Exemptions from Coverage (Idaho).

organizations, are exempt from workers' compensation laws. However, there are also many states that classify these workers as employees for purposes of workers' compensation coverage. The best practice when faced with this issue is to research the applicable state law.

Employers Who Wrongfully Deny Workers' Compensation Coverage

What happens when an employer is required to have workers' compensation coverage, but fails to provide it? What about situations where the employer had insurance coverage, but allowed it to lapse or failed to pay the insurance premium? The simple answer is that the employer remains liable for workers' compensation coverage. The general procedure followed in most states is: If the employer allows the workers' compensation policy to lapse, the state Workers' Compensation Board is notified. In fact, the board is notified whenever a policy is issued, modified, or canceled. If the board receives notice that a policy was canceled, but no information about how and when the company obtained a new policy, the employer faces fines for every day it goes without a policy. The daily fine can be several hundred dollars and can add up quickly. Added to that, if any employee is injured on the job during this period, the company must pay all medical bills. The same rule applies to companies who refuse to pay legitimate claims or wrongfully deny workers' compensation claims. However, there are some important limitations on this rule. For instance, if the employer can show that the employees qualify as "casual," then they are not required to have workers' compensation coverage.

Checklist

A small business owner files W-2 forms for six employees. He files 1099 forms for various other people who assist him in his work. He has avoided purchasing Workers' Compensation Insurance (WCI) coverage during the 2 years his business has been up and running. Defending his refusal to purchase coverage, he states that his business has limited funds. What information can be shared with him in order to convince him of the consequences of noncompliance?

1. What will happen if his neglect to purchase coverage is discovered?

    Employers bound by law to carry Workers' Compensation Insurance, but fail to do so, will be "issued a Stop Work Order" while further investigations are underway. *http://www.mass.gov/dia/Deskcan/erguide.pdf*

2. Will he owe anything for the amount of time he refused coverage when, by law, it was required?

    The employer will pay "up to three times" the premium he would have incurred during the course of the prior 2 years. If the calculated fine is less than $50,000, he will then be required to pay "up to $50,000" instead.
    http://www.dolir.mo.gov/wc/forms/wc-106-AI-07.pdf

3. If an employee is injured while performing duties on the job for the employer, what can happen?

    If an employer is not covered by Workers' Compensation Insurance, an injured employee may file suit against the employer.
    http://www.vwc.state.va.us/employers_guide.htm

4. Is it a possibility that the employer could lose his business if he does not obtain WCI coverage?

    Yes. Employers who have not purchased WCI will be prohibited from conducting business in the state pending the procurement of a workers' compensation policy.
    http://www.wcc.ne.gov/faqs/f35.htm

5. What other fines could he be facing?

    If an action is brought against the employer, and the employer appeals the action, he will be liable, upon conviction, for interest on the fine/penalties accrued over the course of the appellate proceedings.
    http://www.rilin.state.ri.us/statutes/Title28/28-36/28-36-15.HTM

6. Will coverage be required for his "1099 employees?"

    Yes, as long as both the duties they perform and the manner in which they perform those duties are under the direct control of the employer.
    http://www.comp.state.nc.us/ncic/pages/bus&ind.htm

7. Due to his business's funds being limited, can he take a percentage out of each of his employee's paychecks to help cover the cost of the premiums?

    No. Employers are responsible for the entire cost of WCI premiums. If he takes out a percentage of his employee's paychecks, he will be guilty of committing a misdemeanor. *http://www.wcc.state.md.us/Gen_Info/FAQ%20Employers.html*

8. What other way could his noncompliance be discovered?

    If an employee is injured, he or she can conduct a search of the employer's business to discover whether or not he is covered by Workers' Compensation Insurance. For the "Illinois Employer's Insurance Coverage Search" visit
    https://www.ewccv.com/cvs/

What Is Casual Employment?

Workers' compensation does not apply to casual employment. What qualifies as "casual employment?" The definition is often deliberately vague to give courts as much flexibility as they can in considering the issues. The general consensus is that casual employment is work that is only occasional or periodic with no fixed interval and no set times. The term *casual employee* does not mean someone who takes the job lightly, but someone who is not guaranteed a job at all and never knows when the next job will come along. Casual employees have no set times to come to work and/or no scheduled days to appear. The determination of casual employment is not based on whether or not the casual employee receives some kind of compensation for appearing. Instead, it is based on what the person does and when he or she does it. Consider Example 3-3 on page 82.

Actually, defining casual employment can present some unique problems for appellate courts. Given the dizzying array of potential jobs, it is difficult to come up with a single definition that fits all situations. Compare the definitions of casual employment provided in Exhibit 3-6 for a sample of the complexities involved.

A "casual employee" or workman is one who has entered the employment of another to render a particular service that is not continuous or regular but only occasional or incidental to the employment."[7]

"As to what constitutes an employment casual in character, it is obvious that the term 'casual' is not capable of scientific definition. Involved in it are the ideas of fortuitous happening and irregularity of occurrence; it denotes what is occasional, incidental, temporary, haphazard, unplanned. Applying it as practically as possible to the subject of employment, it may be said in general that if a person is employed only occasionally, at comparatively long and irregular intervals, for limited and temporary purposes, the hiring in each instance being a matter of special engagement, such employment is casual in character. On the other hand, even though an employment is not continuous, but only for the performance of occasional jobs, it is not to be considered as casual if the need for the work recurs with a fair degree of frequency and regularity, and, it being thus anticipated, there is an understanding that the employee is to perform such work as the necessity for it may from time to time arise. Even if there be but a single or special job involved, this does not conclusively stamp the employment as casual. If the work is not of an emergency or incidental nature but represents a planned project, and the tenure of the service necessary to complete it and for which the employment is to continue is of fairly long duration, the employment is not casual, and it is immaterial that the accident to the employee for which compensation is sought may occur within a very short period after his entry upon the work."[8]

EXHIBIT 3-6

Two Views of "Casual Employment."

> **EXAMPLE 3-3**
>
> Which of the following scenarios involve a "casual" employment scenario?
>
> 1. John does occasional work for a construction company. He helps frame houses, but does not work when the weather is bad. When the weather is good, he usually has a job on a crew working for ABC Construction Company. However, there are times when the company doesn't call.
> 2. Darrell does occasional work around town for different companies. Sometimes he cleans parking lots, and other times he'll work construction. He also doesn't work when the weather is bad, and he is never sure when his next job will be.
>
> Which one of these scenarios qualifies as casual employment, and which one qualifies under workers' compensation? If you answered that #1 qualifies under workers' compensation and #2 does not, you are correct. In #1 John has regular work for a specific company. The fact that he doesn't work all the time depends on the weather and some other conditions, but he usually has a job with specific duties and for a specific company. He is covered under workers' compensation.
>
> In #2 the situation is different. In Darrell's scenario, he does not work for a specific company and does not have a specific job when he does work. Basically, Darrell does odd jobs for local companies and, as a result, he is not covered under workers' compensation. What happens if Darrell gets injured on a job? He must pay his own medical bills. Of course, he can always sue the company he was working for when he got injured, but he will not be able to handle a claim through the workers' compensation system.

Other examples of casual employment include employment for a single task, like cleaning out a factory. If the employment ends when the job is over, then the person performing it is a casual employee and is not covered under workers' compensation. Consider Example 3-4.

> **EXAMPLE 3-4**
>
> Kyle is 16 and the son of the owner of a tire and auto service company. Kyle comes in every so often to help out, usually during his time out of from school, such as spring break. He can come and go as he pleases and none of the other employees knows when he will be there. One day, as Kyle is putting new tires on a rim, a customer's car suddenly rolls toward him and runs over his foot. He has numerous broken bones and files a workers' compensation claim. Is he covered under workers' compensation law?
>
> *Answer:* Because Kyle had no specified days of the week to report to work and no set times when he is there, he is a casual employee and not entitled to workers' compensation benefits.

EMPLOYEES UNDER WORKERS' COMPENSATION

So far, our discussion has focused on the statutory definition of employer under workers' compensation laws. In this section, we will examine the issue of the definition of employee under those same statutes.

Regular Employees

The provisions of the Workers' Compensation Act apply to anyone who could be classified as a regular employee. That term has been interpreted in a very broad manner. A regular employee is not necessarily someone who works at the company every day. A regular employee can be anyone who routinely works for the company, even on a seasonal basis. The rule here is simple. The courts will count anyone who may potentially qualify as an employee in order to determine if the employer falls under the workers' compensation statutes. When it is a close call, the courts will always side with the employees and require coverage under the workers' compensation statute.

Employees Who Do Not Qualify for Workers' Compensation

The same statutes that provide who is covered under workers' compensation also describe the individuals that do not qualify as employees. Consider Exhibit 3-7.

"Employee" excludes the following:

Any person who is employed by his or her parent, spouse, or child
Any person performing services in return for aid or sustenance only, received from any religious, charitable, or relief organization
Any person holding an appointment as deputy clerk or deputy sheriff
Any person performing voluntary services at or for a recreational camp
Volunteer coaches
Volunteer ski lift operators (this one is from California where they must have a lot of ski lifts)
Student athletes
Law enforcement officers (they have their own form of workers' compensation)

EXHIBIT 3-7
Defining Employee.

Compensation

One of the key elements that must be considered in determining the question of any person's employment status is the simple question of compensation. Generally speaking, uncompensated workers do not fall under the jurisdiction of workers' compensation statutes. Under this rule, a worker who is paid even a marginal sum is covered under workers' compensation laws; volunteer workers are not. By this definition, there are even situations where prison inmates may fall under the jurisdiction of state workers' compensation statutes.

Domestic Workers

Another question that often comes up in the context of employer-employee status has to do with domestic workers. These are the people who act as maids, cooks, and housekeepers for others. They work in homes. Are they covered by workers' compensation? Put another way, if you hire a maid, do you have to pay workers' compensation insurance premiums? The answer is no. Domestic workers are excluded from state workers' compensation laws. However, there are exceptions to that rule. For example, a homeowner might voluntarily enroll in the workers' compensation system and then all domestic staff would be covered. In most situations, workers in a private home do not fall under workers' compensation laws unless there are more than four domestics employed. That means a homeowner who has a cook and a maid is not required to provide workers' compensation coverage. However, if this homeowner has a staff of four or more domestic workers, then the homeowner must provide workers' compensation coverage.

Odd Jobs

When individuals or companies hire an individual to perform a single task, such as clearing away debris from gutters, this person does not qualify as an employee. Instead, this situation falls under the category of casual employment and, if the individual is injured, he or she would not be entitled to workers' compensation coverage.

Professional Athletes

Do professional athletes and the owners of professional sports teams qualify as employees and employers? Interestingly enough, the answer is yes. If a professional athlete is injured while performing his or her duties, then the athlete is covered under workers' compensation laws. Of course, some professional athletes are so well paid that the amount that they might receive under workers' compensation benefits would not be worth applying for, but the fact remains that they are covered.

Subcontractors

Over the years, there have been many cases that have tested the limits of definitions under the workers' compensation system. One of those issues involves subcontractors. In a typical contractor-subcontractor relationship, a general contractor is brought in, perhaps to build a house or work on some project and that general contractor hires subcontractors to carry out specialized work. For example, suppose that you want to build your own house. You hire a general contractor to take care of the project and the general contractor hires subcontractors to do things like frame the house and install drywall, heating, and air conditioning and the hundreds of other things that a new home requires. Suppose one of these subcontractors is injured on the job? Is the subcontractor considered to be an employee under workers' compensation laws? Because this was such a murky issue for so many years, with courts trying to decide if the subcontractor was strictly an employee of the general contractor or not, most states changed their laws and created the special category of "statutory employer." Under this definition, a general contractor is considered to be an employer, but only for the purposes of workers' compensation law. Once that change was made, subcontractors were allowed to file workers' compensation claims under the general contractor's insurance provider. The result of this ruling was that general contractors were protected from civil lawsuits by subcontractors, at least for on-the-job injuries. After all, if the subcontractor qualifies as an employee, that means that employee is barred from bringing a civil suit against the employer. However, the rule changes when the worker is classified as an independent contractor.

Independent Contractors

As we have already seen, if a person is classified as an employee, or even a subcontractor, he or she is covered under workers' compensation. However, that rule does not apply to independent contractors. An **independent contractor** is a freelance agent—a person who controls how he or she will actually perform the job and has little or no direct supervision from a boss, manager, or anyone else who might qualify as an employer. See Exhibit 3-8.

Independent contractor

A person or business that performs work or provides services to another and is not subject to the other person's control as the means of carrying out that work or service.

EXHIBIT 3-8

Court Definitions of "Independent Contractor."

> "When one exercising an independent employment contracts to do a piece of work according to his own judgment and methods, and without being subject to his employer except as to the result of the work, and who has the right to employ and direct the action of the workmen, independently of such employer and freed from any superior authority in him to say how the specified work shall be done or what laborers shall do as it progresses, he is clearly an independent contractor.
>
> "The vital test is to be found in the fact that the employer has or has not retained the right of control or superintendence over the contractor or employee as to details."[9]

The problem with being classified as an independent contractor is that if a person qualifies as one, then he or she is not covered under the workers' compensation system. That has both positive and negative aspects. The positive side is that if a person is classified as an independent contractor, he or she can bring a civil suit against the contractor or person for whom he or she is working. If the independent contractor wins a case like that, he or she can receive a great deal more from a jury award than the ultimate award in a workers' compensation case. On the other hand, the independent contractor might also lose the case and receive nothing. The jury might rule against the independent contractor and there would be no outside source to pay for medical bills or lost wages. Given the positive and negative aspects, most individuals who work on construction sites or manufacturing plants would probably choose to fall within the workers' compensation system rather than outside it. However, determining independent contractor status often raises tricky issues.

Determining Independent Contractor Status

Courts have been presented with the question of defining independent contractor status for decades, and they have come up with some basic guidelines to answer the question. If the answer to any of the court's questions is yes, then the person is an employee, not an independent contractor.

Question Number 1: Does the employer have the right to control how the employee actually did the job?

If the answer is yes, then the person is an employee and is covered by workers' compensation. If the answer is no, then he or she is an independent contractor and does not fall under the jurisdiction of state workers' compensation laws.

Question Number 2: Is the worker substantially economically dependent on the employer?

Before we can answer this question, we must define "substantially economically dependent." If the worker's sole means of support comes from jobs with this contractor, then he or she is substantially economically dependent on the contractor and qualifies for workers' compensation. This is true no matter what the parties believe or what they call themselves. A worker who refers to himself as an independent contractor may actually qualify as an employee under state workers' compensation rules.

EXAMPLE 3-5

Cal installs drywall. Drywall is a tricky business and there are lots of general contractors who refuse to do it. Instead, they call in a specialist. Cal is considered to be the Picasso of drywall. When Cal gets through mudding a board, no one can even tell where the screws went in. Each installation is a thing of beauty. Cal works for general contractors all over the city. He never knows which company he will be working for during any given week.

One day, while working on scaffolding for an arched ceiling, Cal falls and severely injures his back. Can Cal file for workers' compensation under the general contractor's insurance coverage?

The question is straightforward. If Cal is an employee, he can file and have everything taken care of. If Cal is an independent contractor, then he cannot file and he will have to rely on his own health insurance (which Cal does not have).

How would we answer the two-step questions set out above to answer the question of Cal's status?

Question Number 1: Does the employer have the right to control how the employee actually did the job?

Does the general contractor actually tell Cal how to put up the drywall; how to mud and tape it? No. In fact, the whole reason that Cal is brought is because the contractor specifically does not want to do that part of the job. The general contractor would prefer to leave the whole thing to Cal. Under this question, Cal qualifies as an independent contractor, not an employee; he is not covered by workers' compensation. But what about the second question?

Question Number 2: Is the worker substantially economically dependent on the employer?

The facts clearly show that Cal works for several different companies. He is not economically dependent on any single company. Cal is an independent contractor and does not fall under the jurisdiction of the state workers' compensation system.

> **SIDEBAR**
>
> "It is common practice in certain trades for one party to agree for a reward to complete a certain work or undertaking, and then to enter into subcontracts with various parties providing for the execution by them respectively of specified parts of the whole work or undertaking, so that the whole or part thereof would be done by such subcontractors and their assistants. In this manner the principal contractor would avoid in part the responsibility for accidents happening in the carrying out of the work or undertaking. If this responsibility were so shifted upon parties too weak financially to meet it, and who had not secured compensation to their employees in one of the ways required by the statute, an injured workman, proceeding at common law or under the Workmen's [sic] Compensation Act, would obtain neither

Some states do not make these distinctions about independent contractors. Instead, they refer to the difference between employers and contractors. In the states that rely on the definition of a contractor as someone who is not covered by workers' compensation, broader rules are followed. For instance, if the all of the work is done on the employer's premises, these states will consider the person to be an employee (and covered by workers' compensation). These states also follow what some refer to as the "tool rule." Under the tool rule, if the employer furnishes all of the tools and resources for the worker, then the worker is an employee and covered under workers' compensation. If the employer does not furnish these tools—and the worker does—then the worker is an independent contractor and must pay any injuries under his or her own insurance. Consider Example 3-6.

New Restrictions on Employers Under Workers' Compensation

In recent years, states have created new rules regarding employers and how they provide workers' compensation insurance coverage. One of those restrictions involves self-insurance.

> **EXAMPLE 3-6**
>
> Anne is in the business of training individuals how to use proprietary software. She travels all over the country and works with both small and large companies. She works with a company called "Professional Teach'em" that books her travel arrangements and arranges her schedule after she decides which jobs she will accept. However, she also works with a company that provides her with the latest training in the newest version of the software that she teaches. In fact, the company requires her to take two refresher courses each year before she is allowed to teach any new courses. Is Anne an independent contractor and thus covered under workers' compensation, or is she an independent contractor and therefore must arrange for her own medical coverage?
>
> *Answer:* The test for whether or not a person is an independent contractor goes to the actual performance of the job. There is no evidence here that anyone has the right to control how Anne does her job, only that she complete specific training on a specific date. Even though works with a company that arranges for her travel, she is still an independent contractor, because she can pick and choose what jobs she will take.

Self-Insurers

Companies that meet minimum financial standards are permitted to become **self-insurers**. A self-insurer is exactly what its name suggests: It is a company that acts as its own insurance company. Self-insurers have in-house claims' agents and pay out workers' compensation benefits from their own budget instead of paying premiums to an insurance company. The benefits are obvious: They save the money that they would ordinarily pay out to an insurance company. However, because individual states require that a company prove that it has several million dollars on hand to fund their self-insurance schemes, most companies do not meet the minimum requirements. If they fail to properly fund the program for the entire time that they claim status as a self-insurer, then they will face the same punishments as a company that does not have workers' compensation coverage in the first place. States require annual filings for companies that want to act as self-insurers. These filings must prove that they have adequate financial resources to meet the claims that could be made by their employees. See Exhibit 3-9.

Proof of Workers' Compensation Coverage

In addition to requiring specific information from self-insurers, many states have begun implementing new programs and restrictions on companies in order to prove that they have adequate workers' compensation coverage. One of the most popular restrictions involves building permits.

Many states have created laws that specifically prevent local counties from issuing business licenses, building permits, sewage certificates, and other local county paperwork until the company produces proof that it has workers' compensation coverage. In fact, most states now have a form that a company must show on demand that specifies that it has filed annual proof of workers' compensation coverage and that it has paid its insurance premium.

> (a) Prior to issuing a building permit pursuant to section 29-263 a local building official shall require proof of workers' compensation coverage for all employees.[11]

SIDEBAR

compensation nor damages. Furthermore, difficult questions arose with reference to whether the workman was the servant of the principal contractor rather than of his immediate employer, depending largely upon who had power to hire and discharge, to direct and control the workmen, and a variety of other circumstances. In order to obviate these contingencies, and more certainly to assure the workman his contemplated compensation, the statute has imposed … a liability to pay upon the principal contractor, although he might not have been held at common law the employer of the injured workman."[10]

■ **Self-insurer**
A company that acts as its own workers' compensation insurance provider.

EXHIBIT 3-9
Proof of Workers' Compensation Coverage.

> **CASE EXCERPT**
>
> **DETERMINING EMPLOYEE STATUS FOR COLLEGE ATHLETES**
> *Graczyk v. Workers' Comp. Appeals Bd.*, 184 Cal.App.3d 997, 229
> Cal.Rptr. 494 (Cal.App. 2 Dist., 1986)
>
> LILLIE, Presiding Justice.
>
> Petitioner Ricky D. Graczyk (applicant) seeks review of the decision of respondent Workers' Compensation Appeals Board that he was not an employee of respondent California State University, Fullerton (CSUF) when injured in a football game while he was a student at CSUF. We conclude that the Board correctly determined applicant was not an employee of CSUF.
>
> Applicant allegedly sustained injuries to his head, neck and spine while playing varsity college football for CSUF on September 9, 1978, as well as in the period from August 7, 1977, through November 27, 1978.
>
> Trial of his application was bifurcated, and the matter was submitted on the issue whether he was an employee of CSUF within the meaning of the statutory definition of employee (Lab.Code, §§ 3351, 3352).
>
> The evidence established that applicant enrolled as a student at CSUF in the fall of 1977, following completion of high school. Football scouts from CSUF and two other universities recruited him; however, he chose CSUF because it was "close to my mom and the rest of my family." He commenced studies and playing football immediately upon enrollment. Representatives of the CSUF football program encouraged applicant to apply for financial aid. During his first year as a student, he received financial aid, including a college opportunity grant of $1,100 a year from the state, a supplementary grant of approximately $800 from CSUF, and a student loan. Other than the student loan, the grants he received in the first year were based upon financial need and academic achievement, and were unrelated to athletic achievement.
>
> In applicant's second year at CSUF, he received an athletic scholarship in the amount of $1,600 a year, payable in monthly installments. The athletic coach determined recipients of athletic scholarships based on athletic progress and value to the football team; and the scholarship funds were raised by alumni and business groups. Applicant had intended to continue playing on the football team even had he not received the athletic scholarship. The scholarship was for a full year and could not be terminated unless the recipient quit the team, dropped out of school, or failed to maintain academic standards. The scholarship was intended to meet
>
> *Continued*

costs of room and board, but there was no control over the manner in which the recipient spent it. Applicant understood that it was to be used for student expenses, and he so used it. The WORKERS' COMPENSATION JUDGE found that applicant was an employee of CSUF, concluding in essence that he was an employee within the statutory definition of employee as interpreted in *Van Horn v. Industrial Acc. Com.* (1963) 219 Cal.App.2d 457, 33 Cal.Rptr. 169; and that although section 3352, subdivision (k), excluding student athletes as employees, is constitutional, it was enacted in 1981 and could not properly be applied retroactively to deprive applicant of his vested right to employee status under the law existing at the time of his injury.

The Board granted reconsideration and found (in a 2-1 decision) that applicant was not an employee of CSUF. The Board's determination was based on interpretation of the relevant statutes defining 'employee.' Thus, the Board noted the general requirement (§ 3600) of the existence of "employment" as a prerequisite to workers' compensation coverage, as well as the general statutory definition of "employee" (§ 3351) and the statutory definition of persons excluded from the general definition of employee (§ 3352). The Board concluded that the Legislature's 1981 amendment of section 3352, adding subsection (k) thereto and expressly declaring the amendment retroactive, could properly be applied retroactively to exclude applicant from the statutory definition of an employee entitled to benefits under the workers' compensation law. The Board's dissenting panel member stated that he "would find that Labor Code Section 3352(k) may not constitutionally be applied to deprive applicant of a vested right."

In support of his contention that the Board erred in finding that he was not an employee of CSUF, applicant asserts he had a "vested right" in employee status under the law existing at the time of his injuries as established in *Van Horn v. Industrial Acc. Com.*, supra, 219 Cal.App.2d 457, 33 Cal.Rptr. 169, and hence he could not be deprived of it retroactively by the Legislature's 1981 amendment to section 3352. The retroactive operation of a civil statute is by no means unusual, and no constitutional objection exists to such operation save where a vested right, or the obligation of a contract, is impaired. To determine whether applicant had a vested right of action, we must look to the unique nature of the workers' compensation law in California.

California workers' compensation law (§ 3200 et seq.) is a statutory system enacted pursuant to constitutional grant of plenary power to the Legislature to establish a complete and exclusive system of workers' compensation. It is "an expression of the police power" (§ 3201) and has been upheld as a valid exercise of the police power.

Continued

The right to workers' compensation benefits is "wholly statutory" and is not derived from common law. This statutory right is exclusive of all other statutory and common law remedies, and substitutes a new system of rights and obligations for the common law rules governing liability of employers for injuries to their employees. Rights, remedies and obligations rest on the status of the employer-employee relationship, rather than on contract or tort.

In enacting the workers' compensation law as an expression of the police power pursuant to the constitutional grant of plenary power, the Legislature has defined employee status in sections 3351 and 3352. In essence, section 3351 defines persons included in the definition of "employee," and section 3352 defines persons excluded therefrom. An employee excluded from compensation benefits under section 3352 retains his right to maintain a civil action for damages against his employer.

In 1963, at the time of the decision in *Van Horn v. Industrial Acc. Com.*, supra, 219 Cal.App.2d 457, 33 Cal.Rptr. 169, the section 3352 exclusionary definition of employee did not refer to athletes among the occupational groups then excluded from employee status. *Van Horn* (id.) held that a student athlete who was killed in an airplane crash while returning to California with members of the college football team and college officials was an employee within the meaning of the section 3351 definition and the section 3357 presumption that any person rendering service for another, unless expressly excluded by statute, is presumed to be an employee. The *Van Horn* opinion made no reference to the section 3352 exclusionary statute.

Apparently in a response to the *Van Horn* decision (1 Herlick, Cal. Workers' Comp. Law, supra, § 2.11, pp. 30–31), the Legislature in 1965 amended section 3352, adding former subdivision (j) (presently subd. (g), see fn. 3, supra), which provides that "'Employee' excludes . . . [a]ny person, other than a regular employee, participating in sports or athletics who receives no compensation for such participation other than the use of athletic equipment, uniforms, transportation, travel, meals, lodgings, or other expenses incidental thereto." The 1965 amendment was "designed to clarify the position of those who sponsor athletic events or participants in various forms of athletics, [the exclusions being] predicated on the absence of the usual elements of the employment relationship."

In 1977–1978, applicant sustained the alleged injuries herein. In 1981, the Legislature, again taking cognizance of the *Van Horn* decision (see fn. 4, infra), further amended section 3352, attempting to more specifically clarify the exclusion of athletic participants by adding present subdivision (k), which provides that "'Employee' excludes . . . [a]ny student participating as an athlete in amateur sporting events

Continued

sponsored by any public agency, public or private nonprofit college, university or school, who receives no remuneration for such participation other than the use of athletic equipment, uniforms, transportation, travel, meals, lodgings, scholarships, grants-in-aid, or other expenses incidental thereto." The Legislature expressly declared the act "an urgency statute necessary for the immediate preservation of the public peace, health, or safety within the meaning of Article IV of the Constitution" (Stats.1981, ch.21, § 13, p. 49), and stated that "The Legislature finds and declares that the provisions of law set forth in Sections 8, 9, and 10 of this act, which respectively amend Sections 3352 and 3852 of the Labor Code and add Section 3706.5 to the Labor Code, do not constitute a change in, but are declaratory of, the existing law. These provisions shall apply to all claims filed for injuries occurring prior to the effective date of this act."

Since the 1963 *Van Horn* decision was based on section 3351 without any reference or determination as to section 3352, and since in 1965 the Legislature in response to the *Van Horn* decision and prior to the 1977–1978 date of applicant's injuries added former subdivision (j) clarifying the section 3352 exclusionary definition of athletes as employees, the law relating to employee status was in flux, and applicant did not at the time of his injury have a vested right in the *Van Horn* interpretation of the employee status statutes.

Moreover, applicant's inchoate right to benefits under the workers' compensation law is wholly statutory and had not been reduced to final judgment before the Legislature's 1981 addition of subdivision (k) further clarifying the employee status of athletes. Hence, applicant did not have a vested right, and his constitutional objection has no bearing on the issue. Where a right of action does not exist at common law, but depends solely on statute, the repeal of the statute destroys the inchoate right unless it has been reduced to final judgment, or unless the repealing statute contains a saving clause protecting the right in pending litigation. Because it is a creature of statute, the right of action exists only so far and in favor of such person as the legislative power may declare.

Thus, although the law in force at the time of the injury is determinative of a person's right to recovery of compensation benefits, this general rule is subject to circumstances where the legislative intent is to the contrary, provided that in making substantial changes which enlarge or diminish existing rights and obligations, the Legislature's intent to do so retroactively must be clear. Here, the Legislature clearly stated its intent that its 1981 amendment to section 3352 further clarifying the statutory definition of employee status of athletes be retroactive.

For the foregoing reasons, we conclude that applicant did not have a vested right in employee status at the time of his injury; and hence no constitutional objection exists to retroactive operation of the 1981 statute.

Continued

We also consider respondents' contention that irrespective whether applicant's right be characterized as "vested" or "unvested," retroactivity of the Legislature's declaration that its 1981 statutory amendment to section 3352 be retroactive is justified by police power "policy factors."

"Vested rights are not immutable; the state, exercising its police power may impair such rights when considered reasonably necessary to protect the health, safety, morals and general welfare of the people." Hence, the constitutional question, on principle, is not whether a vested right is impaired by a change of law, but whether such a change reasonably could be believed sufficiently necessary to the public welfare as to justify the impairment.

In determining whether a given retroactive provision contravenes due process in impairing a vested right, certain policy factors are considered, such as the significance of the state interest served by the law, the importance of the retroactive application of the law to the effectuation of that interest, the extent of reliance upon the former law, the legitimacy of that reliance, the extent of actions taken on the basis of that reliance, and the extent to which the retroactive application of the new law would disrupt those actions. Where retroactive application is necessary to subserve a sufficiently important state interest, the inquiry need proceed no further.

In *Flournoy* (supra), the court weighed these policy factors, balanced the great public interest and the importance of its retroactive application against a right which had not been grievously impaired, and concluded that the legislative declaration of retroactivity was not unconstitutional.

Here, as previously indicated, the state has a significant, if not a compelling interest in defining the employer-employee status, such status in fact being the very cornerstone of the Legislature's enactment of a complete and exclusive workers' compensation system in exercise of its police power pursuant to the constitutional grant of plenary power. Retroactive application of the 1981 amendment to section 3352 clearly subserved this compelling state interest, as evidenced by the legislative history (fn. 4, supra) to effectuate that interest by clarifying the statutory definition excluding athletes as employees under the 1965 amendment to section 3352. Also, the 1981 amendment legitimately relied on the former law as set forth in section 3352.

Thus, all of the policy factors are in favor of the Legislature's declaration of retroactivity except the extent to which retroactive application would disrupt employee status rights of persons in applicant's position. As to disruption of such rights, we have noted that persons excluded from workers' compensation by the section 3352 exclusionary definition of employee retain their right to maintain a civil action for damages. In addition, the 1981 amendment to section 3352 was not

Continued

"surprise legislation" in light of the existence of the 1965 amendment thereto excluding athletes as employees. Thus, whatever right a person in applicant's position may have had when the Legislature further amended the athletic exclusion definition in 1981 was not "grievously impaired"; and a weighing of the policy factors establishes that the legislative declaration of retroactivity is not unconstitutional.

The June 27, 1985 Decision After Reconsideration of Respondent Workers' Compensation Appeals Board is affirmed.

Case Questions:

1. What limitations did Graczyk have on spending his football scholarship?
2. Did receipt of this scholarship turn Graczyk into an employee of the college? Why or why not?
3. Is the right to receive workers' compensation benefits derived from common law or statutory law? Why is that determination important?
4. Does the fact that benefits are a "vested" right have an impact on the court's decision? Why or why not?

ETHICAL CONSIDERATION:
The Attorney-Client Privilege

The attorney-client privilege is considered to be one of the most important aspects of legal practice. The privilege protects attorneys from being compelled to answer questions or provide details about a client's case, even if the attorney is subpoenaed and called to the stand to be cross-examined. If the attorney invokes the privilege concerning matters covered by the privilege, then the attorney cannot be held in contempt or otherwise penalized for failure to answer such questions.

A question often arises about how far this privilege extends. For instance, is a paralegal protected by a similar privilege? The answer is no. There are some jurisdictions that have held that the presence of the paralegal during an attorney-client discussion may actually waive or eliminate the privilege. That being true, a paralegal cannot refuse to answer questions about conversations with a client. As a result, the paralegal should ensure that the attorney-client privilege is not waived under any circumstances. Because the conversations between the attorney and the client are supposed to be private, the paralegal should make sure that they remain so. The best way to do this is not to discuss any client business away from the office. Unless given permission to do so, it is a good idea to refuse to state that a particular person is even represented by the attorney. Discussing client business with other paralegals, family members, and court personnel might result in a ruling that the privilege has been breached and the client may no longer have that protection. Given that the attorney-client privilege, like doctor-patient confidentiality, is such a core component of the service that the attorney provides, you should never discuss client affairs with anyone other than the attorney and relevant office personnel. Information such as that provided in Exhibit 3-10 would also be considered privileged.

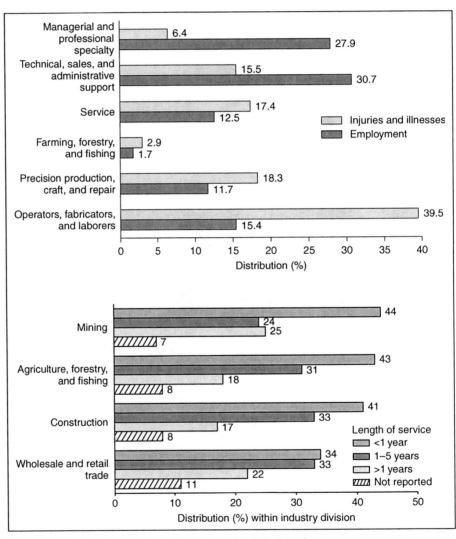

EXHIBIT 3-10 Worker Health Chartbook 2004 (3 sheets).

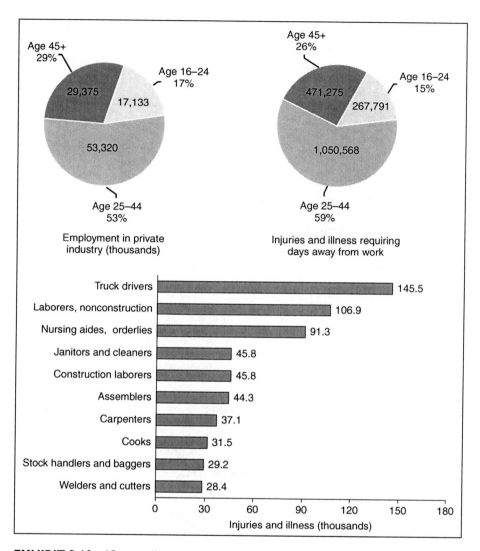

EXHIBIT 3-10 *(Continued)*

CHAPTER SUMMARY

The definition of employer and employee is extremely important in order to figure out who is and who is not covered under the workers' compensation statute. An employer is someone who has workers. Employers must pay into the workers' compensation fund, either by becoming self-insurers or by obtaining workers' compensation insurance. An employee is defined as someone who works regularly for a company. When a person qualifies as an employee under workers' compensation, it means that he or she is entitled to file a claim through the system when injured on the job.

■ KEY TERMS

Employer

Self insurer

Independent contractor

Statutory employer

■ REVIEW QUESTIONS

1. Who qualifies as an employer under workers' compensation?
2. What is a "statutory employer?"
3. In Example 3-5, if Cal refers to himself as an "independent contractor," does that change the analysis? Explain your answer.
4. Is there a minimum number of employees that an employer must have before the employer qualifies under workers' compensation? Explain.
5. What is the rule about paying workers' compensation benefits when an employee has multiple employers?
6. Do partners qualify as employees of one another? Explain.
7. Do charities qualify as employers under workers' compensation statutes? Explain your answer.
8. What sanctions are brought to bear on employers who do not provide workers' compensation when they are legally required to do so?
9. What is casual employment?
10. What is a regular employee?
11. Do workers' compensation statutes apply to seasonal or temporary workers? Explain.
12. What is the rule about domestic workers and workers' compensation coverage?
13. Do subcontractors qualify as employees under workers' compensation statutes? Why or why not?

14. Why is the classification as an independent contractor important under workers' compensation laws?
15. What are some tests that courts apply to the question of whether or not a person qualifies as an independent contractor?
16. What is a self-insurer?
17. What restrictions have states imposed in order to ensure that employers have appropriate workers' compensation insurance coverage?

QUESTIONS FOR REFLECTION

Is the definition of employer and employee too restrictive? Should the definition be expanded to include anyone who works for another? Explain your answer.

WEB SITES

Louisiana Workers' Compensation Board
http://www.laworks.net/bus_oworkers' compensationa.asp

Workers' Compensation Board of Indiana
http://www.in.gov/workcomp/

Arkansas Workers' Compensation Commission
http://www.aworkers' compensationc.state.ar.us/

PRACTICAL APPLICATIONS

How does your state define employer and employee for purpose of workers' compensation coverage? Does your state have a specific minimum number of employees that an employer must have before it qualifies under the statute?

END NOTES

[1] Farrell at 277, 330 N.W.2d 397.
[2] (Mississippi Sec. 71-3-5).
[3] AMJUR WORKERS § 91.
[4] *Kirkland v. Riverwood Intern. USA, Inc.*, 681 So.2d 329 (La. 1996).
[5] *O'Donnell v. R.M. Shoemaker & Co.*, 816 A.2d 1159 (Pa.Super. 2003).

6 (Idaho) I.C. § 72-212.

7 *Porter v. Mapleton Elec. Light Co.*, 183 N.W. 803, 805 (Iowa 1921).

8 *Cochrane v. William Penn Hotel*, 339 Pa. 549, 16 A.2d 43 (Pa. 1940).

9 *Hayes v. Board of Trustees of Elon College*, 224 N.C. 11, 15, 29 S.E.2d 137, 140 (N.C. 1944).

10 *Para v. Richards Group of Washington Ltd. Partnership*, 339 Md. 241, 661 A.2d 737 (Md. 1995).

11 Sec. 31-286b, Connecticut Code.

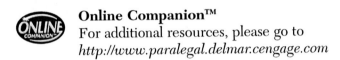

Online Companion™
For additional resources, please go to
http://www.paralegal.delmar.cengage.com

Injuries Under Workers' Compensation

CHAPTER 4

CHAPTER OBJECTIVES

At the completion of this chapter, you should be able to:

- Describe the types of injuries that are covered under workers' compensation laws
- Define the regulations that govern the reporting of injuries occurring on the job
- Describe how injuries are considered to be "arising out of" employment
- Explain the concept of detour and frolic
- Describe occupational illnesses

INTRODUCTION TO INJURIES

In this chapter, we will focus on what qualifies as a job-related injury. We will also examine the related issues of reporting injuries. In order to be compensable under workers' compensation, an injury must arise out of employment duties and in the course of employment. We will define these terms with precision and then examine actions that may exclude an injury from coverage, including detour, frolic, and other employee actions. It is the responsibility of the employee to demonstrate that an injury was work related. When this threshold has been met, the employee is entitled to medical treatment and other treatment, all provided through the employer's workers' compensation fund or insurer. On the other hand, if the employer can show that the employee was engaged in some action that did not arise out of employment, or that the employee was intoxicated, engaged in horseplay, or other actions, the employer may be able to exclude the employee from coverage.

DEFINING INJURIES UNDER WORKERS' COMPENSATION

When an injury occurs, employers are legally obligated to respond quickly by providing medical assistance. Depending on the severity of the injury, the employee may be taken to a hospital emergency room or directed to seek medical treatment at a later date. The employer is not permitted to counsel the employee from seeking medical attention or to make its own determination that the employee does not need any treatment. In addition to ensuring prompt treatment for an injured employee, the employer is also responsible for reporting the accident. The report might go directly to the company owner in a small company or the Human Resources Director in a larger company. In turn, the HR Director must file a report of the incident with the insurance provider as well as the state agency responsible for administering workers' compensation.[1] However, these are not the only individuals who are required to report accidents. The employee also has responsibilities.

When the employee is injured, it is the employee's responsibility to immediately report the incident to his or her supervisor. Failure to report the accident can have disastrous consequences for the employee's future workers' compensation claim. For instance, if the employee waits too long to report the accident, he or she may be statutorily barred from bringing a claim. The actual deadline varies from state to state, but can be as minimal as ten days. Time limits are important for other reasons. For instance, an employee who waits more than 2 years in most states to file a claim is barred from bringing the action. See Exhibit 4-1.

(a) Except as provided in subsection (c) of this section, if a covered employee suffers an accidental personal injury, the covered employee, within 60 days after the date of the accidental personal injury, shall file with the Commission:

(1) a claim application form; and

(2) if the covered employee was attended by a physician chosen by the covered employee, the report of the physician.

(b)(1) Unless excused by the Commission under paragraph (2) of this subsection, failure to file a claim in accordance with subsection (a) of this section bars a claim under this title.[2]

EXHIBIT 4-1
§ 9-709. Accidental Personal Injury—Claim Application (Maryland).

Reporting the employee's accident is an important step for both the employee and the employer, however, this discussion begs the question: what is an injury, at least as that term is defined under workers' compensation law? That is the topic of the next section.

Checklist

A woman was severely injured during an automobile accident. Her husband has come to our firm wanting to know if the circumstances surrounding those injuries qualify her to receive compensation under the Workers' Compensation Act. What are some of the questions that we should obtain answers to?

1. Was the injury caused by an accident?

   An injury must be caused by an accident in order for the claimant to receive compensation under the Workers' Compensation Act. *http://www.ops.state.nc.us/emprsk/wc/handbook/bk-intro.html*

2. Could she be proven to have been "at work" at the time of the incident?

   If so, the requirement that all work-related injuries must "arise out of the course of employment" can be proven, as she will be able to show that her whereabouts satisfy the question of "origin of the risk." *http://www.legis.state.la.us/*

3. Is travel one of his wife's expected job functions?

   Her injury was caused during an automobile accident; therefore, if her employer required her to travel, "a causal connection between [her] injury and the conditions under which [she] work[ed]" exists. *http://www.co.fresno.ca.us/.../agendas/2006/022706/022706%20Disability%20Retirement%20Law%20Resource.pdf*

4. Did the incident occur during her working hours?

   For her injuries to be compensable under the Workers' Compensation Act, "in the course of employment" must be satisfied. If the incident occurred during normal working hours, that requirement may be met. *http://www.cbs.state.or.us/wcb/2006/review/jul/0406938a.pdf*

5. Is common-law language used under the statute?

   Common-law language differs from the terms used most often under the various Workers' Compensation Acts. "[S]cope of employment" common-law language, is to be recognized as meaning the same as "in the course of employment." *Jefferson v. T.L. James & Co.*, 420 F.2d 322 (5th Cir. 1969)

6. Was her commute necessary to abide by a specific order given to her by the employer and did it occur during her work hours?

    For injuries to be compensable, when sustained away from the normal place of work, the claimant must show that she was not engaging in a personal matter, but rather was performing job duties, despite not being "in or about the premises." *http://dir.alabama.gov/docs/law/wc_480-5-5-.02.pdf*

7. Did the incident occur during her commute to or from work?

    Under the Workers' Compensation Act, the claimant would not be able to receive compensation if the incident occurred during her commute either to or from work. Only policemen and firefighters are given an exception. *http://www.senate.mo.gov/05info/BTS_Web/Bill.aspx?SessionType=R&BillID=126*

8. Does she show any possible signs of having developed an anxiety disorder?

    If a mental disorder results from an injury, which meets qualifications under the Act, the disorder may be compensable as long as said injury can be found to have been the "proximate cause" of the disorder. If she claims that her mental disorder rose out of loss of employment, due to suffering injuries, that would not satisfy the criteria under the Act; and, therefore, reparation under the Workers' Compensation Act would be denied. *http://www.legislature.state.tn.us/*

Injuries "Arising out of" and "In the course of" Employment

Before we address specific examples of what constitutes a work-related injury, we must address a more fundamental question. Under workers' compensation law, an injury must satisfy two legal requirements before it will be considered for compensation. These two legal elements are:

1. That the injury "**arises out of**" the employee's job duties and
2. That the injury occurred during "**in the course of**" employment.

Defining "Arising out of"

Workers' compensation statutes in every state impose the requirement that an employee's injury must arise out of the workplace. This simple requirement is the core of the workers' compensation system—that employees surrender the right to bring tort actions against their employers in exchange for coverage of work-related injuries through the workers' compensation system. As we have already seen, this arrangement protects employers from civil suits, but it also imposes on them requirements to care for injured workers. However, the cornerstone of this entire arrangement is the requirement that the injury

Arises out of

The requirement under workers' compensation law that before an injury will be compensated, it must be directly tied to the worker's job duties.

In the course of

The requirement that an injured worker was carrying out duties on behalf of the employer at the time of the injury.

occur on-the-job. If not, the employer has no responsibility to provide medical coverage for the employee. Instead, the employee must either fall back on his or her own resources or on another form of medical insurance.

At first glance, the two requirements that the employee's injury must arise out of and occur in the course of employment are both obvious and difficult to define. An employee who falls while carrying out work duties will be covered by workers' compensation, but what about the employee who has stopped for a drink of water or a bite of food? What about employees who are on a break when they receive their injuries? What rules do we follow when the employee is running an errand for the company? Because of the many different activities that employees carry out, simply defining "arising out of" employment duties can involve a protracted analysis.

Simply put, before an employee can receive compensation for an injury that happens at work, the employee must prove that the injury arose out of the employee's job duties. The employee has to prove that there is a direct cause and effect between his or her job duties and the injury. In many instances, this is a straightforward proposition. Consider the facts in Example 4-1.

Courts have been very liberal in their interpretations of injuries that arise out of employment. Essentially, appellate courts have held that if the employee is acting within the scope of his job duties, then any injury he or she receives will be compensable under workers' compensation law. Scope of job duties includes not only the basic job requirements, but also any related activities. Later in this chapter, we will see that this concept has been expanded to include foreseeable employee activities including trips to the bathroom, eating, drinking, and many other activities. Defining the phrase "arising out of" takes us into the actual duties assigned to the employee and the actions of the employee when the injury occurred. If the employer can show that the employee was not engaged in work-related activity, such as carrying out a personal errand, or engaged in frolic, detour, or

> **SIDEBAR**
>
> "Arising out of employment" is a term almost always seen in close conjunction to "in the course of employment." See Exhibit 4-2.

EXAMPLE 4-1

Maria is driving home from work one afternoon; she stops at the grocery store to buy dinner and slips inside the store and injures herself. Is that injury compensable under workers' compensation?

Answer: No. Maria is clearly not at work and we have already seen that entire purpose behind the workers' compensation scheme is to provide a safety net for employees who are injured on the job. Because Maria is clearly not at work, then workers' compensation issues do not arise.

EXHIBIT 4-2

Injury Under California Law.

> "Injury" includes any injury or disease arising out of the employment, including injuries to artificial members, dentures, hearing aids, eyeglasses, and medical braces of all types; provided, however, that eyeglasses and hearing aids will not be replaced, repaired, or otherwise compensated for, unless injury to them is incident to an injury causing disability.[3]

other activity, then the employee is not acting within the scope of his or her job duties and the resulting injury did not arise out of employment. In addition to establishing that the injury arose out of employment duties, the employee must also prove that the injury occurred within the course of employment. The analysis of course of employment takes into account a different perspective on workers' compensation cases.

Defining "In the course of"

An employee is responsible for showing that the injury he or she received occurred during the course of employment. Broadly defined, this phrase indicates that the employee's injury was a consequence of job duties and was not caused by the employee's negligence, or during a period of time where the employee was not carrying out company business. If the employee can show that he or she was actively engaged in employment duties, or closely related activities, then the employee can establish that the injury occurred during the course of job-related duties. If, on the other hand, the employer can show that the employee was not engaged in work-related actions, either because the employee was not on the job site, not authorized to carry out certain actions, or carrying out personal functions, then the employer can ask the workers' compensation board to refuse to pay the employee's claim. See Exhibit 4-3.

We will address these last two scenarios and several others as we explore exactly what constitutes a work-related injury. Consider Example 4-2 and Example 4-3.

EXHIBIT 4-3

Defining Injury for Workers' Compensation Purposes (Florida).

> "Injury" means personal injury or death by accident arising out of and in the course of employment, and such diseases or infection as naturally or unavoidably result from such injury. Damage to dentures, eyeglasses, prosthetic devices, and artificial limbs may be included in this definition only when the damage is shown to be part of, or in conjunction with, an accident. This damage must specifically occur as the result of an accident in the normal course of employment.[4]

EXAMPLE 4-2

Suppose Maria is on her lunch break; she goes to the grocery store, slips and injures herself. In the Example 4-1, she was clearly not at work or doing any work-related activities, so we could be confident in our analysis that workers' compensation laws did not apply. However, are the issues still as clear? Consider Example 4-3.

EXAMPLE 4-3

In this scenario, Maria stops by the grocery store at the direction of her employer in order to pick up some items for a work function. She falls and injures herself. Are her injuries compensable under workers' compensation?

TYPES OF INJURIES UNDER WORKERS' COMPENSATION

The types of injuries that an employee can receive on the job are almost as numerous and diverse as the people who receive them. However, we can classify injuries into broad categories, showing how a particular injury either is or is not covered under workers' compensation. We will begin with a general definition of "injury" under workers' compensation statutes.

For purpose of workers' compensation, an injury is defined as any harm suffered by an employee that arises out of and during the course of employment. This definition is broad enough to encompass the definition of injury found in most state workers' compensation statutes. With this working definition in mind, we will now proceed to a delineation of specific types of injuries and consider how workers' compensation laws apply. See Exhibit 4-4.

> The employer must pay compensation or furnish benefits required by this chapter if the employee suffers an accidental compensable injury or death arising out of work performed in the course and the scope of employment. The injury, its occupational cause, and any resulting manifestations or disability must be established to a reasonable degree of medical certainty, based on objective relevant medical findings, and the accidental compensable injury must be the major contributing cause of any resulting injuries.[5]

EXHIBIT 4-4

When the Employer Must Pay for Benefits for On-the-Job Injuries (Florida).

Checklist

What questions must be answered in order to determine whether or not an injury meets the criteria under the Workers' Compensation Act?

1. If a claimant's injuries arose out of a motor vehicle accident, did they occur during a brief detour where the purpose of such detour was personal rather than "in the course of" his/her employment? Is the claimant either a policeman or a firefighter?

    Typically, commuting to and from one's home does not meet requirements under the Workers' Compensation Act. An exception is made for both policemen and firefighters due to the exigency of when they are called upon to work. However, a restriction does pertain to this category of employees. If they detoured from the necessary course, and were found to have been engaging in frolic when an injury transpired, that injury would not be compensable under the Workers' Compensation Act. http://wcc.state.ct.us/CRB/1997/3159crb.htm

2. Did the injury result from a claimant's active role in "horseplay?"

    An injury is no longer considered to be "in the course of employment" if the claimant was involved in horseplay. http://www2.iwd.state.ia.us/dwc/wcdecisions.nsf/13f598daaee1d21286256e7d00734325/90d86aca6c33d22f862572b1005cb8dc!OpenDocument

3. Is a medical professional able to show a relationship between a claimed mental injury and a claimant's work?

    Once the ordinary provisions of the Act are met, "arising out of employment" and "in the course of employment," psychological injuries are only compensable under the Act when they can be shown to be "the result of a triggering physical event." Where the correlation between the claimed mental injury and a claimant's work is ambiguous, a medical professional must declare that such a correlation does in fact exist. http://www.courts.state.pa.us/OpPosting/CWealth/out/2058CD06_7-10-07.pdf

4. Did an assailant cause the claimant's injury? If so, was the assailant a co-employee?

    For an injury to be compensable under the Act, it must be caused by an accident. Assault on an employee is considered to be an accident, as long as the claimant is not found, in any way, to have known about, or brought about, the assault. http://links.jstor.org/sici?sici=0008-221(195410)42%3A4%3C531%3ACTICFI%3E2.0.CO%3B2-P

5. If the injured worker is claiming that a disorder was caused by an injury, is he or she able to receive compensation for the disorder?

    The evidence must show an unmistakable relationship between the two, "an injury and a [consequential] disorder." *Hogan v. Twin City Amusement Co.*, 193 N.W. 122 (1923)

6. Was the claimant proven to be under the influence at the time the injury occurred? If so, did his or her employer promote the act that resulted in the claimant becoming inebriated?

   If a claimant can be found to have been intoxicated at the time of injury, compensation is denied under the Act. However, an employer has no grounds to deny the claimant compensation, due to intoxication, if the employer permitted any act that resulted in the claimant's intoxicated state. *McCarty v. Workmen's Comp. Appeals Bd.*, 12 Cal. 3d 677, 117 Cal. Rptr. 65, 527 P.2d 617 (1974)

7. What needs to be determined before an employee is eligible to receive compensation when claiming an occupational disease?

   To prove occupational disease, the employee must show that in any other area of his or her life, the conditions that would cause such a disease were never present. In other words, these conditions can only be found in his/her place of work. *http://www.publications.ojd.state.or.us/A98806.htm*

8. Did the injury transpire during his or her lunch or restroom break?

   If so, the claimant may be eligible to receive compensation. Lunch and restroom breaks are personal but do not fall under any list of disqualifying deviations from the "scope of employment." According to the "personal comfort doctrine," such breaks are necessary "because they improve the efficiency of the employee and thereby benefit the employer." *http://www.appealsboardreporter.com/articles/ABR01-20051210-004.htm.aspx*

Travel to and from Work

In most circumstances, an employee is not covered for injuries received traveling to or returning from the workplace. This is considered to be an employee's personal business and, because the employee is not carrying out any work-related activity, simple commuting will not qualify as arising out of employment. The reasoning behind this rule is that it avoids a potential flood gate of cases. After all, personal injury cases arising in automobile accidents are some of the most common type of lawsuits in the United States. Allowing such claims to be brought through the workers' compensation system would deplete the relatively small resources of the system. Such cases have nearly overwhelmed the regular court system.

However, the rules change when the employee is required to travel as part of his or her job. Then, the employee is often covered under the workers' compensation system while traveling, even when the employee has completed his or her job duties for the day and is returning to a hotel. In this situation, because the employee is away from home on company

> **EXAMPLE 4-4**
>
> Sally is a traveling salesperson. While driving to her hotel after a successful sales meeting, she is injured. Does her injury qualify for workers' compensation coverage?
>
> *Answer:* Yes. Traveling employees fall into a special category and considered to be going about the employer's business, even when not actually "at work." As long as Sally's injury arises out of a risk, which is reasonably foreseeable or related to her job duties, then the injury is covered.[6]

business, nearly all of the employee's travel activities are carried out for the business. Here, an automobile accident will often come under the heading of an injury covered by workers' compensation.

In Example 4-4, Sally's injuries are compensable under workers' compensation laws because Sally is a traveling representative of the company. Sally's injuries in the auto accident are considered to be job related. However, the rule changes completely when the employee's actions are classified as frolic or detour.

Frolic

An employee is not covered for an injury that occurs while he or she is engaged in **detour** or **frolic**. Frolic refers to an employee's actions that are not related to his or her job. When an employee is engaged in frolic, he or she is carrying out personal business and not work-related business. If the employee is carrying out personal duties, even while the employee is on company time, then the resulting injury is not covered under workers' compensation laws. Frolic consists of an employee engaging in personal business; he or she is not conducting any actions related to job duties and is often away from the job site. In such a situation, requiring the employer to compensate the employee for an injury would not only be an injustice, it might actually encourage other employees to carry out personal errands on company time, realizing that any injury they receive will be compensated out of the workers' compensation insurance fund. See Exhibit 4-5.

Detour

The terms frolic and detour are often used in conjunction with one another. A detour is a side errand or a temporary departure of the employee from work-related activities. While on the detour, the employee is no longer covered under workers' compensation and any injury he or she receives must be paid from the employee's own funds or through the employee's personal medical coverage.

Detour

To set aside work-related activities and embark on a persona errand.

Frolic

To engage in an activity for fun or personal pleasure.

> (1) RECREATIONAL AND SOCIAL ACTIVITIES.—Recreational or social activities are not compensable unless such recreational or social activities are an expressly required incident of employment and produce a substantial direct benefit to the employer beyond improvement in employee health and morale that is common to all kinds of recreation and social life.
>
> (3) DEVIATION FROM EMPLOYMENT.—An employee who is injured while deviating from the course of employment, including leaving the employer's premises, is not eligible for benefits unless such deviation is expressly approved by the employer, or unless such deviation or act is in response to an emergency and designed to save life or property.
>
> (4) TRAVELING EMPLOYEES.—An employee who is required to travel in connection with his or her employment who suffers an injury while in travel status shall be eligible for benefits under this chapter only if the injury arises out of and in the course of employment while he or she is actively engaged in the duties of employment. This subsection applies to travel necessarily incident to performance of the employee's job responsibility but does not include travel to and from work as provided in subsection (2).

EXHIBIT 4-5
Deviation from Employment (Florida).

Dual Purpose Trips

In some instances, it is not always easy to classify an employee's actions. For instance, if an employee is requested to carry out a specific action and engages in personal activities at the same time, what effect does this have on the analysis? Referred to as **dual purpose trips**, an employee is carrying out both job-related activity and personal errands at the same time. The dual purpose doctrine has existed for decades. Justice Cordozo refined and expanded on the dual purpose doctrine in the seminal case of *Marks' Dependents v. Gray*, 251 N.Y. 90, 167 N.E. 181 (1920).

Dual purpose trip
A trip undertaken by an employee that has both work-related and personal aspects.

> We do not say that service to the employer must be the sole cause of the journey, but at least it must be a concurrent cause. To establish liability, the inference must be permissible that the trip would have been made though the private errand had been cancelled . . . The test in brief is this: If the work of the employee creates the necessity for travel, he is in the course of his employment, though he is serving at the same time some purpose of his own . . . If, however, the work has had no part in creating the necessity for travel, if the journey would have gone forward though the business errand had been dropped, and would have been cancelled upon failure of the private purpose, though the business errand was undone, the travel is then personal, and personal the risk.

> **EXAMPLE 4-5**
>
> Maria commutes to work and passes the local post office both coming to and from her office. One day, her supervisor asks her to pick up some stamps for the office mail on her way home. While she is driving toward the post office, she is injured in a car wreck. Is she covered by workers' compensation?
>
> *Answer:* No. Although this is a close question, most jurisdictions have ruled that because Maria was already going by the post office, her supervisor's request did not cause her to alter her route or to cause her to do anything that she would not have done on her daily commute. Would the answer be different if Maria were injured walking into the post office?

Under the dual purpose doctrine, if an employee is engaged in work-related activity while also carrying out personal duties, the employee will come under the coverage of workers' compensation laws. However, if the employee completely diverts from work-related actions, such as engaging in frolic or detour, then any injury received after that point in time would not be covered. Consider Example 4-5.

Horseplay

If an employee is engaged in horseplay with other employees, those injuries are not covered under workers' compensation law either. Workers' compensation only covers injuries related to work, not an employee's irresponsible actions.

Psychological Injuries

Does the definition of injury encompass psychological injuries? The topic of psychological injury has a long and interesting history. In personal injury cases, many states recognize that a plaintiff can seek damages from the defendant for loss of sleep, emotional trauma, and other related psychological stresses. However, does the same rule apply to workers' compensation cases? In most states, the answer is yes. An employee may be compensated for psychological injuries, but only when the psychological trauma is directly related to a work injury. See Exhibit 4-6.

> A psychiatric injury shall be compensable if it is a mental disorder which causes disability or need for medical treatment, and it is diagnosed pursuant to procedures promulgated under paragraph (4) of subdivision (j) of Section 139.2 or, until these procedures are promulgated, it is diagnosed using the terminology and criteria of the American Psychiatric Association's Diagnostic and Statistical Manual of Mental Disorders, Third Edition-Revised, or the terminology and diagnostic criteria of other psychiatric diagnostic manuals generally approved and accepted nationally by practitioners in the field of psychiatric medicine.[7]

EXHIBIT 4-6
Defining Psychiatric Injuries.

Acts of God or Nature

What effect do acts of God or nature have on a determination of coverage for injuries? As a general rule, an employee who is injured by a hurricane, earthquake, or other natural disaster is not considered to be injured on the job and therefore workers' compensation will not pay for medical expenses. However, this general rule is subject to interpretation. For instance, if human interference exacerbates an injury, then workers' compensation coverage may apply. Suppose that actions by other workers undermine a structure's fundation and that structure then collapses in high winds while employee A is at work? Many states would recognize such an injury as work related and provided coverage. Consider the factual scenarios in Examples 4-6 and 4-7.

EXAMPLE 4-6

Mario is a member of a five person team working to remove a tree. His company, Trees 'R Us, qualifies as a business under state workers' compensation laws and the company does provide workers' compensation coverage. As the team works on the tree, they loosen the roots in an attempt to push the tree north, away from the parking lot. However, sudden, gale force winds begin and push the tree south. The tree falls and lands on Mario. His leg and pelvis are broken. Is this injury covered under workers' compensation?

Answer: Because the workers contributed to the loosening of the tree roots, this is not entirely an act of God/Nature. Therefore, Mario's injuries must be paid out of the company's workers' compensation fund.

> **EXAMPLE 4-7**
>
> Sidney is at work in a tobacco processing plant and gale force winds suddenly begin blowing. The roof of the building is lifted by the winds and then it drops, killing several employees and severely injuring Sidney. Are his injuries classified as arising out of his job duties?
>
> *Answer:* No. This is a case of an act of God/Nature and there is no interfering human action that has exacerbated the injury. Sidney must rely on his own medical insurance to pay for his injuries.

Assault

When an employee is injured on the job by a battery committed by another employee, those injuries are usually covered under workers' compensation. However, there are a small percentage of cases that argue against this point, at least where the injured employee provoked the assault. In that situation, courts have held that because the employee provoked the other person, the employee was acting outside the scope of his or her duties and therefore the resulting injury is not defined as work related.

Preexisting Injuries

Another complexity arises when an employee has a preexisting injury and then receives a new injury to the same area. In typical tort analysis, a preexisting injury in the same place as the new injury dramatically decreases or completely eliminates the plaintiff's eventual recovery. However, the rules in workers' compensation cases are different than the approach used in tort cases. Preexisting conditions are generally covered in a workers' compensation claim, as long as the current injury was sustained during the course of employment. This means that if the worker begins the new job with a preexisting injury and there is a new incident that re-injures this previous injury, workers' compensation will provide medical coverage for the injury. See Exhibit 4-7.

However, the same limitations apply in this context as in any other workers' compensation case: The employee must be engaged in work-related activity. If not, there is no coverage, whether there is a preexisting injury or not.

Subsequent Injury

If a new incident leads to complications to a preexisting injury, what is the rule when an employee develops complications from a new injury? Suppose, for

> If an injury arising out of and in the course of employment combines with a preexisting disease or condition to cause or prolong disability or need for treatment, the employer must pay compensation or benefits required by this chapter only to the extent that the injury arising out of and in the course of employment is and remains more than 50 percent responsible for the injury as compared to all other causes combined and thereafter remains the major contributing cause of the disability or need for treatment. Major contributing cause must be demonstrated by medical evidence only.[8]

EXHIBIT 4-7

Treatment for Preexisting Injuries.

example, that an employee is injured during the course of his or her employment, but then complications arise during the treatment of that injury? In nearly every such situation, workers' compensation coverage will provide medical and other treatment for the new, or subsequent injury, provided that the new injury is directly related to the original injury. If the subsequent injury is not related, then it is not compensable under workers' compensation law. Consider Example 4-8.

Suicide

Self-inflicted wounds are not compensated under workers' compensation. Suicide is, by its very definition, self-inflicted killing of oneself and should, therefore, always be excluded from workers' compensation coverage. However, even this circumstance has exceptions that can result in coverage. Some states have awarded compensation when the claimant (or the claimant's family) can show that the suicide was a result of the stresses and emotional factors from the work place.[11]

EXAMPLE 4-8

Manny is a truck driver and is at company headquarters one day in order to attend a birthday party. He hurries down a set of stairs because he is late for the party, slips on the stairs, and falls. Last year, he injured the same knee in an automobile accident. Doctors testify that a person without Manny's previous injury would not have sustained an injury. Does Manny's new injury qualify under workers' compensation?

Answer: No. Manny is not performing any work-related activities and there is no indication that the stairs were unsafe or hazardous. The result in this case may change, however, when the personal comfort doctrine is applied.[9]

> **SIDEBAR**
>
> The term "the bends" derived from a line of women's clothing that had just been introduced in New York City with crossed straps on the back, and many women complained about the pain the straps caused across their shoulders and back. One worker commented that the pain that he felt was "just like the bends in those Greek dresses." The name stuck and the term is still used today when deep-sea divers suffer the same malady.

> **EXAMPLE 4-9**
>
> Ingrid is injured at work and there is no question that her injury is work related. However, while she is recuperating from her injury, she develops stomach ulcers that she attributes to the stress and worry about her condition, as well as a reaction to the pain treatment for her original injury. Is this new or subsequent injury that would fall under the jurisdiction of workers' compensation?
>
> *Answer:* No. Unless the claimant can show a clear connection between a new condition and the original injury, it does not fall within the definition of injury or subsequent injury under workers' compensation law.[10]

Intoxication

A worker who is intoxicated on the job will not receive workers' compensation benefits from an injury. It is important to point out that there are two types of intoxication: voluntary and involuntary. Voluntary intoxication is a complete bar to workers' compensation benefits, but involuntary intoxication is not. Involuntary intoxication is a result of the employee's exposure to chemicals, fumes, or other substances that can cause the employee to exhibit poor balance, bad judgment, and general impairment. When the employee can show that the intoxication was not voluntary, then he or she will be entitled to benefits under workers' compensation that are directly tied to the actions the employee carried out while under the influence.[12]

Occupational Diseases

■ **Occupational disease**
A disease or condition that arises out of working conditions.

Occupational diseases have a long history. The men who constructed the footings for the Brooklyn Bridge developed a mysterious illness known as "the bends." This disease was caused by nitrogen air bubbles in their blood—the intense atmospheric pressure that comes from being so far underwater. They actually worked inside the huge footings that supported the bridge. The intense atmospheric pressure would cause nitrogen to form in their bloodstreams, and when they came back to the surface, these nitrogen bubbles would expand and stop blood from flowing to parts of their bodies. The condition was very painful. See Exhibit 4-10.

You might think that it is obvious that an occupational disease should be compensated under worker's compensation law. However, the issues surrounding occupational diseases can be quite complex and often do not yield to a simple analysis. First, there is the definition of the phrase "occupational disease." See Exhibit 4-8.

> "Occupational disease" means a disease contracted in the course of employment, which by its causes and the characteristics of its manifestation or the condition of the employment results in a hazard which distinguishes the employment in character from employment generally, and the employment creates a risk of contracting the disease in greater degree and in a different manner from the public in general.[13]

EXHIBIT 4-8

Defining Occupational Disease (Ohio).

Defining Occupational Diseases

The most basic definition of occupational disease is any illness or condition that is caused by or aggravated by the nature of a particular employee's work. This does not mean that when an employee gets sick at work that the condition is automatically assumed to be an occupational disease. Instead, the employee must show that the condition was something that he or she was routinely exposed to and was part of normal job duties. Under this definition, a legal secretary would be entitled to make a claim for carpal tunnel syndrome because typing is part of his or her job duties, while the attorney might have difficulty bringing a similar claim, when typing is not normally part of his or her duties.

Many states have created a list of specific illnesses that are presumed to be occupational diseases for people who work with particular substances, like asbestos or silica dust. People who contracted these illnesses are presumed to have a valid workers compensation claim. However, this does not mean that if a person comes up with an illness not on the approved list, it will not be covered under workers' compensation. Instead, claims are taken on a case-by-case basis, with the burden on the employee to prove that a particular condition was brought about by working conditions. If the employee can show a causal connection between the illness and the job duties, he or she is likely to make a valid case. If the employee cannot show that direct connection, then he or she will not receive workers' compensation benefits.

Activities Not Strictly Related to Work

What analysis is involved when an employee is injured in an incident that occurs at the workplace, but is not related to his or her work duties, at least in a strict sense? There are many activities engaged in by employees that are not strictly related to their job duties. If the employee is injured in carrying one of these actions out, what effect will it have on his or her workers' compensation coverage? Suppose, for example, that the employee is on a break or eating lunch or any of a hundred activities that are do not further work duties but are engaged in every day by workers. Courts have developed several doctrines to address this issue. The most prominent of these is the personal comfort doctrine.

Personal Comfort Doctrine

Under the **personal comfort doctrine**, an employee who is injured carrying out an activity normally associated with working conditions will be compensated under workers' compensation statutes. Under the personal comfort doctrine, the courts impose an element of foreseeability to the worker's injury.[14] Foreseeability is a concept that is usually seen more often in tort law than in workers' compensation law. It is based on a premise that a person's natural and ordinary actions should form part of the analysis surrounding the resulting harm. Foreseeability is not usually considered in workers' compensation cases, where the focus is generally on whether or not the worker's injuries fall within and arise out of work duties. However, the development of the personal comfort doctrine arose out of situations where employees were injured going to bathrooms to relieve themselves, stepping outside for a smoke break or doing any of a number of actions that would not qualify as either frolic or detour, but also do not fall within the strict definition of work related activities.

Suppose that a worker has stepped outside the business establishment for a breath of fresh air or to take a smoke break and is injured. Under the personal comfort doctrine, those actions are directly tied to the activities at work and would, therefore, come under the heading of a work-related injury and would be compensable under workers' compensation.

The personal comfort doctrine accounts for a large number of cases where a worker is considered to be covered under workers' compensation when the worker obtains refreshments, takes a break, or engages in other activities that do not, at first, appear to be work-related and is injured while engaging in this activity.

Examples of activities that fall under the personal comfort doctrine and would be deemed covered when an employee is injured while performing them are as follows:

- Drinking
- Eating

Personal comfort doctrine

A legal principle that allows an injured employee to recover under workers' compensation laws for an injury arising out of actions that were not directly related to duties, but arose out of the reasonable needs of any employee.

> **EXAMPLE 4-10**
>
> Ted is a truck driver who stays at work after closing time to install a new antenna on his personal vehicle. As he kneels down to install the antenna brace on his bumper, he slips and tears his knee joint. Does the personal comfort doctrine make this an injury that is covered under workers' compensation?
>
> *Answer:* No. Ted was not carrying out work duties, or any activity reasonably related to those duties. The shop was closed, it was after hours, and he was working on his personal vehicle. All of these factors lead to a conclusion that the personal comfort doctrine does not apply.

- Adjusting clothing
- Obtaining additional clothing because of excessive cold in the workplace[15]

Emergencies

What standard applies in situations where an employee is injured during an **emergency**? Here our discussion assumes that an emergency is an event that is different than a disaster, such as an act of God or of nature. Instead, an emergency refers to a sudden danger caused by human action. If an employee is injured in an emergency, do workers' compensation statutes treat this situation as analogous to acts of God or relate the incident to a work related injury? In nearly all situations, injuries incurred in emergencies are compensable under workers' compensation. This is true even when employees are acting beyond the scope of their duties, such as attempting to save other employees or safeguarding property. There is also a strong public policy argument for bringing such injuries under the scope of workers' compensation. After

Emergency
A sudden, dangerous condition caused by human action or inaction.

> **EXAMPLE 4-11**
>
> Terry is at work and bites down on a piece of candy at the reception desk. Is this an on-the-job injury under workers' compensation?
>
> *Answer:* Although eating candy is not a central part of Terry's duties, under the personal comfort doctrine, the activity was reasonably incidental to job duties and is covered under workers' compensation law.

> **EXAMPLE 4-12**
>
> George works for a local company and one evening, after hours, he is just leaving for home when he sees someone breaking into the office. He rushes inside, confronts the burglar, and is severely beaten. He files for workers' compensation coverage. Do his actions constitute an injury?
>
> *Answer:* Yes. The rules about coverage change slightly in emergency situations and George's actions in attempting to protect company property qualify as a work-related injury.[16]
>
> Also, if an employee is acting within the scope of employment and attempting to preserve and maintain the employer's property from damage and is injured doing so, it is usually covered under a workers' compensation claim. See Exhibit 4-9.

all, society wishes to encourage individuals to protect their coworkers and to make reasonable efforts to save them when they are in danger. A ruling that such actions fall outside the workers' compensation system might easily discourage the very actions that we, as a society, encourage in every other context. Consider Example 4-12.

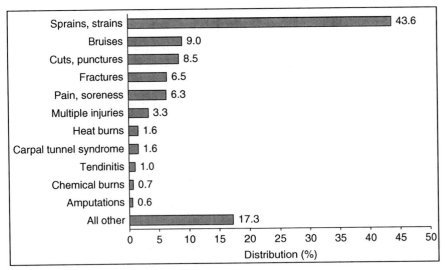

EXHIBIT 4-9 Distribution of Injury and Illness Cases with Days Away from Work.

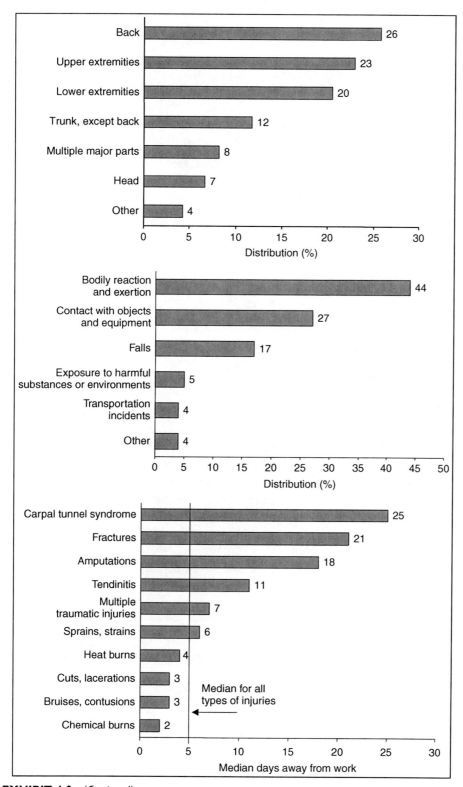

EXHIBIT 4-9 (Continued)

> **CASE EXCERPT**
>
> ## IS AN OFF-DUTY INJURY EVER COVERED UNDER WORKERS' COMPENSATION?
>
> *City of Stockton v. Workers' Comp. Appeals Bd.*[17]
>
> SCOTLAND, P. J.
>
> This case poses the question whether a police officer who injured his leg while off duty, playing in a pickup game of basketball at a private facility, is entitled to workers' compensation benefits.
>
> A workers' compensation judge (WCJ) concluded the injury arose out of and occurred in the course of the police officer's employment because, in the WCJ's view, the officer reasonably believed that "his participation in cardiovascular activities such as basketball were [sic] expected by his employer." In a two-to-one decision, the Workers' Compensation Appeals Board denied the employer's petition for reconsideration.
>
> The police officer's employer then petitioned for, and we issued, a writ of review. We now shall annul the award of workers' compensation benefits.
>
> As we will explain, when an employee is injured during voluntary, off-duty participation in a recreational, social, or athletic activity, Labor Code section 3600, subdivision (a)(9) provides that the injury is not covered by workers' compensation, unless the activity was "a reasonable expectancy of" the employment or it was "expressly or impliedly required by" the employment. General assertions that the employer expects an employee to stay in good physical condition, and that the employer benefits from the employee's doing so, are not sufficient for worker's compensation coverage since that would impose virtually limitless liability for any recreational or athletic activity in which the employee chooses to participate—a result that would run afoul of the limitation set forth in Labor Code section 3600, subdivision (a).
>
> Turning to the facts of this case, we conclude the evidence does not support a finding that Officer Jenneiahn subjectively believed that his employer expected him to engage in an occasional pickup game of basketball in order to stay in shape. In any event, such a subjective belief would have been objectively unreasonable under the circumstances here. Thus, it cannot be said that the specific activity during which he was injured was a reasonable expectancy of, or was expressly or impliedly required by, his employment. For this reason, the Workers' Compensation Appeals Board erred in concluding that Jenneiahn's injury was covered by workers' compensation.
>
> *Continued*

FACTS

Sean Jenneiahn is employed as a police officer by the City of Stockton (the City). He engages in additional employment by officiating at high school basketball and baseball games.

The City's police department has a regulation stating that police officers shall maintain good physical condition. However, after an officer is hired, the department does not require any physical fitness tests or examinations. According to the record in this case, no officer has ever been fired or otherwise disciplined for not being physically fit.

Officer Jenneiahn was not aware of the regulation requiring physical fitness, although he remembered that the application for employment said an officer must be physically fit to do the job. Some of his training officers advised him to stay in shape, and Jenneiahn believed that officers should remain physically fit. He did so by jogging and running, doing cardiovascular workouts, and playing basketball and softball.

The City's police officers are not given time to work out while on duty. However, in the basement of the police department, the City maintains a gymnasium and workout facility that is available for officers' use. Officer Jenneiahn did not use the department's facility because he preferred to work out elsewhere when he was not on duty.

While off duty and playing in a basketball game, Officer Jenneiahn hyperextended his leg and suffered a fracture of the tibia plateau.

The facility where the injury occurred is owned and operated by the Stockton Police Officers' Association (SPOA), not by the City. The facility, which has a gymnasium, kitchen, bar, pool tables, basketball court, barbeque facility, and racquetball court, is used for a variety of social, recreational, and athletic activities. SPOA members can use it whenever they want as part of their union dues.

When the SPOA facility opened, the City's Chief of Police issued a special order strictly prohibiting officers from visiting the facility for any reason while on duty, including taking meal breaks or using the restrooms.

The basketball game in which Officer Jenneiahn was playing when he was injured was not an employer-sponsored event. In fact, it was not a scheduled event at all. The game was described as a pickup game; Jenneiahn went to the SPOA facility and got into a game with others who were there. At the time, he had not been playing very much basketball. He was staying in shape by running and officiating at basketball games. He testified that he would have been in shape regardless of whether he played basketball.

Continued

DISCUSSION

I

The question whether workers' compensation benefits should be received for injuries suffered by an employee during off-duty recreational or athletic pursuits has arisen often.

In *Liberty Mut. Ins. Co. v. Ind. Acc. Com.* (1952) 39 Cal.2d 512, 247 P.2d 697 (hereafter *Liberty Mutual*), the claimant was a live-in employee at a recreational resort. When not performing his duties, he could participate in any of the recreational activities available in the area, including swimming in a pool created by a dam across a stream. He was injured while diving into the pool. Because the pool was located beyond the area under its control, the employer could not prohibit the employee from swimming in the pool. (*Id.* at pp. 515–516, 247 P.2d 697.) The California Supreme Court concluded the injury was not covered by workers' compensation because it occurred while the employee "was engaged in a personal recreational activity on his own free time in an area without the orbit of his employment and beyond the control or dominion of his employer." (*Id.* at p. 517, 247 P.2d 697.) The court observed that to hold otherwise would make compensation coverage virtually limitless. (*Id.* at p. 518, 247 P.2d 697.)

The same conclusion was reached in *Fireman's Fund Etc. Co. v. Ind. Acc. Com.* (1952) 39 Cal.2d 529, 247 P.2d 707 (hereafter *Fireman's Fund*), where the claimant, a live-in cook and housekeeper, was injured during a walk. It was her custom to take short walks once or twice a day, and she had been advised to do so by the employer's doctor. On the day of the injury, she informed her employer that she was going for a walk. The employer told the employee not to go too far. (*Id.* at pp. 530, 531, 247 P.2d 707.) The Supreme Court found the injury was not compensable because it occurred while the employee was "walking on a public road as an act of recreational diversion of her own free choice and when off-duty from her work." (*Id.* at p. 535, 247 P.2d 707.) The court rejected her argument that she "was following her medical adviser's recommendation as to a suitable exercise, and so was conditioning herself to perform better the duties of her employment." (*Id.* at p. 534, 247 P.2d 707.) The court explained: "[I]f such theory should be adopted as sufficient to establish the necessary causal connection with the employment, then any injury sustained by an employee in a recreational activity would be compensable."

In *United Parcel Service of America, Inc. v. Industrial Accident Commission* (1959) 172 Cal.App.2d 73, 342 P.2d 41, the Court of Appeal concluded that an employee

Continued

who was injured in a foot race at a company picnic was not entitled to worker's compensation because "the intangible value of improvement in the employee's health or morals that is common to all kinds of recreation and social life" is not sufficient to make an injury compensable. (*Id.* at pp. 74, 75, 76–77, 342 P.2d 41; see also *State Farm Fire & Casualty Co. v. Workers' Comp. Appeals Bd.* (1981) 119 Cal.App.3d 193, 197, 173 Cal.Rptr. 778.)

And in *City of Los Angeles v. Workers' Comp. Appeals Bd.* (1979) 91 Cal.App.3d 759, 154 Cal.Rptr. 379 (hereafter *City of Los Angeles*), the Court of Appeal concluded that worker's compensation did not apply to injuries suffered by a police officer while weightlifting at home in preparation for a physical fitness test. (*Id.* at pp. 761, 766, 154 Cal.Rptr. 379.) The Workers' Compensation Appeals Board had found compensation was appropriate because the officer was required to undergo a physical fitness test for which he was preparing. (*Id.* at p. 762, 154 Cal.Rptr. 379.) The Court of Appeal disagreed, stating: "There is a wide variety of occupations in which it is necessary for the employee to maintain or improve physical or mental proficiency in order to continue employment or qualify for advancement. The variety of activities which might be thought to serve those purposes is infinite. When the self-improvement activity is voluntary, off the employer's premises and unregulated, the employer can have little knowledge of the physical risks involved, and no opportunity to minimize or protect the employee against such risks. These circumstances strongly militate in favor of classifying such activities as personal in the absence of some connection with employment other than hoped-for personal improvement. The fact that the employer tested the fitness of the employee periodically should not by itself make a self-improvement program an industrial activity." (*Id.* at p. 764, 154 Cal.Rptr. 379, fn. omitted.)

In 1978, the Legislature acted on the question by adding to Labor Code section 3600 a provision that is now subdivision (a)(9) of the section. (Further section references are to the Labor Code, with references to subdivision (a)(9) of section 3600 cited simply as subdivision (a)(9).) Section 3600 provides generally that an injury is covered by worker's compensation benefits when, at the time of the injury, "the employee is performing service growing out of and incidental to his or her employment and is acting within the course of his or her employment" and "the injury is proximately caused by the employment, either with or without negligence." (§ 3600, subds. (a)(2) & (a)(3).) However, subdivision (a)(9) sets forth a limitation. To be compensable, the injury must be one that "does not arise out of voluntary participation in any off-duty recreational, social, or athletic activity not constituting part of the employee's work-related duties, except where these activities are a reasonable expectancy of, or are expressly or impliedly required by, the employment."

Continued

The statutory scheme was construed in *Ezzy v. Workers' Comp. Appeals Bd.* (1983) 146 Cal.App.3d 252, 194 Cal.Rptr. 90 (hereafter *Ezzy*). The Court of Appeal noted that what is now subdivision (a)(9) was added by the Legislature in reaction to decisions that had allowed workers' compensation for injuries suffered by employees during off-duty activities where the activities "were reasonably foreseeable or expectable in the work setting." (*Id.* at p. 261, 194 Cal.Rptr. 90.) The court concluded the subdivision was "intended to draw a brighter line delimiting compensability by replacing the general foreseeability test with one of 'reasonable expectancy' of employment" (ibid.), a test that is met when the employee subjectively believes his or her participation in the activity is expected by the employer, and the belief is objectively reasonable. (*Id.* at p. 260, 194 Cal.Rptr. 90.)

The claimant in *Ezzy* was injured while playing in a regularly scheduled league softball game sponsored by her employer's law firm. (*Ezzy*, supra, 146 Cal.App.3d at p. 257, 194 Cal.Rptr. 90.) While the Court of Appeal considered the case to be close, it found the injury was compensable because (1) the claimant, a part-time law clerk in her second year of law school, was particularly vulnerable to pressure or suggestion that she play, (2) she felt she was essentially "drafted" to play when a partner handed her a t-shirt and schedule and told her that the team would see her at the next game, (3) female employees were pressured to play so the team would not forfeit due to the league's requirement that a team have four women on the field at all times during a game, (4) the firm paid for all equipment, t-shirts, and post-game refreshments, and hosted an awards banquet for players, (5) the firm benefited through improved office cooperation, spirit, morale, and camaraderie, and (6) the firm had not posted or read to its employees the provisions of what is now subdivision (a)(9). (*Id.* at pp. 257–258, 263–264, 194 Cal.Rptr. 90.)

In *Hughes Aircraft Co. v. Workers' Comp. Appeals Bd.* (1983) 149 Cal.App.3d 571, 196 Cal.Rptr. 904 (hereafter *Hughes Aircraft*), the Court of Appeal further considered what is now subdivision (a). Noting legislative history shows the provision's purpose is "to ensure that an employer could provide voluntary off-duty recreational, social and athletic benefits for his employee's personal use without also bearing the expense of insuring the employee for workers' compensation benefits during participation in those activities" (*Id.* at p. 575, 196 Cal.Rptr. 904), the court found that the Legislature intended to exclude from coverage any injuries that are only remotely work-related, so as not to deter employers from subsidizing, sponsoring, or encouraging personal employee activities of a recreational or social character.

The claimant in *Hughes Aircraft* suffered a slip and fall injury while attending an annual off-premises, off-duty holiday party that was subsidized 90 percent by the

Continued

employer. The employer organized the event to foster an atmosphere of togetherness, but attendance was wholly voluntary. An employee's position would not be enhanced by attendance, and there would not be any adverse consequence if an employee did not attend. (*Hughes Aircraft*, supra, 149 Cal.App.3d at pp. 572, 573, 196 Cal.Rptr. 904.) The Workers' Compensation Appeals Board awarded compensation based solely on its view that the employer obtained a direct benefit from the party. (Ibid.) The Court of Appeal held "it was incorrect as a matter of law to conclude that the existence of a direct benefit to the employer could be used to circumvent the express terms" of now subdivision (a)(9). (*Id.* at p. 575, 196 Cal.Rptr. 904.)

Since Hughes Aircraft, a number of published decisions applying what is now subdivision (a)(9) have found that injuries suffered in recreational, social, or athletic settings were covered by workers' compensation.

In *Smith v. Workers' Comp. Appeals Bd.* (1987) 191 Cal.App.3d 127, 236 Cal.Rptr. 248 (hereafter *Smith*), a math teacher suffered fatal injuries while windsurfing at a math club picnic. (*Id.* at pp. 129–130, 236 Cal.Rptr. 248.) The Court of Appeal considered the question "extremely close," but concluded that certain factors tipped the balance to compensability: (1) the teacher was classified as temporary and, thus, was vulnerable to pressure or suggestion that he participate to improve his chances of being rehired; (2) the club was an official school club, and the picnic was an annually scheduled event; (3) teachers were encouraged to participate in school club activities; (4) annual evaluations of teachers were based in part on their willingness to participate in club activities; (5) the event benefited the school by promoting better student-teacher relationships; (6) math club funds were used to provide food and refreshments; and (7) students were required to submit parental permission slips in order to participate. (*Id.* at 141, 236 Cal.Rptr. 248.)

In *Wilson v. Workers' Comp. Appeals Bd.* (1987) 196 Cal.App.3d 902, 239 Cal.Rptr. 719 (hereafter *Wilson*), the claimant was a police officer who injured his ankle while running at a junior college track. As a member of the police department's special emergency response team (SERT), he had to pass physical tests four times a year in order to remain on the team. The tests included a requirement that officers over the age of 35 must be able to run two miles in 17 minutes. A SERT supervisor testified he told SERT officers that they would have to engage in off-duty exercise to pass the tests. (*Id.* at pp. 904, 908, 239 Cal.Rptr. 719.) The Court of Appeal held the injury was compensable because "[i]t would be completely unrealistic to conclude that off-duty running was not expected" of a SERT member over 35 years old who wanted to pass the SERT tests. (Id. at p. 908, 239 Cal.Rptr. 719.)

Continued

In *Kidwell v. Workers' Comp. Appeals Bd.* (1995) 33 Cal.App.4th 1130, 39 Cal.Rptr.2d 540 (hereafter *Kidwell*), the Court of Appeal found compensable an injury suffered by a California Highway Patrol (CHP) officer while she was practicing a standing long jump at home. The standing long jump was a required protocol of the CHP's annual, mandatory fitness test. In past years, she had passed the fitness tests except for the standing long jump. Her failure to pass the standing long jump had significant consequences, including the loss of a $130 per month salary differential, loss of eligibility for certain assignments and overtime, issuance of a "fitness plan," and an entry in her performance evaluation. (*Id.* at pp. 1132, 1133 & fn. 4, 39 Cal.Rptr.2d 540.) Under the circumstances, the court concluded that it would be "patently unreasonable" to find the CHP did not expect the claimant to practice for the standing long jump test. (*Id.* at p. 1139, 39 Cal.Rptr.2d 540.)

On the other hand, a number of published decisions applying what is now subdivision (a)(9) have found that injuries suffered in recreational, social, or athletic settings were not covered by workers' compensation.

In *Meyer v. Workers' Comp. Appeals Bd.* (1984) 157 Cal.App.3d 1036, 204 Cal.Rptr. 74 (hereafter *Meyer*), a car salesman was injured while driving for a weekend visit to his supervisor's place near the Colorado River. (*Id.* at p. 1039, 204 Cal.Rptr. 74.) The Court of Appeal concluded the injury was not compensable because (1) the employer did not subsidize or sponsor the event, and it was not regularly scheduled—it was just an informal invitation by a supervisor, (2) while the visit might foster improved morale, this is true of every social event and, therefore, it is not sufficient to impose compensability, and (3) there was insufficient evidence of pressure exerted to attend the outing. (*Id.* at p. 1043, 204 Cal.Rptr. 74.) Simply stated, the "trip, although initiated by a supervisor, was not a reasonable expectancy of the employment." (*Id.* at p. 1044, 204 Cal.Rptr. 74.)

In *Todd v. Workers' Comp. Appeals Bd.* (1988) 198 Cal.App.3d 757, 243 Cal.Rptr. 925 (hereafter *Todd*), the claimant suffered a knee injury while playing basketball on the employer's premises during a lunch break. The employer allowed employees to install a basketball hoop and backboard, and apparently condoned the games. (*Id.* at pp. 759, 760–761, 243 Cal.Rptr. 925.) The Court of Appeal concluded the injury was not covered by workers' compensation because there was no substantial evidence the employee "reasonably believed he was expected to participate in basketball games during his lunch break, or that participation was expressly or impliedly required by the employment." (*Id.* at p. 760, 243 Cal.Rptr. 925.)

Continued

In *Taylor v. Workers' Comp. Appeals Bd.* (1988) 199 Cal.App.3d 211, 244 Cal.Rptr. 643 (hereafter *Taylor*), the claimant was a police officer who was injured at a city-owned gymnasium while playing in a pickup game of basketball during his lunch hour. Although the police department expected officers to keep themselves in good physical condition, it provided no formal training sessions or guidelines, and there were no formal physical fitness tests. The department had issued a general order that athletic injuries would be considered to be suffered on duty if they were suffered in a pre-approved athletic event, but that workers' compensation benefits would not be awarded without advance approval of the event. (*Id.* at pp. 213, 214–215, 244 Cal.Rptr. 643.) The Court of Appeal found that participation in the pickup game was voluntary, and it was not reasonably expected or required by the officer's employment. (*Id.* at p. 215, 244 Cal.Rptr. 643.) The court added that it is reasonable to permit an employer to limit its liability for athletic injuries, as had the department. "To hold otherwise would in effect render the employer potentially liable for any injury sustained in any recreational or athletic activity if the activity contributed to the employee's physical fitness. Such broad potential liability would be contrary to the legislative intent of section 3600, subdivision (a)(9)." (*Id.* at p. 216, 244 Cal.Rptr. 643.)

In *Tensfeldt v. Workers' Comp. Appeals Bd.* (1998) 66 Cal.App.4th 116, 77 Cal.Rptr.2d 691, the claimant was a city water department employee who injured his knee while playing basketball with other department employees at a city gymnasium during the workday. The game was conducted during working hours because the employees had finished their job assignments early. (*Id.* at p. 119, 77 Cal.Rptr.2d 691.) The Court of Appeal held the injury was not covered by workers' compensation. The fact the employee was not technically off duty at the time did not change the fact that participation was voluntary and was not reasonably expected or required by the employer. (*Id.* at pp. 126–127, 77 Cal.Rptr.2d 691.)

II

The authorities discussed in part I, ante, illustrate the rule that when an employee is injured during voluntary, off-duty participation in a recreational, social, or athletic activity, the injury is not covered by workers' compensation, unless the activity was "a reasonable expectancy of, or [was] expressly or impliedly required by, the employment." (§ 3600, subd. (a)(9).)

In applying the reasonable expectancy test, we first consider whether the employee subjectively believed that participation in the activity was expected by the employer. (*Ezzy*, supra, 146 Cal.App.3d at p. 260, 194 Cal.Rptr. 90.) This issue is a question of fact, which we review under the substantial evidence rule. (*Meyer*, supra, 157 Cal.App.3d at p. 1042, 204 Cal.Rptr. 74.)

Continued

We then determine whether the employee's belief was objectively reasonable. (*Ezzy*, supra, 146 Cal.App.3d at p. 260, 194 Cal.Rptr. 90.) This issue is a question of law that we determine independently. (*Meyer*, supra, 157 Cal.App.3d at p. 1042, 204 Cal.Rptr. 74.)

In considering these issues, we must focus our attention on the specific activity in which the employee was involved when the injury occurred. This is so because subdivision (a)(9) is not intended to replace the basic requirement that to be compensable, (1) an injury must occur while the employee is performing service growing out of and incidental to his or her employment and acting in the course of employment, and (2) the employment must be the proximate cause of the injury. (§ 3600, subd. (a)(2) & (3); *Wilson*, supra, 196 Cal.App.3d at p. 905, 239 Cal.Rptr. 719.) Subdivision (a)(9) was intended to limit, rather than to expand, the scope of liability that an excessively liberal application of the basic test might support. (*Meyer*, supra, 157 Cal.App.3d at pp. 1040–1041, 204 Cal.Rptr. 74; *Hughes Aircraft Co.*, supra, 149 Cal.App.3d at p. 575, 196 Cal.Rptr. 904.)

Indeed, unless courts require a substantial nexus between an employer's expectations or requirements and the specific off-duty activity in which the employee was engaged, the scope of coverage becomes virtually limitless and contrary to the legislative intent of subdivision (a)(9). (*Taylor*, supra, 199 Cal.App.3d at p. 216, 244 Cal.Rptr. 643; see also *Fireman's Fund*, supra, 39 Cal.2d at p. 534, 247 P.2d 707; *City of Los Angeles*, supra, 91 Cal.App.3d at p. 764, 154 Cal.Rptr. 379.)

Accordingly, general assertions that it would benefit the employer for, or even that the employer expects, an employee to stay in good physical condition are not sufficient to require workers' compensation for injuries suffered by the employee during any recreational or athletic activity in which the employee chooses to participate. (*Taylor*, supra, 199 Cal.App.3d at p. 216, 244 Cal.Rptr. 643; see also *Fireman's Fund*, supra, 39 Cal.2d at p. 534, 247 P.2d 707; *City of Los Angeles*, supra, 91 Cal.App.3d at p. 764, 154 Cal.Rptr. 379.)

The decisions that have allowed workers' compensation pursuant to subdivision (a)(9) have generally found the employer expected the employee to participate in the specific activity in which the employee was engaged at the time of injury. In *Ezzy*, the employer expected the employee to play on the law firm's softball team in a regularly scheduled game, and that is what she was doing when she was injured. (*Ezzy*, supra, 146 Cal.App.3d at pp. 257–258, 263–264, 194 Cal.Rptr. 90.) In *Wilson*, the employer expected the employee to engage in off-duty running in order to pass the running test to which he was subjected four times a year, and he was running when injured. (*Wilson*, supra, 196 Cal.App.3d at

Continued

p. 908, 239 Cal.Rptr. 719.) In *Kidwell*, the employer expected the employee to practice the standing long jump in order to meet its testing requirements, and that is what she was doing when injured. (*Kidwell*, supra, 33 Cal.App.4th at p. 1139, 39 Cal.Rptr.2d 540.)

We also must look for specific conduct of the employer that would reasonably convey to the employee that participation in a particular activity is expected. Again, general assertions of benefit to the employer, or that the employer condones or allows the activity, are insufficient. (*Todd*, supra, 198 Cal.App.3d at p. 760; *Meyer*, supra, 157 Cal.App.3d at p. 1043, 204 Cal.Rptr. 74; *Hughes Aircraft*, supra, 149 Cal.App.3d at p. 575, 196 Cal.Rptr. 904.)

Decisions that have found employee injuries compensable under subdivision (a)(9) have found specific conduct by the employer with respect to the activity at issue. In *Ezzy*, a partner of the law firm handed the employee a t-shirt and schedule and said the team would see her at the next game. While this was less than a direct order, it was not a mere invitation to play should she so desire. (*Ezzy*, supra, 146 Cal.App.3d at pp. 257, 258, 194 Cal.Rptr. 90.) In *Smith*, the teacher's annual evaluation was based in part on his willingness to participate in student club activities. (*Smith*, supra, 191 Cal.App.3d at p. 141, 236 Cal.Rptr. 248.) In *Wilson*, the employer required the employee to pass a specific running test four times a year. (*Wilson*, supra, 196 Cal.App.3d at p. 908, 239 Cal.Rptr. 719.) In *Kidwell*, a standing long jump was part of the employer's mandatory fitness testing program and there were significant adverse consequences for failure. (*Kidwell*, supra, 33 Cal.App.4th at p. 1139, 39 Cal.Rptr.2d 540.)

III

Turning to the facts of this case, we first conclude the evidence does not support a finding that Officer Jenneiahn subjectively believed that his employer expected him to engage in an occasional pickup game of basketball.

Officer Jenneiahn remembered that his employment application said an officer must be fit to do the job, some of his training officers advised him to stay in shape, and he believed that an officer should be in shape to do the job. However, he knew that he was not subject to any kind of physical fitness testing or examination, and he was not aware of any officer having been disciplined for not being physically fit.

Moreover, Officer Jenneiahn did not incorporate games of pickup basketball into a training regimen. He played only occasionally, maybe once a month. He believed that basketball was not necessary to maintain his physical fitness; he stayed in shape by running and through his officiating job at high school games.

Continued

And he testified that he was in shape regardless of the occasional pickup basketball game.

In addition, the pickup game in which Officer Jenneiahn was playing when injured was wholly unconnected to his employer. It was in a private facility that was not owned or operated by the employer. The game was not part of a league or other scheduled event. There is nothing in the record to suggest the employer in any way sponsored, encouraged, condoned, or was even aware of the activity. In fact, the employer had issued a directive prohibiting any employee from using the private facility for any reason during the employee's work hours.

In sum, the evidence does not establish that Officer Jenneiahn believed that his employer expected him to participate in the game of pickup basketball. The record establishes only his belief that it was a good idea for a police officer to stay in good physical condition, and his leap to a conclusion that any physical activity in which an officer chooses to engage must be covered by workers' compensation. Such a belief is far too broad and inconsistent with the legislative intent of subdivision (a)(9).

We also conclude that even if there was evidence that Officer Jenneiahn subjectively believed his employer expected him to play in a pickup game of basketball, this belief would not have been objectively reasonable. The game had no connection whatsoever to the employer. It was conducted in a private facility over which the employer had no control. It was not a scheduled activity, and the employer did nothing to sponsor, encourage, or condone the activity. Although the employer expected its officers to maintain sufficient general physical fitness necessary to perform their duties, it did not subject officers to any form of physical fitness testing, let alone testing on the skills utilized in playing basketball. And Jenneiahn knew that playing basketball was unnecessary to his physical fitness for the job.

On this record, it is readily apparent that playing in the off-duty pickup game of basketball was a wholly voluntary choice by Officer Jenneiahn. His employer did not exert any form of pressure to make his choice less than voluntary. The general, and reasonable, expectation that a police officer will maintain sufficient physical fitness to perform his or her duties is not a sufficient basis to extend workers' compensation coverage to any and all off-duty recreational or athletic activities in which an officer voluntarily chooses to participate.

DISPOSITION

The award of workers' compensation benefits is annulled, and the matter is remanded to the Workers' Compensation Appeals Board with directions to enter

Continued

an order denying such benefits. The parties shall bear their own costs in the proceedings before this court.

Case Questions:

1. Did the police department expect Jenneiahn to stay in good physical shape?
2. Does the ruling in this case center on Jenneiahn's subjective belief that his employer actually wanted him to engage in outside physical activities?
3. How does the court address the police department's regulation requiring police officers to stay in good physical shape?
4. Is it significant that the police department maintained a work out facility?
5. According to the court, does access to the basketball court, other amenities and membership in the gym make Jenneiahn's basketball games a work-related activity?
6. Would the result have been different if the basketball game had been scheduled? What if the game had been between various off-duty police officers?
7. Would the result have been different if the police department had organized a basketball tournament and the officer had been injured in this tournament?

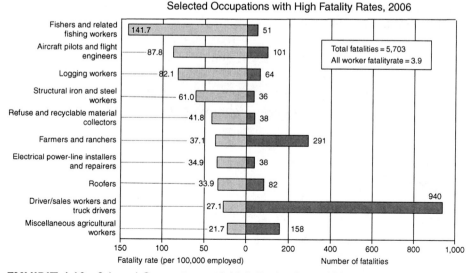

EXHIBIT 4-10 Selected Occupations with High Fatality Rates, 2006.

ETHICAL CONSIDERATION:
Staying Current in the Law

One of the most important things you can do as a legal professional is to continuously read and keep abreast of changes in workers' compensation law. It makes a great deal of sense for you to stay current in workers' compensation if your firm specializes in it. You can do this by reading legal newspapers and legal magazines, but the best way is to read the most recent decisions of the courts in your jurisdiction. Reading recent decisions keeps you in tune with the latest developments in workers' compensation law. When you constantly improve your knowledge and understanding of recent decisions in the law, you can make yourself even more valuable to an attorney. Sometimes you can even save the attorney from an embarrassing mistake—and make yourself that much more indispensable to the firm.

CHAPTER SUMMARY

In this chapter, we have learned that an employee who was injured on the job must prove that the injury arose out of and in the course of his or her job duties. Employees who are running personal errands or are performing non-job-related activities are not covered under worker's compensation and if they are injured will not be compensated under the system. There is often conflict about how to define work-related activities, requiring courts to develop various doctrines to address the issue of what qualifies as an on-the-job injury and what activities will qualify as frolic or detour, which are not covered. Some injuries qualify as occupational diseases and may or may not be compensable under workers' compensation depending on the nature of the injury and the causal connection between the employee's activities and the reported injury.

KEY TERMS

Arises out of
Detour
Dual purpose trip
Emergency

Frolic
In the course of
Occupational disease
Personal comfort doctrine

REVIEW QUESTIONS

1. How do workers' compensation laws describe an on-the-job injury?
2. What types of injuries are covered under workers' compensation laws?
3. Describe the regulations that govern the reporting of an on-the-job injury.
4. Explain the rules governing how and when an employee will receive medical treatment for an on-the-job injury.
5. Compare and contrast the doctrines of increased risk and actual risk.
6. How does a preexisting injury affect the analysis for a new on-the-job injury?
7. Define an injury "in the course of" employment.
8. Explain the rules for injuries occurring when an employee is traveling to or from work.
9. Compare and contrast the detour and frolic.
10. What is a dual purpose trip?
11. What is the personal comfort doctrine?
12. Explain how emergencies affect the analysis of whether or not an injury arises out of the course of employment.
13. How does an employee's intoxication affect a ruling about an on-the-job injury?
14. Explain the legal impact of suicide on the analysis of on-the-job injuries.
15. List and explain various occupational diseases.

QUESTION FOR REFLECTION

Does the workers' compensation system define "injury" too broadly or too restrictively? Discuss your answer.

WEB SITES

California Department of Health Services Prevention Services Program
http://www.dhs.ca.gov/ps/deodc/default.asp
This site provides a good overview of occupational diseases.

Law Guru
http://www.lawguru.com/faq/22.html
This site provides some excellent information about workers' compensation law in one of our most populous states (California).

IWIF
http://www.iwif.com/
This site is dedicated to providing information about workers' compensation insurance.

Texas Workers' Compensation Commission
http://www.tdi.state.tx.us/wc/indexwc.html
This site provides some excellent workers' compensation forms for claims arising under Texas law.

Nebraska's Workers' Compensation Court
http://www.wcc.ne.gov/
Explore this site to learn more about the workers' compensation system in Nebraska.

New Hampshire Department of Labor
http://www.labor.state.nh.us/workers_compensation.asp
Check out this site to learn more about the workers' compensation system in New Hampshire.

PRACTICAL APPLICATIONS

1. Are stress headaches, ulcers, or hearing conditions recognized as work-related injuries in your state? Research your state's workers' compensation laws and provide an analysis of the applicability of these various maladies.

2. Is the personal comfort doctrine recognized in your state? If so, what activities fall under the doctrine? If not, is there a similar doctrine or other approach used that will compensate employees for activities on the job that are not strictly work-related?

END NOTES

[1] *Howard County Ass'n for Retarded Citizens, Inc. v. Walls*, 288 Md. 526, 418 A.2d 1210 (Md. 1980).

[2] MD Code, Labor and Employment, § 9-709.

[3] California Labor Code 3208.

[4] Title XXXI, Chap 440.02, Florida.

[5] Florida Workers Comp. Statutes, 440.09 (1).

[6] *Thompson v. Keller Foundations, Inc.*, 29 Fla. L. Weekly D2159a (Fla. 1st DCA Sept. 27, 2004).

7 California Labor Code 3208.3(a).
8 Florida Workers Comp. Statutes, 440.09(b).
9 *Duvall v. J&J Refuse,* —— Ohio —— (2005) [2005 WL 121710].
10 *Duda & Sons, Inc. v. Kelley,* 900 So. 2d 664 (2005).
11 AMJUR WORKERS § 337.
12 *Reddick v. Grand Union Tea Co.,* 296 N.W. 800 (Iowa 1941).
13 Ohio Statutes, Chap 4123.01 (F).
14 *Holly Hill Fruit Products v. Krider,* 473 So. 2d 829 (1985).
15 *Chambers v. Adm Bureau of Workers' Compensation,* 164 Ohio App. 397 (2005).
16 *Martinez v. Workers' Comp. Appeals Bd.,* 15 Cal.3d 982, 127 Cal.Rptr. 150 (Cal. 1976).
17 38 Cal.Rptr.3d 474 (2006).

Online Companion™
For additional resources, please go to
http://www.paralegal.delmar.cengage.com

Benefits Under Workers' Compensation

CHAPTER 5

CHAPTER OBJECTIVES

At the completion of this chapter, you should be able to:

- Explain the medical benefits available under workers' compensation systems
- Describe the important differences between temporary and permanent partial disability
- Define how an injured employee qualifies as permanently totally disabled
- Explain the death benefits available to an injured employee's family
- Discuss the role of workers' compensation schedules in determining compensation amounts

INTRODUCTION

In this chapter, we will examine the types of benefits available to an employee who is injured on the job. These days, an injured employee can expect any of several different types of benefits, and we will examine each in this chapter. Employees who suffer from work-related injuries or illnesses can expect the following benefits:

- Medical treatment
- Disability payments

- Vocational rehabilitation
- Death payments

Although there is variation from state to state as to both the nature and extent of these benefits, there are many similarities. We will focus on those features that are generally the same from jurisdiction to jurisdiction, keeping in mind that there may be variations on the specifics in your state. Once we examine the types of benefits available, we will also explore exactly how such benefits are awarded; calculate disability payments; discuss the distinctions between temporary and permanent, partial, and permanent disabilities; and finally consider actions that may result in a termination of benefits.

MEDICAL BENEFITS

One of the first concerns of any injured employee is the medical treatment that he or she will receive. Medical and wage benefits are the primary reason to have workers' compensation insurance in the first place and they continue to play a central role in modern practice. Statutes that authorize medical treatment for injured or sick workers emphasize that an employee is entitled to receive medical treatment that is reasonably necessary to cure the injury, relieve the symptoms and place the worker back on the road to making a full recovery, when that is possible. This medical treatment includes visits to doctors, treatment by nurses, dentists, chiropractors, and other medical professionals.[1]

In the first moments after an injury, an employee should receive first aid and then whatever medical treatment is required and necessary. The obligation to provide medical treatment arises from workers' compensation statutes. The duties imposed by these statutes are straightforward: the employer has the obligation to provide medical benefits and the employee has the obligation of cooperating with the medical treatment.[2] See Exhibit 5-1.

However, workers' compensation has never been seen as a parallel structure to a personal injury lawsuit. Workers' compensation statutes were not designed to give full satisfaction to the injured employee or even to make an injured employee whole again. The purpose was simply to provide a statutory safety net that would provide some system to provide medical and wage benefits to injured employees.[6] As a result, they are generally prohibited from seeking damages for pain and suffering and do not have property rights in their benefit awards. The first provision excludes the type of awards that juries often award individuals for the inconvenience, discomfort, and pain associated with an injury received in a negligence action. Although some states do include an element of pain and suffering in their

EXHIBIT 5-1

Summary of Services Under Medical Benefits.

> Injured employees are entitled to receive specialized medical treatment, including the services of specialists, such as:
>
> - Hearing specialist[3]
> - Neurologist[4]
> - Nurse
> - Home health care nurse
> - Chiropractor
> - Dentist
>
> However, medical benefits do not provide for payments to an injured employee's:
>
> - Maids
> - Servants
> - Individuals who carry out odd jobs
> - Housekeeping services[5]
> - Expert witness to help prepare a workers' compensation case

award computations, most do not. A ruling that "benefits are not property rights" prevents an injured employee from suing for a reinstatement of an award based on constitutional principles in the same way that a person might sue for the seizure of personal property by the government.

An employee's right to receive medical benefits arises from his or her qualification under the workers' compensation statutes and the fact that the injury is work-related. When employees seek and pay for medical treatment on their own, statutes provide that they should be reimbursed for these expenses, as long as the treatment is reasonably necessary.[7] They include initial diagnoses and examinations to discover what the injured employee is suffering from and examinations for the early signs of an occupational illness or disease. The injured employee has the right to receive surgical care and follow-up, again without the prior authorization of the employer. The final determination about the employee's care rests with the attending physician, followed by review of the Workers' Compensation Board.

Waiving Medical Benefits

Employees and employers are authorized to enter into agreements where the employee waives his or her right to receive medical benefits. However, such an agreement cannot be a condition of employment, cannot be forced on the employee, and must be reviewed and approved by the Workers' Compensation Board.[8]

Physical Rehabilitation

In addition to providing medical services, state workers' compensation statutes usually include provisions requiring the employer to pay for splints, crutches, wheelchairs, and other medical apparatus, always within the limitation that the apparatus is reasonably required to help cure the employee's condition or relieve its symptoms. These same statutes may require the employer to provide prosthetic devices, such as artificial limbs, glass eyes, hearing aids, and even dentures. Some appellate decisions also provide that the employee must be provided with the cost of the electricity to run such devices, vans to transport them, or modifications to the employee's home to house them.

Transportation

In addition to payments for specific medical treatments, workers' compensation statutes also provide for employee reimbursement for travel expenses directly related to receiving them. Travel expenses include gasoline and even meals when the travel distance is extensive and requires the injured employee to be away from home for some time. Interestingly enough, when a doctor prescribes a "change of climate" for an employee, such as ordering him or her to move to a less humid environment, these costs may also be assessed against workers' compensation medical payments.

Non-Standard Injuries or Illnesses

So far, our discussion about medical benefits has focused on what is and what is not covered under most workers' compensation statutes. However, there are times when the employee's injury cannot be categorized so easily. How are benefits paid when the employee has a preexisting condition or has an unusual injury? For instance, what happens in situations where there is more than one injury?

Preexisting Injuries or Illnesses

There are situations where an employee is already suffering from one injury or illness, continues to work, perhaps on a reduced work load, and then receives a new injury. How does this affect the benefits that he or she is entitled to receive under workers' compensation laws? What happens in situations where a person suffers from a prior illness and then he is totally disabled when injured on the job?

Over the years, courts have been presented with many of these factual situations and they have developed some general approaches to deal with them.

The first rule that courts follow in workers' compensation cases is to treat each injury as separate and distinct from one another, at least when it comes to awards for injuries. An injured employee is legally permitted to receive multiple awards for multiple injuries. If two injuries occur at different times, then the employee is entitled to receive two benefit checks.

The second rule that the courts use is as follows: They will not consider the injuries separately when it comes to their impact on the employee. Suppose that an employee is prone to migraines. She takes prescribed medication for her migraines and these are not considered to be a work-related injury. However, one day she suffers a blow to her head that makes her migraines much worse. Now, instead of once or twice a week, she gets them almost every day. Will her award be different from an award to someone who has never had a headache in her life? The answer is yes.

The workers' compensation system takes employees as it finds them. If some employees have greater susceptibility to specific injuries than do others, the system will still provide compensation and benefits. If the end result of that approach is that an employee is classified as totally disabled for an injury that would ordinarily have resulted in a determination of partial disability, then the system simply absorbs those costs.

However, the rules change when the on-the-job injury, combined with the previous injury or illness, only results in a finding of partial disability. In that case, there must be a separate inquiry into the two distinct health issues: the on-the-job injury and the previously existing injury or illness. There must be some showing that the current injury aggravated the previous injury. If there is no evidence to support an aggravation of the preexisting condition, the employee's previously existing injury will not be part of the assessment of compensation and benefits for the on-the-job injury.

The "Healing Period"

The "**healing period**" is a term that is used to describe the time that an injured employee needs to recover from an injury or illness. The employee is entitled to receive temporary disability payments during the healing period. Once the employee has recovered from the injury or illness, or has reached a maximum possible recovery, the healing period is over. The employee is then entitled to receive permanent partial or permanent total disability

Healing period

The time during which an injured employee can recover from an accident or illness and receive workers' compensation benefits.

payments, depending on the extent of the injury. We will define and explain these terms in the next section.

DISABILITY PAYMENTS

In addition to providing medical benefits and payments to doctors and other health professionals, the workers' compensation system also provides wage compensation for an injured employee. The amount that the employee receives depends on several factors, including his or her actual earnings and the classification of the employee's injuries as temporary or permanent. These benefits are paid to the injured employee during his or her recuperation and also provide for payments to the employee's dependents in the event of the employee's death. The four classifications for disability payments are:

1. Temporary Partial Disability
2. Permanent Partial Disability
3. Temporary Total Disability
4. Permanent Total Disability

Temporary Partial Disability

Calculating benefits for **temporary partial disability** is always more complicated than figuring them for temporary total disability. After all, with total disability, the employee cannot work. But, by its very definition, a temporary partial disability does not disqualify the worker from all work, just from some work. A person might not be able to work at his or her previous position, but could qualify to work at a less strenuous job. In fact, as we will see later, when an employee qualifies as temporarily partially disabled, and less strenuous work is available, the employee must accept it. Consider Example 5-1 on page 144.

▪ **Temporary partial disability**
A condition where an injured employee is unable to perform his or her previous job, but may be able to carry out more limited duties.

Temporary Total Disability

A worker who has a **temporary total disability** is unable to do any type of work at all. That is a high threshold and must be certified by a qualified medical examiner, usually the employee's doctor. In order to meet that standard, the claimant must show that he or she has been disabled to such an extent, by an injury received on-the-job, that he or she is unable to do any other work. This does not mean that the claimant is unable to care for himself or is unable to do regular household chores. Total disability is always gauged according to

▪ **Temporary total disability**
When a worker receives an injury or suffers from a work-related illness that leaves him or her unable to perform any type of meaningful work.

EXAMPLE 5-1

Carrie grosses $1000 a week at her job. One day, she injures her back at work. After receiving treatment, her employer finds her work that is less strenuous for her back, but she only grosses $500 a week. She falls into the category of temporary partial disability. Under the provisions of the statute found in Exhibit 5-2, what would be her weekly disability payment?

Answer: Carrie is entitled to 66 percent of her gross pay, or $660 per week. Reduce this award by what she is currently earning, $500 a week, and then her final award will be $160 a week. The calculation is always based on gross income, not after-tax and other deductions.

EXHIBIT 5-2

Temporary Partial Disability (Florida).

(a) Subject to subsection (7), in case of temporary partial disability, compensation shall be equal to 80 percent of the difference between 80 percent of the employee's average weekly wage and the salary, wages, and other remuneration the employee is able to earn postinjury, as compared weekly; however, weekly temporary partial disability benefits may not exceed an amount equal to 66 2/3 percent of the employee's average weekly wage at the time of accident.

(c) When an employee returns to work with the restrictions resulting from the accident and is earning wages less than 80 percent of the preinjury average weekly wage, the first installment of temporary partial disability benefits is due 7 days after the last date of the postinjury employer's first biweekly work week. Thereafter, payment for temporary partial benefits shall be paid biweekly no later than the 7th day following the last day of each biweekly work week.[9]

---

employment, not the activities that the worker carries on in his or her personal life. See Exhibit 5-3.

When an employee qualifies for temporary total disability, most states make a weekly award that is 66 percent of the employee's gross income for as long as the period of temporary total disability lasts. This benefit is intended only for a limited period of time. If the employee's condition does not improve, then he or she will be reclassified as permanently disabled and the claim will be administered according to the method used for those computations. Temporary total disability payments are based on the finding that the worker is unable to do any work, anywhere. If the injured employee is unable to find gainful employment because of the injury, then he or she qualifies for temporary total disability. Not all states use the 66 percent mark; some are higher and some are lower. See Exhibit 5-4.

> "Temporary total disability" means that period of time an employee is temporarily and totally incapacitated from performing employment at any gainful employment or occupation for which he is reasonably suited by experience or training.[10]

EXHIBIT 5-3

Defining Temporary Total Disability (Wyoming).

If the employer can show that the employee can do some work, then the employee does not qualify for temporary total disability. Instead, the employee would fall into the category of temporary partial disability.

Differentiating Between Temporary and Permanent

Making a clear distinction between the words "temporary" and "permanent" has been a preoccupation of the court system for decades. In most states, "permanent" has come to mean a condition that will last into the conceivable future and one that will not improve over time. If there is a possibility that the condition will improve or that it will only last for a relatively short period of time, then it is considered to be a temporary disability, even if this temporary situation lasts for several years.

Permanent Partial Disability

When we come to the issue of **permanent partial disability** awards, then we enter the world of schedules. Workers' compensation statutes have to be very specific about benefits paid out for particular types of injuries. Reading the statutes sometimes sounds like the script of a horror movie. Consider the wording of Ohio's schedules in Exhibit 5-5.

As you can see from the **schedules**, at various points in time lawmakers have actually had to make a determination about which fingers are more valuable than other fingers. For instance, the loss of a person's thumb will earn more in compensation than will the loss of a ring finger. These determinations

■ **Permanent partial disability**

A work-related injury that leaves a worker with a permanent condition that will not resolve itself over time.

■ **Schedule**

A listing of specific actions or bodily losses and a corresponding monetary award for each.

> For temporary total disability under paragraph (a)(i) of this section, the award shall be paid monthly at the rate of two-thirds (2/3) of the injured employee's actual monthly earnings at the time of injury but not to exceed the statewide average monthly wage for the twelve (12) month period immediately preceding the quarterly period in which the injury occurred as determined pursuant to W.S. 27-14-802 with one-half (1/2) of the monthly award paid on or about the fifteenth of the month and one-half (1/2) paid on or about the thirtieth of the month.[11]

EXHIBIT 5-4

Temporary Total Disability Payments (Wyoming).

> **4123.57 Partial disability compensation.**
>
> Partial disability compensation shall be paid as follows.
>
> Except as provided in this section, not earlier than twenty-six weeks after the date of termination of the latest period of payments under section 4123.56 of the Revised Code, or not earlier than twenty-six weeks after the date of the injury or contraction of an occupational disease in the absence of payments under section 4123.56 of the Revised Code, the employee may file an application with the bureau of workers' compensation for the determination of the percentage of the employee's permanent partial disability resulting from an injury or occupational disease.
>
> Whenever the application is filed, the bureau shall send a copy of the application to the employee's employer or the employer's representative and shall schedule the employee for a medical examination by the bureau medical section. The bureau shall send a copy of the report of the medical examination to the employee, the employer, and their representatives. Thereafter, the administrator of workers' compensation shall review the employee's claim file and make a tentative order as the evidence before the administrator at the time of the making of the order warrants. If the administrator determines that there is a conflict of evidence, the administrator shall send the application, along with the claimant's file, to the district hearing officer who shall set the application for a hearing.
>
> The administrator shall notify the employee, the employer, and their representatives, in writing, of the tentative order and of the parties' right to request a hearing. Unless the employee, the employer, or their representative notifies the administrator, in writing, of an objection to the tentative order within twenty days after receipt of the notice thereof, the tentative order shall go into effect and the employee shall receive the compensation provided in the order. In no event shall there be a reconsideration of a tentative order issued under this division.
>
> If the employee, the employer, or their representatives timely notify the administrator of an objection to the tentative order, the matter shall be referred to a district hearing officer who shall set the application for hearing with written notices to all interested persons. Upon referral to a district hearing officer, the employer may obtain a medical examination of the employee, pursuant to rules of the industrial commission.
>
> (A) The district hearing officer, upon the application, shall determine the percentage of the employee's permanent disability, except as is subject to division (B) of this section, based upon that condition of the employee resulting from the injury or occupational disease and causing permanent impairment evidenced by medical or clinical findings reasonably demonstrable. The employee shall receive sixty-six and two-thirds per cent of the employee's average weekly wage, but not more than a maximum of thirty-three and one-third per cent of the statewide average weekly wage as defined in division (C) of section 4123.62 of the Revised Code, per week regardless of the average weekly wage, for the number of weeks which equals the percentage of two hundred weeks. Except on application for reconsideration, review, or modification, which is filed within ten days after the date of receipt of the decision of the district hearing officer, in no instance shall the former award be modified unless it is found from medical or clinical findings that the condition of the claimant resulting from the injury has so progressed as to have increased the percentage of permanent partial disability. A staff hearing officer shall hear an application for reconsideration filed and the staff hearing officer's decision is final. An employee may file an application for a subsequent determination of the percentage of the employee's permanent disability. If such an application is filed, the bureau shall send a copy of the application to the employer or the employer's representative. No sooner than sixty days from the date of the mailing of the application to the employer or the employer's representative, the administrator shall review the application. The administrator may require a medical examination or medical review of the employee. The administrator shall issue a tentative order based upon the evidence before the administrator, provided that if the administrator requires a medical examination or medical review, the administrator shall not issue the tentative order until the completion of the examination or review.
>
> The employer may obtain a medical examination of the employee and may submit medical evidence at any stage of

EXHIBIT 5-5 Schedule for Permanent Partial Losses (Ohio). *Reprinted courtesy of the Ohio Bureau of Workers' Compensation.*

are based in part on a recognition that the loss of one part of the body can be more difficult to adapt to than others.

Defining Partial Disability

As far as the court system is concerned a person is partially disabled when he or she can still work, even though the disability prevents the person the process up to a hearing before the district hearing officer, pursuant to rules of the commission. The administrator shall notify the employee, the employer, and their representatives, in writing, of the nature and amount of any tentative order issued on an application requesting a subsequent determination of the percentage of an employee's permanent disability. An employee, employer, or their representatives may object to the tentative order within twenty days after the receipt of the notice thereof. If no timely objection is made, the tentative order shall go into effect. In no event shall there be a reconsideration of a tentative order issued under this division. If an objection is timely made, the application for a subsequent determination shall be referred to a district hearing officer who shall set the application for a hearing with written notice to all interested persons. No application for subsequent percentage determinations on the same claim for injury or occupational disease shall be accepted for review by the district hearing officer unless supported by substantial evidence of new and changed circumstances developing since the time of the hearing on the original or last determination.

No award shall be made under this division based upon a percentage of disability which, when taken with all other percentages of permanent disability, exceeds one hundred per cent. If the percentage of the permanent disability of the employee equals or exceeds ninety per cent, compensation for permanent partial disability shall be paid for two hundred weeks.

Compensation payable under this division accrues and is payable to the employee from the date of last payment of compensation, or, in cases where no previous compensation has been paid, from the date of the injury or the date of the diagnosis of the occupational disease.

When an award under this division has been made prior to the death of an employee, all unpaid installments accrued or to accrue under the provisions of the award are payable to the surviving spouse, or if there is no surviving spouse, to the dependent children of the employee, and if there are no children surviving, then to other dependents as the administrator determines.

(B) In cases included in the following schedule the compensation payable per week to the employee is the statewide average weekly wage as defined in division (C) of section 4123.62 of the Revised Code per week and shall continue during the periods provided in the following schedule:

For the loss of a first finger, commonly known as a thumb, sixty weeks.

For the loss of a second finger, commonly called index finger, thirty-five weeks.

For the loss of a third finger, thirty weeks.

For the loss of a fourth finger, twenty weeks.

For the loss of a fifth finger, commonly known as the little finger, fifteen weeks.

The loss of a second, or distal, phalange of the thumb is considered equal to the loss of one half of such thumb; the loss of more than one half of such thumb is considered equal to the loss of the whole thumb.

The loss of the third, or distal, phalange of any finger is considered equal to the loss of one-third of the finger.

The loss of the middle, or second, phalange of any finger is considered equal to the loss of two-thirds of the finger.

The loss of more than the middle and distal phalanges of any finger is considered equal to the loss of the whole finger. In no case shall the amount received for more than one finger exceed the amount provided in this schedule for the loss of a hand.

EXHIBIT 5-5 (Continued)

from going back to previous job. A person who is classified as being partially disabled:

- Must have some form of physical disability
- Must be able to work at gainful employment while still coping with this disability and
- Must have documented loss in earning capacity related to the disability

> For the loss of the metacarpal bone (bones of the palm) for the corresponding thumb, or fingers, add ten weeks to the number of weeks under this division.
>
> For ankylosis (total stiffness of) or contractures (due to scars or injuries) which makes any of the fingers, thumbs, or parts of either useless, the same number of weeks apply to the members or parts thereof as given for the loss thereof.
>
> If the claimant has suffered the loss of two or more fingers by amputation or ankylosis and the nature of the claimant's employment in the course of which the claimant was working at the time of the injury or occupational disease is such that the handicap or disability resulting from the loss of fingers, or loss of use of fingers, exceeds the normal handicap or disability resulting from the loss of fingers, or loss of use of fingers, the administrator may take that fact into consideration and increase the award of compensation accordingly, but the award made shall not exceed the amount of compensation for loss of a hand.
>
> For the loss of a hand, one hundred seventy-five weeks.
>
> For the loss of an arm, two hundred twenty-five weeks.
>
> For the loss of a great toe, thirty weeks.
>
> For the loss of one of the toes other than the great toe, ten weeks.
>
> The loss of more than two-thirds of any toe is considered equal to the loss of the whole toe.
>
> The loss of less than two-thirds of any toe is considered no loss, except as to the great toe; the loss of the great toe up to the interphalangeal joint is co-equal to the loss of one-half of the great toe; the loss of the great toe beyond the interphalangeal joint is considered equal to the loss of the whole great toe.
>
> For the loss of a foot, one hundred fifty weeks.
>
> For the loss of a leg, two hundred weeks.
>
> For the loss of the sight of an eye, one hundred twenty-five weeks.
>
> For the permanent partial loss of sight of an eye, the portion of one hundred twenty-five weeks as the administrator in each case determines, based upon the percentage of vision actually lost as a result of the injury or occupational disease, but, in no case shall an award of compensation be made for less than twenty-five per cent loss of uncorrected vision. "Loss of uncorrected vision" means the percentage of vision actually lost as the result of the injury or occupational disease.
>
> For the permanent and total loss of hearing of one ear, twenty-five weeks; but in no case shall an award of compensation be made for less than permanent and total loss of hearing of one ear.
>
> For the permanent and total loss of hearing, one hundred twenty-five weeks; but, except pursuant to the next preceding paragraph, in no case shall an award of compensation be made for less than permanent and total loss of hearing.
>
> In case an injury or occupational disease results in serious facial or head disfigurement which either impairs or may in the future impair the opportunities to secure or retain employment, the administrator shall make an award of compensation as it deems proper and equitable, in view of the nature of the disfigurement, and not to exceed the sum of ten thousand dollars. For the purpose of making the award, it is not material whether the employee is

EXHIBIT 5-5 *(Continued)*

When it comes to determining permanent disability, there is a mixture of both a factual and medical finding. Physicians are often requested to make a finding of the injured worker's permanent impairment. Here, the doctor attempts to calculate a percentage of loss for the injury. Nerve damage might gainfully employed in any occupation or trade at the time of the administrator's determination.

When an award under this division has been made prior to the death of an employee all unpaid installments accrued or to accrue under the provisions of the award shall be payable to the surviving spouse, or if there is no surviving spouse, to the dependent children of the employee and if there are no such children, then to such dependents as the administrator determines.

When an employee has sustained the loss of a member by severance, but no award has been made on account thereof prior to the employee's death, the administrator shall make an award in accordance with this division for the loss which shall be payable to the surviving spouse, or if there is no surviving spouse, to the dependent children of the employee and if there are no such children, then to such dependents as the administrator determines.

(C) Compensation for partial impairment under divisions (A) and (B) of this section is in addition to the compensation paid the employee pursuant to section 4123.56 of the Revised Code. A claimant may receive compensation under divisions (A) and (B) of this section.

In all cases arising under division (B) of this section, if it is determined by any one of the following: (1) the amputee clinic at University hospital, Ohio state university; (2) the rehabilitation services commission; (3) an amputee clinic or prescribing physician approved by the administrator or the administrator's designee, that an injured or disabled employee is in need of an artificial appliance, or in need of a repair thereof, regardless of whether the appliance or its repair will be serviceable in the vocational rehabilitation of the injured employee, and regardless of whether the employee has returned to or can ever again return to any gainful employment, the bureau shall pay the cost of the artificial appliance or its repair out of the surplus created by division (B) of section 4123.34 of the Revised Code.

In those cases where a rehabilitation services commission recommendation that an injured or disabled employee is in need of an artificial appliance would conflict with their state plan, adopted pursuant to the "Rehabilitation Act of 1973," 87 Stat. 355, 29 U.S.C.A. 701, the administrator or the administrator's designee or the bureau may obtain a recommendation from an amputee clinic or prescribing physician that they determine appropriate.

(D) If an employee of a state fund employer makes application for a finding and the administrator finds that the employee has contracted silicosis as defined in division (X), or coal miners' pneumoconiosis as defined in division (Y), or asbestosis as defined in division (AA) of section 4123.68 of the Revised Code, and that a change of such employee's occupation is medically advisable in order to decrease substantially further exposure to silica dust, asbestos, or coal dust and if the employee, after the finding, has changed or shall change the employee's occupation to an occupation in which the exposure to silica dust, asbestos, or coal dust is substantially decreased, the administrator shall allow to the employee an amount equal to fifty per cent of the statewide average weekly wage per week for a period of thirty weeks, commencing as of the date of the discontinuance or change, and for a period of one hundred weeks immediately following the expiration of the period of thirty weeks, the employee shall receive sixty-six and two-thirds per cent of the loss of wages resulting directly and solely from the change of occupation but not to exceed a maximum of an amount equal to fifty per cent of the statewide average weekly wage per week. No such employee is entitled to receive more than one allowance on account of discontinuance of employment or change of occupation and benefits shall cease for any period during which the employee is employed in an occupation in which the exposure to silica dust, asbestos, or coal dust is not substantially less than the exposure in the occupation in which the employee was formerly employed or for any period during which the employee may be entitled to receive compensation or benefits under section 4123.68 of the Revised Code on account of disability from silicosis, asbestosis, or coal miners' pneumoconiosis. An award for change of occupation for a coal miner who has contracted coal miners' pneumoconiosis may be granted under this division even though the coal miner continues employment with the same employer, so long as the coal miner's employment subsequent to the change is such that the coal miner's exposure to coal dust is substantially decreased and a change of occupation is certified by the claimant as permanent. The administrator may accord to the employee medical and other benefits in accordance with section 4123.66 of the Revised Code.

EXHIBIT 5-5 (*Continued*)

leave a worker with some movement in a hand, but certainly not the same percentage that he or she had prior to the injury. In such a situation, the doctor will assign a 100 percent value to the worker's pre-injury condition, then attempt to gauge the percentage of loss following the injury or illness. This is certainly

> (E) If a firefighter or police officer makes application for a finding and the administrator finds that the firefighter or police officer has contracted a cardiovascular and pulmonary disease as defined in division (W) of section 4123.68 of the Revised Code, and that a change of the firefighter's or police officer's occupation is medically advisable in order to decrease substantially further exposure to smoke, toxic gases, chemical fumes, and other toxic vapors, and if the firefighter, or police officer, after the finding, has changed or changes occupation to an occupation in which the exposure to smoke, toxic gases, chemical fumes, and other toxic vapors is substantially decreased, the administrator shall allow to the firefighter or police officer an amount equal to fifty per cent of the statewide average weekly wage per week for a period of thirty weeks, commencing as of the date of the discontinuance or change, and for a period of seventy-five weeks immediately following the expiration of the period of thirty weeks the administrator shall allow the firefighter or police officer sixty-six and two-thirds per cent of the loss of wages resulting directly and solely from the change of occupation but not to exceed a maximum of an amount equal to fifty per cent of the statewide average weekly wage per week. No such firefighter or police officer is entitled to receive more than one allowance on account of discontinuance of employment or change of occupation and benefits shall cease for any period during which the firefighter or police officer is employed in an occupation in which the exposure to smoke, toxic gases, chemical fumes, and other toxic vapors is not substantially less than the exposure in the occupation in which the firefighter or police officer was formerly employed or for any period during which the firefighter or police officer may be entitled to receive compensation or benefits under section 4123.68 of the Revised Code on account of disability from a cardiovascular and pulmonary disease. The administrator may accord to the firefighter or police officer medical and other benefits in accordance with section 4123.66 of the Revised Code.
>
> (F) An order issued under this section is appealable pursuant to section 4123.511 of the Revised Code but is not appealable to court under section 4123.512 of the Revised Code.
>
> Effective Date: 08-06-1999; (SB 7) 06-30-2006

EXHIBIT 5-5[12]   (Continued)

not an exact science. Evaluating a disability is the function of the Workers' Compensation Board in general and the Administrative Law Judge in particular. We will discuss the role of the ALJ in a future chapter. Reaching a final determination of an employee's injury must then take into account the medical evidence and testimonial evidence from the injured employee and any others. The final award involves a balancing of these various factors. Obviously, the more parts of the employee's body that are affected, the greater the final award. That may be small comfort to someone who has lost an eye and a leg and is receiving 350 weeks of workers' compensation benefits. Consider Example 5-2.

One question that frequently arises concerns the tax consequences of such an award. Workers' compensation benefit awards are not taxable as income under either federal or state tax laws.

Permanent Total Disability

If partial disability is defined as the ability to do some work while being subject to a disability, total disability means that a claimant is unable to do any work at all.

A worker is considered to be totally disabled when he or she is unable to obtain reasonable gainful employment or unable to carry out the activities associated with a substantial portion of any employment. Essentially, in order to justify a finding of **permanent total disability**, an injured worker must be unable to do any type of meaningful work. In that situation, the worker would

Permanent total disability

An injury that leaves a worker unable to return to work or to engage in any other meaningful work for the balance of the worker's life.

> **EXAMPLE 5-2**
>
> Maria makes $18.32 an hour. She works 40 hours a week and her gross pay is $728 per week. If Maria suffers permanent total loss of one of her arms, how much will she receive in workers' compensation benefits?
>
> Maria's weekly salary is $728. Multiply that amount by 66 percent. The result is $480.48. That is the amount that Maria is entitled to receive for a single week. However, what is her total award? We can see from the statute above that Maria is entitled to receive 225 weeks of benefits for the loss of an arm. Multiply 225 by $480.48 = $109,008. If that sounds like a lot of money, consider that Maria will never be able to use her arm again and this money is supposed to compensate her for the rest of her life, even if she is in her mid-twenties.

be entitled to receive a maximum of 70 percent of his or her previous wages for a total of 450 weeks, at least under New Jersey law.

Lump Sum Disability Payments

In some cases, a Workers' Compensation Board may authorize the payout of the entire amount of the injured worker's compensation in a single payment. This is referred to as a **lump sum payment** and must be authorized by state statute.[13] When this payment is made, the employer's total obligation to the injured employee for medical benefits is extinguished. A worker might want to receive the entire balance of his or her compensation in a single check, but experience has shown that this money quickly disappears. Many Administrative Law Judges now opt for weekly payments, if only to protect the worker from his or her own impulses to spend a sudden windfall.

Lump sum payment
Payment of the entire balance of a worker's benefits in a single transaction.

Awards for Pain and Suffering

Workers' compensation benefits are not awarded on the basis of **pain and suffering**. In civil cases, it is common for the plaintiff to request a special monetary award based on the pain and suffering caused by the defendant's negligence. However, workers' compensation benefits are restricted to loss of future income and payment of medical expenses. The formula is supposed to be simple: The claimant receives a percentage of the income he or she would have earned if the employee had been able to continue working. There is also a schedule showing specific amounts for the loss of eyes, fingers, or limbs that does not depend on earning capacity. However, some states have modified

Pain and suffering
The physical, emotional, and mental stress from an injury.

their approach to pain and suffering in workers' compensation cases, at least when the pain is so severe that it actually qualifies as an impairment. In such a case, the pain itself is compensable as a temporary or permanent disability.

Workers' compensation benefit awards do not take into account other losses that are frequently recognized in negligence cases, such as hedonic damages. Hedonic damages are payments to an injured party in recognition of his or her loss of enjoyment in life. A person who is in pain, suffering from the loss of body parts, or is unable to do many of the activities the rest of us take for granted, frequently become depressed and unable to find joy or excitement in their day-to-day existence. In a civil case, such losses would justify additional damage awards. However, that is not the case in workers' compensation cases. The statutes that authorize compensation awards do not permit additional payments for the loss of enjoyment in life.[14]

Earning Capacity

Part of the calculations involved in a workers' compensation case involves calculating the worker's **earning capacity**. This is also referred to as earning power. By whatever term that is used, the determination is always based on the same thing: What did the employee earn before the injury and what can the employee earn after the injury? The difference in these two figures is the loss of earning capacity or earning power. Benefits under workers' compensation, such as temporary partial disability and temporary total disability, are based on the calculation of the injured employee's reduction in earning capacity. Workers' compensation benefit awards are always based on a percentage of what the employee earned prior to the injury. For instance, in the earlier example involving Maria, her state compensated based on 66 percent of her former weekly gross salary. Most states have caps on the payment. As an example, the state might mandate that an injured employee could receive 66 percent of his or her former salary or $500, whichever is less. Under this ruling, the most that an injured employee could receive per week is $500. If it turns out that 66 percent of his or her weekly salary is less than $500, then that is the amount the employee would receive.

Many states have a two-pronged approach to making award determinations: functional disability and impact on earning capacity. Functional disability is a purely physical determination of the employee's limitations. Here, the analysis focuses on the actual physical problem suffered by the employee, including percentage of loss, maximum possible improvement, and other physiological features. The second part of the analysis takes into account these physical issues and then makes a separate determination that reaches a conclusion about the impact that the physical issues have on the worker's employability. If he or she is injured to such an extent that most

■ **Earning capacity**

The total amount that a worker can earn based on training, education, and experience.

types of employment are out of reach, then this justifies a finding of complete loss of earning capacity.[15]

The actual payment of the awards can occur in any of a number of ways. For instance, the injured employee might receive regular disability payments until such time that a medical doctor determines that he or she is able to return to work. At that time, benefits might cease completely. If, on the other hand, a doctor determines that the claimant has achieved maximum possible recovery and still is unable to return to work, then the employer or the employer's insurance company might award a lump sum payment to the employee based on a calculation of the benefits available and the workers' compensation schedule that lists specific amounts for the loss of particular parts of the body.

Awards for Multiple Injuries

It is possible under state workers' compensation law to receive multiple awards for multiple injuries. For instance, a worker might be receiving temporary partial disability payments for one injury and performing work for his or her employer when the employee is injured again. Under this scenario, it is possible for the employee to receive benefits in two different cases for two different injuries.

Disfigurement

What happens in situations when a person not only loses the function of some part of his or her body, but also is disfigured by the injury? You will notice that disfigurement is not listed on the schedule of injuries covered by workers' compensation provided in Exhibit 5-5. However, most states do allow injured workers to recover for disfigurement. What the states do in this situation is to allow the parties or the judge to determine an amount to compensate the employee for the disfigurement and then refer to the schedules for the loss of other parts of the body. The final award would include an amount for the disfigurement and an amount from the loss. In some cases, the Workers' Compensation Board might rule that a person is so disfigured by an injury that for all practical purposes the employee has sustained a permanent partial disability and make an award on that basis.[16]

> **SIDEBAR**
>
> Defining Serious Disfigurement
> A serious disfigurement in fact is a disfigurement that mars and hence adversely affects the appearance of the injured employee to such extent that it may be reasonably presumed to lessen his opportunities for remunerative employment and so reduce his future earning power.[17]

Preexisting Conditions

As we have already seen, a person who suffers from a preexisting condition is still entitled to receive workers' compensation benefits if he or she should receive an additional injury to that same area. The rule is simple: Workers' compensation benefits are permissible even when a normal person would not have been injured by the same occurrence. Persons of special susceptibility are still allowed to receive benefits for aggravation of preexisting conditions.[18]

Checklist: Benefits

A client has come to our firm with specific questions about the benefits she can receive under workers' compensation. Here is a checklist of issues (and answers) that we can provide.

1. What type of benefits am I eligible to receive?

    An injured worker can receive temporary disability benefits, medical benefits and permanent disability benefits. The actual amount of benefits is based on the state average weekly wages and the wage that the employee was receiving prior to the injury. When it comes to medical benefits, these vary from state to state, with some states allowing an injured worker the right to choose her own doctor for treatment, while others require the worker to use a different doctor. Final awards for permanent disability are based on a disability rating provided by the doctor and a schedule of payments set out in state statutes.

2. What exactly happens when a claim gets filed?

    The usual procedure is for the company to forward the claim on to its insurance provider. The provider will investigate a claim and make an award based on a formula mandated under state law. Of course, the provider might decide to controvert the claim and that means the case will go for a hearing.

3. What types of injuries are covered under workers' compensation?

    Just about every on-the-job injury is covered under workers' compensation. There is no requirement, for instance, that a person must have suffered an accident. Coverage also extends to repetitive stress injuries—carpal tunnel syndrome and chronic backache are two examples—and illnesses that can be caused by working conditions.

4. How are benefits paid?

    The basic system is that workers' compensation provides replacement income for the injured worker while he or she recovers, pays for medical expenses related to the injury or illness and even provides vocational rehabilitation to help an injured worker learn new skills. Benefits can also include additional training, educational opportunities, and a job placement service. The important thing to keep in mind is that nobody gets rich receiving workers' compensation benefits. They are designed to provide modest assistance.

5. How much will I get in benefits?

    Let's suppose that a worker is temporarily injured. In that situation, the worker would receive two-thirds of his or her weekly salary, up to a specific amount. For instance, if you made $500 a week, then your benefits would be 2/3 of $500 or $330. All states have a maximum cut off rate so that will receive either two-thirds of his or her salary or a maximum of $X per week, whichever is smaller.

If a person is permanently disabled, the calculations are different. In that case, the Administrative Law Judge will fashion an award that takes into account the nature of the disability, the worker's ability to do other work, and a doctor's certification concerning what total percent of permanent disability the injured worker has. Once those determinations have been made, the board will award weekly benefits for a set period or provide a lump sum payment.

6. Can I use my own doctor?

   In some states, an employee can see his or her own doctor, but only if he or she has made such a request before any injury occurs. In many other states, the employee is referred to a doctor paid by the employer's insurance carrier. This doctor will make a report to the provider that can have a huge impact on the benefits you receive in your case. The doctor's findings (or rating) will help the board determine the total amount of permanent damage and award benefits accordingly.

7. Can I get my prescriptions filled at my own pharmacy?

   Many states have passed laws that specifically force injured employees to fill their prescriptions at approved pharmacies. The insurance provider cannot prevent you from receiving the prescriptions that you were receiving before the injury.

8. How long will it take to get reimbursed for my out-of-pocket costs, such as filling prescriptions?

   There are no statutory guidelines about how quickly an insurance provider must reimburse an injured worker; that can translate into a long wait. Many states have amended their laws to force insurance companies to reimburse unchallenged claims within 45 days of receipt.

VOCATIONAL REHABILITATION AND JOB PLACEMENT SERVICES

In some states, workers' compensation benefits not only pay for medical treatment and compensate for lost wages, but also pay for retraining and vocational rehabilitation. Retraining for other work is not part of the medical benefits package under state workers' compensation law and must be authorized separately. When it is, a worker who is unable to return to his or her former occupation could receive limited funds for retraining in order to learn a different job skill. Vocational rehabilitation benefits often include provisions that allow a worker to return to college or a trade school to learn a new skill set. Additional training can include speech therapy, psychological intervention, and cognitive retraining. If the worker refuses to take part in vocational rehabilitation, then the workers compensation board is justified in either reducing or suspending benefits.[19]

Job Placement Services

In addition to vocational rehabilitation and educational services, many states also offer a job placement service that tries to match injured employees with jobs where they can use their new skills.

DEATH BENEFITS

Workers' compensation statutes also provide death benefits for employees who die as a result of injury or illness. These **death benefits** provide for funeral expenses and payments to the employee's spouse and children. See Exhibit 5-6 for an example of death benefits. Under such a statute, a worker who died within one year of the incident that brought about his or her death would be entitled to funeral expenses totaling $7,500 and 50 percent of the deceased's income until the spouse dies.

When an employee dies because of a work-related illness or injury, this is often referred to as the "last sickness" and is compensable under workers'

■ **Death benefit**

An award made to a deceased worker's family to defray the costs of burial and to provide additional income.

---

(1) If death results from the accident within 1 year thereafter or follows continuous disability and results from the accident within 5 years thereafter, the employer shall pay:

    (a) Within 14 days after receiving the bill, actual funeral expenses not to exceed $7,500.

    (b) Compensation, in addition to the above, in the following percentages of the average weekly wages to the following persons entitled thereto on account of dependency upon the deceased, and in the following order of preference, subject to the limitation provided in subparagraph 2., but such compensation shall be subject to the limits provided in s. 440.12(2), shall not exceed $150,000, and may be less than, but shall not exceed, for all dependents or persons entitled to compensation, 66 2/3 percent of the average wage:

        1. To the spouse, if there is no child, 50 percent of the average weekly wage, such compensation to cease upon the spouse's death.

        2. To the spouse, if there is a child or children, the compensation payable under subparagraph 1. and, in addition, 16 2/3 percent on account of the child or children.[20]

EXHIBIT 5-6

Compensation for Death (Florida). *Adapted from WESTLAW. Reprinted with permission.*

> Should the employee die from some other cause than the injury, payments of compensation to which the deceased would have been entitled to under section 306(c)(1) to (25) shall be paid to the following persons who at the time of the death of the deceased were dependents within the definition of clause (7) of section 307 and in the following order and amounts:
>
> (1) To the surviving widow or widower if there are no children under the age of eighteen.
>
> (2) To a surviving widow or widower and a surviving child or children in which event the widow or widower shall receive one-half and the surviving child or children shall receive the other half.
>
> (3) To a surviving child or children if there is no surviving widow or widower.[21]

EXHIBIT 5-7

Payments to Survivors in Event of Death from Cause Other than Injury (Illinois). *Adapted from WESTLAW. Reprinted with permission.*

compensation laws. Death benefits operate independently of medical or other benefits and are the only benefits that also apply to the deceased worker's family.

An interesting question arises when deciding exactly who is and who is not considered to be part of the deceased worker's family. In recent years, for example, some states have recognized that homosexual couples have a constitutional right to marriage, while many other states have specifically outlawed the union. The question about the deceased worker's children has a longer track record and has been resolved for decades. An illegitimate child, for instance, is just as entitled to death benefits as is a legitimate child. However, live-in lovers and non-married couples do not qualify to receive spousal benefits. (See this chapter's Case Excerpt.) It remains an open question whether states that recognize the legitimacy of homosexual marriages will also award workers' compensation death benefits to the survivors of this union.

Some states provide no death benefits when an employee dies from some cause other than the on-the-job illness or injury. Other states, such as Illinois allow a limited form of death benefit whenever an employee dies. See Exhibit 5-7.

DENIAL OR TERMINATION OF BENEFITS

Once they are awarded, workers' compensation benefits can be denied or terminated for any of a number of reasons. The most common reasons to terminate benefits are:

- The employee recovers and is able to return to work or
- The employee has achieved maximum recovery and will not improve any further

When the employee recovers and is able to return to work, he or she is no longer entitled to receive any workers' compensation benefits, other than lost wages, assuming that there is no change in the employee's earning capacity. On the other hand, if the employee is injured to such an extent that he or she will only recover to a certain point and will never get better again, then the employee is entitled to permanent total disability payments.

However, there are other reasons for terminating benefits. For instance, a worker who provides false information to the Workers' Compensation Board may have benefits terminated, as will an employee who refuses medical treatment.

False Representations by the Employee

An employer is justified in denying workers' compensation benefits when an employee makes false representations, but only when these representations affect the injury. Suppose, for instance, that a worker gives false information on a job application? This, by itself, will not justify denial of a workers' compensation claim. However, the situation changes when the false information relates to the injury. Obviously, a worker who files a false claim of accident will have his or her benefits denied. Similarly, a worker who exaggerates the claim may also face the same disposition.

Some states follow a far more rigid rule when it comes to false information, even when that information is contained on a job application. Louisiana, for example, has workers' compensation statutes that specifically provide that an employee who makes false statements on his or her work application will face denial of coverage under the workers' compensation system. Because states have rules that vary considerably, the courts in the United States have come up with a 3-part test to determine when an employee forfeits workers' compensation benefits by making false statements. That test states that benefits can be denied when all three of the following circumstances are present:

1. The employee knowingly and willfully made false statements about his or her physical condition.
2. The employer relied on that statement in hiring the employee.
3. There was a direct connection between the statement and the injury.

Proof of all three of these elements is required before an employer can request that an employee's workers compensation benefits be terminated. The first element, that the employee knowingly made a false statement, is a fairly straightforward element. Under this test, not all false statements justify a denial of benefits. The employee must make a false statement about his or her physical condition. If the employee claims to have skills that he or she really does not have, that will not justify termination of workers' compensation benefits. Instead, the employee's false statement must be about prior injuries or current physical condition. If the employee injured his or her back on the previous job, fails to admit that on the job application, and then receives another back injury, the false statement would be enough to terminate benefits. The second element, that the employer relied on this statement, is important because there are certain types of physical conditions that have no bearing on someone's job performance. Suppose, for example, that the job application form contains a sentence that reads: "I can lift over 50 pounds. Yes. No." The employee circles "Yes," knowing full well that in his physical condition it would be extremely difficult, if not impossible, for him to lift that amount of weight. However, because he's been hired as a software designer, the employer will be hard-pressed to say that it relied on that statement in hiring the employee. After all, being able to lift heavy weights is not a job requirement for a software developer.

The third and final element concerning false statements on a job application or resume concerns the causal connection between the statement and the new injury. If the employee denies having a slipped disc and injures his or her back while on the job, there would be a direct, causal connection between the statement and the injury. The employer can show that it made a reasonable request of the employee, relying on information that proved to be false. If any one of these three elements is missing, false statements on a resume or job application cannot terminate an employee's workers' compensation benefits.

Refusing Medical Treatment

In addition to denial of benefits based on false statements, employees may also have their benefits terminated under the workers' compensation system if they refuse reasonable medical or surgical treatment. If the treatment available is generally accepted by the medical community and the workers' compensation board determines that the employee's refusal to submit to the treatment is unreasonable, then the worker's benefits will be terminated. Some states are reluctant to go that far. Instead of terminating the benefits, they simply suspend benefits during the time when the employee is refusing treatment. They reinstate benefits as soon as the employee agrees to undergo the procedure. Of course, if the employee never agrees, his or her benefits are never reinstated.

What qualifies as "unreasonably refusing" to undergo medical procedures? The answer to that question actually varies depending on the facts of the case. For instance, if the procedure is minimal, the Workers' Compensation Board is more likely to rule that the employee is being unreasonable when he or she refuses to undergo it. On the other hand, if the procedure involves intensive surgery or dangers to the employee, the refusal might not be considered unreasonable. These cases always involve a balancing act between the employee's actions and the possible dangers of the procedure. If the employee's refusal to undergo medical treatment results in further complications, the employer is under no responsibility to pay for these medical problems.

Illegal Aliens, Immigration Status

A worker who is hired is entitled to receive workers' compensation benefits, even if it turns out that the worker is an illegal alien, or has lied about his immigration status. Some states have changed the first part of this equation by specifically excluding illegal aliens from receiving any type of state-based aid, but many still compensate injured workers regardless of immigration status.

CASE MANAGEMENT ISSUES IN WORKERS' COMPENSATION

The primary goal of the workers' compensation system is to provide injured workers with medical treatment and benefits reasonably related to the work injury. Employers do not have the option of picking and choosing among the benefits that they will carry. Instead, statutes require and they provide these benefits. However, the employer is not in the best position to monitor the employee's progress or even qualified to pass judgment on the best course of treatment. Because employees in many states also have the right to choose their medical providers, there is an innate tension between the two parties: The employer would obviously prefer to limit medical expenses as much as possible and would certainly choose to work with a medical providers with the same attitude, while employees would just as obviously prefer to receive the maximum amount of treatment from the medical providers with whom they have already established a relationship. One way of addressing these conflicting issues is to create the position of case manager.

Case Manager

Case management refers to the process of reviewing the injured worker's medical treatment to ensure that it is achieving the goals of the workers' compensation system, while simultaneously making the most efficient use of resources. While we will use the term "**case manager**" to refer to this individual, it is important to note that that term is not universally applied.

Case manager
A person, often a medical professional who is responsible for managing the care administered to an injured worker by reviewing all medical records, procedures, and claims and is also responsible for interacting with the worker's medical and legal personnel.

Different states may use different terms to describe this individual. Regardless of the title, a case manager is hired by the employer (or employer's insurance provider) and serves the same role that has come to be common in almost all other forms of medical insurance: overseeing medical treatment, suggesting alternative (and less costly procedures), and limiting other procedures.

Most states require that case managers must be licensed by the state. Many also require that the case manager have a medical background. Vermont, for example, requires that case managers must be Registered Nurses. The premise here is that when the case manager is a medical professional, he or she will have a better understanding of the best practices to be followed in caring for the injured worker and will also be aware of the practices that can be both costly and a inefficient in reaching the goal of healing the worker. A case manager with a medical background can spot questionable medical procedures and will have greater insight into potential medical fraud. On the other hand, some critics allege that requiring the case manager to be a medical professional assures that all CMs will be drawn from a pool of individuals already biased in favor of the medical profession and less likely to make decisions based on economics.

Case managers may work directly for insurance carriers or may work as independent contractors for companies that have contractual relationships with insurance carriers. They are paid by the insurance carrier and that has prompted other critics to allege that case managers have a vested interest in siding with the employer in contested issues, just to ensure that they will continue to work with the carrier in future cases. In order to address potential conflicts of interest between employers, employees, and carriers, case managers in most states are required to present injured workers with a **disclosure statement**, specifically detailing the case manager's relationship with the carrier. See Exhibit 5-8.

In some cases, the various phases of the claim are divided between a case manager and an insurance examiner. In this case, an insurance examiner is an employee of the Workers' Compensation Board and is responsible for reviewing claims, authorizing medical treatment, and preparing documents to settle non-contested claims. The insurance examiner may also have additional duties, including:

- Contacting the employer
- Investigating the claim
- Sending documentation to Workers' Compensation Board
- Paying indemnity until claimant reaches maximum medical improvement (MMI)
- Paying medical bills

Disclosure statement
A document reviewed and signed by an injured worker that explains the role of the case manager and explains that the case manager is employed by the employer.

> **CASE MANAGER DISCLOSURE STATEMENT**
>
> I, Deborah Bolstridge, am a Case Manager who is employed by ABC Insurance Company to assist you with returning to work. My goal is to help you return to work as quickly and as safely as possible.
>
> Case managers are provided as a service to you at no cost. The costs for my services are compensated by ABC Insurance Company. In order to carry out my duties I may need to do some or all of the following:
>
> - Contact your employer to discuss your job description and duties. I may also need to discuss work alternatives for you that may involve less strenuous duties than your previous work position. My contact may be by telephone, e-mail, or other electronic communication.
> - Contact your physician, physician's assistant, nurse caretaker or other medical service provider in order to discuss your current condition, your prognosis, possible alternate treatments, and accommodations to improve your chances at making a recovery. However, it is important for you to understand that I generally do not come with you when you seek medical treatment of any kind.
> - Prepare a report to ABC Insurance Company detailing your care, your treatment, and your prospects for recovery. My report will also contain results, recommendations and options. I generally make such a report every thirty (30) days. Whenever I submit a report to ABC Insurance Company, I will also make one available to you within a reasonable period of time.
>
> By singing this from, you agree that you have read it, understand its provisions and have no additional question about the role of a case manager in your workers' compensation case.
>
> _____   _____
> Employee Signature   Date
>
> _____   _____
> CM Signature   Date

EXHIBIT 5-8

Case Manager Disclosure Statement.

- Resolving the claim
- Closing the file. See Exhibit 5-9.

CATASTROPHIC CLAIMS

Most states classify work-related injuries as either catastrophic or non-catastrophic. This classification scheme is more than semantics. If an injury is categorized as catastrophic, it can have a huge impact on the benefits paid to the injured worker and can determine whether or not the worker will

> The Case Manager should have a medical history of the worker. Answers to the following questions should also be available:
>
> - Any indications of repeated workers' compensation claims?
> - Has a return to work order been issued?
> - Are there any discrepancies in reported injuries, such as switching sides for original injury?
> - Will employer be able to take injured worker back in a reduced capacity?
> - Does the injured worker have a history of non-compliance?
> - Are there mental/psychiatric/social issues?
>
> *Summary of Duties of Case Manager*
>
> - Contact the claimant
> - Obtain medical records
> - Input data into managed care data computer system
> - Act as liaison with all medical providers
> - Communicate with legal community
> - Contact medical vendors as needed

EXHIBIT 5-9

Information Necessary for Efficient Case Management.

receive a broad range of additional benefits not normally granted to non-catastrophic injuries. However, before we can discuss the benefits awarded to workers suffering from catastrophic injuries, we must first address the fundamental issue of what qualifies as a catastrophic injury.

What Qualifies as a Catastrophic Claim?

In general, a catastrophic injury is any injury that involves severe head injuries, burns, paralysis, amputations, blindness, or any other injury that prevents the injured worker from returning to any meaningful type of work. Most states provide that a worker who has injuries that qualify as catastrophic will receive two-thirds of his or her average weekly wage for as long as the disability lasts. In catastrophic injuries, the disability is likely to last for the remainder of the injured worker's life. There are additional procedural issues that arise in catastrophic injuries. For instance, the employer may be required to bring in rehabilitation specialists who are experts in handling catastrophic injuries and may also be required to modify the injured worker's residence. Home modification programs will widen doorways to accommodate wheelchairs, install safety railings, modify bathrooms, and build ramps, among other items.

CASE EXCERPT

IS A NON-MARRIED PARTNER ENTITLED TO WORKERS' COMPENSATION DEATH BENEFITS?

Rainey v. Whitewater Engineering[22]

OPINION

BRYNER, Chief Justice.

I. INTRODUCTION

The Alaska Workers' Compensation Act provides that when an employee suffers a work-related death, the employee's surviving widow or widower is eligible for death benefits. When Sharon Ranney sought death benefits after the work-related death of her long-term partner, Gary Stone, the Alaska Workers' Compensation Board ruled that she was not eligible for benefits because she and Stone had never been married. Ranney challenges this ruling, arguing that the board misinterpreted the workers' compensation act and violated her rights to privacy and equal protection under the Alaska Constitution. We affirm the board's decision, holding that the decision correctly interpreted the act and did not deprive Ranney of her constitutional rights, since denying spousal death benefits to Ranney did not substantially burden her freedom to have an unmarried intimate relationship with Stone and was fairly and substantially related to the act's goal of providing quick, efficient, fair, and predictable benefits to families of deceased workers at a reasonable cost to employers.

II. FACTS AND PROCEEDINGS

Sharon Ranney and Gary Stone became romantically involved in the spring of 1995 and moved in together that fall. Although Stone and Ranney were never legally married, they lived together as a couple until Gary Stone's death in April 1999.

While together they shared a joint checking account. They were jointly listed in the Cordova telephone book. And they purchased various kinds of machinery together—a small sawmill, a crane, and a truck. Stone also purchased a life-insurance policy and named Ranney the primary beneficiary. Although Ranney worked off and on throughout their relationship, she depended on Stone's income to maintain her standard of living. Ranney submitted many affidavits from friends attesting to the couple's intent to get married. And Ranney testified that Stone bought her a wedding ring in 1997 and that he formally proposed to her in March of 1999.

Continued

In April 1999 Stone was killed in a work-related accident while employed by Whitewater Engineering. Ranney then filed a claim for death benefits as Stone's "unmarried spouse." Whitewater and its insurer, Fremont Compensation/Cambridge Integrated Services Group, controverted Ranney's claim on the ground that she was never Stone's wife and that she was therefore not entitled to benefits under the act.

In addressing Ranney's claim, the Alaska Workers' Compensation Board noted that AS 23.30.215 provides for the payment of death benefits to the "widow or widower or a child or children of the deceased." Because the act defines "widow" to include "only the decedent's wife living with or dependent for support upon the decedent at the time of death, or living apart for justifiable cause or by reason of the decedent's desertion at such a time," the board reasoned that Ranney would qualify as "the decedent's wife" only if she had actually been married to Stone. Since Ranney had never married Stone, the board concluded that she was ineligible for benefits as his "wife."

After appealing to the superior court, which affirmed the board's decision, Ranney filed this appeal.

III. DISCUSSION

On appeal, Ranney argues that the unmarried partners of deceased employees are eligible to receive death benefits under the workers' compensation act. Moreover, if the act does not cover unmarried but committed relationships like hers and Stone's, Ranney asserts, it violates her rights to privacy and equal protection under the Alaska Constitution.

The Act's Express Language

Ranney argues that, as Stone's "[u]nmarried, [d]ependent [w]idow," she is entitled to death benefits under the Alaska Workers' Compensation Act. Whitewater responds that because Ranney was never married to Stone, she fails to qualify as his "widow," and so cannot properly claim benefits under the act.

When interpreting a statute, "we consider its language, its purpose, and its legislative history, in an attempt to 'give effect to the legislature's intent.'" Although "[w]e have rejected a mechanical application of the plain meaning rule," we have placed a heavy burden on parties who urge us to adopt an interpretation that appears contrary to a statute's plain language.

The workers' compensation act specifies that where a work-related injury causes an employee's death, death benefits are payable to "a widow or widower or a child or children of the deceased." If there is no widow or widower and there are no children, then benefits must be paid to specified members of the extended family.

Continued

The act defines "widow" as "only the decedent's wife living with or dependent for support upon the decedent at the time of death, or living apart for justifiable cause or by reason of the decedent's desertion at such a time." The act does not define "wife," but does provide that "'married' includes a person who is divorced but is required by the decree of divorce to contribute to the support of the former spouse."

Ranney contends that the act's definition of "wife" could plausibly be read to include unmarried cohabitants, so that they would fall within the definition of "widow."

We disagree. The Alaska legislature has directed that [w]ords and phrases shall be construed . . . according to their common and approved usage. Technical words and phrases and those which have acquired a peculiar and appropriate meaning, whether by legislative definition or otherwise, shall be construed according to the peculiar and appropriate meaning. AS 01.10.040(a).

Because "wife" has not been defined statutorily and has no technical meaning in the present context, we look to common usage, where the word ordinarily refers to a married woman. "Marriage" has been defined by statute. The Alaska Marriage Code provides:

(a) Marriage is a civil contract entered into by one man and one woman that requires both a license and solemnization.
(b) A person may not be joined in marriage in this state until a license has been obtained for that purpose as provided in this chapter. A marriage performed in this state is not valid without solemnization as provided in this chapter. AS 25.05.011.

We have previously held that this definition of marriage does not recognize common law marriage. Thus, neither common usage nor legislative definition suggests that people in Ranney's position—unmarried cohabitants—should be considered "wives" or "husbands" under the workers' compensation act.

Moreover, the detailed benefits scheme set out in the workers' compensation act suggests that the legislature did not intend to include unmarried cohabitants as beneficiaries. Alaska Statute 23.30.215 provides that if there is a widow or widower and/or children, they are entitled to benefits. If there is no widow or widower and no children, death benefits may go to the employee's parents, grandchildren, brothers, and sisters if they were "dependent upon the deceased at the time of injury."

Where a statute expressly enumerates the things or persons to which it applies, we often invoke the principle of statutory construction expressio unius est exclusio alterius. This principle "establishes the inference that, where certain things are designated in a statute, 'all omissions should be understood as exclusions.'" We

Continued

have indicated that "the case for application of expressio unius est exclusio alterius is particularly compelling, where ... the scheme is purely statutory and without a basis in the common law." In the context of the workers' compensation act, which creates a detailed and complicated scheme for requiring employers to provide support to some surviving members of the employee's family, it is appropriate to apply this canon of interpretation. Because the act includes a detailed list of beneficiaries, the failure to include unmarried cohabitants suggests their exclusion.

Ranney nonetheless contends that "[t]he concept of 'family' is changing," so that she should be included within the definition of family. She notes that state law in many instances includes unmarried persons within its definition of spouse. She cites Alaska's regulations for adult public assistance, which include within the definition of spouse "unmarried persons who live together and hold themselves out to the community as husband and wife." And she points to similar language in Alaska's childcare assistance program and its disaster relief regulations. She argues that these programs are "intended to prevent people from going hungry or homeless." Because "workers' compensation death benefits serve a very similar purpose," she contends, a similarly broad definition of family should be read into the workers' compensation act.

But as Whitewater correctly observes in response, under the regulations cited by Ranney the non-traditional family members qualify precisely "because the regulations expressly allow them to do so." At most, these regulations illustrate that agencies are capable of expanding the meanings of common terms when they intend to do so. It may be true that the act's purpose is analogous to the purposes of the various public assistance programs cited by Ranney. But where those programs include non-traditional family members, they do so expressly. Here if the legislature had intended to include unmarried cohabitants in its definition of "widow," it similarly could have done so expressly. Accordingly, it appears that the legislature's intent, as manifested in the statutory language, was to limit beneficiaries to those expressly enumerated in the statute. As Stone's unmarried cohabiting partner, Ranney is not eligible for death benefits under the act's language.

Ranney further argues that the purpose of the act is to compensate dependents for a worker's death. She insists that in light of this purpose, the distinctions created by the statute between married and unmarried "wives" should be ignored. Yet compensating dependents is not the act's singular purpose. The act's broader purpose is to provide a system of compensation that is "quick, efficient, fair and predictable"—and is not unreasonably expensive for employers.

As Whitewater points out, allowing unmarried partners to receive benefits would require the board to distinguish between relationships that were sufficiently

Continued

serious to merit the award of benefits and those that were not. Whitewater also notes that requiring such a fact-intensive inquiry could substantially delay the award of benefits and undermine the quick and predictable award of benefits.

The legislature could have adopted a system that required that each relationship be scrutinized on an individual basis to determine whether death benefits should be granted. But it did not. Instead, it engaged in the traditional legislative practice of line drawing. The legislature apparently determined that the potentially increased precision of requiring an ad hoc decision in all cases would be so administratively costly that the system would better be served by using a more formal rule—in this case requiring marriage—for determining which relationships require the payment of benefits. By adopting marriage as the primary criterion for determining when an intimate partner qualifies for benefits, the legislature has determined that legal marriage is an adequate proxy for the more particularized inquiry concerning whether a relationship is serious enough or the partner is sufficiently dependent to justify awarding benefits.

As with all line drawing, particularly where social welfare legislation is involved, the precise point where the line is drawn may seem arbitrary, and there may be "close cases at the margins." But this does not mean that line drawing is impermissible. This kind of line drawing—which involves balancing the benefits of greater precision against its costs and determining how the workers' compensation system can best provide support for workers and their families—is within the legislature's competence. We decline Ranney's invitation to substitute our judgment for the legislature's.

CONCLUSION

For the foregoing reasons, we AFFIRM the decision of the board denying death benefits to Ranney.

Case Questions:

1. What was the relationship between Sharon Ranny and Gary Stone?

2. Why does Ranny claim that she qualifies as Stone's widow?

3. What is *expressio unius est exclusio alterius* and what relationship does it have to the issues raised in this case?

4. Ranny argues that the concept of "family" has changed in recent decades. How does the court respond to that argument?

5. If Ranny had been the illegitimate daughter of Stone, she would be entitled to receive benefits, but not as his live-in lover. How does the court reconcile those two situations?

ETHICAL CONSIDERATION:
Avoiding Conflicts of Interest

A conflict of interest is any issue that arises between the client and the law firm where the client's interest may not be the most important consideration. The most obvious form of conflict of interest is when one attorney represents both sides in a case. An attorney cannot be adequately representing either party's interests when they are on opposing sides. The attorney would have access to potentially damaging information and it would be virtually impossible to maintain client confidentiality. But conflicts of interest rarely involve something as simple as representing both the employer and the employee in the same workers' compensation case. Instead, conflict of interest issue may be more insidious.

Suppose, for example that an attorney is the business partner of the employer while representing an injured employee. There may be no direct connection between the business interests and the issues in the pending claim, but that is not the standard to which attorneys—and paralegals—must adhere. Ethical rules for both attorneys and paralegals emphasize avoiding even the appearance of a conflict of interest. Paralegals are often called upon to review the roster of clients to make sure that any newly acquired client does not have an interest that runs counter to that of a previous client. This is one practical reason why attorneys specialize in representing either employers or injured workers. There is no bare to representing an employee in one action and an employer in another, but the potential for a conflict of interest is often great enough for an attorney to avoid such cases.

One method of avoiding potential conflicts of interest is by performing a "conflicts" check. Paralegals, attorneys, and secretaries routinely review new files to make sure that no potential conflicts are involved. There is even legal software available to help with this process.

CHAPTER SUMMARY

The award of workers' compensation benefits can involve complicated issues. The amount that an injured worker receives depends on numerous factors, including the determination of whether the injury is temporary or permanent and whether it is recognized under the workers' compensation schedules. The schedules make specific awards for the loss of particular parts of the body, awarding more money for eyes and hands and less money for fingers and toes. Compensation benefits can be denied for refusing medical treatment or by making false statements, but not for legitimacy or immigration status.

KEY TERMS

Case manager
Death benefit
Disclosure statement
Earning capacity
Healing period
Lump sum payment

Pain and suffering
Permanent partial disability
Permanent total disability
Schedule
Temporary partial disability
Temporary total disability

REVIEW QUESTIONS

1. What medical benefits are available under workers' compensation?
2. What types of medical professionals can assist a worker who is covered under workers' compensation?
3. Can a worker waive his or her right to medical benefits? Explain.
4. What types of physical rehabilitation may an injured worker receive?
5. Is a preexisting injury compensable under workers' compensation law? Why or why not?
6. What is the "healing period?"
7. Explain temporary partial disability.
8. What is the distinguishing characteristic between temporary partial disability and temporary total disability?
9. What is the usual compensation rate for temporary total disability?
10. What are workers' compensation schedules?
11. What are lump sum payments?
12. Can a workers' compensation benefit payment take into account the employee's pain and suffering? Explain your answer.
13. What are "hedonic" damages?
14. How do workers' compensation statutes define earning capacity?

15. May an injured worker receive workers' compensation benefits for facial disfigurement? When would such an award be authorized?
16. What is vocational rehabilitation?
17. Explain workers' compensation death benefits.
18. Under what circumstances may an injured employee have his or her benefits denied?

QUESTIONS FOR REFLECTION

1. The workers' compensation system was originally envisioned as a safety net for injured workers. Does that premise still apply? Do workers now view the system as something more? Explain your answer.
2. Does the rationale for awarding death benefits to widows/widowers change when the deceased worker has a life partner, but not a legally recognized spouse? Should non-married partners be allowed to collect the same benefit? Why or why not?

WEB SITES

Minnesota Department of Labor and Industry (Temporary partial disability payments)
http://www.doli.state.mn.us/sdstpd.html

Montana Permanent Partial Disability
http://data.opi.mt.gov/bills/mca/39/71/39-71-703.htm

Washington State Workers' Compensation Benefits
http://www.lni.wa.gov/ClaimsIns/Claims/default.asp

Vermont Department of Labor
http://www.labor.vermont.gov/Business/WorkersCompensation/tabid/114/Default.aspx

PRACTICAL APPLICATION

1. Does your state allow workers' compensation awards to non-married couples? Visit your state's web site (found in the Appendix) and locate the answer.
2. What is the schedule amount in your state for a worker's loss of an arm?

■ END NOTES

1. *Newberry v. Youngs*, 163 Neb. 397, 80 N.W.2d 165 (1956).
2. *City of San Francisco v. Workmen's Comp. App. Bd.*, 2 Cal. 3d 1001, 88 Cal. Rptr. 371, 472 P.2d 459 (1970).
3. *Davis v. Conger Life Ins. Co.*, 201 So. 2d 727 (Fla. 1967).
4. *Bailey v. Smelser Oil & Gas, Inc.*, 620 So. 2d 277 (La. 1993).
5. *South Coast Const. Co. v. Chizauskas*, 172 So. 2d 442 (Fla. 1965).
6. *Doss v. Food Lion, Inc.*, 267 Ga. 312, 477 S.E.2d 577 (1996).
7. *Staggs v. National Health Corp.*, 924 S.W.2d 79 (Tenn. 1996).
8. *Irvine v. Perry*, 78 Idaho 132, 299 P.2d 97 (1956).
9. West's F.S.A. § 440.15.
10. WY ST § 27-14-102.
11. WY ST § 27-14-403.
12. Oh. St. § 4123.57.
13. *Melcher's Case*, 125 Me. 426, 134 A. 542 (1926).
14. *Lang v. Nissan North America, Inc.*, 170 S.W.3d 564 (Tenn. 2005).
15. *Second Injury Fund of Iowa v. Shank*, 516 N.W.2d 808 (Iowa 1994).
16. *Wilkes v. Resource Authority of Sumner County*, 932 S.W.2d 458 (Tenn. 1996).
17. *Davis v. Sanford Const. Co.*, 247 N.C. 332, 101 S.E.2d 40 (N.C.1957).
18. *Braewood Convalescent Hospital v. Workers' Comp. Appeals Bd.*, 34 Cal. 3d 159, 193 Cal. Rptr. 157, 666 P.2d 14 (1983).
19. *Bender v. Deflon Anderson Corp.*, 298 A.2d 346 (Del. Super. Ct. 1972).
20. West's F.S.A. § 440.16.
21. 77 P.S. § 541.
22. 122 P. 2d 214 (2005).

Online Companion™

For additional resources, please go to
http://www.paralegal.delmar.cengage.com

The Workers' Compensation System

CHAPTER 6

CHAPTER OBJECTIVES

At the completion of this chapter, you should be able to:

- Explain how a workers' compensation case is presented
- Discuss discovery in workers' compensation cases
- Define the powers of the administrative law judge
- Explain how a workers' compensation case is scheduled
- Compare and contrast benefit review conferences and arbitration hearings

INTRODUCTION TO THE WORKERS' COMPENSATION SYSTEM

In this chapter, we will address the issue of contested disputes between the employee and the employer concerning workers' compensation benefits. We will discuss contested hearings, including how the parties prepare for the hearings, the paperwork involved in bringing a claim, and when and how the hearings are actually conducted. We will begin by addressing the issue of benefit disputes and how they lead to workers' compensation hearings.

Benefit Disputes

The vast majority of workers' compensation cases are uncontested. This means that the employer and employee are satisfied with the benefit arrangement that comes when an employee is injured. However, there are situations where the parties may wish to contest the benefit arrangement. This is especially true when there is a death. See Exhibit 6-1. Workers' compensation benefit disputes can arise for any of a number of reasons, including:

- Employer contests the award of benefits to employee
- Employee's benefits are terminated by action of the Workers' Compensation Board
- Employee's medical provider declares that the employee is ready to return to work

When the parties are unable to resolve the dispute voluntarily, their only option is to request a hearing before the Workers' Compensation Board to make a final determination about benefits.

Either the employee or the employer can request a hearing before the Board when they have a dispute about benefits in a workers' compensation case. Most states have hundreds of such hearings every year. Even though most cases are uncontested, there are still thousands of employees injured every year in every state in the union. With that number of cases, it is no wonder that even with a small percentage contested the workers' compensation system is extremely busy. Because of this caseload, most hearings are set 60 or more days from the time when they are initially filed. It is not unusual for claimants to wait a year before a hearing date is set. During this time, both sides will prepare their case for the hearing. We will discuss that preparation later in this chapter.

FILING A CLAIM

In order to have a hearing under workers' compensation law, either party must officially request a hearing. This filing notifies the Board that there are disputed issues between the employer and employee and puts the Board on notice that these issues cannot be resolved amicably. In many ways, filing a request for a hearing is like filing a pleading in a civil case. See Exhibit 6-2. Although in civil cases the filing is called a Complaint, and in workers' compensation it is called a Request for Hearing, the purpose is the same: It notifies the other side that one party is officially contesting some issue(s) in the case and is requesting a judge be assigned to make a final determination on these issues.

Event or exposure[1]	Fatalities			
	2001-2005 average	2005[2]	2006	
		Number	Number	Percent
Total	5,704	5,734	5,703	100
Transportation incidents	2,451	2,493	2,413	42
Highway	1,394	1,437	1,329	23
Collision between vehicles, mobile equipment	686	718	644	11
Moving in same direction	151	175	152	3
Moving in opposite directions, oncoming	254	265	234	4
Moving in intersection	137	134	138	2
Vehicle struck stationary object or equipment in roadway	27	27	19	([3])
Vehicle struck stationary object, equipment on side of road	310	345	337	6
Noncollision	335	318	297	5
Jack-knifed or overturned–no collision	274	273	248	4
Nonhighway (farm, industrial premises)	335	340	342	6
Overturned	175	182	165	3
Worker struck by a vehicle	369	391	372	7
Rail vehicle	60	83	65	1
Water vehicle	82	88	89	2
Aircraft	206	149	215	4
Assaults and violent acts	850	792	754	13
Homicides	602	567	516	9
Shooting	465	441	417	7
Stabbing	60	60	38	1
Self-inflicted injuries	207	180	199	3
Contact with objects and equipment	952	1,005	983	17
Struck by object	560	607	583	10
Struck by falling object	345	385	378	7
Struck by flying object	50	53	69	1
Caught in or compressed by equipment or objects	256	278	281	5
Caught in running equipment or machinery	128	121	148	3
Caught in or crushed in collapsing materials	118	109	107	2
Falls	763	770	809	14
Fall to lower level	669	664	728	13
Fall from ladder	125	129	129	2
Fall from roof	154	160	184	3
Fall from scaffold, staging	87	82	88	2
Fall on same level	73	84	59	1
Exposure to harmful substances or environments	498	501	525	9
Contact with electric current	265	251	247	4
Contact with overhead power lines	118	112	108	2
Contact with temperature extremes	44	55	53	1
Exposure to caustic, noxious, or allergenic substances	114	136	153	3
Inhalation of substance	56	66	58	1
Oxygen deficiency	74	59	64	1
Drowning, submersion	54	48	50	1
Fires and explosions	174	159	201	4

[1] Based on the 1992 BLS Occupational Injury and Illness Classification Manual. Includes other events and exposures, such as bodily reaction, in addition to those shown separately.
[2] The BLS news release issued August 10, 2006, reported a total of 5,702 fatal work injuries for calendar year 2005. Since then, an additional 32 job-related fatalities were identified, bringing the total job-related fatality count for 2005 to 5,734.
[3] Less than or equal to 0.5 percent.

NOTE: Totals for 2006 are preliminary. Totals for major categories may include subcategories not shown separately. The average count excludes fatalities from the September 11, 2001 terrorist attacks. Percentages may not add to totals because of rounding.

SOURCE: U.S. Department of Labor, Bureau of Labor Statistics, in cooperation with State, New York City, District of Columbia, and Federal agencies, Census of Fatal Occupational Injuries

EXHIBIT 6-1 Fatal Occupational Injuries (Illinois). *Bureau of Labor Statistics, 2004.*

TEXAS DEPARTMENT OF INSURANCE,
DIVISION OF WORKERS' COMPENSATION
7551 Metro Center Drive, Suite 100
Austin, Texas 78744

CLAIM # ____________
Carrier's Claim # ____________

EMPLOYER'S CONTEST OF COMPENSABILITY

1. Employee's Name (Last, First, M.I.)	4. Employer's Name (Last, First, M.I.)	
	5. Employer's Mailing Address (Street or P.O. Box)	
2. Social Security Number - -	City State Zip Code	
3. Date of Injury - -	6. Employer's Telephone No. ( )	7. Insurance Carrier

In accordance with Art. 8308-5.10 of the Texas Workers' Compensation Act, the employer has the right to contest the compensability of an employee's injury if the insurance carrier accepts liability for the payment of benefits.

8. Provide any relevant facts supporting the reason(s) for contesting compensability.

Employer's Signature ____________ Date ____________

Title ____________

Division Date Stamp Here

DWC FORM-4 (Rev. 10/05) Page 1

DIVISION OF WORKERS' COMPENSATION

EXHIBIT 6-2 Employer's Contest of Compensability (Texas). *Reprinted courtesy of the Texas Department of Information, Workers' Compensation.*

Statutes of Limitation

A statute of limitation imposes a time limit on a legal action. Statutes of limitation are common in all legal fields from criminal law to administrative law, and workers' compensation is no different. The premise behind a statute of limitation is that by requiring a party to bring a legal action within a certain time period there is better prospect that the witnesses, files, and evidence will still be available and that there will be some predictability to the legal process. A person or company can know, for instance, that if a legal claim will be brought, it must begin within a specified time period or it will be barred forever. For workers' compensation cases, the generally accepted approach is to impose a limit of 12 to 24 months from the time of the injury until the claim is barred. If an employee fails to file a claim, or an employer fails to contest an award of benefits, that party is barred from seeking further legal redress.

Statutes of limitation are frequently more complicated than they might at first seem. For instance, suppose a person is not immediately aware of the fact that a condition in the workplace is contributing to his or her ill health. In this situation, statutes often provide that the statute of limitations runs from the moment that an employee knew—or should have known—that the illness or injury was work-related. See Exhibit 6-3. There are other issues that can arise when discussing statutes of limitation concerns in workers' compensation cases. For instance, does a ruling about a worker's arm also include an injury to the worker's fingers? For a resolution of that question, see this chapter's Case Excerpt.

Notice of Hearing

Parties receive a notice of the hearing, which also goes to their attorneys if they are represented. In cases where the parties are represented by an attorney, it is common to have a pre-hearing conference at least a week prior to the actual hearing. The notice of hearing serves to give all parties the date, time, and location of the hearing.

---

(1) Except to the extent provided elsewhere in this section, all employee petitions for benefits under this chapter shall be barred unless the employee, or the employee's estate if the employee is deceased, has advised the employer of the injury or death pursuant to s. 440.185(1) and the petition is filed within 2 years after the date on which the employee knew or should have known that the injury or death arose out of work performed in the course and scope of employment.[1]

EXHIBIT 6-3

Time Bars to Filing Petitions for Benefits (Florida) *Adapted from WESTLAW. Reprinted with permission.*

Filing Forms

There are many forms required to contest a workers' compensation benefit award—or the failure to make an award—as well as to carry out other actions. Forms are important in workers' compensation because the hearings are heavily weighted toward administrative issues. See Exhibit 6-4. As a result, many states have statutes that require all information to be completed on the required

COMMONWEALTH OF PENNSYLVANIA
DEPARTMENT OF LABOR AND INDUSTRY
BUREAU OF WORKERS' COMPENSATION
1171 S. CAMERON STREET, ROOM 103
HARRISBURG, PA 17104-2501
(TOLL FREE) 800-482-2383
TTY 800-362-4228

CLAIM PETITION FOR WORKERS' COMPENSATION

EMPLOYEE SOCIAL SECURITY NUMBER

DATE OF INJURY

MONTH DAY YEAR

PA BWC CLAIM NUMBER (IF KNOWN)

EMPLOYEE

First Name
Last Name
If Deceased - Dependent or Guardian
First Name
Last Name
Address
Address
City/Town State Zip
County
Telephone ( )

EMPLOYER

Name
Address
Address
City/Town State Zip
County
Telephone ( ) FEIN

VS. **INSURER or THIRD PARTY ADMINISTRATOR** (if self-insured)

Name
Address
Address
City/Town State Zip
Telephone ( ) Bureau Code
County
Claim # FEIN

1. Complete description of injury or illness including all parts of body affected. (If you are seeking additional compensation from the Subsequent Injury Fund for total disability as a result of a previous permanent loss, or loss of use of one hand, one arm, one foot, one leg or one eye, and a subsequent injury causing loss, or loss of use of, another hand, arm, foot, leg or eye, you must also submit form LIBC-375.)

2. If occupational disease, give the last date of employment (MONTH - DAY - YEAR) and/or last date of exposure (MONTH - DAY - YEAR).

3. Give date of injury or onset of disease (MONTH - DAY - YEAR).

4. How did the injury or disease happen?

5. Did injury or disease occur on employer's premises? ☐ Yes ☐ No Where? (Be specific.)

6. Notice of your injury or disease was served on your employer on (MONTH - DAY - YEAR) in the following manner:

7. What was your job title at the time of injury or disease?

362 1197-1

EXHIBIT 6-4 Claim Petition for Workers' Compensation (Pennsylvania).

8. Were you working for more than one employer at the time of your injury? ☐ Yes ☐ No If Yes, list additional employers:

9. Did this problem cause you to stop working? ☐ Yes ☐ No If Yes, give date. [MONTH] - [DAY] - [YEAR]

10. Are you back to work with the same employer? ☐ Yes ☐ No If Yes, ☐ Regular Job ☐ Other Job / Give Title.

11. Are you working with another employer? ☐ Yes ☐ No If Yes, give name and address of new employer:

12. What were your wages at the time of injury? $ _____ ☐ Hour ☐ Day ☐ or Week

13. If you have returned to work since your injury or illness, are you earning ☐ More ☐ Same ☐ Less than you were at the time of injury? Current earnings $ _____ ☐ Hour ☐ Day ☐ or Week

14. I am seeking payment for (check all that apply):

   ☐ Loss of Wages
      ☐ Partial disability from [MONTH-DAY-YEAR] to [MONTH-DAY-YEAR]
      ☐ Full disability from [MONTH-DAY-YEAR] to [MONTH-DAY-YEAR]
   ☐ Medical bills (give name of doctor/hospital, address, type of treatment and bill in space below).
   ☐ Counsel fees to be paid by the employer.
   ☐ Loss or loss of use of arm, hand, finger, leg, foot or toe.
   ☐ Disfigurement (scars) of head, face, or neck.

   ☐ Loss of sight.
   ☐ Loss of hearing.

15. Other _____

16. Is there other pending litigation in this case? ☐ Yes ☐ No If Yes, explain below:

PLEASE ENTER MY APPEARANCE FOR PETITIONER:

Attorney Name

PA Attorney ID Number

Firm Name

Address

Address

City/Town   State   Zip Code

Telephone (   )

Date of Petition
[MONTH] - [DAY] - [YEAR]
A copy of this petition has been sent to the employer.

Signature
☐ Employee   ☐ Attorney

NOTICE: This Petition must be filled out as fully as possible. The original must be sent to the Bureau of Workers' Compensation, 1171 South Cameron Street, Room 103, Harrisburg, PA 17104-2501. A copy must be sent by you to the employer. Information on the completion of this form may be obtained by calling the Bureau of Workers' Compensation Helpline at 800-482-2383.

Any individual filing misleading or incomplete information knowingly and with intent to defraud is in violation of Section 1102 of the Pennsylvania Workers' Compensation Act and may also be subject to criminal and civil penalties through Pennsylvania Act 165.

LIBC-362 REV 4-02

362 1197-2

EXHIBIT 6-4   *(Continued)*

forms. If the information is not complete, the form will not be processed and will be returned to the offending party with a request that all information be completed before it is resubmitted. Some states even go further and will dismiss a claim if forms are not adequately completed. See Example 6-1.

> **EXAMPLE 6-1**
>
> Theo works in Human Resources for ABC Inc. and has received notice that an employee wishes to contest a denial of workers' compensation benefits. Theo completes the form found in Exhibit 6-2; however, he leaves the section "Provide any relevant facts supporting the reason(s) for contesting compensability" blank. Based on what you have learned this far in the chapter, will the workers' compensation board accept the form?
>
> *Answer:* Leaving such an important and critical portion of the contest of compensability form blank will surely result in a rejection of the form, and if the matter is not rectified, the employer's contest of benefits may be dismissed as well. The practical result is that the employer will be deemed to have consented to the employee's request for benefits.

PREPARING FOR THE HEARING

Both parties will carry out extensive preparations before appearing at the hearing. See Exhibits 6-5 and 6-6. They will interview witnesses, pin down testimony, investigate the medical records, and carry out discovery. **Discovery** is the process that both parties use to learn facts about the allegations raised by the other party. Through discovery, the parties can request that the other party hand over all of the important details about the case, prior to the hearing. Like civil cases, discovery issues are extremely important and form the basis of the intensive preparation for the hearing.

■ **Discovery**

The exchange of information between both sides in a contested hearing.

Discovery in Workers' Compensation Hearings

It would be incorrect to assume that the rules that govern discovery in civil cases are identical to the rules that govern discovery in workers' compensation cases. There are many jurisdictions that have modified discovery rules in workers' compensation cases by strictly limiting it or even by attempting to completely bar it. In civil cases, for example, discovery is broad and pervasive. A party can file interrogatories, requests for admission, request for production of documents, evidence and things, requests to visit real property in dispute, and several other documents. The theory underlying such broad discovery in civil cases is that the more the parties know about the case, the more likely they are to settle prior to trial. However, that principle is challenged in workers' compensation cases where lengthy discovery only extends the time it takes to settle the issues and allows attorneys to bill more time. However, limiting discovery brings its own disadvantages. One need only look at criminal law.

Discovery in criminal cases is far more limited than it is in civil cases. In criminal cases, the defendant is entitled to receive a copy of the

COMMONWEALTH OF PENNSYLVANIA
DEPARTMENT OF LABOR AND INDUSTRY
BUREAU OF WORKERS' COMPENSATION
1171 S. CAMERON STREET, ROOM 103
HARRISBURG, PA 17104-2501
(TOLL FREE) 800-482-2383
TTY 800-362-4228

DEFENDANT'S ANSWER TO CLAIM PETITION UNDER PENNSYLVANIA WORKERS' COMPENSATION ACT

Social Security Number: ________ - ________ - ________

Date of Injury ________ / ________ / ________
MM DD YYYY

PA BWC Claim Number: ________________ (IF KNOWN)

Employee

First Name ________ Last Name ________
Street 1 ________
Street 2 ________
City/Town ________ State ________ Zip Code ________ - ________
County ________ Telephone (____) ____ - ________

VS.

Employer

Name ________
Street 1 ________
Street 2 ________
City/Town ________ State ________ Zip Code ________ - ________
County ________
Telephone (____) ____ - ________ FEIN ________

Insurer or Third Party Administrator (if self-insured)

Name ________
Street 1 ________
Street 2 ________
City/Town ________ State ________ Zip Code ________ - ________
Telephone (____) ____ - ________ Bureau Code ________
County ________
Claim Number ________ FEIN ________

TO YOUR HONORABLE JUDGE:

In answer to the captioned claim, the Defendant respectfully pleads as follows: (Answers must be identified by numerical order in direct response to corresponding numbered allegations on claim petition.)

NOTICE: This answer should be clearly completed (preferably typed) and original mailed directly to the office of the Judge to whom the case is assigned. Answers must be filed within 20 days. Every fact alleged in the claim petition not specifically denied by this answer shall be deemed to be admitted.

(OVER)

LIBC-374 REV 5-04 (Page 1)

EXHIBIT 6-5 Defendant's Answer to Claim Petition Under Pennsylvania Worker's Compensation Act. *Reprinted courtesy of the Pennsylvania Bureau of Worker's Compensation.*

As a matter of further defense, the Defendant states the following:

_____
_____
_____
_____
_____
_____
_____
_____
_____
_____
_____
_____
_____
_____
_____
_____
_____
_____
_____
_____
_____
_____

WHEREFORE, the Defendant requests that the claim petition be dismissed or in the alternative disallowed.

Defendant

First Name	Last Name
Signature	
Date: ___/___/___ MM / DD / YYYY	

Attorney

Signature	
Date: ___/___/___ MM / DD / YYYY	

PLEASE ENTER MY APPEARANCE FOR DEFENDANT:
Attorney

First Name	Last Name
Firm Name	
Street 1	
Street 2	
City/Town	State	Zip Code
Telephone	PA Attorney ID Number

Any individual filing misleading or incomplete information knowingly and with intent to defraud is in violation of Section 1102 of the Pennsylvania Workers' Compensation Act and may also be subject to criminal and civil penalties through Pennsylvania Act 165 of 1994.

Auxiliary aids and services are available upon request to individuals with disabilities.
Equal Opportunity Employer/Program

LIBC-374 REV 5-04 (Page 2)

EXHIBIT 6-5 (Continued)

CARRIER'S RESPONSE
Michigan Department of Labor & Economic Growth
Workers' Compensation Agency
PO Box 30016, Lansing, MI 48909

Social Security Number	Date of Birth	Employee Name		
Employee Address (Street No. and Name)		Employee City	State	Zip Code
Date(s) of Injury		Insurance Company/TPA Claim Number		
Employer		Insurance Company or TPA (If self-insured)		
Employer Address (Street No. and Name)		Insurance Company Address (Street No. and Name)		

City	State	Zip Code	City	State	Zip Code
Federal ID Number			NAIC or Self-Insurance Number		

1. Do you dispute that the injury or disability is work related? ☐ Yes ☐ No
2. Do you dispute that the claimant is disabled? ☐ Yes ☐ No
3. List reasons supporting your position in the space provided.

4. Have you had the claimant medically examined in connection with this claim? ☐ Yes ☐ No
   If yes, give name and address of individual who performed the examination.

5. **Do you certify that to the best of your knowledge all existing medical records of the carrier or employer contained in your file that are relevant to this claim have been furnished to the claimant and/or the claimant's attorney? ☐ Yes ☐ No**

Claims person/attorney to whom correspondence should be sent	Attorney ID Number (If applicable)
Claims office/attorney address	Telephone No. (Include area code)
Preparer Signature	Date

The Department of Labor & Economic Growth will not discriminate against any individual or group because of race, sex, religion, age, national origin, color, marital status, disability, or political beliefs. If you need assistance with reading, writing, hearing, etc., under the Americans with Disabilities Act, you may make your needs known to this agency.	Authority: Workers' Disability Compensation Act, Section 418.222 Completion: This form is to be submitted by the carrier within thirty (30) days after the carrier's receipt of a completed Application for Mediation or Hearing. Penalty: Failure to complete shall prohibit that party from proceeding.

WC-251 (8/05)

EXHIBIT 6-6 Carrier's Response (Michigan). *Reprinted courtesy of the Michigan Workers' Compensation Agency.*

charges against him, any scientific or other reports, and any evidence that might possibly show that the defendant is innocent. Using the same approach in workers' compensation arguably creates more hearings than it resolves.

Discovery, whether in workers' compensation cases or other types of litigation was created to avoid the kind of trial by surprise that makes for an interesting and dramatic presentation but does not promote judicial efficiency. It also runs counter to the basic philosophy of providing workers' compensation benefits in the first place: to provide legitimately injured workers with compensation. As a result, the discovery methods that are commonly applied in these cases tend to focus on the narrow issues of the employee's physical condition.

Types of Discovery

Although there are some jurisdictions that specifically prohibit discovery in workers' compensation cases (such as New York City), most permit it. The most common types of discovery include:

- Depositions
- Interrogatories
- Request for production of medical records
- Request for independent medical examination

Depositions

Deposition

The oral questioning of a witness, under oath, conducted by an attorney before a court reporter.

A **deposition** is a face-to-face session between the attorneys and the witnesses in the case. Conducted before a court reporter, the entire session is recorded or transcribed. Once the witness is sworn in, the attorneys may question the witness about any issues involved in the case. Depositions occur long before the hearing is ever set. There is no judge present during a deposition. If the attorneys have any objections about questions raised, they may reserve them for discussion during the hearing. The questions and answers are transcribed by a court reporter. Later, the court reporter will produce a transcript of the session that both sides in the case can refer to in order to prepare for the hearing. In workers' compensation cases, the transcript of some witnesses, such as doctors, can be used in place of live testimony. This saves the medical profession a lot of time (from having to constantly appear at hearings), and it also saves the parties a lot of money. Doctors and specialists bill heavily for in-court testimony and presenting it through a transcript, usually read by a member of the legal team, saves that cost. Deposition transcripts can also be used to contradict the live testimony of a witness.

Video Depositions

Another option to presenting the live testimony of a physician or specialist is to record the doctor's deposition in a video and play it for the Administrative

> **(Employer to Employee) Interrogatory Question #1**
> Explain in precise terms exactly why you believe that you are unfit to return to work. Provide lists of any medical personnel, medical records, findings, or other documentation that you believe supports your claim.

EXHIBIT 6-7
Sample Interrogatories.

Law Judge at the hearing. The use of video depositions has skyrocketed in recent decades and the ease and convenience of digital video will only make this practice even more common. A video deposition records the question and answer session between the attorneys and witness in exactly the same way as the traditional written transcript does, but it allows the witness to refer to graphs and other visual aids and makes the entire presentation considerably more interesting.

Interrogatories

Unlike depositions, **interrogatories** are written questions that are sent between the parties in a workers' compensation case. Witnesses never receive interrogatories. The parties must respond in writing to each question posed. Interrogatories serve an important function in helping to pin down important points in the parties' versions of the case. See Exhibit 6-7 for an example.

Interrogatories
Written questions posed by one party to another.

Request for Production of Medical Records

Both sides in a workers' compensation case have the right to request that the other side produce medical records pertinent to the issues in the case. Employees must sign waivers that allow their medical providers to issue these records to others. In some cases, the employee may have to sign several different types of waivers to satisfy recent changes in legislation concerning patient rights. See Exhibit 6-8.

Request for Independent Medical Examination

In addition to answering questions and producing records, the employer also has the right to request that the employee receive an independent medical examination. The employee must go to this examination, although the employee is allowed to request a more convenient time or location to actually conduct the examination. The medical examination will be carried out by a physician selected by the employer or, when the employee disputes the choice of doctor, a physician chosen from a panel or one selected by the workers' compensation board. This doctor's final report will be issued to both the employer and employee and will contain the doctor's final opinion about

EXHIBIT 6-8

Utah Rule R602-2. Adjudication of Workers' Compensation and Occupational Disease Claims.

> R602-2-1. Pleadings and Discovery.
>
> 1. Upon filing the answer, the respondent and the petitioner may commence discovery. Discovery allowed under this rule may include interrogatories, requests for production of documents, depositions, and medical examinations. Discovery shall not include requests for admissions. Appropriate discovery under this rule shall focus on matters relevant to the claims and defenses at issue in the case. All discovery requests are deemed continuing and shall be promptly supplemented by the responding party as information comes available . . .
>
> 3. Upon reasonable notice, the respondent may require the petitioner to submit to a medical examination by a physician of the respondent's choice . . .
>
> 5. Requests for production of documents are allowed, but limited to matters relevant to the claims and defenses at issue in the case, and shall not include requests for documents provided with the petitioner's Application for Hearing, nor the respondent's answer . . .
>
> 9. Any party who fails to obey an administrative law judge's discovery order shall be subject to the sanctions available under Rule 37, Utah Rules of Civil Procedure.

the state of the employee's health, the likely recovery, and the percentage of permanent impairment, should there be any.

Refusal to Abide by Discovery

What happens in situations where either party refuses to comply with discovery requests? The answer is simple: The Administrative Law Judge presiding over the case is allowed to impose sanctions. Although the judge could order a monetary fine for each day that a party fails to respond, most judges opt for a different approach. Workers' compensation rules allow a judge to prohibit a party from presenting evidence on a contested issue or even to dismiss certain claims. Obviously, such a ruling could be devastating for the party and the threat of this remedy is usually enough to force a party to abide by the court's ruling.

Reviewing the Workers' Compensation File

All claimants, both employers and employees, have the right to see the entire contents of the employee file. But this right is only limited to the interested parties in the case. The employee's files are not public records and cannot be viewed by someone who simply has a general interest in workers' compensation cases. In order to view the file, there must be a case pending before the Board and only the contesting parties can view it. Interestingly enough, most

Workers' Compensation Boards do not make copies of files and mail them out. Instead, they make the file "available." What this means is that if either party wants to see the file, they can travel to the Board's headquarters and take a look at it there. The parties can make copies, but the Board usually refuses to make the copies and mail them out to the parties.

Adding Documents to the File

Either party is free to add documents to the file. An employee might wish to supplement the file with additional medical reports and findings, while the employer might have its own doctor's findings sent in to be added to the file. The reason that parties would want to supplement the file is that the ALJ reviews this file before and during the hearing and the parties know that it is always a good idea to give the judge as much information about their version of the case as possible.

A party seeking to add material to the Workers' Compensation Board file must do so in writing and use the appropriate form. Most states also have rules that require a party to submit additional material to the file at least five days before the scheduled hearing. If the party submits it after that deadline, the material will not be considered.

WORKERS' COMPENSATION HEARINGS

There are several procedural steps that must occur before a hearing is held. See Exhibits 6-9 and 6-10. We have already seen that one or both of the parties must request a hearing, but many states have also created intervening conferences and hearings that must be completed before a contested hearing is permitted. These intervening steps include the benefit review conference and the arbitration hearing.

Benefit Review Conference

A **benefit review conference** (BRC) is often the first step toward a full-blown workers' compensation hearing. The benefit review conference is an informal affair, where the employee meets with a representative of the employer—or the employer's workers' compensation insurance provider—to discuss the issues raised by either the employer or employee. The purpose of the benefit review conference is to settle a benefit dispute without having to engage in a protracted hearing. If the parties can reach a settlement of the issues, they put in writing in an agreement. The agreement is signed by all parties and will be controlling if further issues arise between the employer and employee. If, on the other hand, the parties are unable to resolve their disputes, the next step may be an arbitration hearing or a hearing before an Administrative Law Judge.

Benefit review conference

An informal meeting between employer, employee, and the employer's insurance provider to discuss compensation issues.

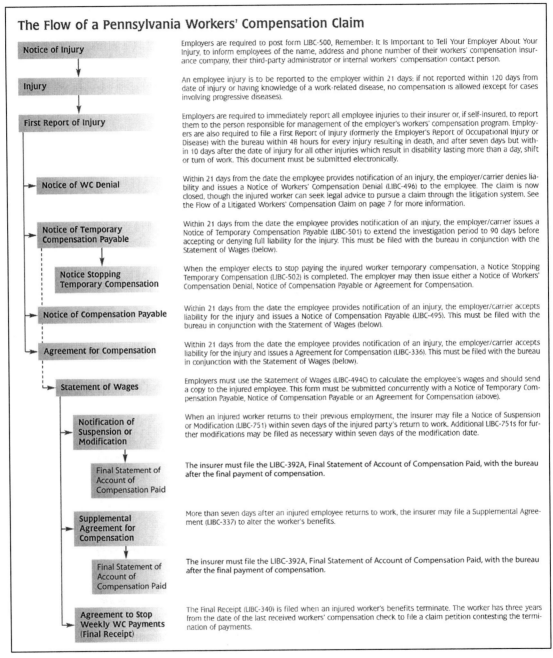

EXHIBIT 6-9 The Flow of a Pennsylvania Workers' Compensation Claim.

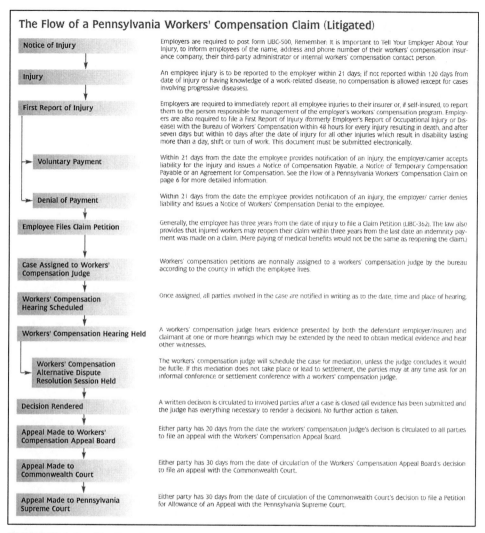

EXHIBIT 6-9 (Continued)

Arbitration Hearings

Many states have instituted **arbitration hearings** in a further attempt to resolve disputes between employers and employees. Like benefit review conferences, the purpose of the arbitration hearing is to find a way of resolving the issues between the parties without recourse to a contested hearing. See Exhibit 6-11. Unlike a benefit review conference, an arbitration hearing has a third party present: the arbitrator. This person works with the parties to coax them into resolving their disputes. If they reach an agreement, they will again

■ **Arbitration hearing**

A hearing by a neutral third party to determine contested issues between two parties.

Worker's Compensation Claim Flow

REGULAR CLAIMS

Report of Injury by the Employee (Approximately 200,000 annually)	An employee makes a report to his or her employer of a work-related injury or illness as soon as possible after the accident or becoming aware of the injury. Generally, the employee has two years to report an injury. If the employer knew or should have known about the injury, the claim for an accidental injury can be made within the 12-year statute of limitations. There is no time limit for filing a claim for occupational disease.
Report of Injury to the Insurer and Worker's Compensation Division (Approximately 60,000 lost-time claims reported annually)	An employer is required to report all work injuries or illnesses to its workers compensation insurance carrier within 7 days after actual knowledge of the injury. The insurance carrier must file all injury reports involving lost-time compensable claims with Wisconsin Worker's Compensation Division within 14 days after the date of injury. The employer will also report claims to its insurer that only require medical services in order to have the insurer make those payments.
Payment for Lost-time or Permanent Disability (Approximately 53,000 compensable claims annually)	The employer's insurance carrier is expected to make 80% of the first payments of compensation within 14 days of the date of injury. However, in cases requiring an investigation, it may take longer. If compensation is denied, insurers must notify the claimant within 7 days, explain their decisions and include rights to have a formal hearing before an Administrative Law Judge (ALJ). After the initial payment, compensation payments are made regularly and are calculated on a weekly basis. Generally they are based upon two-thirds of the average weekly wages earned in the year prior to the date of injury.

DISPUTED CLAIMS

Injured Worker Files Application for a Hearing (Approximately 7,000 annually)	An injured worker has twelve years from the date of injury or the date of last payment to file an application for a formal hearing before an ALJ. The Division may attempt to resolve some of these disputes through informal mediation conducted by its paralegal staff. For disputes involving an applicant who is not represented by an attorney, the Division usually conducts a pre-hearing conference with an ALJ to narrow the issues and explain the hearing process
Hearings are Scheduled (Approximately 6000	Workers' compensation applications for hearings are normally assigned to the ALJ on a first-in, first-out basis. Hearings

EXHIBIT 6-10 Workers' Compensation Claim Flowchart (Wisconsin).

Hearings are Scheduled (Approximately 6000 hearings are scheduled annually)	≫	Workers' compensation applications for hearings are normally assigned to the ALJ on a first-in, first-out basis. Hearings are generally held in the municipality requested by the applicant. Once assigned, all parties involved in the case are notified in writing as to the date, time and place of hearing
WC Hearing Held (Approximately 1,200 hearings are held annually)	≫	An ALJ hears evidence presented by both the defendant and claimant at one or more hearings. Most disputes are resolved with one hearing. About two-thirds of all requests for a hearing are settled without an actual hearing. Many are compromised or stipulated.
Decision Rendered	≫	The ALJ issues a decision within 90 days after the close of the record. This usually means 90 days after the hearing. The typical decision is issued in less than 45 days.
Appeal to Labor Industry Review Commission (LIRC) (Approximately 500 are reviewed annually)	≫	Either party may file a petition for review with the Labor and Industry Review Commission (LIRC) within 21 days after the ALJ issues a decision.
Appeal made to Circuit Court (Approximately 125 annually)	≫	Either party may start an action in the circuit court of the county in which he or she resides within 30 days after the LIRC decision.
Court of Appeals (Approximately 5 annually) (Approximately 5 annually)	≫	Either party may appeal to the Court of Appeals within 45 or 90 days depending on when the notice of entry of judgment is served.
Wisconsin Supreme Court	≫	Either party may file a petition for review with the Supreme Court within 30 days of the date of the Court of Appeals

EXHIBIT 6-10 (*Continued*)

STATE OF ILLINOIS	)	☐ Injured Workers' Benefit Fund (§4(d))
	)	☐ Rate Adjustment Fund (§8(g))
COUNTY OF _____	)	☐ Second Injury Fund (§8(e)18)
		☐ None of the above

ILLINOIS WORKERS' COMPENSATION COMMISSION
19(b-1) ARBITRATION DECISION

_____   Case # _____ WC _____
Employee/Petitioner

v.

_____
Employer/Respondent

An *Application for Adjustment of Claim* was filed in this matter, and a *Notice of Hearing* was mailed to each party. The petitioner filed a *Petition for an Immediate Hearing Under Section 19(b-1) of the Act* on _____. The respondent filed a *Response* on _____. The matter was heard by the Honorable _____, arbitrator of the Commission, in the city of _____, on _____. After reviewing all of the evidence presented, the arbitrator hereby makes findings on the disputed issues checked below, and attaches those findings to this document.

DISPUTED ISSUES

A. Was the respondent operating under and subject to the Illinois Workers' Compensation or Occupational Diseases Act?

B. Was there an employee-employer relationship?

C. Did an accident occur that arose out of and in the course of the petitioner's employment by the respondent?

D. What was the date of the accident?

E. Was timely notice of the accident given to the respondent?

F. Is the petitioner's present condition of ill-being causally related to the injury?

G. What were the petitioner's earnings?

H. What was the petitioner's age at the time of the accident?

I. What was the petitioner's marital status at the time of the accident?

J. Were the medical services that were provided to petitioner reasonable and necessary?

K. What amount of compensation is due for temporary total disability?

L. Should penalties or fees be imposed upon the respondent?

M. Is the respondent due any credit?

N. Other _____

ICArbDec19(b-1) 6/08   100 W. Randolph Street #8-200 Chicago, IL 60601 312/814-6611   Toll-free 866/352-3033   Web site: www.iwcc.il.gov
Downstate offices: Collinsville 618/346-3450   Peoria 309/671-3019   Rockford 815/987-7292   Springfield 217/785-7084

EXHIBIT 6-11 Illinois Workers' Compensation Commission 19(b-1) Arbitration Decision. *Reprinted courtesy of the Illinois Workers' Compensation Commission.*

FINDINGS

- On _____, the respondent _____ **was** operating under and subject to the provisions of the Act.
- On this date, an employee-employer relationship   *did*   exist between the petitioner and respondent.
- On this date, the petitioner   *did*   sustain injuries that arose out of and in the course of employment.
- Timely notice of this accident   *was*   given to the respondent.
- In the year preceding the injury, the petitioner earned $ _____ ; the average weekly wage was $ _____ .
- At the time of injury, the petitioner was _____ years of age, *single* with _____ children under 18.
- Necessary medical services   *have*   been provided by the respondent.
- To date, $ _____ has been paid by the respondent for TTD and/or maintenance benefits.

ORDER

- The respondent shall pay the petitioner temporary total disability benefits of $ _____ /week for _____ weeks, from _____ through _____ , as provided in Section 8(b) of the Act, because the injuries sustained caused the disabling condition of the petitioner, the disabling condition is temporary and has not yet reached a permanent condition, pursuant to Section 19(b-1) of the Act.
- The respondent shall pay $ _____ for medical services, as provided in Section 8(a) of the Act.
- The respondent shall pay $ _____ in penalties, as provided in Section 19(k) of the Act.
- The respondent shall pay $ _____ in penalties, as provided in Section 19(l) of the Act.
- The respondent shall pay $ _____ in attorneys' fees, as provided in Section 16 of the Act.
- In no instance shall this award be a bar to subsequent hearing and determination of an additional amount of temporary total disability, medical benefits, or compensation for a permanent disability, if any.

RULES REGARDING APPEALS Unless a party 1) files a *Petition for Review* within 30 days after receipt of this decision; and 2) certifies that he or she has paid the court reporter $ _____ for the *final* cost of the arbitration transcript and attaches a copy of the check to the *Petition*; and 3) perfects a review in accordance with the Act and Rules, then this decision shall be entered as the decision of the Commission.

STATEMENT OF INTEREST RATE If the Commission reviews this award, interest at the rate set forth on the *Notice of Decision of Arbitrator* shall accrue from the date listed below to the day before the date of payment; however, if an employee's appeal results in either no change or a decrease in this award, interest shall not accrue.

_____   _____
Signature of arbitrator   Date

ICArbDec19(b-1) p. 2

EXHIBIT 6-11   (*Continued*)

put into writing in what some states refer to as an Arbitration Agreement and others simply as an agreement. No matter what the final product is called, it will contain a description of the contested issues and the manner in which the issues were resolved by the parties. Part of the agreement will be a waiver of the **contested case hearing** (CCH).

> **Contested case hearing**
>
> A formal hearing, conducted by an Administrative Law Judge or other official, to make a final determination about benefit awards and other issues.

Hearings

Workers' compensation hearings are not held in courts. Instead, they are held in conference rooms or at the branch offices of the state workers' compensation board. As a result, they tend to be less formal than trials held in courtrooms. The actual hearing is usually held in a large room instead of a courtroom, and unlike trials that continue to follow rules of etiquette established centuries ago, workers' compensation hearings lack the gravity of a trial and in many ways feel more like meetings than a formal resolution of important legal matters.

Location of the Hearing

Most states provide offices located around the state for the actual hearings. Multiple sites are provided as a way to decrease the travel time and other discomforts associated with long trips. There is no requirement that the hearings must take place at a courthouse or near the location where the actual injury occurred. It is common for workers' compensation hearings to be held a conference rooms, empty offices, and other buildings.

Hearing Date

Hearing dates can be, and often are, reset from the original date provided in the notice of hearing. Hearings may be delayed for any of a number of reasons, including the express request of the parties or the unavailability of certain witnesses. Either party can file a **motion for continuance** requesting that the hearing date be set at a later time.

> **Motion for continuance**
>
> A motion by one side requesting that a court hearing be delayed to a future date.

Canceling the Hearing

The party who requested the hearing also has the right to cancel the request. As long as the other party consents to the cancellation, the case will be removed from the docket. However, if any of the parties still wish to contest any of the issues raised in the case, the case will remain set for a hearing.

Representation at the Hearing

Although it is not necessary for an employee to have an attorney representing him or her at the hearing, it is an excellent idea. Most states require that a representative must be a member of the State Bar, while some allow nonlawyers to represent others. In most jurisdictions, the employee is faced with only two possibilities: *pro se* representation or representation by an attorney. *Pro se* is the term given to individuals who choose to represent themselves. All injured workers have the right to represent themselves, although an individual who is not trained in legal methodology rarely achieves the results that an attorney can achieve. *Pro se* claimants are not entitled to any special accommodations in the hearing; they are, in fact, held to the same standard as attorney representatives.

The standards do not change. As the hearing is conducted, the judge will make rulings on evidence in the same way, regardless of whether or not the parties have attorneys to represent them. Most states also have rules that prohibit uninsured employers from representing themselves. In those states, employers that have violated the workers' compensation statutes by failing to provide insurance must appear at the hearing with a member of the State Bar to represent them.

Pro se
(Latin) "For himself." A person who is not represented by an attorney and chooses to represent himself or herself.

Compensating Attorneys

The pay arrangements for the attorneys involved in the case vary depending on which side the attorney is representing. Attorneys who represent employees commonly work on a **contingency fee**. This is a fee based on the total recovery in the case. The normal contingency fee is one-third of the total employee's recovery. This means that if the employee wins $10,000 as a result of the hearing, his or her attorney is entitled to $3333. Of course, if the employee receives nothing, then the attorney receives no fee. Contingency fee arrangements force attorneys who represent claimants to seriously evaluate the merits of each of their cases before taking them. An attorney who routinely loses workers' compensation cases will be unable to sustain his or her practice and certainly will not be able to pay employees, rent, or bills for other necessities.

Contingency fee
An attorney's fee that is based on a percentage of the total recovery in a case.

Attorneys who represent employers are paid an hourly wage. Such an attorney might charge $150 to $300 per hour (or even higher). Although this sounds like a great deal of money, part of the attorney's fee pays for administrative expenses, including office rent, secretarial support, supplies, legal malpractice insurance and, of course, taxes.

The pay structures place the attorneys in different attitudes toward a workers' compensation case. The claimant's attorney would like to settle the case as soon as possible so that he or she can receive payment, while the employer's attorney has no overpowering need to settle the case so quickly. Of course, both attorneys are bound by strict ethical codes that govern how they conduct the case and how they protect the interests of their clients, but the pay arrangements for the attorneys certainly contribute to the tactics each uses throughout the case.

Many states have implemented separate code systems to monitor attorneys. For instance, Illinois creates an attorney code number for all attorneys who practice before the Workers' Compensation Board. Once issued, the attorney would simply provide his or her code number on all documents and forms filed with the board, instead of providing name, address, telephone number, and state bar number. See Exhibit 6-12.

ILLINOIS WORKERS' COMPENSATION COMMISSION
100 WEST RANDOLPH STREET #8-200
CHICAGO, IL 60601-3227
312-814-6500
WWW.IWCC.IL.GOV

APPLICATION FOR IWCC ATTORNEY CODE NUMBER

Attorney Firm Name _____

Address _____

Suite/P.O. Box _____

City, State, Zip _____

E-mail Address _____

Telephone _____

Illinois ARDC Registration Number _____

RETURN TO: Yvonna Castronova
Public Information Unit
Illinois Workers' Compensation Commission
100 W. Randolph St. #8-200
Chicago, IL 60601
yvonna.castronova@illinois.gov

Assigned Attorney Code number _____

Date Assigned _____

EXHIBIT 6-12 Application for IWCC Attorney Code Number (Illinois).

Evidentiary Rules

Rules of evidence refer to the type of evidence that the judge can consider in the case. In most civil and criminal cases, hearsay evidence, or the repeated statement of someone who is not present, is not allowed. However, in workers' compensation hearings, the evidentiary rules are relaxed. Workers' compensation hearings can consider hearsay and other testimony that would never be admissible in a civil or criminal trial. The reason for this liberal approach to evidence is that workers' compensation hearings are supposed to determine benefits, not guilt or innocence, or even civil liability.

Checklist—Preparing for a Workers' Compensation Hearing

Suppose that a client has come to our firm and wants to know what he or she should do to prepare for the upcoming workers' compensation hearing. Here is a checklist of items to go through with the client:

1. Be prepared for the fact that case might settle at the last minute.

   There is something about an impending hearing that tends to make both sides in a contested case suddenly wish to be more reasonable. The employer/insurance carrier might be worried about losing the claim; the client might be worried about not being awarded anything.

2. Witnesses should be present.

   No matter how friendly a witness is, no matter how supportive to the client's case, make sure that all witnesses will be present at the hearing. The best way to make sure that they come is to subpoena them. Subpoena forms are available through the Workers' Compensation Board.

3. Documentation is essential.

   Always tell the client to bring any and all documentation that has any bearing on any issue in the case. The rule here is simple: If you aren't sure if it's important, bring it anyway. Remind the client not to make notes and other marks on the documents. They may be admitted during the hearing and handed over to the judge for review.

4. Always, always arrive on time.

   The best rule with clients is to tell them "on time is late." This means that if the client has a hearing scheduled for 9 a.m. and he or she plans on arriving at 9 a.m., the client is already late. The hearing begins at the appointed time and the client should already be present and ready to go. Tell clients to arrive at least 30 minutes early. It gives them a chance to settle down and focus on the issues, and it helps to alleviate a bit of anxiety.

5. Paper and pens must be available.

   It is always important for the clients to have paper and pens with them. That way they can take notes during the proceedings, and if they need to communicate with the attorney, they can write a note and slide it over to the attorney instead of trying to whisper things to the attorney during the hearing.

6. Be prepared for stress.

   Hearings can be very stressful. Advise clients to get plenty of sleep the night before the hearing and to eat healthy meals for breakfast and lunch. They should also take short walks during the breaks in the hearing, if their physical disability allows such a thing.

ADMINISTRATIVE LAW JUDGES

Workers' compensation hearings are held before Administrative Law Judges. In this section, we will address exactly what an Administrative Law Judge is, the powers that this person possesses and how Administrative Law Judges function in the workers' compensation system.

The Administrative Law Judge (ALJ) plays a role similar to the one played a traditional judge in a civil or criminal case. However, unlike other types of cases, the ALJ not only acts as the judge, but also as the jury. Because there are never any juries impaneled in workers' compensation cases, the judge must decide issues of fact and make a determination about who should win the case.

Powers of the ALJ

Like most judges, Administrative Law Judges have the power to make rulings on the issues in the case and can enforce those rulings against all parties. The judge has the power to rule for or against either party and can dismiss specific issues raised by parties were even entire cases. Many of the powers associated with ALJs are similar to the powers of any civil or criminal judge. However, there are important differences.

Administrative Law Judges do not wear robes. Instead, they wear suits. Because workers' compensation hearings are informal, they usually don't bang gavels either. What they do is take notes and ask questions as the attorneys present their cases. At the conclusion of the case, the Administrative Law Judge has the power to enter a ruling against either party. This ruling usually comes within 60 days of the hearing and is presented as a Summary of the Case or Findings of Fact. Under either name, this document contains the judge's decisions about the important facts in the case and the judge's ruling based on those facts.

Communicating with Administrative Law Judges

Just as in other types of cases, the ALJ is not allowed to meet privately with either side while the case is pending. This is called an ***ex parte meeting*** and is strictly prohibited. Administrative Law Judges cannot give advice to employers or employees because that would be a violation of judicial ethics.

If it becomes necessary to communicate with an Administrative Law Judge while a workers' compensation case is pending, the best and perhaps only way to do it is in writing. Whenever one side sends correspondence to the judge, they should always send a copy to the other side.

> **Ex parte meeting**
> A meeting with a judge without the other side present

Requesting a Different Judge

There are provisions under workers' compensation statutes that allow either party to request a change of Administrative Law Judge. Normally, the request must be made at least 30 days prior to the hearing date and must set out specific reasons why the party is requesting a different judge. When such a request is filed by either party, a different ALJ must hear the motion and consider its merits. If the new Administrative Law Judge finds that there are no valid reasons to change judges, then the original judge will be reassigned to the case. There are times when the ALJ might file his or her own request to be removed from a case. In situations where the judge knows the parties personally, sitting on the case would create an impermissible appearance of impropriety and under the judicial code of ethics the judge must remove himself or herself from the case.

Administrative Law Judge's Role at the Hearing

The ALJ will usually schedule several hearings on a particular day. In some of these cases, the parties will settle their issues before the hearing ever starts, so it makes sense to schedule several hearings on a particular day. If the earlier cases settle, the ALJ can still hear the remaining cases. The ALJ usually has years of experience in hearing such cases and therefore moves things along pretty quickly. Most ALJs are former workers' compensation attorneys, so they know the system from both perspectives. Administrative Law Judges have the power to force the attorneys to stop questioning witnesses about particular issues, and they even have the power to force the attorneys to stop talking entirely. They are paid employees of the state Workers' Compensation Board and have no vested interest in how the case comes out. For instance, they are not authorized to receive a percentage of the award or an additional fee for dismissing a case. Such a practice would play against the neutral role that the ALJ is supposed to maintain throughout the proceedings.

CONDUCTING THE HEARING

A workers' compensation hearing, often referred to as a contested case hearing (CCH), resembles a trial in superficial ways. It is a formal hearing conducted before an Administrative Law Judge, division hearing officer, or some other official empowered to make final rulings on the issues pending in the case. When the actual hearing begins, it falls to the party who originally requested the hearing to begin the presentation. The common practice is for both attorneys to make some preliminary remarks about the case and then for the party who requested the hearing to begin presenting testimony and evidence.

Presenting a workers' compensation case is like presenting any case: The only way to do it is through witnesses and evidence. Attorneys are not allowed to offer their opinions about the case. Instead, they must call witnesses to the stand and present documents to the court that they believe prove their case.

Witnesses

There are always witnesses who appear in workers' compensation cases. These witnesses include anyone who has personal knowledge about the issues in the case. This will obviously include the employee. In fact, the employee may be the first person to testify. He or she will tell the judge about the accident and then any other issues involved in the case. Other witnesses are called to testify through the court's subpoena power.

Subpoenas

Subpoena
An order directing a person to appear at a hearing at a specific date and time.

A **subpoena** is a court order compelling a witness to appear at a specific date and time. See Exhibit 6-13. If a party wishes to issue a subpoena, it must obtain a subpoena form from the Workers' Compensation Board and then ensure that it is properly served on a witness. Properly served refers to the process of hand delivering the subpoena to the witness. Attorneys for both sides routinely subpoena everyone, even the employee's friends and others who say that they intend to be present at the hearing anyway. The best practice is to issue subpoenas to friendly witnesses just to make sure that the court has some leverage over a witness who suddenly changes his or her mind about appearing at the hearing. The parties are not required to pay for subpoenas, although they may have to pay a process server or sheriff's deputy to actually

> **SUBPOENA FOR WITNESS**
>
> VWC File No.
>
> Case of
>
> COMMONWEALTH OF VIRGINIA,
> VIRGINIA WORKERS' COMPENSATION COMMISSION
>
> To the Sheriff of the City/County of
>
> **WE COMMAND** that you summon:
>
> to appear before the Virginia Workers' Compensation Commission at
>
> on the _____ day of _____, 20 _____, at _____ to give evidence on behalf of the _____ in the controversy pending before this Commission between _____, Claimant, and _____, Defendants.
>
> Failure to appear as directed is punishable by the penalty prescribed by law. **Witness**, the **Virginia Workers' Compensation Commission**, this the _____ day of _____, 20 _____.
>
> VIRGINIA WORKERS' COMPENSATION COMMISSION
>
> IRIS C. PEACE, Clerk
>
> _____
>
> Fee for serving subpoena to be paid by:
>
> _____
>
> **ATTENTION SHERIFF**: Please return notice of service to the <u>Virginia Workers' Compensation Commission, Office of the Clerk, 1000 DMV Drive, Richmond, VA 23220</u>.

EXHIBIT 6-13
Witness Subpoena (Virginia).

serve the subpoena. Some states do not allow parties to serve subpoenas themselves and require sheriff's deputies to do it. In that case, the party may be required to pay a minimal fee for the service.

Direct Examination

At the hearing, the attorney who subpoenaed the witness calls that person to the stand and asks that witness questions. The witness is sworn in and the rules about perjury and false statements apply. The attorney questions the

EXHIBIT 6-14
Presentations in a Contested Hearing.

> In a contested hearing, both the employer and employee may:
> - Present oral testimony from witnesses and parties
> - Cross-examine witnesses presented by the other side
> - Introduce evidence, such as photographs, reports, and other materials
> - Request and receive discovery materials

Direct examination
The questioning of a witness to present proof of matters contested in a hearing.

Cross examination
The questioning of a hostile or opposing witness.

witness about what he or she knows of the case and tries to prove specific things about the case through the person's testimony. This process is called **direct examination**. Once the first attorney is finished asking questions, the attorney representing the other side has the right to ask questions. This is called cross-examination. See Exhibit 6-14.

Cross Examination

Cross examination is the process of questioning an opposition witness to discovery potential bias, lack of knowledge or to raise other points. Cross examination may be brief or it may be extensive, depending on the nature of the witness's testimony on direct examination. The case proceeds in this fashion, from witness to witness with each one questioned first on direct examination and then on cross examination until the first party has presented all of its witnesses and evidence. At that point, the second attorney presents his or her case in exactly the same way.

Rule of Sequestration

Rule of sequestration
A rule that requires witnesses, who have been subpoenaed to testify, to remove themselves from the courtroom while other witnesses testify.

The **rule of sequestration** applies in workers' compensation cases as much as it does in civil and criminal cases. This rule prohibits witnesses from being seated in the courtroom while other witnesses are testifying. Witnesses are not permitted to hear what other witnesses say. The reason for the rule is simple: Witnesses tend to modify their testimony as they hear others speak. If they are not familiar with what previous witnesses have said, their version is more likely to be as the witness remembers it and not as he or she has recently heard someone else recount it.

Refusal to Testify

What happens if a witness has been properly served with a subpoena and refuses to testify? The party who served the subpoena can request the ALJ to issue a warrant for the witness's arrest. The judge may issue a bench warrant to compel the witness to appear, although such drastic remedies are rarely needed.

INITIAL AND FURTHER HEARINGS

There are often practical difficulties involved in bringing all witnesses and parties together at the same day and time. Faced with these logistical problems, Administrative Law Judges often schedule two hearings: an initial hearing and a **secondary** or **further hearing** where the other people can testify. The initial hearing is where the employer and employee will testify, and the further hearing is where the witnesses who had legitimate excuses for missing the first hearing can testify. By allowing two possible hearing dates, the ALJ can avoid scheduling problems that might delay the entire case.

> **Secondary hearing**
> Also known as a **further hearing;** an additional hearing held on issues raised in a workers' compensation case.

Recording the Hearing

The actual hearing will be recorded. Sometimes, a court reporter is present and stenographically recording everything that is being said. Modern stenographic machines come with computer chips that allow them to do instant transcription. Some hearings are transcribed in real time and the participants can connect to the room's computer network and see a transcript of witness testimony on their laptops. In other hearings, the testimony is recorded on a tape recorder and replayed at a later date in order to create a written transcript.

Concluding the Hearing

Once both sides have present all of their evidence and witnesses, the ALJ "deems the case submitted," and then has up to 60 days to issue a ruling. During this time, the ALJ will research applicable laws and cases and review the hearing transcript and the file before reaching a decision about whether or not to award benefits in the case.

Settling Workers' Compensation Cases

A workers' compensation case may settle at any point during the proceedings. There is no prohibition against settling the case before, during or even after a hearing. In fact, it is quite common for the parties to reach an accommodation minutes before the hearing is scheduled to occur. There is something about the prospect of a final decision in the case that often encourages both parties to present a more reasonable position than they have maintained in the weeks and months leading to the hearing date.

> **CASE EXCERPT**
>
> ## HOW WORKERS' COMPENSATION JUDGES DEFINE "BODY PARTS"
> *Blue Bell, Inc. v. Speakman*[2]
>
> Opinion by ROBERT DICK BELL, Presiding Judge.
>
> Petitioners, Blue Bell, Inc. (Employer) and Liberty Mutual Insurance Co., seek review of an order of a three-judge panel of the Workers' Compensation Court (Panel). The Panel affirmed a trial court order finding Respondent Maggie M. Speakman (Claimant) sustained a change of condition for the worse to her right arm and awarding medical treatment. For the reasons set forth below, we sustain in part and vacate in part the Panel's order.
>
> In March of 1987, Claimant filed a Form 3 alleging cumulative trauma injuries to both hands and wrists, right arm, and right hand and thumb. In December, 1988, Claimant filed an amended Form 3 alleging injuries to both hands, both arms, her shoulders and her neck. Notably, the amended Form 3 did not mention either of Claimant's thumbs. By order dated June 19, 1990, the Workers' Compensation Court held Claimant suffered job-related cumulative trauma injuries to "the RIGHT AND LEFT HANDS, RIGHT AND LEFT ARMS (with radicular symptoms into both shoulders and neck)...." The date of her last hazardous exposure was found to be May 8, 1985. Claimant was awarded both Temporary Total Disability (TTD) and Permanent Total Disability (PTD) benefits.
>
> In 2004, Claimant initiated the present proceedings by seeking an order finding she had sustained a change of condition for the worse to both her hands and left arm. Employer admitted a change of condition to the right wrist and agreed to authorize surgery thereon. Employer also agreed to a court appointed independent medical examination to determine whether Claimant had sustained a change of condition for the worse to her left arm. However, Employer denied Claimant's requests for a finding of change of condition for the worse and medical treatment to both hands to the extent Claimant was seeking treatment for her thumbs. Specifically, Employer argued because Claimant never sought a finding of injuries to or PPD rating for her thumbs in the original proceeding, the statute of limitations and the theory of waiver operated to foreclose any claim for injuries to Claimant's thumbs.
>
> The trial court denied Employer's statute of limitations and waiver defenses and awarded Claimant medical treatment, including surgery, to her right arm. The court specifically held the June 19, 1990, Order's "finding of injury to claimant's RIGHT HAND AND LEFT HAND includes all body parts below the ELBOW and includes claimant's FOREARMS, WRISTS, FINGERS and THUMBS." The trial court
>
> *Continued*

specified Employer's "defense denying that the THUMBS were not adjudicated as part(s) of the HAND(S) by the Court in its June 19, 1990, Order is DENIED." The trial court reserved for future determination whether Claimant suffered a change of condition for the worse to her left arm. Employer appealed to the three-judge panel, which affirmed the trial court's ruling by a two-to-one vote.

Employer raises two propositions of error on review. First, Employer urges the Panel erred in awarding medical treatment to Claimant's right arm. Both parties argued before the Panel and now agree on appeal that the order should have authorized treatment to Claimant's right wrist, rather than to her right arm. It appears the Panel committed something akin to a scrivener's error when it authorized treatment to Claimant's right "arm." See *Townsend v. Dollar Gen. Store*, 1993 OK CIV APP 164, ¶ 28, 864 P.2d 1303, 1308. Therefore, the Panel's order is hereby modified to correct the error to accurately reflect treatment was authorized for Claimant's right "wrist." *Id.*

Employer also argues the Panel erred in ruling Claimant's thumbs were included in the 1990 Order. Workers' compensation laws are purely creatures of statute. The Workers' Compensation Court "can act only by authority of statute. Thus, any allowance of benefits or the restriction upon an award must be given, if at all, by statute." Furthermore:

> A statute-of-limitation issue ordinarily presents a mixed question of fact and law. Even though the trial court's factual determinations relative to the statutory time bar [if supported by any competent evidence] will not be independently reviewed, application of the 85 O.S.1991 § 43 time bar to render a claim not remediable is a conclusion of law and hence is subject to de novo review by this Court. *Sneed v. McDonnell Douglas*, 1999 OK 84, ¶ 9, 991 P.2d 1001, 1004.

Employer argues Claimant had two years from the date of her last hazardous exposure to file a workers' compensation claim for any injuries to her thumbs. 85 O.S.2001 § 43. At both the time of Claimant's last hazardous exposure to trauma and when she brought the present action, thumbs were scheduled members—separate from hands—under the Workers' Compensation Act. 85 O.S. § 22(3)(a) (1981 & 2001). Because Claimant failed to file a claim for any injury to her thumbs for nearly twenty years after her last hazardous exposure, Employer contends § 43 bars any recovery.

Claimant responds that a finding of an injury to the "hand" covers any and all parts of the arm below the elbow. Thus, Claimant urges, her right thumb was included in the court's 1990 finding of an injury to the right hand. As support for her argument, Claimant cites *Wilkerson Chevrolet, Inc. v. Mackey*, 1961 OK 267, 366

Continued

P.2d 422. In *Wilkerson*, the claimant's wrist and forearm were injured when an automobile hood fell on it. Medical evidence revealed the claimant fractured his wrist and the trial court awarded PPD benefits for disability to the hand. The employer argued any disability was "due to the elbow" and not the accidental injury. (Although unclear in the opinion, it appears the claimant may have suffered an elbow injury in a separate job-related accident then pending in another workers' compensation proceeding.) The Court held "[t]he evidence is undisputed that claimant sustained an accidental injury to the wrist and forearm. Any injury below the elbow may be compensable as a disability to the hand." *Id*, 366 P.2d at 424. The Court did not cite any authority for the latter proposition.

The *Wilkerson* opinion has been cited twice in published opinions. One opinion is clearly inapplicable here. In the other case, City of *Okla. City v. Pool*, 1978 OK 96, 580 P.2d 989, the claimant also suffered a fractured wrist and was awarded benefits for disability to the hand. On appeal, the employer argued it should not have been assessed certain deposition costs because the doctor's report was unclear whether disability was to the arm or the hand and because the wrist is not a scheduled member under § 22. In affirming the award, the Court referred to language in § 22(3) regarding amputations. That section provides in relevant part:

> Amputation between the elbow and the wrist shall be considered as the equivalent of the loss of a hand.... Amputation at or above the elbow shall be considered as the loss of an arm. *Wilkerson* and *Pool* are distinguishable from the facts of the present case. Both were appeals from an original order awarding benefits for an injury to the hand where the claimant suffered a fractured wrist. Unlike the present case, neither opinion involved a motion to reopen a case for a change of condition for the worse on a scheduled member not specified in the trial court's original order awarding workers' compensation benefits. It appears *Wilkerson* and *Pool* were based upon the amputation language in the Act. Because an amputation of part of an arm between the wrist and the elbow is considered the loss of a hand, it logically follows that a mere injury to the same part of the arm should only be compensated as an injury to the hand. On this basis, we believe the *Wilkerson* language is inapplicable to the instant case.

When a matter is set for hearing on permanent disability, the claimant must indicate what injuries are to be heard and which specifically reserved. If no injuries are reserved, all injuries are deemed at issue when the case is heard. *Id*. at ¶ 14, 854 P.2d at 380, citing *Friar v. Sirloin Stockade, Inc.*, 1981 OK 117, 635 P.2d 597. Accord *University of Okla. v. Steinberg*, 2001 OK CIV APP 91, 29 P.3d 618 (res

Continued

judicata barred reopening case for bladder and bowel problems where claimant was aware of such problems at time of trial, Form 3 did not allege injury to such body parts and order adjudicated PPD for injury only to the back and neck). See also *Sneed v. McDonnell Douglas*, 1999 OK 84, 991 P.2d 1001 (statute of limitations barred shoulder injury claim where claimant knew of shoulder pain when he filed his Form 3 for arm and hand injuries but did not list shoulders); *Smith v. Matrix Serv. Inc.*, 2001 OK CIV APP 75, 25 P.3d 298 (statute of limitations barred recovery for neck injury where claimant was aware of injury but failed to specify same on Form 3 which listed other specific body parts).

In the case at bar, Claimant's amended Form 3 gave no notice of any injuries to her thumbs. Claimant admitted she had problems with her thumbs in 1985 and that they have gradually gotten worse over time. However, Claimant did not seek a finding of injury to either thumb at trial. In fact, the 40 page trial transcript contains no mention of Claimant's thumbs. The medical reports introduced at trial noted Claimant's prior right thumb surgery, but did not include a specific finding of injury or give a PPD rating with respect to either of Claimant's thumbs. Finally, the trial court's June 19, 1990, order did not mention Claimant's thumbs.

On the basis of the foregoing, we conclude the Panel erred in holding Claimant's thumbs were included in the original order awarding benefits for injuries to Claimant's hands. Thumbs and hands are separately compensable members under the Act and case law dictates scheduled members are deemed at issue in the original proceeding unless specifically reserved. Claimant did not mention any injury to her thumbs nor did she reserve such issue in the original proceeding. Accordingly, the statute of limitations has run on any claim Claimant had for injuries to her thumbs.

VACATED IN PART, SUSTAINED IN PART AS MODIFIED.

HANSEN, J., and JOPLIN, J., concur.

Case Questions:

1. Explain the differences in the claims raised in 1988 and 2004 by the claimant.
2. Why did the Workers' Compensation Board deny coverage for the claimant's thumbs?
3. What is the claimant's stance regarding the coverage of her thumb as part of her hand?
4. According to the court, how is a motion for change of condition different than an original order awarding benefits?
5. Was it significant that the claimant never sought a finding of injury to her thumbs in the original claim?

ETHICAL CONSIDERATION:
Judicial Ethics

Judges, including Administrative Law Judges, are required by state court rules and their own ethical codes to be neutral and objective in all suits. This means that a judge cannot play favorites during the course of the hearing. The judge cannot, for example, side with one party's interpretation during the hearing, and require the other side to change the judge's predisposition. Instead, a judge is supposed to be objective, consider all of the evidence and arguments, and reach a decision that is fair. If an Administrative Law Judge were to act the way that some judges on television shows routinely act, that judge's decisions would be routinely overturned on appeal and the judge would undoubtedly be hauled before an ethics review board.

CHAPTER SUMMARY

When employers and employees have benefit disputes, they are entitled to file for a hearing to request an Administrative Law Judge to make a final determination about the contested issues. Workers' compensation hearings are held in conference rooms, not in courthouses. The evidentiary rules used to conduct the hearings are more relaxed than those used in regular civil or criminal trials. Attorneys who represent the parties in these hearings are compensated in different ways. Employee-attorneys are usually paid a contingency fee, while employer-attorneys are usually paid an hourly wage. The Administrative Law Judge makes decisions about the contested issues. Prior to the hearing, the parties are permitted to engage in discovery to learn more about the other side's version of the case. The actual hearing is conducted much like a trial, with witnesses testifying and exhibits offered to prove allegations in the case.

KEY TERMS

Arbitration hearing
Benefit review conference
Contested case hearing
Contingency fee
Cross examination
Deposition
Direct examination
Discovery

Ex parte meeting
Interrogatories
Motion for continuance
Pro se
Rule of sequestration
Secondary hearing
Subpoena

REVIEW QUESTIONS

1. How does a party dispute workers' compensation benefits?
2. What is a notice of hearing?
3. What are the powers of an Administrative Law Judge?
4. What is discovery?
5. Explain the difference between interrogatories and depositions.
6. How do statutes of limitation apply to workers' compensation hearings?
7. How do the rules of discovery in workers' compensation cases compare with the rules in civil cases?
8. What is a video deposition?
9. What is a request for production of medical records?
10. What are the consequences for a party who refuses to abide by the discovery rules?
11. What is a benefit review conference?
12. What is the difference between an arbitration hearing and a contested hearing?
13. Where are workers' compensation cases normally held?
14. What is *pro se* representation?
15. Explain the two different methods for compensating the attorneys who represent employees and employers.
16. What is an Administrative Law Judge?
17. How are contested workers' compensation hearings carried out?
18. What is the difference between direct examination and cross examination?
19. What is a subpoena?
20. What is the rule of sequestration?

QUESTIONS FOR REFLECTION

1. Should workers' compensation hearings be made more formal, so that they more closely resemble a trial with all of the rights that a trial would bring to the proceedings? Explain your answer.
2. Is it wise for a person to represent himself or herself at a workers' compensation hearing? Are there benefits to *pro se* representation that having an attorney would not bring to the proceedings?

WEB SITES

Bureau of Labor Statistics—Work-related injuries
http://www.bls.gov/iif/#tables

Texas Division of Workers' Compensation—Dispute Resolution
http://www.tdi.state.tx.us/wc/information/dispute.html

Wisconsin Department of Workforce Development
http://www.dwd.state.wi.us/wc/workers/claim_flow.htm

Industrial Commission of Arizona
http://www.ica.state.az.us/workers'.htm

State of Florida Division of Administrative Hearings
http://www.jcc.state.fl.us/jcc/

Rhode Island Workers' Compensation Court
http://www.courts.state.ri.us/workers/defaultnew-workers.htm

State of South Carolina Workers' Compensation Commission
http://www.wcc.state.sc.us/

PRACTICAL APPLICATIONS

Locate your state's forms for requesting a hearing and to supplement a compensation file. What information is required to complete the forms?

END NOTES

1 West's F.S.A. § 440.19.

2 2006 WL 1892433 (Okla.Civ.App. Div. 1, 2006).

Online Companion™
For additional resources, please go to
http://www.paralegal.delmar.cengage.com

Workers' Compensation Insurance

CHAPTER 7

CHAPTER OBJECTIVES

At the completion of this chapter, you should be able to:

- Discuss the basic features of an insurance policy
- Explain the various types of workers' compensation insurance programs
- Discuss how a company qualifies as a self-insurer
- Explain the role of state agencies in regulating workers' compensation insurance
- Define how insurance rates are set

INTRODUCTION TO INSURANCE

The basic scheme behind insurance is deceptively simple: Individuals (policy holders) make payments (premiums) to the insurance company, which pools the money and uses this pool of money to pay out any claims made by a policyholder. This arrangement spreads the risk of loss so that no one individual must bear the brunt of a large financial loss. Insurance companies are often seen as an important element of the economy, since they guarantee that businesses and individuals will be able to recover from devastating losses, such as fires or automobile collisions. Without insurance, business owners would have no way of reestablishing themselves after a catastrophe. Given this crucial economic importance and the fact that insurance companies have a great deal of leverage when dealing with the individual policyholder, all states have passed legislation restricting and regulating insurance companies.

Without insurance, there are only three possible methods to compensate an individual for a loss. They are (1) the individual bears the total burden, (2) the individual who caused the loss pays for it, and (3) a statute provides that some other agency, such as Workers' Compensation Insurance Fund, pays the loss.

Insurance companies have existed for centuries. Lloyd's of London, the world's most famous insurance company, has existed since 1688. Although it originally sold tea, it swiftly moved into the business of insuring merchants.

Insurance coverage is a type of contract between an individual (the insured) and an entity (the insurance company). The insured pays a **premium** (often a specific, monthly amount) in exchange for the insurance company's promise to pay (or **indemnify**) for the insured's property loss, medical bills, funeral expenses, liability, etc., up to a specified total amount.

If the insurance policy is a contract, then what is the insured receiving in exchange for his or her premium payments? Actually, the insured receives three benefits:

1. The insurance company agrees to compensate the insured for specific losses covered by the policy.
2. The insurance company agrees to provide an attorney to the insured should the insured be sued for any actions covered by the policy.
3. The insurance company agrees to act as a **fiduciary** (one bound by legal and ethical duties to act in the best interests of another) in handling the insured's policy matters.

If the insurance company breaches any of these promises, then it has violated the terms of a contract (or policy), and the insured is entitled to bring suit to enforce the policy.

The typical insurance policy has several component parts. These include the declarations page, the insurance agreement, a definitions section, and any exclusions. The typical workers' compensation policy often includes a section detailing the duties of an insured after an employee accident or injury and information about how to file a claim. There are usually general provisions in the policy that deal with issues such as bankruptcy of the insured and subrogation rights of the insurance company. **Subrogation** refers to the power of the insurance company to sue in the name of the policyholder to recoup the money it paid out on the insurance claim.

Premium

The insured's payment to the insurance company.

Indemnify

Payment to the insured for a loss covered in the insurance contract.

Fiduciary

A relationship in which one person, or entity, is obligated to act in a trustworthy relationship to the other. A fiduciary has the duty to act in the best interests of the other. A common example of a fiduciary relationship is the attorney-client relationship.

Subrogation

The right of an insurance company to bring suit to reclaim funds it has indemnified.

WORKERS' COMPENSATION INSURANCE

We will now move from a general discussion of insurance to the specific issue of workers' compensation insurance. In many ways, workers' compensation insurance is just like any other type of insurance. If you drive a car, you will be familiar with these principles because workers' compensation, like automobile insurance, is required by law.

When an employer falls under the jurisdiction of the Workers' Compensation Act, the employer must provide coverage by enrolling in the state-based program, obtaining private insurance, or qualifying as a self-insurer. States have different threshold requirements for requiring workers' compensation insurance, with some states requiring it when an employer has three or more employees, while others requiring it when an employer has any employers. Workers' compensation statutes not only require that coverage must exist, but also that employers post a notice to that effect so that all employees will be aware of the fact that the company is covered by workers' compensation insurance. See Exhibits 7-1 and 7-2.

The basic purpose of workers' compensation insurance is to protect workers. But workers' compensation insurance also protects the employer. If the employer did not have workers' compensation insurance, then the employer would be required to pay the employee's total medical bills and other benefits directly out of its own budget. That amount would vary depending on the employee's injury, but it would certainly be greater than the cost of a monthly insurance premium. So workers' compensation insurance, besides being a requirement of state law, also makes good economic sense. An employee is ensured so that his or her work-related injury or illness will be compensated, and the employer has the assurance that an injured worker's medical bills and benefits will not come directly from its working capital.

Workers' compensation insurance is like any other insurance. A company arranges a policy with an insurer and pays a monthly premium for the policy. Like any other insurance policy, workers' compensation insurance continues in effect until the insured decides to cancel it, the insured fails to make premium payments, or the insurance company decides that it will not renew a policy.

However, workers' compensation insurance does have some important differences from other types of insurance. For one thing, it is required by statute. An employer that does not arrange for workers' compensation insurance is in violation of the law and will face fines and sanctions, such as being required to pay all of an injured employee's benefits directly. Unlike other types of insurance, which can have widely different provisions from company to company, workers' compensation insurance must provide some basic protections. If the insurance company does not offer to reimburse injured

> **Form 16 NJ A**
>
> **POSTING NOTICE**
>
> The law requires every insured employer to post and maintain notices naming the company insuring its compensation liability "in a conspicuous place or places in and about the employer's place of business." The form of notice is prescribed by the Commissioner of Insurance and shall be clearly printed on a minimum of 90# index, 8½" by 11" in size. The content and arrangement of items must be consistent with the layout shown below. In accordance with 3:2-1 a duplicate filing must be made before the form is placed in use.
>
> ---
>
> **NOTICE**
>
> The undersigned employer hereby gives notice that the payment of compensation to employees and their dependents has been secured in accordance with the provisions of the Employer's Liability Insurance Law, Title 34, Chapter 15, Article 5, Revised Statutes New Jersey, by insuring with the
>
> ( ) Insurance Company
>
> for the period
>
> Beginning .... Ending ....
> Employer ....
>
> *In accordance with the above cited law, notice of compliance must be posted and maintained conspicuously in and about the employer's workplaces.*
>
> Form 16 NJ A

EXHIBIT 7-1 Posting Notice Workers' Compensation Insurance (New Jersey). *Reprinted courtesy of the State of New Jersey.*

employee's medical benefits, or refuses to provide legal counsel for a litigated claim, then the state will prevent the company from issuing any new policies and may reform previously issued policies to bring them into conformance with existing state law.

Because state law mandates workers' compensation insurance, once the policy is issued and the company pays its premiums there are no lapses or periods of interrupted coverage. A policy remains in effect for the entire term. With other types of insurance there are grace periods before the coverage kicks in. That is not the case with workers' compensation insurance. Once the premium is paid, the coverage begins.

NOTICE TO EMPLOYEES

NOTICE TO EMPLOYEES

The Commonwealth of Massachusetts
DEPARTMENT OF INDUSTRIAL ACCIDENTS
600 Washington Street, Boston, Massachusetts 02111
617-727-4900 - http://www.mass.gov/dia

As required by Massachusetts General Law, Chapter 152, Sections 21, 22 & 30, this will give you notice that I (we) have provided for payment to our injured employees under the above-mentioned chapter by insuring with:

_____
NAME OF INSURANCE COMPANY

_____
ADDRESS OF INSURANCE COMPANY

_____
POLICY NUMBER   EFFECTIVE DATES

_____
NAME OF INSURANCE AGENT   ADDRESS   PHONE #

_____
EMPLOYER   ADDRESS

_____
EMPLOYER'S WORKERS' COMPENSATION OFFICER (IF ANY)   DATE

MEDICAL TREATMENT

The above named insurer is required in cases of personal injuries arising out of and in the course of employment to furnish adequate and reasonable hospital and medical services in accordance with the provisions of the Workers' Compensation Act. A copy of the First Report of Injury must be given to the injured employee. The employee may select his or her own physician. The reasonable cost of the services provided by the treating physician will be paid by the insurer, if the treatment is necessary and reasonably connected to the work related injury. In cases requiring hospital attention, employees are hereby notified that the insurer has arranged for such attention at the

_____
NAME OF HOSPITAL   ADDRESS

TO BE POSTED BY EMPLOYER

EXHIBIT 7-2 Notice to Employees Regarding Workers' Compensation (Massachusetts).

But workers' compensation insurance is also unusual for other reasons. For one thing, it is a "limited policy." A limited policy is insurance that has numerous exclusions and only focuses on a very narrow area of coverage. Workers' compensation insurance provides coverage for injured workers exclusively. It does not provide coverage for other claims brought against the company. Workers' compensation insurance only indemnifies accidental injuries that occur within the scope of the job. The policy does not cover situations where customers or other non-employees are injured on the premises or by the actions of employees. The employer must obtain other insurance to provide coverage for those issues.

Workers' compensation insurance is also different from other policies because of the legal definition of "accepting a claim." In other types of insurance, when a claim is made, the insurer can review the case and make a determination about coverage. If it denies coverage, there may be litigation to determine if the insurer's decision was correct. But in workers' compensation there is a built in presumption that the claim is valid until some evidence is presented to contest that fact. The practical result is that all claims are considered valid and accepted as long as they meet the requirements under workers' compensation law. Of course, the insurer always has the right to contest a fraudulent claim, but the point here is that claims are presumed to be valid unless someone can prove otherwise.

Multiple Workers' Compensation Insurance Policies

In some circumstances, employers may have more than one workers' compensation insurance provider. There are several reasons why multiple policies make sense. For one thing, state law may allow it and spreading out the risk, especially for a big company, is always a good idea. One insurance company might not be willing to cover a large company's entire workers' compensation insurance needs, simply because of the sheer volume of potential claims. But spreading this danger among two or more insurance companies might make the situation a lot more palatable for insurance providers. In some cases, for example, a big company might insure different operations with different insurance companies. There are no prohibitions against doing so, as long as each policy meets the minimum standards set out under state workers' compensation law.

The Requirement to Provide Insurance

The state has the power to regulate workers' compensation insurance in order to make sure that employers obtain it and employees benefit from it. There are a variety of ways that an employer can obtain workers' compensation insurance, including:

- Enroll in a state-based insurance program
- Purchase private insurance
- Qualify as a self-insurer

Enrollment in a State-Based Insurance Program

Most states have some form of state-based insurance fund. Employers can enroll in the program by paying fees. Once they have joined the system, it works much like any insurance policy. The state fund will pay workers' compensation benefits and medical expenses for injured employees. The state, like private insurance companies, will also invest the fees it obtains in order to generate additional income. For state-based insurance coverage, the Workers' Compensation Board collects fees from all employer members and pools these funds in much the same way that any insurance company would. Claims are paid out of this fund. It is important to note, however, that not all states provide state-based funds. Connecticut, for example, allows only private insurance and self-insurance programs.

An interesting question arises about the classification of a state-based workers' compensation insurance fund. Does it qualify as a state agency, a trust fund or some other program? The question goes beyond academic classification. If the program is considered to be a kind of state agency, then it is bound by state administrative codes, including the prohibition against earning profits. State and federal agencies are not supposed to be profit-making ventures. Most authorities agree that the state-based workers' compensation program is a trust fund. That designation carries specific legal requirements. A trust fund is a pool of money that must be carefully held for the benefit of another. The person, or governmental agency, in charge of the trust cannot use the funds for other purposes. The designation as a trust fund protects the state workers' compensation program from being used to fund other governmental initiatives. Because state programs are classified as trusts, governments have not been allowed to use the workers' compensation fund in order to make up for budgetary short falls or to fund other government programs.

Most states give employers the option of enrolling in the state-based workers' compensation insurance program, obtaining private insurance or becoming a self-insurer. However, some state-based workers' compensation insurance arrangements do not provide these options. Instead, the state mandates that all employers must belong and they must pay the required fees. Other states opt for a middle of the road approach: they insist on payments into the state-based fund, but allow the employer to obtain additional private workers' compensation insurance coverage.

Purchasing Private Insurance

The second option for an employer is to purchase private insurance. There are many insurance companies that issue workers' compensation insurance policies. These companies operate in exactly the same way as any other insurance company. They evaluate risks and potential profits before deciding to issue a policy. The process of evaluating the risks involved is called **underwriting**. An underwriter evaluates various factors, including the inherent risks of the employer's business, the history of work injuries at the company facilities, previous claims, and numerous other factors. The end result of the underwriting analysis is a decision of the amount of risk that the insurance company will take on by granting a policy to a specific employer. If the insurer decides that the risk is too great, it will refuse to issue the policy. In that event, the employer may have no other option than to become a self-insurer.

> **Underwriting**
> The process of reviewing many different factors to determine the risk of investment.

Self-Insurance

Large companies have a third option when it comes to workers' compensation. They can become **self-insurers**. The employer acts as its own insurer, evaluating claims, paying benefits, and administering its program in much the same way that a private insurance company would. Why would a company want to become a self-insurer? The answer comes down to pure economics. Even taking on the additional expenses and employees to handle their workers' compensation claims, a company can still save more money than if it simply obtained private insurance coverage. This is especially true if the company has a large pool of employees or is engaged in dangerous manufacturing processes.

> **Self-insurer**
> A statutory provision that allows companies that meet minimum financial requirements to act as their own insurers.

A company wishing to become a self-insurer must have a net worth of $1 million dollars and post a bond to cover that amount. Once the bond is posted with the state, the company can begin operating its workers' compensation service as an in-house program. The $1 million threshold effectively precludes many smaller companies who do not have that total net worth. These companies must seek private insurance or enroll in the state program.

Requirement to Invest Funds Collected

Whether a company enrolls in the state system, obtains private insurance, or acts as a self-insurer, it will become involved in investing the funds acquired. Like all other types of insurance, the premiums collected must be reinvested in profit-making ventures. Most insurance companies invest their funds in government bonds. These are considered safe investments

EXHIBIT 7-3 Standard Coverage Form, Group Self-Insurance (Georgia). *Reprinted courtesy of the Georgia State Board of Workers' Compensation.*

```
WC-11 STANDARD COVERAGE FORM
```
GEORGIA STATE BOARD OF WORKERS' COMPENSATION

Use form WC-11 to:

To notify Board of coverage of new fund member, complete Sections A and C.
To notify Board of changes/activity, (as listed in Section B) complete A, B, and C.

Mail to: Coverage Section
State Board of Workers' Compensation
270 Peachtree Street, NW
Atlanta, GA 30303-1299
404-656-3692

INSTRUCTIONS FOR COMPLETING FORM WC-11

SECTION A:

1. ENTER COMPLETE CORPORATE NAME (IF NAME HAS CHANGED, PUT NEW NAME HERE).
2. ENTER ADDRESS OF CORPORATE OFFICE (IF ADDRESS HAS CHANGED, PUT NEW ADDRESS HERE).
3. ENTER TYPE OF BUSINESS (I.E. general contractor, retail sales, restaurant, landscaping, etc.).
4. ENTER ORIGINAL EFFECTIVE DATE OF INSURED MEMBER.
5. ENTER DOING BUSINESS AS (dba) NAME WHEN DIFFERENT FROM CORPORATE NAME. COMPLETE SEPARATE FORM WC-11 FOR EACH DIFFERENT (dba) NAME.
6. ENTER ADDRESS OF (dba) LOCATION (IF MORE THAN ONE LOCATION, USE SEPARATE FORM WC-11).
7. ENTER HERE IF A FRANCHISE OR "CHAIN" USES A STORE NUMBER TO IDENTIFY A SPECIFIC LOCATION.
8. ENTER POLICY NUMBER ISSUED WHEN INSURANCE IS PURCHASED.

SECTION B: CHECK EXACT ACTION(s) BEING TAKEN AND GIVE EFFECTIVE DATE OF ACTION.

1. ADD DOING BUSINESS AS (dba) NAME AS SHOWN IN SECTION A - (5).
2. ADD LOCATION ADDRESS AS SHOWN IN SECTION A - (6).
3. CANCEL CORPORATE NAME AS IN SECTION A - (1).
4. CANCEL DOING BUSINESS AS (dba) NAME AS SHOWN IN SECTION A - (5).
5. CANCEL LOCATION ADDRESS AS SHOWN IN SECTION A - (6).
6. EFFECTIVE DATE OF REINSTATEMENT.
7. CORPORATE NAME PRIOR TO NAME CHANGE.
8. DOING BUSINESS AS (dba) NAME PRIOR TO NAME CHANGE.
9. OLD CORPORATE ADDRESS PRIOR TO ADDRESS CHANGE.
10. OLD DOING BUSINESS AS (dba) ADDRESS PRIOR TO ADDRESS CHANGE.

SECTION C:

1. COMPLETE GROUP SELF-INSURANCE FUND NAME - DO NOT USE ABBREVIATIONS OR INITIALS.
2. NAME AND ADDRESS OF THIRD PARTY ADMINISTRATOR PROCESSING CLAIMS.
3. NAME AND PHONE NUMBER (WITH EXTENSION) OF PERSON COMPLETING FORM - DO NOT USE INITIALS.

IF YOU HAVE QUESTIONS PLEASE CONTACT THE STATE BOARD OF WORKERS' COMPENSATION AT 404-656-3818 OR 1-800-533-0682 OR VISIT http://www.sbwc.georgia.gov
WILLFULLY MAKING A FALSE STATEMENT FOR THE PURPOSE OF OBTAINING OR DENYING BENEFITS IS A CRIME SUBJECT TO PENALTIES OF UP TO $10,000.00 PER VIOLATION (O.C.G.A. §34-9-18 AND §34-9-19).

| WC-11 | REVISION . 07/2006 | 11 | STANDARD COVERAGE FORM |

EXHIBIT 7-3 *(Continued)*

with a reliable return. Investment of insurance premiums is not only encouraged, but also actually required, especially for state-based workers' compensation funds. The reason for the requirement is simple mathematics. The money collected from employers is usually not enough to cover the actual costs to administer the program, pay salaries, benefits, medical bills, and all of the other expenses associated with the workers' compensation system. As a result, investment becomes necessary to generate additional income. See Exhibit 7-3.

STATE REGULATION OF WORKERS' COMPENSATION INSURANCE

Workers' Compensation Boards have a great deal of authority when it comes to regulating insurance policies and procedures. The commissioner of the Workers' Compensation Board has the power to issue a set of classifications of risks and premium rates for all insurance companies issuing workers' compensation polices. In some states, the premiums and insurance rates may also fall under the jurisdiction of the state insurance board, which is responsible for all types of insurance issued in the state.

Among the powers of the Workers' Compensation Board is the right to refuse certain companies the option of issuing policies. This effectively cripples an insurance company. As a result, insurance companies that issue workers' compensation policies work hard to make sure that their policies are acceptable to the Board. However, the Board cannot abuse this power by being arbitrary and capricious. The reasons for refusing to allow a specific company to issue new policies must be based on objective criteria and fairly arrived at.

Workers' Compensation Boards can regulate all of the following with respect to insurance coverage:

- Rates
- Premiums
- Classifications

Rates

An insurance rate is the fee structure that is assigned to a particular company, based on several different factors and a formula that takes into account all of the following:

- Potential claims by employees
- Expenses/losses of the insurer
- Profits to be made from premiums

These factors are all part of a simple question: Will the insurance company make a profit by issuing a policy to this company? If the answer is yes, then the company will go forward. If the math points to a loss (or not as great a profit) then the insurance company may decide against issuing workers' compensation policies.

Premiums

The premium is the regular monthly payment that the insured makes to the insurance company. Employers must pay premiums in order to maintain their insurance coverage in the same way that we must pay our homeowner's or auto insurance premiums in order to keep those policies in place.

Calculating Premiums

When an insurance company calculates the base premium for a company, it bases its calculations on the employer's payroll. The more employees a company has, the higher the premium. Smaller companies are charged lower premiums. The higher premium for larger companies builds a reserve that can be used to pay out any claims. Obviously, the company with more employees has a much higher potential for making claims. But there are other factors to consider in setting premiums. For instance, there is the danger of the company's business.

Risk Exposure

Different companies have different levels of risk based on what they do. Some jobs have inherent risks that are much greater than others. For instance, compare and contrast the duties of an oil rig worker and an office worker. Obviously, the company that employs the oil rig workers will pay a much higher workers' compensation insurance premium than the company that employs officer workers.

Classifications

Insurance companies often address the issue of risky jobs by creating a classification system that groups extremely dangerous companies together. Every company in this group would pay a higher insurance premium than companies classified as lower risk.

Refusal to Pay Benefits

When an insurance company wrongfully withholds benefit payments to an injured worker, the state has the right to impose sanctions against the insurance company. In North Carolina, for example, an insurer would be subject to fines after failing to pay a claim 14 days after it was made. Although other

FORM 130

The Commonwealth of Massachusetts
Department of Industrial Accidents – Department 130
600 Washington Street – 7th Floor, Boston Massachusetts 02111
Info. Line 800-323-3249 ext. 470 in Mass. Outside Mass. - 617-727-4900 ext. 470
http://www.mass.gov/dia

COMPLAINT OF IMPROPER CLAIMS HANDLING AGAINST AN INSURER

DIA Board # (If Known):

The purpose of this form is to request the Department of Industrial Accidents (DIA), Office of Claims Administration to conduct a preliminary investigation into the claims handling practices of an Insurer. Upon completion of our investigation you will be notified of our findings. Please note- The DIA can only determine if the matter should be further investigated by the Division of Insurance. The DIA can **NOT** award damages or any type of award or compensation to a complainant.

1. Complainant's Name (Last, First, MI):
2. Complainant's Telephone Number:
3. Complainant's Address (No. and Street, City, State, Zip Code):
4. DIA Board Number (if known):
5. Date of Injury (mm/dd/yyyy):
6. Complainant's Social Security Number*:
7. Name of Complainant's Attorney:
8. Telephone Number of Complainant's Attorney:
9. Attorney's Address:
10. Employer's Name & Address (No. and Street, City, State, Zip Code):
12. Name & Address of Insurer's Attorney:
13. Telephone Number of Insurer's Attorney:
14. Workers' Compensation Insurance Carrier:
15. Insurance Carrier's Case File Number (if known):
16. Claims Representative's Name:
17. Claims Representative's Tel. Number:

NATURE OF COMPLAINT (attach additional sheets if necessary)
Specify dates of complaint, date claim has been paid through, any weeks not paid, etc.

18. Complainant's Signature:
19. Date Prepared (mm/dd/yyyy):

*Disclosure of Social Security Number is Voluntary. It will aid in the processing of documents. Please Print Clearly or Type. Unreadable forms will be returned.

Form 130 - Revised 8/2001 - Reproduce as needed.

EXHIBIT 7-4 Complaint of Improper Claims Handling Against an Insurer (Massachusetts).
Reprinted courtesy of the Massachusetts Department of Industrial Accidents.

> **SIDEBAR**
>
> The link to view employers who are in compliance with state workers' compensation insurance laws in Illinois is: *http://www.iwcc.il.gov/insurance.htm.*

states set different deadlines, many have opted for sanctions against insurance companies that wrongfully withhold payment for workers' compensation claims for either benefits or medical procedures. See Exhibit 7-4.

Verifying Coverage

As a way of streamlining the entire process of both verifying coverage and reporting employers who have violated the law and failed to obtain workers' compensation insurance coverage, most states provide some system that allows individuals to verify workers' compensation insurance for specific employers. Some states, like Illinois, offer an online database that allows anyone with Internet access to check on an individual employer to verify that it has obtained workers' compensation insurance. When the employer is not listed in the database, it is a strong indicator that the company is in violation of workers' compensation statutes and should be reported to the state Workers' Compensation Board.

Penalties for Failing to Maintain Workers' Compensation Coverage

Each state has a section in its workers' compensation statute that provides sanctions, fines, and other penalties for an employer who is required to provide workers' compensation insurance yet fails to do so. These statutes may provide a per day fine of several thousand dollars, criminal sanctions, and a requirement that the employer must pay the injured worker's medical and compensation benefits. See Exhibit 7-5 for an example of a statute penalizing an employer for failing to provide workers' compensation insurance coverage.

EXHIBIT 7-5

Failure to Secure Workers' Compensation Insurance (New York).

> §52. Effect of failure to secure compensation.
>
> 1. (a) Failure to secure the payment of compensation for five or less employees within a twelve month period shall constitute a misdemeanor, and is punishable by a fine of not less than one thousand nor more than five thousand dollars. Failure to secure the payment of compensation for more than five employees within a twelve month period shall constitute a class E felony, and is punishable by a fine of not less than five thousand dollars nor more than fifty thousand dollars in addition to any other penalties otherwise provided by law. It shall be an affirmative defense to any criminal prosecution under this section that the employer took reasonable steps to secure compensation.[1]

PRACTICAL APPLICATIONS OF INSURANCE COVERAGE

Now that we have discussed how insurance policies come into existence, we must address the question of how these policies are interpreted by the parties. Insurance coverage raises a host of legal issues and the cases that interpret insurance policies are legion. Insurance policies have been challenged on every conceivable ground and through the years the court system has come up with some basic approaches to interpreting provisions in such policies.

Policy Ambiguities

We have already seen that an insurance policy is a contract. Like any contract, the language used in the policy is critical. When an issue arises between insurance companies and their customers, the courts always review the policy to determine exactly what rights were negotiated. That is one reason why all insurance policies, especially workers' compensation policies, are long and are written with every possible contingency in mind. After all, insurance companies have been at this for a very long time, and if they want to protect themselves, the policy is the only real place to do it. Unlike other forms of insurance, workers' compensation insurance policies must also be construed in light of the basic reason to issue them in the first place: to provide benefits to injured workers. That means that any policy provision that tries to eliminate statutory obligations will not be implemented. Courts will refuse to honor provisions that attempt to limit medical benefits, lost wage benefits, or any other coverage that falls below the uniform policy requirements in any particular state.

When there is an issue about the wording of a workers' compensation policy, the law requires that the ambiguity be resolved in such a way that the insurance policy provides coverage and protects employees. One of the basic approaches is to construe policy ambiguities against the insurance company and in favor of employee coverage.

The theory is this: Because the insurance company actually drafted the policy, they shall bear the brunt of conflicting or ambiguous clauses contained in it. This rule of construction applies to all workers' compensation policies. The rule guides courts in the approach and analysis that they should use to interpret the numerous provisions in the policy. This approach provides a baseline principle: When in doubt, the courts should construe the policy in favor of a stance that grants the widest possible coverage to as many employees as possible.

The state statutes that mandate the minimum requirements for workers' compensation insurance policies also provide for more mundane issues, including the wording used and even the size of the font in which the policy is printed. It also imposes strict limitations on issues such as exclusions and imposes a strict duty to defend.

Font Sizes

Insurance has been heavily regulated by the states for decades. These regulations affect everything from creating an office of state Insurance Commissioner (or similar title) to the size of the type font used in policies. In fact, many states have statutes that specify not only the size of the type that must be used in the policy, but also require the use of boldface lettering for certain terms. These initiatives are all designed to make the policy easier to read and to avoid the old adage that "large print giveth and small print taketh away." In the past, small print, buried deep in the policy, has been used to disguise policy limitations and other restrictions on the policyholder's rights.

Exclusions

An insurance policy does not apply in all situations. For example, one evening Mary leaves work and gets involved in a traffic accident on the way home. Her injuries are not covered under her employer's workers' compensation policy because that policy limits its coverage to the on the job accidents. The exclusions page actually states this, in bold letters. Workers' compensation insurance policies often contain specific **exclusions**, limiting the policy to injuries incurred in the scope, practice, and implementation of business duties. Any other injuries are not covered.

Of course, the insurance company cannot word its exclusions in such a way as to avoid paying for legitimate claims. The Workers' Compensation Board will see to it that the policy exclusions are not overly broad. If they are, then the Board will refuse to allow the company to insure employers.

Documentation to Be Submitted to the Workers' Compensation Board

Most states require that insurers, employers, and injured workers must submit documentation, forms and other material to the state during the course of a workers' compensation claim. This documentation consists of the various forms required by the Workers' Compensation Board, including the original claim, employer contests of the claim, and other forms detailing various payments of benefits and medical costs. However, this does not mean that all bills and events in a workers' compensation case must be documented

---

Exclusion

The persons, types of losses, or damages not covered by an insurance policy.

with the state. States generally do not require proof of payment by the parties for the following items:

- Travel expenses
- Minor medical bills of $2,000 or less
- Prescriptions
- Ambulance invoices
- Out-of-state claims or providers
- Private-duty-nursing bills
- Nursing-home bills
- Pain-clinic bills
- Rehabilitation services[2]

Duty to Defend

One of the main duties that an insurance company has under its workers' compensation policy is to provide a legal defense when an injured employee contests a claim. This is referred to as the "**duty to defend.**" The insurance company meets this obligation by hiring an attorney to represent the employers in the claim. This attorney will represent the insured throughout the legal action, although he or she is paid by the insurance company. The attorney who represents the insured owes his or her duty to the insured, even though the insurance company is paying for the services.

The duty to defend is triggered when an insured is sued. In a workers' compensation setting, the duty to defend is triggered when an insured company has a dispute filed by an injured employee. In the last chapter, we saw how benefit disputes proceed through the workers' compensation system. Once the process begins, it is the insurance company's responsibility to provide legal counsel to represent the company. Whether or not the employee also hires an attorney is entirely the decision of the employee. In Chapter 6, we saw that the attorneys who regularly represent employers are compensated in a different manner than those who routinely represent employees.

The insurance company's duty to defend is provided by the express terms of the policy. However, questions often arise in specific claims, especially when the claim involves unusual activities, whether the policy provides coverage for such actions. In these situations, an insurance company would prefer some direction from the courts about what its legal obligations are. In cases where the duty is not clear, an insurance company might be compelled to seek a court ruling on the subject before it enters the case. After all, if the insurance company's duty to defend has not been triggered by the facts of

Duty to defend
An insurance company's responsibility to provide legal counsel for its insured against whom an action has been filed.

> **SIDEBAR**
>
> An insurer's duty to defend arises when the claim against the insured sets forth facts representing a risk covered by the terms of the policy.[3]

the case, and the company contests the issues on behalf of the employer, then the insurance company has essentially waived any right to claim that it has no obligation to provide such a defense.

Declaratory Judgments

When an insurance company is faced with the dilemma of trying to decide if it is obligated to provide a defense in a case, it will often file an action referred to as a declaratory judgment (or declaratory action, in some states). This proceeding is similar to a civil lawsuit, but instead of seeking damages from any parties, the action seeks a court determination concerning the rights and obligations of the parties. When the court rules on a declaratory action, the court is making a determination about the rights of the parties who are or may be involved in a pending action. To bring this issue within the framework of workers' compensation claims, an insurance company that has some doubts about whether a particular claim falls under the clauses of its premium might file an action for a declaratory judgment. The attorneys representing the insurance company would argue why they believe that the insurance policy does not apply in this case (and therefore why the insurance company should not be required to hire counsel for the employer to defend the claim). The insurance company would then seek a ruling from the court specifying exactly what the insurance company's obligation is. Should the court review the policy and determine that a particular claim is not covered, then the insurance company has no further obligations in the case and it will be relieved of its duty to defend in a specific claim. On the other hand, if the court determines that the policy provisions are triggered, the insurance company would then enter the case, provide legal counsel, and carry out all other provisions in the policy to protect the legal rights of the employer. Courts have been consistent in ruling that an insurance company's duty to defend is a broad obligation, broader even than its obligation to indemnify for damages. Because of this approach, an insurance company is often on the losing side of litigation when it contests its duty to defend in particular cases.

Checklist: Gathering Evidence and Preparing for a Claim

1. Have a plan in place.

    All employers should have a plan in place that should be implemented when an employee is injured. For instance, the employee should receive immediate medical treatment. After that, the supervisor should contact the insurance provider to report the incident.

2. Question the injured worker.

    As soon as possible, obtain an oral statement from the injured worker about what happened. Try to get as much as detail as possible.
    In addition to getting the details of the incident, also obtain the following information:

    - Employee's full name, including nicknames, maiden names, etc.
    - Current address (the one in the employment file might not be up to date)
    - Phone numbers, including cell phones, beepers, pagers, and e-mail addresses
    - Social Security numbers and driver's license numbers
    - Marital status
    - Sex, date of birth
    - Date of hire
    - Any previous medical issues similar to this one

3. Locate witnesses.

    You should locate any witnesses to the incident and also question them. Have them write out their own statements about what they saw and heard.

4. Record the scene.

    Photograph or videotape the scene where the accident occurred as soon as possible after the incident. A visual record can be invaluable later on.

5. Contact the insurance provider and inquire about an attorney.

    Most insurance companies keep attorneys on retainer, and it's never too early to get legal advice about possible litigation.

6. Gather information about the incident or injury, including:

    - Date, time, and location of injury
    - Type of injury
    - Body part affected, paying particular attention to which side of the body was initially reported as injured
    - What caused the injury? Was it faulty machinery? Employees playing? Carelessness?
    - What precisely was the employee doing at the time of the injury?

CASE EXCERPT

WHEN DOES THE DUTY TO DEFEND PROVISION APPLY?
Lenny Szarek, Inc. v. Maryland Cas. Co.[4]

Justice GORDON delivered the opinion of the court:

Plaintiff, Lenny Szarek, Inc. (Szarek) appeals the grant of summary judgment to defendant Maryland Casualty Company (Maryland) on its counterclaim for declaratory judgment. Szarek contends the circuit court erred in concluding that the territoriality provisions of Maryland's insurance policy precluded coverage for a worker's compensation claim filed in Illinois and that the lack of coverage was clear to the point that Maryland was not even required to provide a defense against such a claim. We agree with Szarek and reverse.

FACTUAL BACKGROUND

Szarek's and Maryland's pleadings reveal the following undisputed facts.

Szarek is a carpentry contractor and an Illinois corporation, headquartered in McHenry County. We take notice that McHenry is one of Illinois' northernmost counties, sharing a border with the State of Wisconsin. Szarek does business in both Illinois and Wisconsin.

On June 23, 1994, Maryland issued a policy of worker's compensation insurance to Szarek, with coverage retroactive to May 23, 1994, and continuing through June 23, 1995. Maryland's policy provided: "We will pay promptly when due the benefits required of you by the workers compensation law." The policy defined "workers compensation law" as follows: "Workers Compensation Law means the workers or workmen's compensation law and occupational disease law of each state or territory named in item 3.A. of the Information Page." Only one state was listed in item 3.A. of the information page: Wisconsin.

Szarek also entered into a separate employer's liability pooling agreement, a form of self-insurance, covering the same period of time as the Maryland policy. The agreement also provided that workers' compensation benefits would be paid "when due the benefits required of you by the workers' compensation law." However, the agreement defined "the workers' compensation law" as "the workers' or workmen's compensation law and occupational disease law of Illinois." The agreement appointed Management Services, Inc. (also known as Risk Management Association, and hereinafter referred to as RMA) as its administrator.

On November 7, 1994, Thomas Cholewinski, a Szarek employee, was hurt while working in Kenosha, Wisconsin. Cholewinski was an Illinois resident and filed

Continued

his worker's compensation claim in Illinois. Szarek tendered this claim to RMA. RMA, unaware of the existence of the Maryland policy at the time, began to pay benefits and incur expenses on the claim in the amount of $33,412.80.

When RMA became aware of the Maryland policy, it tendered the claim to Maryland on January 19, 1996, for ongoing administration, and sought compensation for the benefits it had paid and the costs of administration it had incurred. Maryland, however, denied any liability for Cholewinski's claim on March 8, 1996, explaining it would "not be able to provide benefits on ... the claim under ... its workers' compensation policy issued for the State of Wisconsin." Cholewinski subsequently filed for an adjustment of his claim before the Illinois Industrial Commission, naming Szarek and Maryland as defendants. Maryland did not participate in the proceeding, however, and the final settlement of $22,980.75, reached on April 15, 1997, was paid out of the self-insurance pool. All told, Szarek, through its contributions to the self-insurance pool, paid $69,316.01 for benefits to Cholewinski and for defense against his claim.

Litigation over Maryland's denial of coverage commenced in the law division of the circuit court of Cook County sometime in 1999, originally between RMA and Maryland, but later between Szarek and Maryland in the chancery division. Szarek's complaint alleged that Cholewinski's claim was covered under the Maryland policy, that Maryland had wrongfully failed to defend and indemnify Szarek for the claim, and that, as a result, Szarek paid for the costs of defense and workers' compensation benefits itself. In its answer to the complaint, Maryland denied that Cholewinski's claim fell within the terms of the policy and therefore denied that it owed a defense and indemnification of his claim. Maryland also filed a counterclaim the same day it filed its answer, seeking a declaration from the circuit court that it had no duty to defend or indemnify Szarek against Cholewinski's claim. Maryland conceded that Cholewinski had a valid claim under either Wisconsin or Illinois law, but nevertheless contended that its policy only covered claims brought in Wisconsin.

On June 30, 2003, Szarek moved the chancery court for summary judgment on its complaint. In response, Maryland cross-motioned for summary judgment on its counterclaim. In its motion, Szarek contended that benefits were due under Wisconsin worker's compensation law once Cholewinski was injured in Wisconsin, and therefore Maryland owed coverage. Maryland, on the other hand, argued that the plain language of its policy limited coverage to claims filed in Wisconsin. The chancery court denied Szarek's motion and granted Maryland's motion, stating "the Maryland worker's compensation coverage ... does not apply to the Illinois worker's compensation claim. As a result, Maryland had no obligation to defend Szarek; no obligation to indemnify Szarek and no obligation to make payments to Szarek." Szarek appeals.

Continued

II. ANALYSIS

"To ascertain the meaning of . . . an insurance policy's words . . . a court must construe the policy as a whole." *Outboard Marine Corp. v. Liberty Mutual Insurance Co.*, 154 Ill.2d 90, 108, 180 Ill.Dec. 691, 607 N.E.2d 1204, 1212 (1992). Unambiguous terms of a policy will be applied as written, unless those terms violate public policy. *Villicana*, 181 Ill.2d at 442, 230 Ill.Dec. 30, 692 N.E.2d at 1199. Ambiguities in terms limiting or excluding coverage, however, will be construed against the insurer and in favor of the insured. *Progressive Universal Insurance Co. of Illinois v. Liberty Mutual Fire Insurance Co.*, 347 Ill.App.3d 411, 414, 282 Ill.Dec. 636, 806 N.E.2d 1224, 1227 (2004). A term is ambiguous when it is subject to more than one reasonable interpretation. *Outboard Marine Corp.*, 154 Ill.2d at 108, 180 Ill.Dec. 691, 607 N.E.2d at 1212.

On appeal, Maryland contends that under the language of the policy it is only liable for defense and indemnification of worker's compensation claims as "required" by Wisconsin's worker's compensation act, which it contends means that the claim must be filed in Wisconsin. Szarek, on the other hand, argues that "as required" under Wisconsin's worker's compensation law means that a claim should be evaluated and paid under Wisconsin law regardless of where the claim is filed. Szarek therefore sees the provision not as limiting coverage to claims brought in a particular forum, but rather as a choice of law provision limiting benefits to what would have been granted under the state law specified in the policy. Szarek further contends that the law required Maryland to include an express exclusion in the policy for claims filed outside of Wisconsin, if that was Maryland's desired limitation of coverage, and that public policy demands the negation of provisions limiting the territorial reach of worker's compensation coverage.

These issues, considered under virtually identical policy provisions as that at issue in this case, have produced two divergent lines of decisions. One line of cases agrees with Szarek that alleged territorial limitation provisions are in fact choice of law provisions, not limiting coverage based on where the employee chooses to file his claim, but only to restrict benefit eligibility and to set indemnification limits based on the state law specified in the policy. This line of cases includes *Smith & Chambers Salvage v. Insurance Management Corp.*, 808 F.Supp. 1492 (E.D.Wash.1992). The other line of cases agrees with Maryland that, for there to be coverage, the claim must actually be filed in the state whose law is made to apply in defining the term "worker's compensation law." This line of cases includes *Travelers Insurance Co. v. Industrial Accident Comm'n*, 240 Cal.App.2d 804, 809–10, 50 Cal.Rptr. 114, 118–19 (1966). We perceive the more enlightened view to be reflected in those cases that find the plain meaning of policies providing that benefits will be paid "as required" under a specified state's worker's compensation

Continued

law to only be a choice of law provision, and therefore find that Maryland must indemnify Szarek for the benefits paid to Cholewinski and for the costs of defense against his claim. As a result of this conclusion, we need not address Szarek's claim that Maryland breached its duty to defend. We find the Pennsylvania Supreme Court's decision in Weinberg instructive. Mrs. Gotkin, the employee in Weinberg, was injured in Pennsylvania, but filed a worker's compensation claim in her home state of New Jersey. The State Workmen's Insurance Fund, under which the plaintiff, a Pennsylvania business, was covered, provided that the Fund agreed to "assume the whole liability of this Insured Employer under the Workmen's Compensation Act of Pennsylvania." *Weinberg*, 368 Pa. at 80, 81 A.2d at 908. The policy further provided that its liability for judgments was "confined to the liability arising under the Workmen's Compensation Law, and not otherwise." *Weinberg*, 368 Pa. at 80, 81 A.2d at 908. The *Weinberg* court rejected the Fund's claim that the policy language rendered it liable only for claims filed in Pennsylvania, stating that that view "confused the Fund's liability for the payment of compensation due because of the injury to the employee, and its liability for the payment of a judgment obtained by the employee in an action to enforce payment of compensation." *Weinberg*, 368 Pa. at 80, 81 A.2d at 908. The court explained that at the moment Gotkin was injured she became eligible for Pennsylvania benefits, simultaneously making the employer liable to pay compensation under the Pennsylvania Act. *Weinberg*, 368 Pa. at 81, 81 A.2d at 908–09. Based on that consideration, the court found Gotkin's subsequent, fortuitous choice to file her claim in New Jersey did not impact the employer's liability under the Pennsylvania act. *Weinberg*, 368 Pa. at 81, 81 A.2d at 909. The court therefore concluded that under the Fund's policy, the Fund was liable to assume the defense and indemnification of Gotkin's claim, but only as would have been granted under the Pennsylvania Act, even allowing the complete denial of compensation if the injury would not have been covered under Pennsylvania law. *Weinberg*, 368 Pa. at 81, 81 A.2d at 909; accord *Kacur*, 253 Md. at 509–10, 254 A.2d at 161–62.

In *Kacur*, the employer was a Maryland resident also doing business in Pennsylvania. The employee was injured in Maryland and filed his worker's compensation claim there. The insurer had promised "to pay promptly when due all compensation and other benefits required of the insured by the workmen's compensation law," and specified that the coverage "applied to the Workmen's Compensation Law of each of the following states: PENNSYLVANIA." *Kacur*, 253 Md. at 502, n. 1, 254 A.2d at 157, n. 1. The *Kacur* court observed that a "contract of insurance coverage between the employer and his carrier, may be sufficiently broad as to cover the employer in all situations coextensive with the options open to the injured employee under applicable

Continued

Workmen's Compensation Acts," so long as an insurer is only required to indemnify its insured for the amount allowed under the law of the state specified in the policy. *Kacur*, 253 Md. at 504–05, 254 A.2d at 158. *Kacur* criticized the holding of *Consolidated Underwriters v. King*, a Texas appellate court decision concluding that a similar provision restricted coverage to claims actually filed in a particular forum, which in that case was Louisiana. The *Kacur* court noted Professor Larson's view that the provision in *King* merely served as a choice of law, not a coverage provision. *Kacur*, 253 Md. at 509, 254 A.2d at 161; see 9 A. Larson Workers' Compensation Law § 151.04 at 151-12 (2000) (current edition: "the employer plainly intended to accept compensation liability for all its employees working in the area where decedent worked (Texas). The repeated references to Louisiana in the policy all are attempts to state what law shall govern"). As in *Weinberg*, the court ordered that the insurer indemnify the employer, but only for benefits which would have been allowed under the law of the state specified in the policy. *Kacur*, 253 Md. at 510, 254 A.2d at 161–62; see also *Toebe*, 114 N.J.Super. at 50, 274 A.2d at 826 (rejecting an insurer's argument that *Weinberg* and *Kacur* should not be applied because they "would allow a court to determine what a foreign administrative agency would award as compensation, as the same argument could be made in any conflict of laws case where the court of the forum, in addition to determining the applicable law of another jurisdiction, must also fix damages").

We agree with these courts and hold that the substantially identical language of the Maryland policy should be construed as setting forth only a choice of law provision to be applied regardless of where the claim is filed, and only restricting benefits to the extent that they are payable under Wisconsin law, not restricting coverage to claims filed in Wisconsin. This approach is consistent with the general principle previously noted that where the language of an insurance policy is capable of more than one interpretation it should be construed against the insurer and in favor of coverage. *Outboard Marine Corp.*, 154 Ill.2d at 108, 180 Ill.Dec. 691, 607 N.E.2d at 1212; *Progressive Universal Insurance Co.*, 347 Ill.App.3d at 414, 282 Ill.Dec. 636, 806 N.E.2d at 1227. This approach further comports with the well established principle that "if an insurer does not intend to insure against a risk which is likely to be inherent in the business of the insured, it should specifically exclude such risk from the coverage of the policy," which Maryland could easily enough have done. *University of Illinois v. Continental Casualty Co.*, 234 Ill.App.3d 340, 351, 175 Ill.Dec. 324, 599 N.E.2d 1338, 1346 (1992), quoting *Bremen State Bank v. Hartford Accident & Indemnity Co.*, 427 F.2d 425, 427 (7th Cir.1970); accord *Sieman v. Postorino Sandblasting & Painting Co.*, 111 Mich.App. at 718, 314 N.W.2d at 740 ("the insurer could have written into the policy an express exclusion of coverage under even the law of Wisconsin for cases where

Continued

an employee proceeds in the Michigan compensation system"). Finally, this approach also avoids having an employer's coverage rest totally on the whim of the employee in his choice of the forum state in which to process the claim. See *Duvall*, 117 N.H. at 226, 372 A.2d at 266 ("that the employee, for reasons of his own, chose to file in New Hampshire, is a happenstance which is irrelevant to the question of the insurer's liability"); *Weinberg*, 368 Pa. at 82, 81 A.2d at 909 ("we do not think it can be fairly inferred from the terms of the policy, or that the parties thereto could have contemplated, that the insurer assumed the obligation to save plaintiffs harmless only in case the injured employee instituted proceedings to recover compensation in the state specified as providing the worker's compensation law in the plan and not if, for some purpose of her own, she chose to proceed in some other jurisdiction").

Maryland, however, argues that the appellant's contentions ignore the Illinois case of *Ohio Casualty Co. v. Southwell*, 284 Ill.App.3d 1019, 220 Ill.Dec. 492, 673 N.E.2d 404 (1996). But we fail to see the applicability of that case to the situation here. In our view, the *Southwell* court never sought or claimed to apply Illinois' substantive law in construing the language of the policy. Rather, it felt compelled to apply California substantive law under Illinois' internal conflict of law rules. *Southwell* held that because all the significant contacts with respect to the policy occurred in California, California law controlled the interpretation of the provisions of the policy. *Southwell* concluded that California substantive law must control because California was the domicile of the insured, its employee, and was where the insurance policy was negotiated and delivered. Concluding that the interpretation of that provision was articulated in the California case of Travelers, *Southwell* held: "Pursuant to California law, *Ohio Casualty* the insurer cannot be held liable for *Southwell*'s Illinois workers' compensation claim because the Ohio policy exclusively covers liability for injury under the workers' compensation laws of California." (Emphasis added.) *Southwell*, 284 Ill.App.3d at 1024, 220 Ill.Dec. 492, 673 N.E.2d at 408.

Thus, as Szarek contends, the result in *Southwell* hinged exclusively on the resolution of a choice of law question, the answer to which mandated that California law be used to interpret any and all provisions in the policy. The fact that the *Southwell* court concluded that California's interpretation would not violate Illinois' public policy (*Southwell*, 284 Ill.App.3d at 1023–24, 220 Ill.Dec. 492, 673 N.E.2d at 406–08) only means that California's interpretation did not offend our constitution or any existing statutes or precedents (*American Federation of State, County & Municipal Employees v. State of Illinois*, 124 Ill.2d 246, 260, 124 Ill.Dec. 553, 529 N.E.2d 534, 540 (1988)), which in no way denotes that it determined that Illinois courts, free to consider the meaning of the provision as a matter of first impression under

Continued

Illinois law, should follow California's lead. See *General Casualty Co. v. Carroll Tiling Service, Inc.*, 342 Ill.App.3d 883, 896, 277 Ill.Dec. 616, 796 N.E.2d 702, 712 (2003) (concluding that *Southwell*, resolved by the choice of law determination, was of no significance in interpreting Illinois law).

Finally, Maryland would not have us reach our coverage conclusion by asserting that the cases on which we rely are all premised on the employer being left uninsured in the event the court did not impose coverage on the insurer. See generally *Weinberg*, 368 Pa. 76, 81 A.2d 906; *Kacur*, 253 Md. 500, 254 A.2d 156. As Maryland puts it, "each case . . . stands for the proposition that where an employer would be left uninsured by a contrary holding, public policy will expand a workers compensation policy to cover a claim brought in a non-covered state. No similar situation exists here, since SZAREK is insured through RMA for the claim filed under Illinois law." In support of that contention, Maryland cites to language from *Duvall*, where the court said: "Had the employer desired coverage under the law of New Hampshire it could have obtained such protection through the payment of the additional premium." *Duvall*, 117 N.H. at 227–28, 372 A.2d at 267. We are unpersuaded. It is the specific provisions of the policy that must control, not the availability of other coverage. Moreover, we find Maryland's attempted use of *Duvall* to be disingenuous. The *Duvall* court made its quoted statement, not in response to an employer's claim that it should provide benefits under the policy, but in opposition to the employer's argument that it should indemnify beyond the benefit limits provided under the worker's compensation law of the state specified in the policy. The *Duvall* court still held that the insurer was required to indemnify the employer up to the benefit limit under the worker's compensation law of the state specified in the policy, even though the employee filed in his claim in a different state. *Duvall*, 117 N.H. at 226–27, 372 A.2d at 266–67.

For all the foregoing reasons, we reverse the judgment of the circuit court and remand for a determination as to whether Cholewinski's injuries would have been compensable under Wisconsin''s worker's compensation act. Should the circuit court find that claim eligible for compensation under Wisconsin law, judgment should be entered for Szarek and damages computed based on the benefits schedule of the Wisconsin's worker's compensation act. Finally, if determined by the trial court to be appropriate, the damages may be divided between RMA and Maryland based on established principles of equitable contribution between insurers with overlapping coverage. See *Progressive Insurance Co. v. Universal Casualty Co.*, 347 Ill.App.3d 10, 19, 282 Ill.Dec. 953, 807 N.E.2d at 585 (2004).

Reversed and remanded with instructions.

Continued

Case Questions

1. According to Szarek which state's laws should be followed in paying out the workers' compensation claim in this case?
2. Which party did the chancery court agree with? What reason did that court give for its decision?
3. What does the court of appeals say about construing the unambiguous terms of an insurance policy?
4. What is a "choice of law" provision as it is explained in this case?

ETHICAL CONSIDERATION:
Insurance Fraud

As a legal professional, you must always be on guard for cases that might involve insurance fraud. There are many people who see defrauding an insurance company as a "victimless" crime. See Exhibit 7-6. After all, the insurance company is a large, faceless corporation and committing fraud against such an organization might not seem to be as bad as stealing from a neighbor, at least to some people. There are often signs that a client is engaging in insurance fraud. Some of these signs include:

- The number of days worked and the salary claimed are not consistent with the type of job
- Items on documentation have been crossed out, erased, or been covered with white-out
- The worker's occupation is inconsistent with the employer's business
- Injured worker moves out of state shortly after filing the claim
- There are no witnesses to the injury
- Worker cannot recall specific details of the incident or gets important details wrong

In addition to these warning signs, a paralegal should also be aware that there are medical providers who engage in fraud, often without the client's knowledge. Indicators of medical-provider fraud include:

- A billed service that the injured worker does not recall having received is included

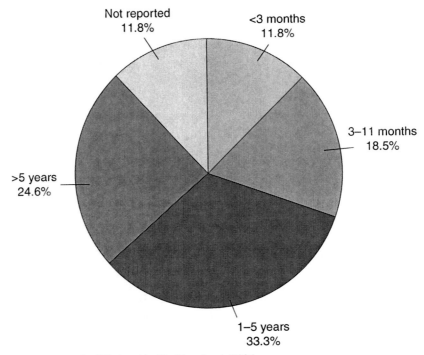

EXHIBIT 7-6 Worker Health Chartbook 2004.

- The medical reports are almost identical even though they are for different patients
- The health-care costs are much higher than one would expect
- The frequency or duration of treatments is much higher than would be expected for a non-catastrophic condition
- Large volume of prescription drugs for relatively minor injury are included

CHAPTER SUMMARY

Insurance is a contract between an insurance company and an insured. Employers obtain workers' compensation insurance in order to meet statutory requirements. They have three possible options in order to satisfy their legal obligations: they can enroll in the state-based program; they can obtain private insurance, or they can become self-insurers. State Workers' Compensation Boards regulate insurance policies and companies, making sure that all policies meet the mandatory minimums. When there are ambiguities in a policy, they are resolved in favor of employees.

KEY TERMS

Duty to defend
Exclusion
Fiduciary
Indemnify
Premium
Self-insurer
Subrogation
Underwriting

REVIEW QUESTIONS

1. Do all workers' compensation insurance policies contain a duty to defend clause?
2. Can an insurance company draft its exclusions in such a way that it prevents most employees from being covered?
3. Explain the basic features of an insurance policy.
4. What is a premium?
5. What is a fiduciary?
6. What is subrogation?
7. Explain the state-mandated features of a workers' compensation insurance policy.
8. What are limited policies?
9. Under what circumstances may a company obtain multiple workers' compensation insurance policies?
10. What are the three basic options open to an employer who wishes to comply with state law requiring workers' compensation insurance coverage?
11. Explain state-based workers' compensation insurance programs?
12. What is underwriting?
13. Explain how a company might qualify to become a self-insurer.
14. How are premiums calculated?
15. How do insurance companies set their rates?

16. What rules and regulations govern font sizes in insurance policies?
17. What are policy exclusions?
18. Explain an insurance company's duty to defend under a workers' compensation insurance policy.

QUESTIONS FOR REFLECTION

1. What principles do courts follow in construing the provisions of insurance policies?
2. Do the laws applying to self-insurance unduly favor large companies over those with smaller assets?

WEB SITES

North Carolina Industrial Commission
http://www.comp.state.nc.us/

Pennsylvania Department of Labor and Industry
http://www.dli.state.pa.us/landi/cwp/view.asp?a=151&q=209835

Virginia Workers' Compensation Commission
http://www.vwc.state.va.us/

Labor Commission of Utah
http://laborcommission.utah.gov/IndustrialAccidents/index.html

Vermont Department of Labor and Industry
http://www.state.vt.us/labind/wcindex.htm

PRACTICAL APPLICATIONS

1. Locate your state's statutes regarding the obligation of employers to provide workers' compensation insurance coverage. What options are available for employers in your state?
2. What type of notice are employers in your state required to post concerning workers' compensation coverage? Do they resemble the notices offered in this chapter from New Jersey or Massachusetts?

END NOTES

[1] McKinney's Workers' Compensation Law § 52.
[2] See *http://www.comp.state.nc.us/ncic/pages/insurer.htm*.

[3] *Fieldcrest Cannon, Inc. v. Fireman's Fund Ins. Co.*, 124 N.C.App. 232, 477 S.E.2d 59 (N.C.App.1996).

[4] 357 Ill.App.3d 584, 829 N.E.2d 871, 293 Ill.Dec. 946 (Ill.App. 1 Dist.2005).

Online Companion™
For additional resources, please go to
http://www.paralegal.delmar.cengage.com

Appealing a Workers' Compensation Award

CHAPTER 8

CHAPTER OBJECTIVES

At the completion of this chapter, you should be able to:

- Explain the function of the Workers' Compensation Appeals Board
- Describe the purpose of a petition for reconsideration
- Define the actions that a Workers' Compensation Board may take when it has appellate authority
- Explain the organization of the state court appellate system
- Describe the powers of appellate courts

INTRODUCTION

In Chapter 6, we addressed the process of presenting a hearing to an Administrative Law Judge. We saw that these hearings are conducted in ways that are similar to a trial: Evidence is presented and witnesses testify. However, there are important differences between workers' compensation hearings and regular trials. For example, the evidentiary rules are more informal and these hearings are not routinely held in courtrooms, but in office buildings. The appeal of a workers' compensation case has the same kinds of similarities and differences. In some ways, appealing a workers' compensation case is very similar to any appeal, but there are also important differences. In this chapter, we will examine both the similarities and critical differences in appellate review of workers' compensation cases. We will also address the issue that crops up in virtually every workers' compensation case: settlement.

SETTLEMENT IN WORKERS' COMPENSATION CLAIMS

There is a strong preference for settling all types of cases, and workers' compensation disputes are no exception. Although there is an understandable urge to think that settling workers' compensation cases would strongly resemble settlement issues in any other civil action, workers' compensation claims raise unique issues. For one thing, the settlement is based on determining the worker's point of maximum medical improvement, whether that means returning to the full range of activities that the worker enjoyed before the injury or some reduced capacity that might well last the remainder of the worker's life. Workers' compensation is designed to replace the income lost from an injury, as well as to provide medical services. See Exhibit 8-1. It was never designed to provide a financial windfall to injured workers. In addition to considerations of the medical and supplemental benefits for injured workers, there are also important issues concerning the payment for legal services incurred by the employee, the employer, and the insurance company.

When an attorney represents the plaintiff in a personal injury case, it is common for the attorney to be paid by **contingency fee**. In a contingency fee arrangement, the attorney receives some percentage of the total recovery. The most common percentage is 33 1/3 percent. Suppose that the plaintiff receives a total recovery of $100,000. The attorney representing the plaintiff would be entitled to $33,333. However, attorney's fees, like many other issues, take on a new complexity in workers' compensation cases. In the simplest example, an injured worker receives a lump sum payment of $50,000. A lump sum payment is an amount paid by the employer (or employer's insurer) in exchange for the worker's dismissal of his or her claim. If an attorney were to receive the traditional 33 1/3 percent of the recovery, the worker's lump sum amount would be $33,350 with $16,650 going to the attorney. Although this is the accepted rate in personal injury and other types of civil cases, many states have balked at allowing such a high rate of recovery in workers' compensation cases. The theory underlying workers' compensation benefits is to provide a safety net for injured or ill workers, and many see such a large recovery by the worker's attorney as a windfall. Attorneys, on the other hand, point out that they provide a nec-

> **SIDEBAR**
>
> "The law favors the settlement of disputes . . . and there exists a strong public policy to minimize needless litigation."[1]

■ **Contingency fee**

A fee that is conditioned on an award. When an award is made, the attorney's fee is based on a percentage of the total award; when no award is made, the attorney is not entitled to any fee.

EXHIBIT 8-1 Settlement Agreement and Application for Approval of Settlement Agreement (Ohio). *Reprinted courtesy of the Ohio Bureau of Workers' Compensation.*

Employer Signature
(Required by ORC 4123.65 unless the employer is no longer doing business in Ohio)

Instructions

Please check one of the following boxes and sign below. Your signature does not waive the employer's right to withdraw consent to the settlement by providing written notice to the employee and the BWC administrator within 30 days after the administrator issues the approval of the settlement agreement.

☐ A. The employer is supportive of and agreeable to a settlement up to the amount listed on the front of this application.

☐ B. The employer does not agree with the requested settlement terms, but will participate with the BWC in the negotiation process.

☐ C. The employer is supportive of and agreeable to settlement of the claims listed on the front of this application. However, the employer will not participate in the settlement negotiations and requests the BWC to negotiate the settlement on behalf of the employer.

☐ D. The employer is not agreeable to settlement of the claim(s) listed on the front of this application.

By signing this agreement, an employer that is currently self-insured acknowledges its obligation to reimburse BWC for the portion of the settlement amount allocated to DWRF costs of the above-referenced claim(s). The DWRF portion of the settlement will be billed to the self-insuring employer, even if the injured worker has not yet been determined to be permanently and totally disabled or currently eligible for DWRF benefits.

Employer signature	Title	Date
Telephone number ( )	Fax number ( )	

Settlement Agreement and Release

As set forth in this agreement, the injured worker for and in consideration of the receipt of the settlement amount approved by the BWC, which sum will be paid from the appropriate fund on behalf of the employer after approval by the BWC administrator, unless within 30 days after such approval the administrator, the employer or the injured worker, withdraws consent to, or unless the Industrial Commission of Ohio (IC) disapproves the agreement, does hereby for him/herself and for anyone claiming by, through or under him/her, forever release and discharge the above referenced employer, its officers, employees, agents, representatives, successors and assigns, the IC, the BWC, the appropriate fund, and all persons, firms or corporations from any or all claims, demands, actions or causes of action incurred on or prior to the date of the approval of this agreement, arising out of Ohio Revised Code Chapter 4121. or 4123., which he/she now has or which he/she hereafter claim to have, whether known or unknown by reason of or in any manner growing out of the claims or parts thereof set forth above. The injured worker further understands and agrees that any amount paid pursuant to this agreement is subject to any valid court-ordered child support. The persons involved with filing this settlement agree that if any claim(s) or part of any claim(s) being settled has been recognized or allowed, then the cost of all medical services, hospital bills, drugs and medicines with date(s) of service or filling of related prescriptions (not to exceed a 30-day supply) provided to the injured worker before the effective settlement date, shall be the responsibility of the state insurance fund, provided such costs result from the allowed conditions of the claims and are properly payable under current medical payment guidelines. The costs of medical services hospital bills, drugs and medicines (not to exceed a 30-day supply) provided to the injured worker on or after the effective date of the settlement date are the responsibility of the injured worker.

☐ By initialing this box, the injured worker acknowledges he or she has read and understands the above statement.

Also as set forth above, the injured worker understands that any settlement amounts allocated for future medical services must be used for medical services before Medicare will consider payment for services for the conditions of the workers' compensation claim.

Settlement of any claim(s) included in this agreement in no way impairs BWC's statutory rights to subrogation recovery. Also, be advised that upon a finding of fraud, the administrator retains the right to rescind this settlement agreement and re-open the claim for an administrative overpayment hearing and referral for criminal prosecution.

Injured worker signature	Date

Power of Attorney

By signing below the injured worker grants a limited power of attorney to the attorney of record for the purpose of receiving the warrant issued because of this settlement agreement.

Injured worker signature	Date
Representative signature	Date

EXHIBIT 8-1 (*Continued*)

essary service and that they should be paid commensurate with their training, ability, experience and, most of all, the protection that they offer when a lone worker goes against a large company and an even larger insurance company. But commentators have pointed out for years that the procedures involved in workers' compensation cases aren't as extensive and usually do not require the same level of intensive discovery and trial preparation as a large civil case and the attorney's fee should reflect that reality. To that end, many states have placed caps on attorneys' fees that limit total recovery to as low as 20 percent. Consider Example 8-1.

Compromise and Release

A **compromise and release** (C&R) is a resolution of a workers' compensation case where the worker releases the claim against the company in exchange for a monetary award. State law governs how a C&R can be created, usually by requiring that the settlement involve a periodic monetary payment to the injured worker over months and even years and that the final settlement must be approved by the Workers' Compensation Board. Many states have either expressly or indirectly discouraged **lump sum** awards because of the temptation that a sudden influx of money can have for some workers. In a case of a periodic payment, the employee would receive a fixed payment and so would his or her attorney.

In creating a C&R, all parties to the litigation must sign and agree to the terms. See Exhibit 8-2. This includes not only the injured worker, but also the employer and the employer's insurance company. The C&R must also be submitted to the Administrative Law Judge or Workers' Compensation Board for final approval. Once approved, the parties are not allowed to renege on the agreement. The injured worker cannot, for example, decide to press his or her case after receiving several payments and then deciding that the amount is not sufficient. However, the C&R can be set aside if the worker was defrauded or tricked into entering the agreement in the first place.

> **Compromise and release**
> Settlement of a workers' compensation case where the employer or insurer pays a specific award to the employee in exchange for the employee's dismissal of his or her claim.

> **Lump sum**
> A single award of money that cancels out the employer's and insurer's obligation to provide any additional payments or benefits in the future for a contested claim.

EXAMPLE 8-1

Erica has settled her case for a weekly award of $233.45. How much will she actually receive if she has an attorney who represented her and the state has enacted a 20 percent cap on attorneys' fees?

Answer: Erica will receive 80 percent of the settlement amount, or $186.76. Her attorney will receive weekly payments of $46.69.

```
                    STATE OF CALIFORNIA
                DIVISION OF WORKERS' COMPENSATION
                WORKERS' COMPENSATION APPEALS BOARD

COMPROMISE AND RELEASE


                                    Case No(s). _____

                                    Social Security No. _____


_____   _____
Applicant (Employee)                Address


_____   _____
Correct Name(s) of Employer(s)      Address(es)


_____   _____
Correct Name(s) of Insurance Carrier(s) Claims Administrator(s)   Address(es)

1. The employee, born _____, claims that he/she was employed at _____,
                                                                              (city)
   _____, as a(n) _____ by the employer(s), and claims to have sustained
      (state)                (occupation)
   injury(ies) arising out of and in the course of employment:
        (State with specificity the date(s) of injury(ies) and what part(s) of body, conditions or systems are being settled.)

   on _____ to _____

   on _____ to _____

   on _____ to _____

   on _____ to _____

   on _____ to _____

        Body parts, conditions and systems may not be incorporated by reference to medical reports.

2. Upon approval of this compromise agreement by the Workers' Compensation Appeals Board or a workers' compensation
   administrative law judge and payment in accordance with the provisions hereof, the employee releases and forever discharges
   the above-named employer(s) and insurance carrier(s) from all claims and causes of action, whether now known or ascertained
   or which may hereafter arise or develop as a result of the above-referenced injury(ies), including any and all liability of the
   employer(s) and the insurance carrier(s) and each of them to the dependents, heirs, executors, representatives, administrators
   or assigns of the employee.  Execution of this form has no effect on claims that are not within the scope of the workers'
   compensation law or claims that are not subject to the exclusivity provisions of the workers' compensation law, unless
   otherwise expressly stated.

3. This agreement is limited to settlement of the body parts, conditions, or systems and for the dates of injury set forth in
   Paragraph No. 1 despite any language to the contrary in this document or any addendum.


DWC WCAB FORM 15 (Rev. 10/2005) (Page 1 of 3)
```

EXHIBIT 8-2 Compromise and Release (California).

Factors to Consider Before Attempting to Settle

All of the parties to a workers' compensation claim will spend some time evaluating the possibility of settling the case before taking it to a full hearing.

Applicant/Employee: _____ WCAB No(s). _____

4. Unless otherwise expressly stated, approval of this agreement RELEASES ANY AND ALL CLAIMS OF APPLICANT'S DEPENDENTS TO DEATH BENEFITS RELATING TO THE INJURY OR INJURIES COVERED BY THIS COMPROMISE AGREEMENT. The parties have considered the release of these benefits in arriving at the sum in Paragraph No. 7. *Any addendum duplicating this language pursuant to* Sumner v WCAB, *48 CCC 369 (1983), is unnecessary and shall not be attached.*

5. Unless otherwise expressly ordered by the Workers' Compensation Appeals Board or a workers' compensation administrative law judge, approval of this agreement does not release any claim applicant may have for vocational rehabilitation benefits or supplemental job displacement benefits.

6. The parties represent that the following facts are true: (If facts are disputed, state what each party contends under Paragraph No. 9.)

   EARNINGS AT TIME OF INJURY $_____

   TEMPORARY DISABILITY INDEMNITY PAID $_____ Weekly Rate $_____

   Period(s) Paid _____

   PERMANENT DISABILITY INDEMNITY PAID $_____ Weekly Rate $_____

   Period(s) Paid _____

   TOTAL MEDICAL BILLS PAID $_____ Total Unpaid Medical Expense to be Paid By: _____

   Unless otherwise specified herein, the employer will pay no medical expenses incurred after approval of this agreement.

7. The parties agree to settle the above claim(s) on account of the injury(ies) by the payment of the **SUM OF** $_____. The following **amounts are to be deducted** from the settlement amount:

   $_____ for permanent disability advances through _____
   (date)

   $_____ for temporary disability indemnity overpayment, if any.

   $_____ payable to _____

   $_____ payable to _____

   $_____ payable to _____

   $_____ payable to _____

   $_____ requested as applicant's attorney's fee.

   LEAVING A BALANCE OF $_____, after deducting the amounts set forth above and less further permanent disability advances made after the date set forth above. Interest under Labor Code §5800 is included if the sums set forth herein are paid within 30 days after the date of approval of this agreement.

8. Liens not mentioned in Paragraph No. 7 are to be disposed of as follows (Attach an addendum if necessary):

DWC WCAB FORM 15 (Rev. 10/2005) (Page 2 of 3)

EXHIBIT 8-2   *(Continued)*

The worker might wish to settle rather than risk the possibility of receiving no award, or, more likely, a substantially reduced award after a hearing. The employer and the employer's insurer will consider settling the case prior to a hearing to avoid the possibility of being saddled with a heavy award. But there

```
Applicant/Employee: _____  WCAB No(s). _____
```

9. The parties wish to settle these matters to avoid the costs, hazards and delays of further litigation, and agree that a serious dispute exists as to the following issues (initial only those that apply). **ISSUES NOT INITIALED BY ALL PARTIES ARE NOT INCLUDED WITHIN THIS SETTLEMENT.**

```
___  ___  earnings
___  ___  temporary disability          COMMENTS
___  ___  jurisdiction
___  ___  apportionment
___  ___  employment
___  ___  injury AOE/COE
___  ___  serious and willful misconduct
___  ___  discrimination (Labor Code §132a)
___  ___  statute of limitations
___  ___  future medical treatment
___  ___  other _____
___  ___  other _____
___  ___  permanent disability _____
___  ___  self-procured medical treatment, except as provided in Paragraph 7
___  ___  vocational rehabilitation benefits/supplemental job displacement benefits
```

Any accrued claims for Labor Code Section 5814 penalties are included in this settlement unless expressly excluded.

10. It is agreed by all parties hereto that the filing of this document is the filing of an application, and that the WCAB may in its discretion set the matter for hearing as a regular application, reserving to the parties the right to put in issue any of the facts admitted herein and that if hearing is held with this document used as an application, the defendants shall have available to them all defenses that were available as of the date of filing of this document, and that the WCAB may thereafter either approve this Compromise and Release or disapprove it and issue Findings and Award after hearing has been held and the matter regularly submitted for decision.

11. **WARNING TO EMPLOYEE: SETTLEMENT OF YOUR WORKERS' COMPENSATION CLAIM BY COMPROMISE AND RELEASE MAY AFFECT OTHER BENEFITS YOU ARE RECEIVING OR MAY BECOME ENTITLED TO RECEIVE IN THE FUTURE FROM SOURCES OTHER THAN WORKERS' COMPENSATION, INCLUDING BUT NOT LIMITED TO SOCIAL SECURITY, MEDICARE AND LONG-TERM DISABILITY BENEFITS.**

THE APPLICANT'S (EMPLOYEE'S) SIGNATURE MUST BE ATTESTED TO BY TWO DISINTERESTED PERSONS OR ACKNOWLEDGED BEFORE A NOTARY PUBLIC

By signing this agreement, applicant (employee) acknowledges that he/she has read and understands this agreement and has had any questions he/she may have had about this agreement answered to his/her satisfaction.

Witness the signature hereof this _____ day of _____, 20_____, at _____

```
_____ (Date)    _____ (Date)
Witness 1                          Applicant (Employee)
_____ (Date)    _____ (Date)
Witness 2                          Attorney for Applicant
_____ (Date)    _____ (Date)
Interpreter                        Attorney for Defendant
                                   _____ (Date)
STATE OF CALIFORNIA
County of _____
```

On this ____ day of _____, 20___, before me, _____, a Notary Public in and for the said County and State, residing therein, duly commissioned and sworn, personally appeared _____ known to me to be the person(s) whose name(s) is/are subscribed to the within Instrument, and acknowledged to me that _he_ executed the same.

In Witness Whereof, I have hereunto set my hand and affixed my official seal the day and year in this Certificate first above written.

_____
Notary Public in and for said County and State of California

DWC WCAB FORM 15 (Rev. 10/2005) (Page 3 of 3)

EXHIBIT 8-2 (Continued)

are other factors for the parties to consider than the possible award amount. The employer and employer's insurer might also consider the costs involved in litigating the claim. Attorneys who represent insurance companies and employers routinely bill by the hour and are not paid on a contingency fee

EXHIBIT 8-3

Billable Hours for A & B Insurance Defense Firm.

1.2	Initial meeting with XYZ Insurance adjuster and discussion of the issues raised by Jane Doe's claim
2.4	Review of medical records, employer's report of injury
1.4	Personal conference with DEF Employer, Inc., Mr. Wilson, who initially investigated injury and took photos of accident area
3.8	Legal research into issues of potential personal injury claim taken outside of workers' compensation claim because of possible product liability issue due to defective chopping and binding machinery that caused injury to Jane Doe
.4	Telephone conference with Mr. Roe, attorney representing Ms. Doe, and discussion of issues raised in her case
4.3	Travel to and active participation in deposition of Ms. Doe
1.0	Prepared deposition digest of Ms. Doe's testimony
.3	Dictation of potential strategies to be used in hearing, based on Ms. Doe's responses at deposition and her obvious discomfort with specific questions
14.8	Subtotal

basis. They will be paid whether the employer and insurer win the case or not. Some law firms have very high hourly rates and a claim that lingers for months could easily rack up enormous legal fees. Consider Exhibit 8-3.

If the law firm that provided the itemized statement of billable hours charges $250 per hour, then the bill for the services provide to date is $3,700. In a contested case, the events—and the billable hours—will continue to mount until the employer or the insurance company might decide that it would be more cost-effective to settle the case before incurring even more attorney's fees.

Evaluation of Claims for Settlement Purposes

In addition to the consideration of attorney's fees, the parties might also consider other issues before entering into settlement discussions. For instance, the attorneys for the insurer/employer and the employee would want to know all of the following:

- Is there a potential for offset by the employee receiving other benefits, such as Medicare, Social Security, personal insurance, or retirement benefits?
- How much has the insurer/employer paid out in medical compensation? (And how much more will be required?)
- Has the employee had other claims? (This could be an indication of a preexisting condition or even of fraud.)
- Is the employee currently employable in some capacity, even if he cannot return to his former occupation?

- What is the likelihood of future medical treatment? How extensive will this future medical treatment be?
- Is the employee facing bankruptcy? (He or she may wish to settle the case after the bankruptcy has been finalized.)

Creating a C&R Settlement

Once the parties have reviewed all of the facts of the case and negotiations have resulted in a settlement of all issues, the parties must then draft a C&R settlement statement to present to the board. The settlement statement must address all of the following issues:

- That all issues pending in the claim have been resolved
- That a specific party has assumed the responsibility for paying a specific amount to the injured worker at specific intervals (or in one lump sum payment, payable on a specific date and in a specific manner)
- That the employee has designated a beneficiary to receive any unpaid benefits upon the employee's death (if such payment are authorized)
- That all attorneys' fees have been satisfied[2]

THE WORKERS' COMPENSATION BOARD

Although states follow different rules and procedures when it comes to the powers, duties, and composition of Workers' Compensation Boards, there are some general components. Most Workers' Compensation Boards consist of seven or more people. These individuals have the responsibility and the power to regulate workers' compensation claims, set rules and regulations, and review decisions by Administrative Law Judges. They act much like an appellate court, reviewing decisions made in hearings and possessing the power to alter those decisions. The most common way for Workers' Compensation Boards to become involved in review of a hearing is through a petition for reconsideration.

Petition for Reconsideration

When one party loses at a workers' compensation hearing, the employee or employer has the right to file a **petition for reconsideration** by the entire Workers' Compensation Board. Within 15 days of the final decision by the ALJ in the hearing, the Board has the power to modify that decision. But the Board will only take that action if someone requests that it do so. The vehicle to make this request is the petition for reconsideration. If no petition is filed, then the Board is not authorized to take action and the original ruling remains in effect.

Petition for reconsideration
A request by a party for a review of a workers' compensation award.

Of course, simply because one of the parties requests a reconsideration does not mean that the Board will grant it. The Board might decide that the original decision in the case is the proper one and make no alterations to the findings. Once a petition is filed, the Board can take any of the following actions:

- Amend the original findings
- Modify the original findings
- Rescind the original findings
- Order a new hearing

The Board's powers to change the original ruling cover all issues raised in the original hearing. If there were multiple findings by the ALJ, and multiple decisions, the Board can amend, modify, or rescind each of them individually. The Board can even decide to modify part of the decision while leaving the rest unaffected.

Deadlines

All states have strict deadlines dictating exactly when a party can file for a petition for reconsideration and when this right has expired. In states that impose a 15-day deadline on petitions for reconsideration, for example, the rules refer to "calendar days," not "business days." A party counts all intervening days, including holidays and weekends, unless the last day falls on a weekend or holiday. In that event, the due date would be the next business day. Consider Example 8-2.

Checklist: Bringing an Appeal

We will assume that our client has lost his case before the Board and now wishes to bring an appeal. What steps are necessary to bring this appeal?

1. File a petition for review of the Board's decision.

    The party who loses in the hearing has a specific time period, usually 20 days from the date of the final ruling to file a petition for a review. If the party does not file the petition, he or she waives any further right to appeal. The petition for review requests the ALJ to reconsider the decision made at the hearing. Usually, the judges do not change their minds and this denial of the petition sets the stage for the rest of the appeal.

2. Include transcripts and other materials with the petition for review.

    In many cases, the party must request that a transcript of the hearing accompany the petition for review. Without the transcript, the judge will simply deny the petition.

> **EXAMPLE 8-2**
>
> Suppose that a final decision in a workers' compensation case was made Friday afternoon, September 5. What is the deadline for filing a petition for reconsideration?
>
> Calendar day computations include weekends and holidays. Fifteen days would include the 6th and 7th (Saturday and Sunday), the following week (the 8th through the 12th), the intervening weekend, and the following week. But these calculations put the 15th day on Saturday, September 20th. Does that mean that the party must file his or her petition for reconsideration on a Saturday? What if the Workers' Compensation Board does not have Saturday hours?
>
> There's a simple answer to this problem: Calendar days include all intervening weekends and holidays, unless the last day falls on a weekend or holiday. In that event, the due date is the next business day. If the due date falls on a Saturday, such as we have in this case, and the following Monday is a state or federal holiday, then the due date would be Tuesday. Of course, it would be prudent to file before the last day of the deadline period, but that is not always possible. In any event, under the 15-day rule, a party would have until Monday, September 22nd to file a petition for reconsideration.

3. Prepare written briefs.

   Once the petition for review has been filed and transcripts have been ordered, the Board will contact the parties and give them a specific deadline for filing written briefs either in support or in opposition to the petition for review. The usual pattern is to give the party requesting the petition 20 days to file a brief. Once filed, the opposing party is given 20 days to respond to the initial brief.

4. The Judge's decision

   The ALJ will file a written decision on the petition, and briefs, within 30 days of the receipt of the final brief in the case. After that, the case will be sent to the entire Board for review.

5. The Court of Appeals

   If the party wishes to contest the decision by the full Board, he or she can file an appeal in the state court of appeals. At that point, it becomes like any other appeal pending before that court and the litigants must follow the precise rules set out by that court. These rules are often quite different than the rules found in bringing an appeal before the Workers' Compensation Board.

THE WORKERS' COMPENSATION APPEALS BOARD

In some states, the final decision by an Administrative Law Judge goes directly to a Workers' Compensation Appeals Board—although they may be known by other names. The Appeals Board acts as the appellate court for workers' compensation decisions and may be a separate entity from the Workers' Compensation Board, or may be simply be another component of that Board. In some states, the Workers' Compensation Board reviews decisions by Administrative Law Judges, while in other states, that duty falls to the Workers' Compensation Appellate Board. For the sake of clarity, we will refer to these as two separate entities (1) the Board, which oversees rule making and procedural and scheduling issues, and (2) a separate Workers' Compensation Appellate Board, which has the power to review the decisions by Administrative Law Judges, make its own finding,s and change the original decision.

The Appeals Board usually consists of five, seven, or nine judges, appointed by the government. They are comprised of odd-numbered groups, so that there is little possibility of a tie when they all consider a single case. (The U.S. Supreme Court is configured with nine justices for the same reason.) The Appeals Board follows its own procedural rules. See Exhibits 8-4 and 8-5.

Procedure at the Workers' Compensation Appeals Board

The Appeals Board resembles the Court of Appeals and Supreme Court that we will discuss later in this chapter. Usually meeting as a panel of three to five judges, the appeals board considers appeals in workers' compensation cases that originally began as petitions for reconsideration and have now ripened into a full blown appeals. This occurs when a party is dissatisfied with the

---

EXHIBIT 8-4

Maine Workers' Compensation Appeals Board.

Appeals. Any party in interest may present a copy of the decision of a hearing officer or a decision of the board, if the board has reviewed a decision pursuant to section 320, to the clerk of the Law Court within 20 days after receipt of notice of the filing of the decision by the hearing officer or the board. Within 20 days after the copy is filed with the Law Court, the party seeking review by the Law Court shall file a petition seeking appellate review with the Law Court that sets forth a brief statement of the facts, the error or errors of law that are alleged to exist and the legal authority supporting the position of the appellant.[3]

```
                    FORM NO. 8-C
                 WORKERS' COMPENSATION
                    NOTICE OF APPEAL
               TO MISSOURI COURT OF APPEALS
               _____ DISTRICT

         BEFORE THE LABOR AND INDUSTRIAL RELATIONS COMMISSION
                        STATE OF MISSOURI
```

_____   )
)
)
                 Claimant,   )
) Injury No.: _____
vs.   )
)
)
_____   ) Appellate Court No.: _____
)
                 Employer.   )

Notice is hereby given that _____ appeals to the Missouri Court of Appeals, _____ District.

_____   _____
Date notice of Appeal filed   Signature of Attorney or Appellant
(to be filled in by Secretary of Commission)

(The appellant(s) must file the original notice of appeal and one copy for the Appellate Court with, and pay the docket fee required by court rule to, the secretary of the commission within the time specified by law. At the same time appellant must serve a copy of the notice of appeal on attorneys of record of all parties other than appellant(s), and on all parties not represented by an attorney. Proof of service shall be made on the original and copy to be filed with the commission.)

                              CASE INFORMATION

TYPE NAME AND BAR ENROLLMENT NUMBER   TYPE NAME AND BAR ENROLLMENT NUMBER
OF APPELLANT'S ATTORNEY   OF RESPONDENT'S ATTORNEY
                                             *List additional respondents on page two of this form

_____   _____

Street _____   Street _____

City _____   City _____

State _____ Zip Code _____   State _____ Zip Code _____

Telephone _____   Telephone _____

TYPE NAME OF APPELLANT   TYPE NAMES OF

_____   Employee: _____

Street _____   Dependents: _____

City _____   Employer: _____

State _____ Zip Code _____   Insurer: _____

                                                      Form 8-C (04-00) AI

EXHIBIT 8-5 Workers' Compensation Appeals Board, Application for Adjudication of Claim.

Date of Commission Award or Decision: _____

Date and County of Accident: _____

(Attach copy of Commission Award or Decision)

Second Injury Fund Involved: ☐ Yes ☐ No

DIRECTIONS TO COMMISSION

A copy of the notice of appeal and the docket fee shall be mailed forthwith to the clerk of the appellate court. The record on appeal shall be prepared and certified within such time as to enable timely filing by the appellant.

PROOF OF SERVICE

I have this day served a copy of this notice of appeal on each of the following persons at the address stated by _____ *(ordinary mail, certified mail, personal service)*:

_____
Signature of Attorney or Appellant

Dated: _____, 20_____

Form 8-C-2 (04-00) AI

EXHIBIT 8-5 *(Continued)*

Workers' Compensation Board's decision on a petition for reconsideration and that party files an appeal, requesting the Appeals Board to nullify the original decision and rule in its favor.

The Workers' Compensation Appeals Board has the exclusive jurisdiction to consider workers' compensation cases. Appellate jurisdiction is the power of a court or some other body to hear cases on appeal. The Workers' Compensation Appellate Board has limited authority. First, and perhaps most obviously, it may only consider issues raised in workers' compensation cases. Second, its authority is only triggered when a workers' compensation is concluded. The Appeals Board has no authority to intervene in a pending case and order a specific outcome. The Appeals Board must wait until the original case is concluded and the Administrative Law Judge has made findings of fact and ordered an award before it has appellate jurisdiction in the case. See Exhibit 8-6. As we have already seen, the Appeals Board may also lack authority in the case until the Workers' Compensation Board has also considered the case. Some states have this intervening step; others do not.

Before the Appeals Board can exercise jurisdiction, all issues pending in the case must be resolved and one party must then contest that award. Appellate jurisdiction has some other important considerations. For one thing, the Appeals Board is also limited in the actions that it may take in a case on appeal. The Appeals Board can amend, modify, rescind, or order a new hearing. Although that might seem to be a great deal of authority, in practical terms it means that the Appeals Board is limited to a review of the materials presented in the hearing, the law that applies to the case, and its own precedents. The Appeals Board does not conduct new hearings to make its findings. In fact, this is an important point to make about appellate courts in general. They are not authorized to consider new evidence. The Appeals Board does not conduct its own hearings, compel witnesses to testify, or consider evidence that was not presented in the original hearing. It is limited to the **record**, consisting of the transcript of the hearing, the evidence presented, and the findings of fact by the Administrative Law Judge. The record also consists of any judicial orders, findings of fact, summaries of evidence presented at the hearing and depositions used during the actual hearing. In workers' compensation hearings, the record can consist of a large number of documents and materials, all of which must be poured over before a final decision is given.

Record
The body of evidence, including testimony, medical evidence, and depositions, presented at a workers' compensation hearing.

All questions arising under this Article if not settled by agreements of the parties interested therein, with the approval of the Commission, shall be determined by the Commission, except as otherwise herein provided.[4]

EXHIBIT 8-6
Workers' Compensation Commission to Determine All Questions (North Carolina).

Actions by the Appeals Board

The members of the Appeals Board review the record created in the hearing before the ALJ and sometimes schedule oral argument where attorneys representing both sides argue why their clients should prevail. The Appeals Board also researches the law and reaches a decision about the propriety of the findings by the Administrative Law Judge. Finally, they write up their findings and distribute the written decision to the parties to explain the basis of their conclusions.

The Appeals Board has 90 days to issue a written decision after a case is filed. Their final written decision must include their findings of fact and discuss the law that applies to these facts. Most appellate courts issue written opinions. They do this so that the parties will understand the basis for the Board's ruling, and also to help guide other attorneys about future cases. Written decisions help parties understand why the Board made its decision, even if the parties are not in agreement with those reasons.

However, the appeals process is not concluded when the Appeals Board issues its written decision. In fact, in many ways, it is just beginning. The party who loses the appeal has the right to appeal to a higher court. Remember, our entire legal system is based on the premise that the actions of a lower court can be appealed to a higher court. The party who loses in the Appeals Board will have the opportunity of appealing to the Court of Appeals.

THE STATE COURT OF APPEALS

In this section, we will consider the structure of the appellate court system on the state level. Before we discuss the state appellate structure, we must first address a more fundamental question: How are the courts in the United States organized? See Exhibit 8-7.

The Organization of Court Systems in the United States

The organization of the court systems in the United States is based on a straightforward premise: The actions of one court can be reviewed (and changed) by another, higher court. Seen this way, the court system, whether

EXHIBIT 8-7

Appeals to the Court of Appeals (Colorado).

> (1) The final order of the director or the panel shall constitute the final order of the division. Any person in interest . . . being dissatisfied with any final order of the division, may commence an action in the court of appeals against the industrial claim appeals office as defendant to modify or vacate any such order.[5]

on the state or federal level, is arranged as a pyramid. At the base of the pyramid are the various trial courts or workers' compensation hearings. These are the courts with which most people are familiar. This is where witnesses testify and evidence is presented. However, there is another layer of the court system that is less well-known, but which is just as important. This is the appellate level.

In most civil and criminal cases, the state appellate court system has two levels: the Court of Appeals and the State Supreme Court. (Not all states use these precise names for these courts, but the basic features are the same, regardless of the actual name ascribed to the court.) Consider Example 8-3.

Courts of Appeal

When a case is appealed it is sent to an appellate court for review. An appellate court can review the case and is authorized to change the findings of the Workers' Compensation Board, but only for specific reasons. Because the employer is the one bringing the appeal in Example 8-3, it must allege grounds that show that the original decision, and subsequent approval by the Workers' Compensation Board, was incorrect and should be overturned.

All states and federal jurisdictions have appellate courts. In most states, the first level of the state appellate court is named the Court of Appeals. For most people, this is the first—and only—level of the appellate court system with which they will ever come into contact. In workers' compensation cases, the state Court of Appeals is actually the second level of the appellate system. The first was the Workers' Compensation Appeals Board. Under this system, a party

---

EXAMPLE 8-3

Brittany is a legal secretary. She has acquired carpal tunnel syndrome because of the extensive typing that she is required to perform on a daily basis. There have been many issues in this case and when attempts at mediating the dispute failed, the claim went to a hearing before an Administrative Law Judge. The judge determined that, based on the medical evidence, Brittany is entitled to permanent total disability and a physical loss rating of 20 percent usage for her wrists. The law firm's insurance carrier hotly disputed this case and when the Administrative Law Judge entered this order, the insurance carrier immediately filed a petition for reconsideration. The Board considered this petition and denied it. Then the employer brought an appeal to the full Appeals Board. The Board supported the original decision and refused to modify or change the award. At this point, if the employer wishes to continue the appellate process, it must enter the state court system.

who wishes to contest an award by a state Workers' Compensation Board would bring his or her appeal to the Appeals Board and then to the state Court of Appeals. There are some states that allow workers' compensation cases to skip the Court of Appeals entirely and go directly to the state Supreme Court, but most follow this format of Appeals Board to Court of Appeals.

Just as we saw in our discussion of Appeals Boards, Courts of Appeal do not retry cases. The losing party is not given the opportunity of presenting new witnesses and evidence that were not presented in the original case. In fact, witnesses never testify before an appellate court. The parties appear before a bank of judges who listen to arguments and consider the written record of what transpired during the hearing. If they believe that an error occurred, they are empowered to change the Board's findings and to modify or completely rescind an award.

Terminology in Appellate Courts

When a case reaches the state Court of Appeals and any higher courts, the terms used to describe the parties also change. Where the parties were originally referred to as employer and employee, or claimant and employer, now they are referred to by the terms "**appellant**" and "**appellee**." The party bringing the appeal is referred to as the appellant, while the party who won at the lower level is referred to as the appellee. This means that the terms can shift as the case moves up through the court system. Consider Example 8-4.

The State Supreme Court

The state Supreme Court is the highest court in the state and decides all issues of state law and the interpretation of the state constitution. It is, in almost all cases, the final authority for the interpretation of workers' compensation statutes. There is one other court that has the final authority on all issues of state and federal law, but we will reserve our discussion of the U.S. Supreme Court until later in this chapter.

■ **Appellant**
The person bringing the current appeal from an adverse ruling in the court below.

■ **Appellee**
The person who won in the lower court.

> **EXAMPLE 8-4**
>
> In Brittany's case, she won at both the original hearing and before the Workers' Compensation Appeals Board. The employer brings the case to the state Court of Appeals. What is Brittany's official term now?
>
> Brittany is the appellee. She won in the lower court, and therefore the employer is the appellant.

Not all states refer to their highest court by the name, "Supreme Court." In New York, for example, the state's highest court is called Superior Court. But by whatever name, this court operates on the same principles. For instance, all of these courts have the authority to decide which cases they will consider. That authority is referred to as **certiorari** or *cert*.

Certiorari

Simply because a party wishes to take his or her case to the state's highest court does not mean that the court will consider the appeal. A party can appeal an award from the Workers' Compensation Appeals Board and can also appeal to the state Court of Appeals, but to get any higher, the party must contend with cert. Certiorari, or cert, is the authority of an appellate court to decide which cases it will hear. Most state Courts of Appeal, on either the state or federal level, do not have this authority. They must hear all appeals brought to them, but state Supreme Courts and the U.S. Supreme Court have the authority to refuse to hear appeals. In fact, they routinely only grant cert in important cases, ones that have statewide impact or that raise important issues about state law. For instance, a state Supreme Court might grant cert in a workers' compensation case that challenges the constitutionality of state statutes.

State Supreme Courts and the United States Supreme Court routinely refuse to hear the vast majority of cases that apply to them for an appeal. In such a situation, they would "deny cert." This decision effectively terminates the appeal by refusing the parties to argue their case. If they "grant cert," on the other hand, it simply means that they will consider the appeal. It does not guarantee who will win. A party could easily request cert, have it granted, and then lose the appeal.

Grounds for Granting Cert

State Supreme Courts only grant cert in cases that the court considers to have important legal significance. Simply because the case is important to the parties themselves does not elevate it to this status. Instead, the parties must demonstrate, when they apply for cert, that the case has broader significance and is important to clear up some critical legal issue. If they are unable to show that significance, the state Supreme Court will probably deny cert.

The Federal Appellate Court System

The federal appellate court system is very similar to the state court system we have just discussed. However, instead of one Court of Appeals, there are 13, scattered across the country. They do not hear appeals from single states.

> **Certiorari**
> (Latin) A writ or order transferring a case from a lower court to a higher court for review.

Instead, the federal system has divided the entire United States and its territories into different circuits. Each Federal Circuit Court of Appeals hears appeals from any states in its region. Like state Courts of Appeal, these courts usually do not have cert authority and must hear every appeal brought before them. Appeals in federal workers' compensation cases go to these courts. There the courts consider issues brought under the Federal Employees' Compensation Act and related issues. Appeals from the Federal Circuit Court of Appeals are heard in the highest court in the federal system: the United States Supreme Court. See Exhibit 8-8 for a list of the federal courts.

The U.S. Supreme Court

The U.S. Supreme Court is the highest court on both the state and federal level. It is the final court of appeals for all federal cases and, when a party loses in a state Supreme Court, that party can appeal to the U.S. Supreme Court, too. However, just like state Supreme Courts, the U.S. Supreme Court turns down, or denies cert, in the vast majority of cases that come before it.

1st Circuit: Maine, Massachusetts, New Hampshire, Rhode Island, and Puerto Rico. Circuit court is located in Boston.

2nd Circuit: Connecticut, New York, and Vermont. Circuit court is located in New York.

3rd Circuit: Delaware, New Jersey, Pennsylvania, and the Virgin Islands. Circuit court is located in Philadelphia.

4th Circuit: Maryland, North Carolina, South Carolina, Virginia, and West Virginia. Circuit court is located in Richmond, Virginia.

5th Circuit: Louisiana, Mississippi, and Texas. Circuit court is located in New Orleans.

6th Circuit: Kentucky, Michigan, Ohio, and Tennessee. Circuit court is located in Cincinnati.

7th Circuit: Illinois, Indiana, and Wisconsin. Circuit court is located in Chicago.

8th Circuit: Arkansas, Iowa, Minnesota, Missouri, Nebraska, North Dakota, and South Dakota. Circuit court is located in St. Louis.

9th Circuit: Alaska, Arizona, California, Hawaii, Idaho, Montana, Nevada, Oregon, Washington, and Guam. Circuit court is located in San Francisco.

10th Circuit: Colorado, Kansas, New Mexico, Oklahoma, Utah, and Wyoming. Circuit court is located in Denver.

11th Circuit: Alabama, Florida, and Georgia. Circuit court is located in Atlanta.

The other two circuits are the District of Columbia Circuit and the Federal Circuit.

EXHIBIT 8-8

Federal Circuits in the United States.

The Court will only grant cert in cases that it considers to have national importance or when a question arises about the interpretation of the U.S or state Constitutions.

BRINGING AN APPEAL

When a party wishes to bring an appeal to a state or federal appellate courts, many of the same rules apply. We have already seen that some courts must grant cert before such an appeal can be brought. In all of these courts, some form of Notice of Appeal is required to actually begin the appellate process.

Notice of Appeal

In order to bring an appeal, a party must file a **Notice of Appeal** or similar document. This notice requests the appellate court to consider the case and also submits reasons why this court has appellate jurisdiction to consider the matter. For instance, the party might state that all issues in the case have been decided, that a final order has been entered in the case, and that the party has requested and has been denied a petition for reconsideration. A notice of appeal also requests that the lower court transfer the record to the appellate court so that the court may have all relevant materials on hand to consider the appeal. Following a notice of appeal, the parties will then file briefs.

> **Notice of Appeal**
> A notice that dockets a case with an appellate court and also requests the transfer of the record from a lower court to the appellate court.

Appellate Briefs

Once an appellate court has decided to hear an appeal, the parties must file briefs. The purpose of the appellant's brief is to explain why the party believes he or she should win. A brief argues a position by discussing the applicable law of the case, the facts of the underlying claim, and how the facts and law support the party's contentions.

Contents of an Appellate Brief

When a person wishes to contest the decision of a lower court, he or she must file a brief with the court. The basic elements of a brief include:
- Title Page
- Statement of Facts
- Enumerations of Error
- Argument
- Conclusion

Title Page

A brief must have a title, or cover page, listing the names of the parties, the appellate docket number, and the name of the court. In the case involving Brittany and her employer, the title page would be captioned, "Law Firm, Appellant v. Brittany Wilson, Appellee."

Statement of Facts

After the cover sheet, the legal team will prepare a Statement of Facts that describes the injury and any important events involved in the workers' compensation case. The statement of facts will discuss the circumstances surrounding the employee's injury, the employee's treatment, the medical evidence, the details of the hearing, and any other relevant details. A statement of facts must be accurate and conform to the record. However, having said that, obviously the parties will play up certain points over others in order to emphasize their positions.

Enumerations of Error

Once the party has set out the basic facts of the case, the next section of the appellate brief contains the Enumerations of Error—which may be known under other terms in different states. This is usually a single, boldfaced paragraph that explains why the court's ruling was wrong. See Exhibit 8-9 for an example.

Argument

The main part of an appellate brief is the Argument. It is this section where the parties set out the applicable law, discuss the facts, and attempt to persuade the court to enter a ruling in its favor. The argument can run to dozens of pages, although modern practice has seen a dramatic reduction in the argument portion of briefs and a tendency to greater conciseness in presenting a party's position.

Conclusion

The Conclusion is a short statement at the end of the brief that reiterates the party's position and requests specific relief. The conclusion reminds the court of the basis of the party's claim and sums up the major points of the party's contentions.

I. The Workers' Compensation Board was in error in granting an award to the employee, given that the available medical research contradicts the employee's claim of carpal tunnel syndrome.

EXHIBIT 8-9

Enumeration of Error.

POWERS OF APPELLATE COURTS

Now that we have discussed the procedure involved in bringing a case on appeal, we will address the specific actions that an appellate court can take in a case on appeal. The options for appellate courts are limited to the following:

- Affirming a decision
- Reversing a decision
- Modifying a decision
- Remanding a case for further proceedings

Affirming a Decision

If the state Supreme Court agrees that the Court of Appeals made the right ruling, it will **affirm** the case. This means that the court agrees with whatever decision was made in the immediate lower court. However, because an action may have gone through several courts and several different decisions, one must read the actual case before deciding exactly what affirming a decision means in a particular context. Consider Example 8-5.

Reversing a Decision

When a higher court reverses a lower court ruling, it issues an order reversing that court's decision and making the appellant the winner in the case. In Brittany's case, a **reverse** of the decision would mean that she would win her case in the state Supreme Court.

Modifying a Decision

Appellate courts are also authorized to create a hybrid decision that partly affirms and partly reverses a lower court's decision. This is common when

Affirm
The appellate court agrees with the verdict, or some ruling, entered in the lower court and votes to keep that decision in place.

Reverse
To reverse a decision is to set it aside; an appellate court disagrees with the verdict, or some ruling, in the lower court and overturns that decision.

EXAMPLE 8-5

Brittany won her case at the original hearing and in the Workers' Compensation Appeals Board. However, she lost in the Court of Appeals. What does it mean when the state Supreme Court affirms the decision?

Answer: It means that Brittany loses, because this court is affirming the decision of the immediate preceding court.

there are numerous issues in the appeal. Modifications are rarely seen in cases where there is only issue on appeal.

Remanding a Case

If an appellate court requires additional information, such as witness testimony or evidence, the only option for the court is to return the case to the Workers' Compensation Board for additional hearings. Appellate courts are not equipped to hear new testimony. When appellate courts **remand** a case, they return it to the Workers' Compensation Board with directions about what type of hearings the Board should have. Once that hearing is held, the case is transferred back to the Supreme Court for further consideration.

Remand

The appellate court requires additional information or an evidentiary hearing; it cannot conduct such a hearing itself, so it sends the case back to the trial court for the hearing and then considers the appeal based on that hearing.

CASE EXCERPT

GRANTING A PETITION FOR REHEARING
Matticks v. W.C.A.B. (Thomas J. O'Hora Co., Inc.)[6]

OPINION BY Judge SMITH-RIBNER.

Joseph Matticks (Claimant) petitions for review of the order of the Workers' Compensation Appeal Board (Board) affirming, as modified, an amended order of Workers' Compensation Judge Howard M. Spizer (WCJ) that granted Claimant's claim petitions for specific loss benefits and payment of medical bills. The issues include whether the Board had authority to grant a petition for rehearing filed by Thomas J. O'Hora Company, Inc. (Employer) and thereafter to reinstate its voluntarily withdrawn appeal; whether Employer waived its right to challenge the WCJ's decision; and whether the WCJ's denial of a credit to Employer for the total disability benefits it paid is supported by substantial, competent evidence.

I

On November 14, 1997, Claimant sustained a spinal cord injury in the course of his employment with Employer as a pipe fitter, and he began receiving total disability benefits pursuant to a notice of compensation payable (NCP), which indicated an average weekly wage of $1118.89 with a weekly compensation rate of $542. On September 22, 2000, Claimant filed three claim petitions seeking payment for nursing care provided by his wife, payment of medical bills from his physicians and benefits for a specific loss of use of both arms.

Continued

Claimant testified before WCJ Howard M. Spizer that he felt pain in his arms while carrying a heavy piece of pipe on November 14, 1997, and that he was admitted to the hospital the next day. Claimant underwent cervical surgery on November 21, 1997, but despite surgery he continued to have pain in his shoulder down into his hands and the conditions of his arms worsened. The WCJ observed that the four digits on Claimant's right hand were bent inward toward his palm and that the thumb was extended upward or outward. Claimant, among other things, was unable to close or open his hands and could not control the left hand or pick up any heavy items. After surgery Claimant participated, unsuccessfully, in a series of occupational therapies, and he relied upon his wife for all of his daily personal care and activities. Claimant's vehicle is equipped with a special key to start the ignition and a tripod over the steering wheel through which he can place his wrists to steer the vehicle, but someone has to open the car door and connect the seat belt.

After his injury, Claimant began treating for depression, and he suffered problems with his bowels and bladder. Claimant's wife, Nancy Matticks, testified that upon the recommendation of Claimant's physician, she quit her full-time job with J.C. Penny Telemarketing, earning $10.71 per hour to provide full personal care for Claimant. Jeanne Wonnell Frye, a registered nurse and an expert in life-care planning, testified on behalf of Claimant that a physical therapist, a certified nurse assistant or an LPN would be paid $11 per hour for the type of personal care services that Claimant's wife provided to him. She related that other than the ability to eat with his hands, Claimant cannot use his hands for other daily activities.

Claimant submitted various medical reports. Dr. Victor T. Ambruso, a board-certified neurosurgeon who examined Claimant in October 1999 and on October 5, 2000, opined that Claimant sustained a neck injury on November 14, 1997 and developed disc herniation and significant compression on the spinal cord over the next few days, eventually leading to central cord syndrome. By the time of the cervical surgery on November 21, 1997 damage to Claimant's spinal cord had already occurred because of a delay in diagnosis, which resulted in permanent plegia, i.e., paralysis, in both upper extremities. Dr. Ambruso stated that on October 5, 2000, Claimant complained of pain in his neck and arm and incontinence of the bowel and bladder and that his examination showed severe damage to the cervical cord starting at the C5-6 level caused by the cord damage sustained in the work injury. Claimant's loss of use of both arms resulted from the central cord syndrome's rendering his extremities useless for all practical intents and purposes, and he was totally disabled from the pain causing him to be totally dependent on his wife for his care. He suffered as well from depression.

Continued

Both parties submitted a medical report from Dr. Robert W. Mauthe, a board-certified physiatrist, who opined that Claimant lost the use of both hands for all practical intents and purposes due to the central cord syndrome. Also he suffered no separate and distinct injury apart from the specific loss due to disc herniation, and although the herniation was corrected the effects thereof remained. According to a report from Dr. Christopher Metzger, a board-certified orthopedic surgeon, Claimant was unable to perform his daily activities due to the central cord syndrome. K. Gendron, Ph.D., a psychologist, opined that Claimant was severely depressed due to the injury and the resulting physical limitations and that he would remain disabled for the rest of his life. Finally, Dr. Edwin Sherwin, a physician board-certified in internal medicine and gastroenterology who had treated Claimant since December 1998, opined that Claimant's abdominal pain, bladder retention and constipation were all related to the neurologic work injury.

In a decision circulated on January 8, 2002, the WCJ stated as follows in Finding of Fact 16:

> After reviewing the evidence this WCJ accepts as credible and persuasive, the report of Dr. Ambruso, is found to be convincing and persuasive, which has been identified as claimant's exhibit number six (6) in which he concludes that the claimant has sustained loss of use of both arms, and not only his hands, as a result of the work injury of November 14, 1997, resulting in a C5–6 central cord injury. This WCJ also finds persuasive and convincing all the other medical reports submitted by the claimant confirming that in addition to the loss of use of his arms, he also has other medical conditions which requires payment for medical services for treatment rendered by Dr. Gendron, for psychological purposes, Dr. Sherwin, for bowel and incontinence purposes, Dr. Kohn, for neurologic purposes, as well as his family physician Dr. Kaville. By accepting Dr. Ambruso's testimony as credible, this WCJ finds that the claimant sustained a specific loss of both arms for all practical intents and purposes, remains totally disabled from any type of employment and requires treatment with regard to the medical conditions set forth in reports submitted by the claimant.

In his amended order circulated on January 25, 2002, the WCJ awarded Claimant specific loss benefits for both arms in the amount of $542 per week for 820 weeks (or 410 weeks for each arm), pursuant to Section 306(c)(3) of the Workers' Compensation Act (Act), Act of June 2, 1915, P.L. 736, as amended, 77 P.S. § 513(3), and a forty-week healing period (twenty weeks for each arm) effective

Continued

October 5, 2000 (the date of Dr. Ambruso's last examination). Employer was ordered to pay the unpaid medical bills and to pay $100 per day seven days a week for personal care services provided by Claimant's wife, effective September 19, 2000. Employer appealed both decisions to the Board.

On June 17, 2002, the parties entered into a compromise and release agreement to resolve Claimant's claim petition for the payment of personal care services provided by his wife. Employer agreed to pay Claimant $350 per week for 820 weeks for personal care services from October 5, 2000 or for the duration of Claimant's life, whichever is shorter. In a decision circulated July 3, 2002, the WCJ approved the agreement and discharged Employer and its insurance carrier "from liability under the Act only as set forth more fully and at length in the compromise and release agreement." WCJ's July 3, 2002 Decision, Conclusion of Law No. 3. In the order, however, the WCJ stated that "[a]ll liability of the employer and/or its insurance carrier under the Act is fully discharged in exchange for the payment of the sums outlined in the compromise and release agreement. . . ."

On October 30, 2002, another attorney from the same law firm that represented Employer sent the Board a letter requesting that Employer's appeal be marked as withdrawn, and the Board withdrew the appeal and closed the record by order dated November 5, 2002. On November 15 Employer's attorney sent the Board another letter requesting reinstatement of the appeal because its withdrawal was made under the mistaken belief that the compromise and release agreement resolved all outstanding claims. The Board denied the request on July 11, 2003, but upon petition by Employer for rehearing/reconsideration the Board vacated its order on November 14 and reinstated Employer's appeal.

The Board subsequently reviewed the merits of the appeal, and it modified the WCJ's decision by granting Employer a credit for total disability benefits it paid under the NCP because Claimant had no disability separate and apart from his arms, which have resolved into a specific loss. In addition, the Board reduced Claimant's healing period for the specific loss of both arms to twenty weeks because the healing periods for both arms are to run simultaneously. The Board affirmed the WCJ's decision in all other respects.

The Court's review is limited to determining whether constitutional rights were violated, whether an error of law was committed, whether a practice or procedure of the Board was not followed or whether the findings of fact are supported by substantial evidence in the record. The appellate role is not to reweigh the evidence or to review witness credibility; rather, the appellate court must simply determine whether the WCJ's findings have the requisite measure of support in the record as

Continued

a whole. The WCJ is free to accept or to reject the testimony of any witness, including a medical witness, in whole or in part.

II

Claimant argues that the Board lacked authority to grant a rehearing and to reinstate Employer's appeal under Section 426 of the Act, added by Section 6 of the Act of June 26, 1919, P.L. 642, 77 P.S. § 871, which provides in part:

> The board, upon petition of any party and upon cause shown, may grant a rehearing of any petition upon which the board has made an award or disallowance of compensation or other order or ruling, or upon which the board has sustained or reversed any action of a referee; but such rehearing shall not be granted more than eighteen months after the board has made such award, disallowance, or other order or ruling, or has sustained or reversed any action of the referee.

Claimant asserts that the Board's order is not an "award or disallowance or other order or ruling" under Section 426. However, the Court is guided by the well-established rule of statutory construction that the clear and unambiguous language in a statute may not be disregarded under the pretext of pursuing its spirit. See Section 1921(b) of the Statutory Construction Act of 1972, 1 Pa.C.S. § 1921(b); *Borough of Glendon v. Department of Environmental Resources*, 145 Pa.Cmwlth. 238, 603 A.2d 226 (1992). Claimant's interpretation would result in a disregard of the express language of Section 426 and thereby reduce the words "other order or ruling" to mere surplusage. More importantly, the Board has broad discretion to grant a rehearing upon cause shown under Section 426 of the Act. *Cudo v. Hallstead Foundry, Inc.*, 517 Pa. 553, 539 A.2d 792 (1988).

In the compromise and release agreement, the parties agreed to discharge Employer from liability to pay for the personal care services provided by Claimant's wife. The two remaining claim petitions were not covered by the agreement. The Board found, and Claimant does not dispute, that Employer's new attorney immediately sought reinstatement of the appeal after realizing the error in withdrawing Employer's appeal. Claimant does not allege prejudice resulting from the Board's decision to grant a rehearing and to reinstate Employer's appeal, and because the undisputed facts in this case establish cause for granting Employer's request the Board did not abuse its discretion in reinstating the appeal.

Next, Claimant argues that Employer waived the issues of its entitlement to a credit for payment of total disability benefits and the propriety of the WCJ's award for the healing period because Employer only listed by numbers the challenged

Continued

findings of fact and conclusions of law in the notice of appeal form filed with the Board. The regulation at 34 Pa.Code § 111.11(a)(2) provides that an appeal must be filed "on a form provided by the Board or on a form containing substantially . . . [a] statement of the particular grounds upon which the appeal is based, including reference to the specific findings of fact which are challenged and the errors of law which are alleged" and that "[g]eneral allegations which do not specifically bring to the attention of the Board the issues decided are insufficient."

Claimant relies on this Court's recent holding in *Jonathan Sheppard Stables v. Workers' Compensation Appeal Board (Wyatt)*, 739 A.2d 1084, 1089 (Pa.Cmwlth.1999), wherein the Court concluded that the employer "utterly failed to raise any of the foregoing claims of error with any degree of specificity in its appeal to the Board." The employer in that case claimed that the WCJ exceeded the scope of the Board's remand order by allowing new testimony, erred in determining that the claimant was in the course of employment at the time of the accident and erred in awarding specific loss benefits due to disfigurement. In its appeal form, the employer merely listed the WCJ's findings that allegedly were in error and were not supported by substantial evidence (Findings 3–8, 12–23); the employer specified as well that the WCJ committed errors of law (Conclusions 2–10); and the employer attached a copy of the WCJ's decision to the appeal form.

Here, Employer followed the identical appeal process utilized by the employer in *Jonathan Sheppard Stables*. Employer's appeal form simply listed WCJ Spizer's findings of fact (Nos. 3–19) that allegedly were not supported by substantial competent evidence and listed the WCJ's conclusions of law (Nos. 2–5) that allegedly contained errors of law. Employer also attached a copy of the WCJ's decision to the appeal form. Based on *Jonathan Sheppard Stables*, the Court is compelled to agree with Claimant that Employer effectively waived its arguments as to the WCJ's disposition of the credit and the healing period because Employer failed to properly preserve those issues in its appeal. The fact that Employer may have argued the issues in its brief to the Board is unavailing as it failed to comply with 34 Pa.Code § 111.11(a). Accordingly, the Court reverses the Board's order to the extent that it granted a credit to Employer for total disability payments and reduced the healing period to twenty weeks as those issues were waived. The Court otherwise affirms the Board's order.

ORDER

AND NOW, this 9th day of March, 2005, the order of the Workers' Compensation Appeal Board is reversed to the extent that it granted Thomas J. O'Hora Company, Inc. a credit for total disability payments it made to Joseph Matticks and reduced his

Continued

healing period from forty weeks to twenty weeks. The Board's order is affirmed in all other respects.

Case Questions:

1. What are the injuries claimed by the injured worker in this case?
2. What services did the claimant's wife provide to him after his injury?
3. What findings did the Workers' Compensation Judge enter about this case after a consideration of the evidence?
4. Why did the attorneys for the employer seek to reinstate the appeal in this case?
5. According to the court, what was the function of the compromise and release agreement in this case?

ETHICAL CONSIDERATION:
Quantity over Quality

One of the problems with specializing in any area of law such as workers' compensation is the temptation to concentrate on the quantity of cases instead of the quality of each claim. There are firms that specialize in workers' compensation cases to the extent that they are referred to as client mills. In mills, client cases are pushed through the office with a minimum of attention to the details and a strong emphasis on settlement. Lawyers and paralegals begin to focus on receiving fees instead of zealously representing the interests of their clients. Clients receive very little personal attention. Client mills are, at best, a questionable practice and may violate any of a number of ethical guidelines. Whether the lawyer represents a lone injured worker or a multinational insurance company, the client deserves quality legal representation. Because workers' compensation is such a specialized area, there is a strong temptation to streamline processes and generate maximum legal fees, either by settling claimant cases quickly or by maximizing billable hours for employers and insurance companies. In either event, when the focus of the practice becomes the profits generated and not the legal rights of the client, the firm is in serious danger of violating ethical practices and providing poor overall service. Such a firm might stay in business for months or years, but eventually such practices will land the firm in trouble. You should be wary of such firms because their poor reputation might reflect on you.

CHAPTER SUMMARY

Unlike other civil or criminal trials, workers' compensation cases are appealed to their own appellate board, commonly referred to as the Workers' Compensation Appeals Board. Whoever loses there can appeal the case through the regular state or federal appellate court system. Most workers' compensation cases go first to the state Court of Appeals. From there, the losing party can appeal to the state Supreme Court, but only if that court grants cert. Appellate courts are limited in the decisions that they can make in cases on appeal. They can affirm, or agree with a lower court's decision. They can reverse, or overturn, a lower court's decision. They can also remand an appeal by sending it back to the Workers' Compensation Board for additional hearings.

KEY TERMS

Affirm
Appellant
Appellee
Certiorari
Compromise and release
Contingency fee
Lump sum
Notice of Appeal
Petition for Reconsideration
Record
Remand
Reverse

REVIEW QUESTIONS

1. How are deadlines calculated for purposes of filing motions and appeals in workers' compensation cases?
2. What is a Petition for Reconsideration?
3. Explain the purpose of the Workers' Compensation Appeals Board.
4. What is appellate jurisdiction?
5. What is an appellate record?
6. Explain how a Workers' Compensation Appeals Board reaches its decision.
7. Describe the process of creating a compromise and release of a pending workers' compensation case.
8. Describe the organization of the court system on the state and federal level.
9. What is the relationship between Courts of Appeal and Workers' Compensation Appeals Boards?

10. Differentiate between the terms used for the parties in a hearing and on appeal.
11. What is certiorari?
12. What grounds does a court consider before deciding to grant certiorari?
13. What are federal circuits?
14. What is a Notice of Appeal?
15. Explain the various components of an appellate brief.
16. Compare and contrast an appellate court's decision to either affirm or reverse a lower court decision.
17. How would an appellate court go about modifying a lower court decision?
18. What is remand?

QUESTIONS FOR REFLECTION

1. What are some of the critical factors that both employers and employees must consider before offering to settle a case?
2. Are there too many levels of appellate review for workers' compensation cases? Explain your answer.
3. Why is it important for a paralegal to understand how an appellate brief is created?

WEB SITES

California Workers' Compensation Appeals Board
http://www.dir.ca.gov/wcab/wcab.htm

Nevada Division of Industrial Relations
http://dirweb.state.nv.us/

Indiana Workers' Compensation Board
http://www.in.gov/workcomp/

State of Wyoming Department of Employment
http://wydoe.state.wy.us/

PRACTICAL APPLICATIONS

Review your state's appellate structure. When a party loses a hearing, where does he or she appeal? Is there a board and an appellate board, or a single appellate step? What requirements must a party meet in order to bring an appeal in your state's system?

END NOTES

1. *Truck Terminal Motels of America, Inc. v. Berks County Bd. of Assessment Appeals*, 127 Pa.Cmwlth. 408, 561 A.2d 1305 (1989).
2. Ohio Admin. Code § 4121-3-15(E)(6).
3. 39-A M.R.S.A. § 322.
4. N.C.G.S.A. § 97-91.
5. C.R.S.A. § 8-43-307.
6. 872 A.2d 196 (Pa.Cmwlth. 2005).

Online Companion™
For additional resources, please go to
http://www.paralegal.delmar.cengage.com

Medical Utilization Issues in Workers' Compensation

CHAPTER 9

CHAPTER OBJECTIVES

At the completion of this chapter, you should be able to:

- Explain initiatives used by employers to reduce the total number of workers' compensation injury claims
- Discuss the use of pre-employment screenings as a way to reduce later injuries
- Discuss medical utilization issues, including effective use of current medical treatments and tracking medical costs
- List and explain the various proposals to change the current workers' compensation system, especially in regard to medical benefits and costs
- Define evidence-based medicine
- Explain various initiatives to investigate fraudulent practices by employers, employees' and medical providers

INTRODUCTION

Throughout this text, we have discussed the workers' compensation system as it exists on both the federal and state levels. However, in this final chapter, we will focus on where the system is going. Specifically, we will examine new initiatives in workers' compensation such as pre-employment screening and then discuss proposals designed to streamline the entire workers' compensation system, including the broad range of medical utilization issues, evidence-based medicine, and proposals for modifying the existing workers' compensation system.

PRE-EMPLOYMENT SCREENING

Most of us know that new job applicants will most likely be required to submit to blood or urine screens to determine if they are taking illegal substances such as narcotics. However, it is now also routine to require job applicants to submit to pre-employment physical testing. The purpose of this testing is to ensure that the worker can perform the routine tasks associated with the job, as well as determine individuals who are at risk for potential workers' compensation claims. An applicant who works in a warehouse might be required to lift 30, 40, or even 50 pounds as dead weight, not only to make sure that the person can actually handle the load, but also to make sure that he or she does not have a bad back that would only be exacerbated by job duties and might lead to a claim. However, **pre-employment screening** has gone beyond simple strength tests. Most employers now hire outside firms to administer a broad range of tests to prospective employees; these tests may include not only lifting designated weights, but also additional tests such as the following:

- Cardiovascular
- Baseline hearing and vision tests
- Blood sugar or proteins (that could indicate an underlying health problem)
- Pulmonary function tests
- Respiratory mask fit testing (if the employee will be working around hazardous materials including paint, mold, asbestos, and other substances)

However, some of the data tracked in pre-employment screenings might not appear to have a direct relationship to the job. For instance, some companies routinely take an applicant's height and weight as part of the physical evaluation process. Studies have shown that chronically overweight individuals tend to suffer from greater incidents of back pain and charting a person's height in relation to weight gives an excellent indication of whether a person is overweight. Some have suggested that tracking this additional data might eventually lead to discriminatory practices against overweight individuals. If they are more likely to have back problems, perhaps companies will refuse to hire them in the first place? Obese individuals have also been shown to have more lost time from work and greater absenteeism than other employees.[1]

Pre-employment screening

Testing and evaluation of an applicant's physical abilities to ensure that he or she can perform the work duties assigned; used to reduce potential workers' compensation claims.

EMPLOYER INITIATIVES TO DECREASE ON-THE-JOB INJURIES

As employers have come to see that simply avoiding injuries and accidents is not enough to reduce workers' compensation claims, many have created new initiatives in an attempt to reduce injuries and illnesses and consequently to lower the number and severity of claims. Attention to worker comfort can pay huge dividends for employers. For instance, one company began taking a proactive approach to workers with persistent migraines. The company authorized employees with migraines to take any necessary medication with a resulting increase in production time and worker efficiency. Treatment to prevent migraines boosts work productivity.[2]

Of course, companies fall under the jurisdiction of various state and federal safety agencies, including the Occupational Safety and Health Administration (OSHA). Compliance with these safety rules and regulations is mandatory. However, when we talk about employer initiatives to reduce danger to employees, we are actually focusing on efforts to go above and beyond the minimum requirements of federal and state agencies. By focusing on making the workplace safer and more conducive to the health of the employee, there is a concomitant increase to the bottom line. Fewer injured workers inevitably translate into higher profits. Following this same vein, some companies have even gone so far as to focus on employee comfort by providing on-site child daycare, medical facilities, and in some very rare instances, quiet rooms where employees can go for brief naps on their breaks. In almost all of these instances, the employers have seen a boost in productivity and efficiency and fewer workers' compensation claims. However, there are other methods to decrease worker injury than those simply focusing on employee issues. Another method is to document potential safety hazards and deal with them before they cause serious injury. This is the purpose of a near miss report.

Near Miss Reports

Near miss report
A report that details a potential problem or an accident or injury that did not actually occur, but would have caused injuries if it had.

Some employers have taken the idea of data collection a step further and are now requiring employees and supervisors to file **"near miss" reports**. These are reports that detail an accident that almost occurred, but did not. At first, it might seem odd to create a report system when an accident did not occur, but such reports can be quite valuable. For instance, if a worker narrowly avoided injury, the circumstances that led to that near miss could be investigated and improved upon before a real injury occurs.

Near miss reports are also an excellent vehicle for workers to report unsafe conditions and to ensure that there is some documentation of the condition. Some Workers' Compensation Boards have near miss reports as part of the forms that they provide to workers and employers.

Enhanced Safety Training

These days, nearly all major companies have established safety training regimens to supplement the standard human resource training for new employees. Mandatory employee safety training can drastically decrease workers' compensation injury claims by simply making employees more aware of potential safety issues and creating a culture of safety in the workplace. Safety training can be as basic as the proper way to lift objects and as complex as how to use specialized equipment such as gas masks, chemical showers, and burn treatment.

MEDICAL UTILIZATION ISSUES

In recent years, the issue of **medical utilization** has become an important trend in workers' compensation cases. In its broadest sense, medical utilization refers to the process of tracking medical treatment and costs, as well as methods to make the system work more efficiently and economically.

Anyone pursuing a workers' compensation claim under any state's system would probably agree that the current system is unnecessarily complex, that it costs too much, that administrative issues drag out the process of finalizing a claim, and that many of its features haven't kept pace with technological advances. Medical utilization programs seek to address some or all of these problems by creating a more streamlined and efficient workers' compensation system—one that responds to the needs of both employers and employees and that takes full advantage of new approaches to medical treatment, cuts through red tape, and ultimately lowers the costs of the system for everyone.

Medical utilization
The review of medical procedures to ensure that they are effective both for medical purposes and for overall cost reduction.

Tracking Medical Costs

Medical utilization studies often focus first on payments: to whom are they made, what are they for, and what costs are associated with the procedures. Before a system can be improved, it must first be understood. The questions that arise from a review of medical costs include:

- Where are the funds collected from employers, and held by insurance companies, actually spent?
- Do the amounts paid out vary from state to state? If so, why?
- Do services vary depending on the workers' financial status?

EXHIBIT 9-1
Medical Costs.

> While the number of claims have continued to decline in recent years, medical costs have continued to spiral out of control. From 1997 to 2002, medical costs per claim increased by 125%, rising from $13,845 to $31,120 per claim. By comparison, national medical inflation grew by 22%.[4]

In an interesting twist, while some states have seen a gradual decline in the number of workers' compensation claims, medical costs have continued to rise at an alarming rate. Some studies show that from 1997 to 2002, medical costs in workers' compensation claims increased by 125%.[3] In states that have enacted medical utilization review, costs incurred by the system have almost always reduced, sometimes by double-digit percentage marks. See Exhibit 9-1.

Income-Based Disparities

There are also studies suggesting that medical utilization would also be helpful in addressing disparities in the treatment received by workers. For instance, numerous studies have shown that workers with higher incomes generally received more medical procedures and generally better care than workers with lower incomes, despite the fact that they are being treated for the same injury. This is true even when the actual cost to the employer/insurance carrier remained the same, whether the claim was made by a high wage earner or a low wage earner.[5]

Because medical utilization review has become a part of a virtually every state's workers' compensation system, closer attention has been paid to the data collected about various injuries and the causes behind them. Perhaps even more important, medical utilization has led to proposals to make changes to the existing workers' compensation system.

> **SIDEBAR**
>
> Carpal Tunnel Syndrome (CTS) patients in different wage groups had significantly different medical costs. The total medical sum accrued by the patient with CTS diagnosis was 12% higher for the above the median wage group than the lower wage group, controlling for type and number of procedures.[6]

PROPOSALS TO CHANGE THE WORKERS' COMPENSATION SYSTEM

In the last few years, many states have promoted various proposals to improve the overall quality and efficiency of workers' compensation systems. In states that have enacted some form of workers' compensation initiative, there have been varying results. In Wisconsin, for example, where medical utilization was made a part of each workers' compensation claim, there was a 16 percent reduction in medical service costs.[7] Over the past few years, there have been many proposals to amend or modify the workers' compensation system. They include:

- Fee schedules for all medical services
- Evidence-based medicine
- Physician training in disability ratings
- Generic drug initiatives
- New and better training programs for claims handlers
- Revised sanctions and fines
- Streamlined grievance procedures
- Better fraud detection

Medical Fee Schedules

Schedules are not a new concept in workers' compensation. We have already seen that most states have statutes that place a specific monetary amount on the loss of a finger, a hand, an arm, and so on. In those situations, the set schedule provides for so many month's of benefits for the injuries or illnesses. **Medical fee schedules** set maximum costs for specific procedures. Implementing a medical fee schedule—as some states have already done—is simply a natural extension of the workers' compensation philosophy. Many medical providers have resisted the switch to predictable fee schedules fearing that their income would decrease dramatically. However, that is not always the case. In states such as Florida that implemented a modified fee schedule for doctors in 2004, prices paid to the doctors in general and surgeons in general actually increased.[8]

In some states, the proposal is even more specific: Tie the medical fee schedules to the index of identical services provided under Medicaid/Medicare. This has the advantage of creating a sense of predictability and relying on a system that has already proven useful for delivering medical services.

In states that propose tying workers' compensation fee schedules to Medicaid/Medicare schedules, there is an automatic update feature. As the fees are raised for Medicaid/Medicare services, they would have a corresponding increase in workers' compensation fee schedules. Like Medicare/Medicaid, such a system would also allow for exceptions to the fee schedule for unusual or rare medical procedures.

In states that do have some form of fee schedule, there is always a question about billing in workers' compensation cases. In fact, one of the primary reasons for creating medical utilization review boards was to review the dramatically different charges sent in by medical providers for the same treatment. The Workers' Compensation Board always has the right to review medical billing and to reduce or completely rule out payment for certain procedures.

Medical fee schedule
A schedule or code of all possible treatments, therapies, and medical services provided along with a maximum payment authorized for each.

One could argue that there has always been a fee schedule in the workers' compensation system; it simply hasn't been very systematic. In states that establish baseline amounts for medical charges instead of creating an actual fee schedule, especially one that is continually updated, there could be a 5- or 10-year lapse in updating the charges for medical procedures. No one is under the illusion that medical costs have remained stagnate for the last 5 or 10 years.

But fee schedules are only one of the ways the workers' compensation system seeks to address spiraling medical costs. Another initiative is one that is already sweeping through the medical field: evidence-based medicine.

Evidence-Based Medicine

■ **Evidence-based medicine**
An approach to medical treatment that focuses on proven data collection, peer review, and scientific analysis.

When medical providers institute an **evidence-based medicine** approach, they focus on data, tracking such things as how long it took for a patient to receive certain medications and the efficacy of delivering certain medicines or treatments within a specified period of time. It was studies based on evidence-based medicine that showed the effectiveness of giving aspirin to recent stroke victims. Evidence-based medicine also seeks to change some of the regional differences seen in treatment for worker injuries. Carpal Tunnel Syndrome, for example, has a wide range of treatment possibilities, even to the point of whether or not it is recognized as a valid condition, depending on the state where it is reported.

In some cases, medical providers, insurance companies, or employers may bring in outside companies to evaluate procedures and practices to see if they can be improved upon. These companies will:

- Examine the number of services per visit and visits per claim
- Focus on medical procedures that have been proven to be effective
- Create independent medical review procedures that allow for the implementation of new and proven medical treatments

Training Physicians in Disability Ratings

■ **Disability rating**
A determination by a medical provider of the percentage of an injured worker's temporary or permanent impairment due to a work-related injury or illness.

We have already seen that a **disability rating** or impairment rating can have profound consequences for an injured worker. For instance, a doctor must determine when an injured worker has reached the point of maximum medical improvement (MMI) and then make a determination of the degree that the employee will remain impaired for the rest of his or her life. In most states, there are no standards to train physicians or other medical providers in disability ratings. This results in a disparate system, with disability ratings depending very much on the outlook and personality of the doctor instead of on the objective factors of the injury or illness. As a result, many states have proposed a comprehensive overview of the disability rating system along with intensive physician training in determining disability.

Most states do not have a program for training physicians in determining disability ratings. As a result, the same injury may receive radically different disability ratings from different doctors. These ratings will affect the injured worker's medical treatment, physical therapy and ultimately the final award of benefits. Creating a disability training program would at least have the benefit of creating more uniform system, although it is unlikely that such subjective findings can ever be made completely uniform.

Generic Drug Initiatives

Most states have already enacted some form of **generic drug** program. Generic drugs are medical compounds that have the same molecular structure as brand name drugs, but are significantly cheaper. In states that have enacted generic drug programs, the requirement is usually that if a brand name drug has a generic equivalent, then the generic must be prescribed. Because the pharmaceuticals developed by major drug companies can only be protected under the patent laws for seven years, when that time has expired, other companies can create duplicates and sell them at considerably lower prices than the original.

New and Better Training Programs for Claims Handlers

One of the biggest causes of delay in processing workers' compensation claims comes from the administration of the claim. Many claims handlers have huge caseloads and many do not receive adequate training, let alone continuing education on a yearly basis. By requiring annual continuing education that will introduce claims handlers to the latest in software and technological advances, there is a far better chance that an individual claim will move more quickly through the system.

Revised Sanctions and Fines Under the Workers' Compensation System

Many states have enacted fines and penalties against employers and insurance companies for a wide variety of infraction, including failure to file initial report of injury, wrongful denial or delay in providing benefits of injured employees, and even sanctions for frivolous appeals. Many states also suffer

---

SIDEBAR

"Evidence-based medicine is a relatively new term referring to the use of peer review, clinical documentation and clinical studies that determine the best course of treatment for a particular condition. All of medicine is headed towards evidence-based medicine, including family practice and specialties. It's going to become the standard of care nationwide. In the near future, it is most likely the way that all physicians will be compensated based on their implementation of evidence-based medical approaches."
— Dr. Ronald Plemmons

Generic drug
A chemical and molecular duplicate of a drug that has an expired patent.

STATE OF CALIFORNIA
Division of Workers' Compensation
PRIMARY TREATING PHYSICIAN'S PERMANENT AND STATIONARY REPORT (PR-3)

This form is required to be used for ratings prepared pursuant to the 1997 Permanent Disability Rating Schedule. It is designed to be used by the primary treating physician to report the initial evaluation of permanent disability to the claims administrator. It should be completed if the patient has residual effects from the injury or may require future medical care. In such cases, it should be completed once the patient's condition becomes permanent and stationary.

This form should not be used by a Qualified Medical Evaluator (QME) or Agreed Medical Evaluator (AME) to report a medical-legal evaluation.

Patient:
  Last Name _____ Middle Initial ____ First Name _____ Sex ___ Date of Birth _____
  Address _____ City _____ State _____ Zip _____
  Occupation _____ Social Security No. _____ Phone No. _____

Claims Administrator/Insurer:
  Name _____ Claim No. _____ Phone No. _____
  Address _____ City _____ State _____ Zip _____

Employer:
  Name _____ Phone No. _____
  Address _____ City _____ State _____ Zip _____

You must address each of the issues below. You may substitute or append a narrative report if you require additional space to adequately report on these issues.

Date of Injury _____   Last date _____   Date of current _____   Permanent & _____
          Date   worked Date   examination Date   Stationary date Date

Description of how injury/illness occurred (e.g. Hand caught in punch press; fell from height onto back; exposed 25 years ago to asbestos):

Patient's Complaints:

STATE OF CALIFORNIA

DWC Form PR-3
(Rev. 06-05)

EXHIBIT 9-2 Primary Treating Physician's Permanent and Stationary Report (Permanent Disability Report)—California Division of Workers' Compensation.

Division of Workers' Compensation
PRIMARY TREATING PHYSICIAN'S PERMANENT AND STATIONARY REPORT (PR-3)

Relevant Medical History:

Objective Findings:
Physical Examination: (Describe all relevant findings; include any specific measurements indicating atrophy, range of motion, strength, etc.; include bilateral measurements - injured/uninjured - for upper and lower extremity injuries.)

Diagnostic tests results (X-ray/Imaging/Laboratory/etc.)

Diagnoses (List each diagnosis; ICD-9 code must be included)   ICD-9
  1. _____   _____
  2. _____   _____
  3. _____   _____
  4. _____   _____

	Yes	No	Cannot Determine
Can this patient now return to his/her usual occupation?	☐	☐	☐
If not, can the patient perform another line of work?	☐	☐	☐

DWC Form PR-3
(Rev. 06-05)

EXHIBIT 9-2 (*Continued*)

STATE OF CALIFORNIA
Division of Workers' Compensation
PRIMARY TREATING PHYSICIAN'S PERMANENT AND STATIONARY REPORT (PR-3)

Subjective Findings: Provide your professional assessment of the subjective factors of disability, based on your evaluation of the patient's complaints, your examination, and other findings. List specific symptoms (e.g. pain right wrist) and their frequency, severity, and/or precipitating activity using the following definitions:

Severity: Minimal pain - an annoyance, causes no handicap in performance.
Slight pain - tolerable, causes some handicap in performance of the activity precipitating pain.
Moderate pain - tolerable, causes marked handicap in the performance of the activity precipitating pain.
Severe pain - precludes performance of the activity precipitating pain.

Frequency: Occasional - occurs roughly one fourth of the time.
Intermittent - occurs roughly one half of the time.
Frequent - occurs roughly three fourths of the time.
Constant - occurs roughly 90 to 100% of time.

Precipitating activity: Description of precipitating activity gives a sense of how often a pain is felt and thus may be used with or without a frequency modifier. If pain is constant during precipitating activity, then no frequency modifier should be used. For example, a finding of "moderate pain on heavy lifting" connotes that moderate pain is felt whenever heavy lifting occurs. In contrast, "intermittent moderate pain on heavy lifting" implies that moderate pain is only felt half the time when engaged in heavy lifting.

		Yes	No	Cannot determine
Pre-Injury Capacity	Are there any activities at home or at work that the patient cannot do as well now as could be done prior to this injury or illness?	☐	☐	☐

If yes, please describe pre-injury capacity and current capacity (e.g. used to regularly lift a 30 lb. child, now can only lift 10 lbs.; could sit for 2 hours, now can only sit for 15 mins.)

1.

2.

3.

4.

DWC Form PR-3
(Rev. 06-05)

EXHIBIT 9-2   *(Continued)*

STATE OF CALIFORNIA
Division of Workers' Compensation
PRIMARY TREATING PHYSICIAN'S PERMANENT AND STATIONARY REPORT (PR-3)

Preclusions/Work Restrictions

Are there any activities the patient cannot do?   Yes ☐   No ☐   Cannot determine ☐

If yes, please describe all preclusions or restrictions related to work activities (e.g. no lifting more than 10 lbs. above shoulders; must use splint; keyboard only 45 mins. per hour; must have sit/stand workstation; no repeated bending). Include restrictions which may not be relevant to current job but may affect future efforts to find work on the open labor market (e.g. include lifting restriction even if current job requires no lifting; include limits on repetitive hand movements even if current job requires none).

1.

2.

3.

4.

5.

6.

Medical Treatment: Describe any continuing medical treatment related to this injury that you believe must be provided to the patient. ("Continuing medical treatment" is defined as occurring or presently planned treatment.) Also, describe any medical treatment the patient may require in the future. ("Future medical treatment" is defined as treatment which is anticipated at some time in the future to cure or relieve the employee from the effects of the injury.) Include medications, surgery, physical medicine services, durable equipment, etc.

Comments:

DWC Form PR-3
(Rev. 06-05)

EXHIBIT 9-2   *(Continued)*

STATE OF CALIFORNIA
Division of Workers' Compensation
PRIMARY TREATING PHYSICIAN'S PERMANENT AND STATIONARY REPORT (PR-3)

Apportionment:

Effective April 19, 2004, apportionment of permanent disability shall be based on causation. Furthermore, any physician who prepares a report addressing permanent disability due to a claimed industrial injury is required to address the issue of causation of the permanent disability, and in order for a permanent disability report to be complete, the report must include an apportionment determination. This determination shall be made pursuant to Labor Code Sections 4663 and 4664 set forth below:

Labor Code Section 4663. Apportionment of permanent disability; Causation as basis; Physician's report; Apportionment determination; Disclosure by employee

(a) Apportionment of permanent disability shall be based on causation.

(b) Any physician who prepares a report addressing the issue of permanent disability due to a claimed industrial injury shall in that report address the issue of causation of the permanent disability.

(c) In order for a physician's report to be considered complete on the issue of permanent disability, it must include an apportionment determination. A physician shall make an apportionment determination by finding what approximate percentage of the permanent disability was caused by the direct result of injury arising out of and occurring in the course of employment and what approximate percentage of the permanent disability was caused by other factors both before and subsequent to the industrial injury, including prior industrial injuries. If the physician is unable to include an apportionment determination in his or her report, the physician shall state the specific reasons why the physician could not make a determination of the effect of that prior condition on the permanent disability arising from the injury. The physician shall then consult with other physicians or refer the employee to another physician from whom the employee is authorized to seek treatment or evaluation in accordance with this division in order to make the final determination.

(d) An employee who claims an industrial injury shall, upon request, disclose all previous permanent disabilities or physical impairments.

Labor Code section 4664. Liability of employer for percentage of permanent disability directly caused by injury; Conclusive presumption from prior award of permanent disability; Accumulation of permanent disability awards

(a) The employer shall only be liable for the percentage of permanent disability directly caused by the injury arising out of and occurring in the course of employment.

(b) If the applicant has received a prior award of permanent disability, it shall be conclusively presumed that the prior permanent disability exists at the time of any subsequent industrial injury. This presumption is a presumption affecting the burden of proof.

(c)(1) The accumulation of all permanent disability awards issued with respect to any one region of the body in favor of one individual employee shall not exceed 100 percent over the employee's lifetime unless the employee's injury or illness is conclusively presumed to be total in character pursuant to Section 4662. As used in this section, the regions of the body are the following:

DWC Form PR-3
(Rev. 06-05)

EXHIBIT 9-2 (Continued)

STATE OF CALIFORNIA
Division of Workers' Compensation
PRIMARY TREATING PHYSICIAN'S PERMANENT AND STATIONARY REPORT (PR-3)

(A) Hearing.

(B) Vision.

(C) Mental and behavioral disorders.

(D) The spine.

(E) The upper extremities, including the shoulders.

(F) The lower extremities, including the hip joints.

(G) The head, face, cardiovascular system, respiratory system, and all other systems or regions of the body not listed in subparagraphs (A) to (F), inclusive.

(2) Nothing in this section shall be construed to permit the permanent disability rating for each individual injury sustained by an employee arising from the same industrial accident, when added together, from exceeding 100 percent.

	Yes	No
Is the permanent disability directly caused, by an injury or illness arising out of and in the course of employment?	☐	☐
Is the permanent disability caused, in whole or in part, by other factors besides this industrial injury or illness, including any prior industrial injury or illness?	☐	☐

If the answer to the second question is "yes," provide below: (1) the approximate percentage of the permanent disability that is due to factors other than the injury or illness arising out of and in the course of employment; and (2) a complete narrative description of the basis for your apportionment finding. If you are unable to include an apportionment determination in your report, state the specific reasons why you could not make this determination. You may attach your findings and explanation on a separate sheet.

DWC Form PR-3
(Rev. 06-05)

EXHIBIT 9-2 (*Continued*)

STATE OF CALIFORNIA
Division of Workers' Compensation
PRIMARY TREATING PHYSICIAN'S PERMANENT AND STATIONARY REPORT (PR-3)

List information you reviewed in preparing this report, or relied upon for the formulation of your medical opinions:

Medical Records:

Written Job Description:

Other:

DWC Form PR-3
(Rev. 06-05)

EXHIBIT 9-2 *(Continued)*

STATE OF CALIFORNIA
Division of Workers' Compensation
PRIMARY TREATING PHYSICIAN'S PERMANENT AND STATIONARY REPORT (PR-3)

Primary Treating Physician (original signature, do not stamp)

I declare under penalty of perjury that this report is true and correct to the best of my knowledge, and that I have not violated Labor Code §139.3.

Signature: _____ Cal. Lic. # : _____

Executed at: _____ Date: _____
              (County and State)

Name (Printed): _____ Specialty: _____
Address: _____ City: _____ State: _____ Zip: _____
Telephone: _____

DWC Form PR-3
(Rev. 06-05)

EXHIBIT 9-2   *(Continued)*

from bizarre or unusual penalty structures. For instance, suppose we have a case in which the total medical costs are approximately $200,000. If the employer or insurance carrier is late on a $10 payment for reimbursement for prescription, the Workers' Compensation Board is permitted to access a 10% penalty or $20,000. As a result, there are many built-in incentives for the employee and employer to have an adversarial relationship about all aspects of workers compensation claim. Some states have suggested mediation or arbitration for some of these issues. Other states have proposed that penalties be tied to the amount in controversy.[9]

Streamlined Grievance Procedures

We have already seen that some states have enacted arbitration hearings that allow disgruntled injured workers to file a grievance against an insurance company, an employer, or even a member of the Workers' Compensation Board. Many states are now considering expanding on these programs and incorporating them into other aspects of a workers' compensation claim.

Better Fraud Detection

The workers' compensation systems in every state have had issues with fraud from the inception of their programs. Fraud comes in a variety of forms, from malingering employees who exaggerate or even manufacture symptoms to doctors who pile on unneeded and costly medical procedures to insurance companies who deliberately delay paying out benefits on claims with obvious merit. All of these practices cost the state workers' compensation systems millions of dollars. Many states have created legislation to dramatically increase penalties for such behavior and to even prosecute these actions.

Of the examples provided in Exhibit 9-3, the two that need further explanation are "legal mills" and "medical mills." These are colloquial terms for the

---

Examples of workers' compensation fraud include the following practices:

- Abusive billing practices such as "up coding"—changing the billing code of a procedure to the highest possible charge
- Billing for services that were never provided
- Legal "mills"
- Medical "mills"
- Employee fraud

EXHIBIT 9-3

Examples of Workers' Compensation Fraud.

law offices that take up questionable cases at best and outright fraudulent cases at worst, all with an eye toward moving as many cases toward settlement as possible and thus increasing the fees paid to the law office. The fact that these cases have questionable merit is not a central issue for a legal mill, although ethically and legally it certainly should be. As far as medical mills are concerned, these are medical offices that essentially do the same thing as a legal mill, churning through patients with questionable illnesses or injuries to bilk insurance companies and employers of as much money as possible. Many times, questionable law firms work hand-in-glove with medical providers of dubious reputation in order to maximize profits for both.

The problem about discussing fraud in a workers' compensation system is that it appears to be a victimless crime. After all, when an injured worker is dealing with a large, faceless corporation, especially an insurance company, most people would tend to side with the injured worker. Bilking the insurance company out of as much money as possible might even be seen as a positive step. However, this attitude fails to take into account that the costs for workers' compensation fraud are inevitably passed on to the rest of society through higher premiums for employers and higher costs for goods when those employers must pass those higher insurance premium costs on through their business models.

CASE EXCERPT

Ryndycz v. W.C.A.B. (White Engineering)[10]

OPINION BY Judge SMITH-RIBNER.FN1

Richard Ryndycz (Petitioner) petitions for review of a decision by the Workers' Compensation Appeal Board (Board) that affirmed the December 7, 2005 decision of Workers' Compensation Judge (WCJ) Francis J. Desimone following a remand. The WCJ again affirmed a utilization review determination finding that chiropractic treatment rendered to Petitioner by Darryl K. Warner, D.C. was reasonable and necessary for forty-four treatments between July 31, 2002 and December 2, 2002 but was not reasonable and necessary for treatments after that. Petitioner questions whether utilization review of medical expenses awarded by WCJ Joseph E. McManus in June 2003 is barred by res judicata and should be subject to collateral estoppel; whether the scope of utilization review is limited to medical services provided within thirty days of a request for review and thereafter; and whether the utilization

Continued

reviewer, the WCJ and the Board considered the reasonableness and necessity of the palliative care rendered to Petitioner.

I

Petitioner suffered a lower back injury on June 18, 2001 in the course of his employment with White Engineering (Employer). Employer did not file a notice of compensation payable (NCP), temporary notice of compensation payable (TNCP) or notice of compensation denial (NCD), but it did refer Petitioner to a panel physician, Barry J. Burton, D.O. It paid Petitioner's medical expenses and transferred him to light duty. Petitioner received chiropractic services for pain from Peter J. Szakacs, D.C. On October 10, 2001, Dr. Burton released Petitioner to full, unrestricted job duties, although Dr. Szakacs permitted only light-duty work. Employer laid off Petitioner on October 26, 2001. In November 2001 he filed a claim petition and in May 2002 filed a penalty petition alleging Employer's failure to file an NCP, TNCP or NCD. They were heard by WCJ McManus.

In a decision of June 19, 2003, WCJ McManus accepted the testimony of Petitioner and Dr. Szakacs in its entirety, rejected the testimony of Dr. Burton and Employer's other witness and granted Petitioner's claim and penalty petitions. He determined that chiropractic services, including Dr. Szakacs' services and those of Dr. Warner amounting to $7747, were provided for treatment of the work injury and that Employer was liable for payment under provisions of the Workers' Compensation Act (Act), Act of June 2, 1915, P.L. 736, as amended, 77 P.S. §§ 1-1041.4, 2501-2626. Also, Employer violated the Act by failing to make available work within Petitioner's restrictions, by failing to issue a timely NCD or to enter into a timely agreement and by unreasonably and unnecessarily delaying payment of compensation benefits. Citing *Williams v. Workmen's Compensation Appeal Board (A.T. & T. Techs., Inc.)*, 144 Pa.Cmwlth.297, 601 A.2d 473 (Pa.Cmwlth. 1991), the WCJ found that Employer should have entered into a supplemental agreement and suspension and that the underlying action was a termination case and not an original claim petition. In *Williams* the Court held that the employer who retained an employee at full pay and modified her duties after the work injury should have executed a compensation agreement and that when she was laid off for economic and seniority reasons Employer should have entered into a supplemental agreement.

WCJ McManus ordered Employer to pay weekly compensation of $322 beginning October 26, 2001 and onward. In addition, Employer was directed to pay: statutory interest of ten percent on all deferred and unpaid compensation; quantum meruit attorney's fees of $7860 not to be deducted from compensation; $2361.80 in reasonable and necessary litigation costs; attorney's fees of

Continued

twenty percent after exhaustion of the quantum meruit fee; for chiropractic services for treatment of the injury consistent with the findings and conclusions and provisions of the Act; and a penalty of fifty percent plus statutory interest on all deferred and unpaid compensation.

Employer appealed to the Board, which affirmed. It determined that WCJ McManus acted within his authority to accept the testimony of Petitioner's witnesses over that of Employer's witnesses. In view of Employer's failure to file a proper document regarding the injury and the WCJ's finding of unreasonable and excessive delay in payment, the Board concluded that Employer had no basis for any contest of Petitioner's claim until it obtained a deposition from Dr. Burton. The Court affirmed on review. *White Eng'g v. Workers' Compensation Appeal Board (Ryndycz)*, (Pa Cmwlth., Nos. 862 and 2133 C.D.2004, filed June 20, 2005). It cited *Johnstown Housing Authority v. Workers' Compensation Appeal Board (Lewis)*, 865 A.2d 999 (Pa.Cmwlth. 2005), where a contest was held unreasonable when the employer had no medical basis to deny the allegations of the claim petition and had paid the claimant's medical expenses and modified his work duties. The Court held that the record supported the conclusion that Employer violated the Act by its delay in paying the awarded benefits.

On July 16, 2003, within thirty days of WCJ McManus' decision, Employer requested utilization review of the treatment provided by Dr. Warner instead of paying his charges. Mark Cavallo, D.C., determined in a report that the treatment was reasonable and necessary for forty-four visits from July 31, 2002 through December 2, 2002 but not for the seventy visits after that through September 17, 2003. Petitioner testified before WCJ Desimone that he has been treated about twice a week since his first treatment on July 31, 2002. He stated that he continues to have difficulty dressing and cannot bend; that his treatment is limited to manipulation and electrotherapy and relieves pain and stiffness; and that his pain worsens if he does not get treatment. Dr. Warner opined that Petitioner has lumbar spine instability involving quite a bit of arthritic damage and degenerative damage to four disc spaces and an unlevel pelvis, with facet damage producing constant pain. The treatment reduces his pain but has not resulted in overall improvement. Dr. Warner made no referrals to any other health care provider; he is not recommending home exercise as it would exacerbate Petitioner's condition; and he ordered no tests other than x-rays. Petitioner's treatment should continue indefinitely, and he cannot perform even sedentary work.

Dr. Cavallo stated that he reviewed office notes for 114 visits. He opined that chiropractic treatments through December 2, 2002 were reasonable and necessary,

Continued

but the records did not show clinical gains after that. He tried three times to contact Dr. Warner by telephone, but he did not return the calls. Michael-Gerard Moncman, D.O., a certified neurosurgeon, reported that he was unable to complete an examination on March 9, 2004 because Petitioner could not or would not sit or lie on an examination table. WCJ Desimone found that Dr. Warner's treatment was not providing any benefit to Petitioner as determined by Dr. Cavallo, and the WCJ said that Dr. Warner's testimony was not credible because he did not consider and address the ineffectiveness of his treatment.

The Board noted on Petitioner's appeal that WCJ Desimone's decision listed WCJ McManus' decision as an exhibit but did not reconcile the differences with that decision. The Board vacated and remanded for WCJ Desimone to address WCJ McManus' June 2003 decision and order and what effect, if any, it had on the present litigation. The parties submitted briefs, and WCJ Desimone admitted an affidavit by Dr. Warner of September 13, 2005, detailing charges from July 31, 2002 through March 14, 2005. The WCJ overruled the objection of Employer and admitted the exhibit in a letter to counsel of September 30, 2005. The WCJ issued a second decision on December 7, 2005 in which he stated in Finding of Fact No. 4 that WCJ McManus found that services were provided by Dr. Warner for which his charges were $7747 and that Employer was liable for payment consistent with provisions of the Act. He pointed out that WCJ McManus did not refer to dates of service by Dr. Warner and that although WCJ McManus made a finding as to the total bill he did not order payment of any specific amount.

WCJ Desimone incorporated his former findings and then concluded that Employer could file its utilization review request within thirty days of WCJ McManus' decision. Despite WCJ McManus' binding determination that the underlying action was a termination case, WCJ Desimone nevertheless concluded to the contrary that Employer's utilization review request was filed in the context of Petitioner's claim petition, thereby allowing Employer to file its request within thirty days of June 19, 2003 retroactive to all treatments. WCJ Desimone again affirmed the utilization review. On Petitioner's second appeal the Board simply stated that it was satisfied with the WCJ's discussion on this point, and it affirmed.

II

Petitioner argues that utilization review should have been limited to medical care provided after June 17, 2003, that is, retrospective only thirty days from the date of filing the request. He quotes *Warminster Fiberglass v. Workers' Compensation Appeal Board (Jorge)*, 708 A.2d 517 (Pa.Cmwlth. 1998), which stated that under Act 44 medical bills may be challenged only through a timely utilization review

Continued

request, and the WCJ and the Board have no jurisdiction until that is decided. That case also quoted 34 Pa.Code § 127.404(b), which provides that if an employer seeks retrospective review, the request must be filed within thirty days of the receipt of the bill or the request is waived, but "if the insurer is contesting liability for the underlying claim, the 30 days in which to request retrospective UR is tolled pending an acceptance or determination of liability." Further, this provision "does not apply to termination petitions because the terms 'acceptance' and 'determination,' when taken together, apply only to claim petitions." *Warminster Fiberglass*, 708 A.2d at 521 n8. Petitioner contends as well that the utilization review did not consider the palliative nature of the care, although such care easing pain and symptoms has been found to be reasonable and necessary pursuant to *Trafalgar House v. Workers' Compensation Appeal Board (Green)*, 784 A.2d 232 (Pa.Cmwlth. 2001). FN4 He notes in his reply brief that Employer concedes that the underlying action was in fact a termination case.

Employer first argues that WCJ Desimone concluded on remand that WCJ McManus' decision has no impact on the utilization review. Although WCJ McManus decided the work-relatedness of the chiropractic treatments and noted $7747 as the charge by Dr. Warner, he could not decide the reasonableness and necessity of treatments because a WCJ has such jurisdiction only in a petition to review a utilization review determination. *Chik-Fil-A v. Workers' Compensation Appeal Board (Mollick)*, 792 A.2d 678 (Pa.Cmwlth. 2002). Moreover, WCJ McManus did not award $7747 for Dr. Warner's charges. Employer claims that substantial evidence exists to support the WCJ's determination as to reasonableness and necessity, and it acknowledges the Trafalgar House holding as to palliative care but states that a utilization reviewer's opinion that treatment is not beneficial is sufficient to support a finding that the treatment is unreasonable and unnecessary. WCJ Desimone noted that the treatment was not accomplishing stated objectives.

The Court first addresses Petitioner's contention that WCJ McManus ordered payment of Dr. Warner's $7747 in charges for his services. The WCJ found that services were in treatment of the work injury and ordered payment "consistent with the provisions of the Act." This did not preclude Employer from asserting any challenge to reasonableness and necessity that it could file in a timely manner pursuant to the provisions of the Act. As to the timeliness of Employer's utilization review request, WCJ McManus held that the underlying proceeding was in the nature of a termination proceeding, not a claim petition. Employer did not dispute that Petitioner was injured at work on June 18, 2001, but it nevertheless failed to file an NCP, TNCP or NCD, and it denied all allegations of the claim petition although

Continued

it had no medical basis to do so. Employer's initial liability was never seriously contested, and but for Employer's violation of the Act it would have been in a payment status under an NCP or an agreement and would have been required to challenge any medical bill within thirty days all along.

As held in *Warminster Fiberglass*, the tolling of the thirty-day period for challenging medical bills does not apply to termination cases. Inasmuch as WCJ Desimone was bound by WCJ McManus' ruling that the underlying action was a termination case, WCJ Desimone erred in his December 2005 decision by allowing Employer to challenge all of the bills submitted by Dr. Warner. The WCJ should have permitted challenges only to the bills submitted after June 17, 2003, that is, no more than thirty days before the filing of the utilization review request, under 34 Pa.Code § 127.404(b). The charges totaling $7747 were for services rendered through March 10, 2003, as indicated by Dr. Warner's Affidavit, Employee Ex. 8. Because those charges are for services rendered well before June 17, 2003, they became final and are not now subject to utilization review. The same applies to charges between March 10, 2003 and June 17, 2003. The Court shall remand for entry of an order calculating the amount of such charges and directing payment.

ORDER

AND NOW, this 18th day of October, 2007, the Court reverses the order of the Workers' Compensation Appeal Board to the extent that it affirmed the decision of Workers' Compensation Judge Desimone allowing *White Engineering* to challenge the award for $7747 in medical expenses of Dr. Darryl K. Warner. The Court otherwise vacates the Board's order and remands this matter for a determination of the total of the bills submitted by Dr. Warner between March 10, 2003 and June 17, 2003, which are not subject to challenge, and for further proceedings for the Workers' Compensation Judge to consider evidence presented of the palliative effect of medical care provided by Dr. Warner.

Case Questions:

1. What is the medical utilization issue in this case?
2. Why did the Workers' Compensation Judge determine that chiropractic treatment in this case was necessary and related to the work injury received by the employee?
3. What determination did the expert witness in this case make about the 114 office visits for chiropractic care?
4. What is the purpose of a utilization review request?
5. What did the petitioner argue about the utilization review and how it should be limited?

ETHICAL CONSIDERATION:
Fraudulent Medical Practices

As this chapter points out, there is a fair amount of fraud and abuse in the workers' compensation system on both the federal and state levels. Fraud appears in many forms, including employee malingering or exaggeration of injuries, employers who use deceptive or delaying tactics to deny benefits, medical providers that charge for services that were never rendered and/or those medical providers that prescribe services that are not needed. In the end, fraudulent practices simply raise the price for everyone involved in the workers' compensation system. See Exhibit 9-4, which provides a table of national health spending. Fraud detracts from the overall benefits paid to legitimate claims, raises insurance rates for employers, and can result in criminal prosecutions in cases where medical providers commit illegal actions in order to boost their final payment from the insurance carrier. No matter where you may end up working in

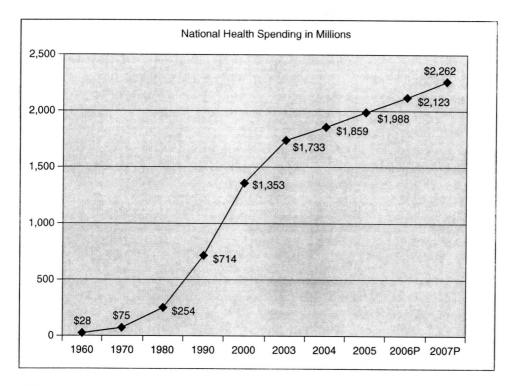

EXHIBIT 9-4 (National Health Spending in Millions).
Note: Selected rather than continuous years of data are shown prior to 2003. Years 2006 forward are CMS projections.
Source: Centers for Medicare and Medicaid Services (CMS), Office of the Actuary; and California HealthCare Foundation.

the worker's compensation system, you should always be aware of and ready to report fraud. If you believe the client has engaged in fraudulent activities, you should bring this to the attention of the attorney with whom you work. If, on the other hand, you are associated with a medical provider that you believe is engaged in fraud, you should contact the appropriate authorities. Failure to take affirmative action on your part could conceivably result in an allegation that you were a party to the fraud in the first place.

CHAPTER SUMMARY

There are many proposals to change various aspects of the workers' compensation system. Employers have initiated programs to prescreen their employees before hiring them, train them better while they are employed, and provide better follow-up and investigation when an injury occurs. Insurance carriers, for their part, have begun insisting on better documentation of injuries and on safety programs and even the creation of a safety officer for various companies. Medical utilization focuses on the appropriate and effective use of medical treatment for injured workers. Many states have implemented medical utilization review boards to oversee the medical treatment provided to injured worker and to restrict certain services that have not proven to be efficacious. All of these efforts are aimed at lowering the costs to administer the workers' compensation system.

KEY TERMS

Disability ratings
Evidence-based medicine
Generic drug
Medical fee schedules

Medical utilization
Near miss report
Pre-employment screening

REVIEW QUESTIONS

1. What are pre-employment screenings?
2. What is medical utilization?
3. Why is it important to track medical costs in workers' compensation cases?

4. List and explain various proposals to change the workers' compensation system.
5. Why is it important to update fee schedules?
6. What is evidence-based medicine?
7. Explain the issues surrounding training physicians in disability ratings.
8. What are generic drugs?
9. How could better training of claims handlers help improve the efficiency of the workers' compensation system?
10. What types of sanctions can be brought against employers or insurance carriers for wrongfully denying benefits?
11. What are some of the proposals to streamline the workers' compensation process?
12. Why is fraud such a big concern in workers' compensation cases?

QUESTIONS FOR REFLECTION

1. Does your state's Workers' Compensation Board have medical utilization as part of its claims process?
2. Should employers be forced to institute policies such as mandatory child day care or emotional counseling, instead of allowing individual employers to decide if they should implement such programs?
3. Based on what you have read in this chapter, which of the proposals to change the workers' compensation system make the most sense to you?

WEB SITE

American College of Occupational and Environmental Medicine
http://www.acoem.org

PRACTICAL APPLICATIONS

Review your state's workers' compensation Internet site and locate information about medical utilization. What does your state require? Locate articles on evidence-based medicine. Explain how this approach to workers' compensation cases could help or hurt claims filed by injured workers. Research the following topic: Are there any pending proposals in your state to modify the state workers' compensation system? If so, what are they?

END NOTES

1. Illness and Injury Among Female Employees at the US Department of Energy. Journal of Occupational & Environmental Medicine. 40(11):994–998, November 1998. Richter, Bonnie S. PhD.
2. American College of occupational and environmental medicine. March 9, 2007.
3. *The Effect of Income on Medical Care Utilization by Injured Workers in California; Abstr AcademyHealth Meet.* 2003; 20: abstract no. 196.
4. The Effect of Income on Medical Care Utilization by Injured Workers in California; Abstr AcademyHealth Meet. 2003; 20: abstract no. 196.
5. The Effect of Income on Medical Care Utilization by Injured Workers in California; Abstr AcademyHealth Meet. 2003; 20: abstract no. 196.
6. *The Effect of Income on Medical Care Utilization by Injured Workers in California; Abstr AcademyHealth Meet.* 2003; 20: abstract no. 196.
7. The Anatomy of Workers' Compensation Medical Costs and Utilization, 6th Edition. Stacey M. Eccleston, Petia Petrova, and Xiaoping Zhao. February 2007. WC-07-02—WC-07-09.
8. The Anatomy of Workers' Compensation Medical Costs and Utilization, 6th Edition. Stacey M. Eccleston, Petia Petrova, and Xiaoping Zhao. February 2007. WC-07-02—WC-07-09.
9. Workers Compensation in California: Questions and Answers. Getting Appropriate Medical Care for Your Injury Prepared for the California Commission on Health and Safety in Workers Compensation, October 2006. Berkeley University.
10. 2007 WL 3023986, *5 (Pa.Cmwlth. 2007).

Online Companion™
For additional resources, please go to
http://www.paralegal.delmar.cengage.com

APPENDIX A

All 50 States' Workers' Compensation Internet Sites and Relevant Federal Sites. Sites are listed alphabetically by state

Alabama	http://dir.alabama.gov/wc/
Alaska	http://labor.state.ak.us/wc/home.htm
Arizona	http://www.ica.state.az.us/
Arkansas	http://www.awcc.state.ar.us/
California	http://www.dir.ca.gov/chswc/chswc.html
Colorado	http://www.coworkforce.com/dwc/
Connecticut	http://wcc.state.ct.us/
Delaware	http://www.delawareworks.com/industrialaffairs/services/WorkersComp.shtml
District of Columbia	http://www.does.dc.gov/does/cwp/view.asp?a=1232&Q=537428
Florida	http://www.fldfs.com/WC/
Georgia	http://sbwc.georgia.gov/02/sbwc/home/0,2235,11394008,00.html;jsessionid=DAD281A8EEF59C7E092AABE262C9D77D
Hawaii	http://hawaii.gov/labor/
Idaho	http://www.iic.idaho.gov/
Illinois	http://www.iwcc.il.gov/
Indiana	http://www.in.gov/workcomp/
Iowa	http://www.iowaworkforce.org/wc/
Kansas	http://www.dol.ks.gov/WC/HTML/wc_ALL.html
Kentucky	http://www.labor.ky.gov/workersclaims/
Louisiana	http://www.laworks.net/WorkersComp/OWC_WorkerMenu.asp

Maine	http://www.maine.gov/wcb/
Maryland	http://www.wcc.state.md.us/
Massachusetts	http://www.mass.gov/dia/
Michigan	http://www.michigan.gov/wca
Minnesota	http://www.doli.state.mn.us/workcomp.html
Mississippi	http://www.mwcc.state.ms.us/
Missouri	http://www.dolir.missouri.gov/wc/
Montana	http://erd.dli.mt.gov/wcclaims/wcchome.asp
Nebraska	http://www.wcc.ne.gov/
Nevada	http://dirweb.state.nv.us/
New Hampshire	http://www.labor.state.nh.us/workers_compensation.asp
New Jersey	http://lwd.dol.state.nj.us/labor/wc/wc_index.html
New Mexico	http://www.workerscomp.state.nm.us/
New York	http://www.wcb.state.ny.us/
North Carolina	http://www.comp.state.nc.us/
North Dakota	http://www.workforcesafety.com/
Ohio	http://www.ohiobwc.com/
Oklahoma	http://www.owcc.state.ok.us/
Oregon	http://wcd.oregon.gov/
Pennsylvania	http://www.dli.state.pa.us/landi/cwp/view.asp?a=138&Q=58929&landiPNav=|#1026
Rhode Island	http://www.courts.state.ri.us/workers/defaultnew-workers.htm
South Carolina	http://www.wcc.state.sc.us/
South Dakota	http://www.state.sd.us/applications/LD01DOL/frameset.asp?navid=&filtertype=1
Tennessee	http://www.state.tn.us/labor-wfd/wcomp.html
Texas	http://www.tdi.state.tx.us/wc/indexwc.html
U.S. Department of Labor	http://www.dol.gov/
Utah	http://www.laborcommission.utah.gov/indacc/indacc.htm
Vermont	http://labor.vermont.gov/Workers/Injured/tabid/110/Default.aspx
Virginia	http://www.vwc.state.va.us/
Washington	http://www.lni.wa.gov/
West Virginia	http://www.wvinsurance.gov/boardofreview/index.htm
Wisconsin	http://www.dwd.state.wi.us/wc/default.htm
Wyoming	http://wydoe.state.wy.us/doe.asp?ID=9

Glossary

Affirm The appellate court agrees with the verdict, or some ruling, entered in the lower court and votes to keep that decision in place.

Appellant The person bringing the current appeal from an adverse ruling in the court below.

Appellee The person who won in the lower court.

Arbitration hearing A hearing by a neutral third party to determine contested issues between two parties.

Arises out of The requirement under workers' compensation law that before an injury will be compensated, it must be directly tied to the worker's job duties.

Assumption of the risk A defense in negligence cases that shows that the plaintiff was aware of the dangers inherent in a specific activity and chose to carry out the action in full knowledge of these dangers.

Benefit review conference An informal meeting between employer, employee, and the employer's insurance provider to discuss compensation issues.

Burial benefit Payment for a portion of an injured worker's burial costs.

Case manager A person, often a medical professional who is responsible for managing the care administered to an injured worker by reviewing all medical records, procedures, and claims and is also responsible for interacting with the worker's medical and legal personnel.

Certiorari A writ or order transferring a case from a lower court to a higher court for review.

Compromise and release Settlement of a workers' compensation case where the employer or insurer pays a specific award to the employee in exchange for the employee's dismissal of his or her claim.

Contested case hearing A formal hearing, conducted by an Administrative Law Judge or other official, to make a final determination about benefit awards and other issues.

Contingency fee An attorney's fee that is based on a percentage of the total recovery in a case. Also, a fee that is conditioned on an award. When an award is made, the attorney's fee is based on a percentage of the total award; when no award is made, the attorney is not entitled to any fee.

Continuation of pay The name for the workers' compensation benefit available to employees under the Federal Employees' Compensation Act.

Cross-examination The questioning of a hostile or opposing witness.

Death benefit Payment to a deceased worker's family. An award made to a deceased worker's family to defray the costs of burial and to provide additional income.

Deposition The oral questioning of a witness, under oath, conducted by an attorney before a court reporter.

Detour To set aside work-related activities and embark on a personal errand.

Direct examination The questioning of a witness to present proof of matters contested in a hearing.

Disability rating A determination by a medical provider of the percentage of an injured worker's temporary or permanent impairment due to a work-related injury or illness.

Disclosure statement A document reviewed and signed by an injured worker that explains the role of the case manager and explains that the case manager is employed by the employer.

Discovery The exchange of information between both sides in a contested hearing.

Dual purpose trip A trip undertaken by an employee that has both work-related and personal aspects.

Duty to defend An insurance company's responsibility to provide legal counsel for its insured against whom an action has been filed.

Earning capacity The total amount that a worker can earn based on training, education, and experience.

Emergency A sudden, dangerous condition caused by human action or inaction.

Employer An individual or company that has employees.

Evidence-based medicine An approach to medical treatment that focuses on proven data collection, peer review, and scientific analysis.

Ex parte meeting A meeting with a judge without the other side present.

Exclusion The persons, types of losses, or damages not covered by an insurance policy.

Exclusive remedy The only legal remedy available to the parties.

Fiduciary A relationship in which one person, or entity, is obligated to act in a trustworthy relationship to the other. A fiduciary has the duty to act in the best interests of the other. A common example of a fiduciary relationship is the attorney-client relationship.

Frolic To engage in an activity for fun or personal pleasure.

Further hearing *See* secondary hearing.

Generic drug A chemical and molecular duplicate of a drug that has an expired patent.

Healing period The time during which an injured employee can recover from an accident or illness and receive workers' compensation benefits.

In the course of The requirement that an injured worker was carrying out duties on behalf of the employer at the time of the injury.

Income benefit Payments made to an injured worker to provide some percentage of income during the worker's rehabilitation or permanent injury period.

Indemnify Payment to the insured for a loss covered in the insurance contract.

Independent contractor A person or business that performs work or provides services to another and is not subject to the other person's control as the means of carrying out that work or service.

Interrogatories Written questions posed by one party to another.

Lump sum A single award of money that cancels out the employer's and insurer's obligation to provide any additional payments or benefits in the future for a contested claim.

Lump sum payment Payment of the entire balance of a worker's benefits in a single transaction.

Medical expense Payment for treatment received by an injured worker for a covered accident or illness.

Medical fee schedule A schedule or code of all possible treatments, therapies, and medical services provided along with a maximum payment authorized for each.

Medical utilization The review of medical procedures to ensure that they are effective both for medical purposes and for overall cost reduction.

Motion for continuance A motion by one side requesting that a court hearing be delayed to a future date.

Near miss report A report that details a potential problem or an accident or injury that did not actually occur, but would have caused injuries if it had.

Notice of Appeal A notice that dockets a case with an appellate court and also requests the transfer of the record from a lower court to the appellate court.

Occupational disease A disease or condition that arises out of working conditions.

Pain and suffering The physical, emotional, and mental stress from an injury.

Permanent partial disability A work-related injury that leaves a worker with a permanent condition that will not resolve itself over time.

Permanent total disability An injury that leaves a worker unable to return to work or to engage in any other meaningful work for the balance of the worker's life.

Personal comfort doctrine A legal principle that allows an injured employee to recover under workers' compensation laws for an injury arising out of actions that were not directly related to duties, but arose out of the reasonable needs of any employee.

Petition for reconsideration A request by a party for a review of a workers' compensation award.

Pre-employment screening Testing and evaluation of an applicant's physical abilities to ensure that he or she can perform the work duties assigned to reduce potential workers' compensation claims.

Premium The insured's payment to the insurance company.

Pro se (Latin) "For himself." A person who is not represented by an attorney and chooses to represent himself or herself.

Product liability A legal theory for a cause of action against a manufacturer or seller of a product that causes injury to a person; liability is not based on fault.

Record The body of evidence, including testimony, medical evidence, and depositions, presented at a workers' compensation hearing.

Remand The appellate court requires additional information or an evidentiary hearing; it cannot conduct such a hearing itself, so it sends the case back to the trial court for the hearing, and then considers the appeal based on that hearing.

Reverse To reverse a decision is to set it aside; an appellate court disagrees with the verdict, or some ruling, in the lower court, and overturns that decision.

Rule of sequestration A rule that requires witnesses, who have been subpoenaed to testify, to remove themselves from the courtroom while other witnesses testify.

Schedule A listing of specific actions or bodily losses and a corresponding monetary award for each.

Secondary hearing Also known as a further hearing; an additional hearing held on issues raised in a workers' compensation case.

Self-insurer A company that acts as its own workers' compensation insurance provider. Also, a statutory provision that allows companies that minimum financial requirements to act as their own insurers.

Statutory employer An individual or company classified as an employer for workers' compensation purposes only.

Subpoena An order directing a person to appear at a hearing at a specific date and time.

Subrogation The right of an insurance company to bring suit to reclaim funds it has indemnified.

Temporary partial disability A condition where an injured employee is unable to perform his or her previous job, but may be able to carry out more limited duties.

Temporary total disability When a worker receives an injury or suffers from a work-related illness that leaves him or her unable to perform any type of meaningful work.

Tort A wrong for which the law provides a remedy.

Underwriting The process of reviewing many factors to determine the risk of investment.

Workers' compensation A system created in the early 20th century to provide minimal medical coverage and benefits for injured workers.

Workers' Compensation Board The governmental unit responsible for administering the workers' compensation system.

Index

A

Accepting a claim, 216
Acts of God, 113
Acts of nature, 113
Administrative Law Judge (ALJ)
  bench warrant, issuing, 202
  communicating with, 199
  "deems the case submitted", 203
  ex parte meeting, 199
  powers of, 198
  request a different judge, 199
  role of, 198, 199–200
Advocate
  becoming an, 55
  compensation, 56
Affirm, 265
Appeals Board
  actions by, 258
  introduction, 254
  jurisdiction of, 257
  limitations, 257
  Maine Workers' Compensation Appeals Board, 254 exhibit, 8–4
  makeup of, 254
  procedure at, 254, 255–256
  Workers' Compensation Appeals Board, application for adjudication of claim, 255 exhibit, 8–5
  Workers' Compensation Commission to determine all questions (North Carolina), 257 exhibit, 8–6
Appellant, 260
Appellate court
  terminology, 260
Appellee, 260
Arbitration hearing, 187, 189
Arises out of, definition of, 104
Assault, 28–29, 114
Assumption of the risk, 4, 26
Attorneys
  application for IWCC attorney code number, 196 exhibit, 6–12
  code systems, 196
  compensating, 195–196
  contingency fee, 195, 243, 249
  rates, 196

B

Battery, 28, 29, 114
Bends, the, 116
Benefit review conference (BRC), 187

Benefits, 8–21
  amount of, determining, 10, 12–13
  burial benefits, 10
  case management issues. *See* Case management issues
  catastrophic claims, 162–163
  classifications of, 143
  death benefits, 10, 157 exhibit, 5–7
    compensation for death (Florida), 156 exhibit, 5–6
    definition of, 156
    homosexual marriages, 157
    last sickness, 156–157
  denial/termination of
    3-part test, 158–159
    common reasons, 157–158
    false representations by employee, 158–159
    illegal aliens, immigration status, 160
    refusing medical treatment, 159–160
  disability payments
    disfigurement, 153
    introduction, 143
    lump sum, 151

309

multiple injuries, 153
permanent partial disability, 145–150
permanent total disability, 150–151
preexisting conditions, 153–154
temporary partial disability, 143, 144 exhibit, 5-2
temporary total disability, 143–145
earning capacity, 152–153
firefighters, 14, 14 exhibit, 1-6
fraud, denying for claims of, 14–15
hedonic damages, 152
income during injury/illness, 9
introduction, 138–139
job placement services, 156
law enforcement, 14, 14 exhibit, 1–6
medical, 139–142
   expenses, 9, 113
   healing period, 142–143
   introduction, 139–140
   non-standard injuries or illnesses, 141
   physical rehabilitation, 141
   preexisting injuries or illnesses, 141–142
   summary of services under medical benefits, 140 exhibit, 5-1
   transportation, 141
   waiving, 140–141
partial disability, defining, 146–150
schedule for permanent partial losses (OHIO), 146–150 exhibit, 5-5
vocational rehabilitation, 155–156
"Benefits are not property rights", ruling, 140

Building permits, proof of coverage, 89, 89 exhibit, 3–9
Burial benefit, 10

C

C and R settlement, 251
   compromise and release, 246–251 exhibit, 8-2
   creating, 251
Carpal Tunnel Syndrome (CTS), 264, 280
Case excerpts
   body parts, defined by judges, 204–207
   college athletes, determining employee status, 90–95
   constitutional protections, 17–20
   due process, 58–65
   duty to defend provision, 230–237
   granting a petition for rehearing, 266–272
   non-married partner, death benefits entitlement, 164–168
   off-duty injury, is it covered, 122–133
   utilization review, 293–298
Case management issues
   case manager, 160–162
   disclosure statement, 161, 162 exhibit, 5-8
   information necessary for efficient case management, 163 exhibit, 5-9
   insurance examiner, 161–162
   introduction, 160
Case manager, 160–162
Casual employee, 81, 82
Casual employment, 79, 81–82, 81 exhibit, 3–6, 85
Catastrophic claims, 162–163
Causation, 25

Centers for Medicare and Medicaid Services (CMS), 54–55
Certiorari (or cert), 261
Claims handlers, new/better training programs for, 281
Common-law influences
   intentional torts
      injuries, caused by coworkers, 29
      introduction, 28–29
   negligence
      assumption of the risk, 26
      duty, 25–26
      introduction, 25
      product liability, 26–28
Compromise and release (C and R), 246–251
Constitutional protections, 5–6
Contested case hearing (CCH). *See* Workers' compensation hearings
Contingency fee, 195, 243, 249
Continuation of pay (COP)
   advantage of, 35
   definition of, 35
   online site for FECA forms, 36–37 exhibit, 2-3
   stopping, 35, 37
Cordozo, Justice, 111
Court of Appeals, 259–260
Coworker injury, 29
Cross examination, 202

D

Damages, 25, 112, 139
Deadlines, 252
Death benefits
   annual death benefits questionnaire (Ohio)13 exhibit, 1–5
   compensation for death (Florida)156 exhibit, 5–6
   definition of, 10, 156
   homosexual marriages, 157

last sickness, 156–157
notice of employees death (California)11 exhibit, 1–3
notice of fatal injury or occupational disease and claim for compensation for death benefits (Texas)12 exhibit, 1–4
payments to survivors, cause other than injury, 157 exhibit, 5–7
Declaratory judgment (or declaratory action), 228
"Deems the case submitted", 203
Defense Base Act (DBA)
   benefits, 57
   coverage, 57
   introduction, 56
Deny cert, 261
Depositions, 184
Detour, 110
Direct examination, 201–202
Disability payments
   disfigurement, 153
   introduction, 143
   lump sum, 151
   multiple injuries, 153
   permanent partial disability, 145–150
   permanent total disability, 150–151
   preexisting conditions, 153–154
   temporary partial disability, 143, 144 exhibit, 5–2
   temporary and permanent, differentiating between, 145
   temporary total disability, 143–145
Disability rating, 282–283
Disclosure statement 161, 162 exhibit, 5–8
Discovery
   civil vs. criminal cases, 180
   definition of, 180
   independent medical examination, request for, 185–186
   medical records, request for, 185
   refusal to abide by, 186
   types of
      depositions, 184
      interrogatories, 185, 185 exhibit, 6–7
      video depositions, 184–185
   Utah Rule R 602-2, 186 exhibit, 6–8
   workers' compensation file
      adding documents to, 187
      availability of, 187
      reviewing, 186–187
   in workers' compensation hearings, 180–184
Disfigurement, 153
Domestic workers, 84
Double-dipper, 54
Dual purpose trips, 111–112
Due process claims, 6
Duty, 25–26
Duty to defend, 227–228

E

Earning capacity
   award determination, 152–153
   calculating, 152
   functional disability, 152
Earning power. *See* Earning capacity
Economic reality test, 72–73
Emergencies, 119–120
Emergency, definition of, 119
Employees
   casual employment, 81–82, 81 exhibit, 3–6
   defining, 83 exhibit, 3–7
   independent contractors, 85–88
   not eligible for workers' compensation
      compensation, question of, 84
      defining employee, 83 exhibit, 3–7
      domestic workers, 84
      odd jobs, 84
      professional athletes, 84–85
      regular, 83
      subcontractors, 85
Employer, definition of, 70
Employers
   casual employment, 81–82, 81 exhibit, 3–6
   charities, 77, 79
   definition of, 70
   economic reality test, 72–73
   employees, minimum number of, 70–71, 72 exhibit, 3–1
   employer status, court doctrines that determine, 72–73
   initiatives to decrease on-the-job injuries, 278–279
   multiple, 71–73
   nonprofit organizations, 77, 79
   restrictions (new) on, 88–89
      proof of workers' compensation coverage, 89, 89 exhibit, 3–9
   self-insurers, 89
   subject to workers' compensation statute
      charities, 77, 79
      employer certification of compliance (Louisiana)75 exhibit, 3–2
      employment relationships under workers' compensation (Indiana)76 exhibit, 3–3
      introduction, 73–74
      nonprofit organizations, 77, 79
      partnerships, 74
      statutory employers, 74–75, 77, 77 exhibit, 3–4
   workers' compensation, failure to provide, 79

Enumerations of error, 264, 264 exhibit, 8–9
Ethical considerations
　attorney-client privilege, 95–97, 96–97 exhibit, 3–10
　avoiding conflicts of interest, 169
　avoiding fraudulent claims, 20–21
　client contact (paralegal), 66
　fraudulent medical practices, 299–300, 297 exhibit, 9–4
　insurance fraud, 237–238
　judicial ethics, 208
　quantity over quality, 272
　staying current in the law, 134
Evidence-based medicine, 281
Evidentiary rules, 197
Exclusion, 226
Exclusive remedy, 5
Ex parte meeting, 199

F

False representations by employee, 158
Federal appellate court system, 261–262
Federal Black Lung Program, 43
　black lung benefits identification card, 44 exhibit, 2–8
　miner's application for benefits, 45–48 exhibit, 2–9
Federal Employees' Compensation Act (FECA)
　criminal sanctions, 41, 41 exhibit, 2–6
　exceptions to, 34–35
　FECA coverage, 32 exhibit, 2–2
　federal workers as of 2004, 31 exhibit, 2–1
　federal workers' compensation system, 32
　Form CA-1, 39–40 exhibit, 2–5
　introduction, 31
　online site for FECA forms, 36–37 exhibit, 2–3
　qualifying for, 33
Federal internet sites, 301–302
Federal programs
　Defense Base Act (DBA), 56–57
　Federal Black Lung Program, 43, 44 exhibit, 2–8, 45–48 exhibit, 2–9
　Medicaid, 49–52
　Medicare, 49–52
　Social Security. *See* Social Security
Federal workers' compensation system
　benefits
　　continuation of pay (COP), 35, 37
　　introduction, 35
　claim for continuance of compensation, 38
　claims, filing, 37–41
　criminal sanctions, 41, 41 exhibit, 2–6
　exceptions to, 34–35
　Federal Employees' Compensation Act. *See* Federal Employees' Compensation Act (FECA)
　Form CA-1, 39–40 exhibit, 2–5
　history lesson, 32–33
　state and federal systems, differences between, 32
Fiduciary, 212
Firefighters, special protections for, 14, 14 exhibit, 1–6
Font sizes, 226
Foreseeability, 118
Fraud
　combating, 21
　denying benefits for, 14–15
　double-dipper, 54
　spotting (telltale signs), 21
Frolic
　definition of, 110
　deviation from employment (Florida), 111 exhibit, 4–5
Functional disability, 152

G

Generic drug, 281
Generic drug initiatives, 281
Grant cert, 261
Grievance procedures, 292

H

Healing period, 142–143
Hedonic damages, 152
Homosexual marriages, 157
Horseplay, 112
Human Resources (HR) Director, 102

I

Illegal aliens, 160
Immigration status, 160
Income benefit, 9
Indemnify, 212
Independent contractors
　court definitions of, 86 exhibit, 3–8
　definition of, 85
　status, determining, 86–88
Indirect employee, 75
Injuries
　accidental personal injury— claim application (Maryland), 102 exhibit, 4–1
　activities not strictly related to work
　　introduction, 117–118
　　personal comfort doctrine, 118–119
　"arising out of", 104–106
　coworker injury, 29
　defining, 102–103

distribution of injury and illness cases with days away from work, 120–121 exhibit, 4–9
emergencies, 119–120
injury under California law, 106 exhibit, 4–2
introduction, 101–102
reporting, 102–103
reporting deadlines, 102
selected occupations with high fatality rates, 2006, 133 exhibit, 4–10
Injuries, types of
acts of God, 113
acts of nature, 113
assault, 114
defined, 107
horseplay, 112
intoxication, 116
occupational diseases, 116–117
preexisting, 114
psychological, 112, 113 exhibit, 4–6
subsequent injury, 114–115
suicide, 115
travel as part of the job, 109–110
travel to and from work, 109–110
   detour, 110
   deviation from employment (Florida), 111 exhibit, 4–5
   dual purpose trips, 111–112
   frolic, 110
treatment for preexisting injuries, 115 exhibit, 4–7
when the employer must pay (Florida), 107 exhibit, 4–4
Insurance examiner, 161–162
Insurance fraud, 20, 21, 237
Intentional torts
coworker injury, 29
examples of, 28–29
tort, definition of, 28
Interrogatories, 185, 185 exhibit, 6–7

In the course of
defining injury for workers' compensation purposes, 106 exhibit, 4–3
definition of, 104, 106
Intoxication, 116
Involuntary intoxication, 116

J
Job placement services, 156

L
Last sickness, 156–157
Law enforcement, special protections for, 14, 14 exhibit, 1–6
Limited policy, 216
Lloyd's of London, 212
Longshore and Harbor Workers' Compensation Act of 1927, 41, 42 exhibit, 2–7
Lump sum, 246
Lump sum payment, 151–152, 251

M
Marks' Dependents v. *Gray*, 111
Maximum medical improvement (MMI), 161, 282
Medicaid
Centers for Medicare and Medicaid Services (CMS), 54–55
coordinating benefits, state and federal level, 54–55
definition of, 52
five tips for SSI or Medicaid hearings, 56 exhibit, 2–11
fraud, 54–55
medical fee schedules and, 281–282
Medicare, comparing to, 52
non-lawyer representation, 55
patient's request for medical payment, 50–51 exhibit, 2–10

qualifying for, 52
Medical benefits
expenses, 9, 113
healing period, 142–143
introduction, 139–140
non-standard injuries or illnesses, 141
physical rehabilitation, 141
preexisting injuries or illnesses, 141–142
transportation, 141
waiving, 140–141
Medical costs, 279 exhibit, 9–1
Medical expense, definition of, 9
Medical fee schedule, 281–282
Medical utilization, 276
Medical utilization issues
definition of, 277
income-based disparities, 280
introduction, 276–277
medical costs, 279 exhibit, 9–1
pre-employment physical testing, 277
pre-employment screening, 276
tracking medical costs, 279–280
Medicare
advocates, 55–56
Centers for Medicare and Medicaid Services (CMS), 54–55
coordinating benefits, on state and federal level, 54–55
definition of, 49–51
fraud, 54–55
Medicaid, comparing to, 52
medical fee schedules and, 281
patient's request for medical payment, 50–51 exhibit, 2–10
Workers' Compensation Medicare Set-aside Arrangement (WCMSA), 54
Motion for a continuance, 194

N

Near miss report, 278–279
Negligence, 25–26
"No fault", 3, 28
"No-fault" arrangement, 3
Notice of Appeal, 263

O

Occupational diseases, 116–117, 117 exhibit, 4–8
Occupational Safety and Health Administration (OSHA), 278
Odd jobs, 84

P

Pain and suffering
  awards for, 151–152
  definition of, 151
  medical benefits and, 139–140
Paralegals
  as advocates, 55–56
  attorney-client privilege, 95–97
  client contact, 66
  client mills and, 272
  compensation, 56
  conflicts of interest, avoiding, 169
  five tips for SSI or Medicaid hearings, 56 exhibit, 2–11
  worker health chartbook 2004, 96–97 exhibit, 3–10
Partial disability, defining, 146–150
Partnerships, 74
Permanent disability, determining, 148–150
Permanent partial disability, 145–150
  schedule for permanent partial losses (OHIO), 146–150 exhibit, 5–5
Permanent total disability, 150–151
Personal comfort doctrine
  definition of, 118
  examples of, 118–119
  foreseeability, 118
Petition for reconsideration, 251–252
  actions possible, 251
  deadlines, 252
Pre-employment physical testing, 277
Pre-employment screening, 276
Preexisting conditions, 153–154
Preexisting injuries, 114, 115 exhibit, 4–7
Premiums, 212, 222
Private insurance, 218
Product liability, 26–28
Professional athletes, 84–85
Pro se, 195
Psychological injuries, 112, 113 exhibit, 4–6

R

Record, the, 257
Regular employees, 83
Remand, 265
Request for a hearing, 176
Reverse, 265
Risk exposure, 222
Robber barons, 32
Rule of construction, 225
Rule of sequestration, 202

S

Schedule, definition of, 145
Schvaneveldt, Norma, 10, 12–13
Scope of employment, 107, 120, 177
Secondary (or further) hearing, 203
Self-inflicted wounds. *See* Suicide
Self-insurance, 88–89, 218
Self-insurer, 89, 218
  proof of workers' compensation coverage, 89 exhibit, 3–9
Serious disfigurement, 153
Settlement
  compromise and release (C and R), 246–249 exhibit, 8–2, 251
  cost of litigation, 246
  evaluation of claims, 250–251
  factors to consider, 247–250, 249 exhibit, 8–3
  introduction, 242
  lump sum payment, 243
  settlement agreement and application for approval of settlement agreement (Ohio), 244 exhibit, 8–1
Settling, 203
Social Security
  advocates, 55–56
  benefits, qualifying for, 48–49
  fraud, 54–55
  history of, 43–44, 47–49
  introduction, 43
  Social Security Disability Insurance (SSDI), 44, 49
  supplementals, 49
  Supplemental Security Insurance (SSI), 43, 49
Social Security Disability Insurance (SSDI), 44, 49
State-based insurance program, 217
State Court of Appeals
  appeals to the Court of Appeals (Colorado), 258 exhibit, 8–7
  appellate briefs, 263–264
  Notice of Appeal, 263
  powers of
    affirming a decision, 265
    modifying a decision, 265–266
    remanding a case, 266
    reversing a decision, 265
State Supreme Court, 260–261
Statutes of limitation, 177
Statutory employer
  definition of, 74

employee status, determining, 77
exemptions from coverage, 78 exhibit, 3–5
factors that determine statutory employee status, 77 exhibit, 3–4
Statutory employers, 74–75, 77
Subcontractors, 85
Subpoenas, 200–201, 201 exhibit, 6–13
Subrogation, 212
Subsequent injury, 114–115
Substantially economically dependent, 87
Suicide, 115
Superior Courts. *See* State Supreme Court
Supplemental Security Income (SSI) fund, 43
Supplemental Security Insurance (SSI), 43, 48, 49, 56

T

Temporary and permanent, differentiating between, 145
Temporary partial disability, 143, 144 exhibit, 5–2
Temporary total disability, 143–145
 defining (Wyoming), 145 exhibit, 5–3
 payments (Wyoming), 145 exhibit, 5–4
Time limits, 102, 102 exhibit, 4–1
Tool rule, 88
Tort, definition of, 28
Trust fund, 217

U

Underwriting, 218
United States court systems
 appellate court terminology, 260
 Court of Appeals, 259–260
 federal appellate court system, 261–262
 federal circuits in the U.S., 262 exhibit, 8–8
 organization of, 258–259
 state Supreme Court, 258–259
 U.S. Supreme Court, 260–261
"Unreasonably refusing", 159–160
U.S. Supreme Court, 260–261

V

Victimless crimes, 20–21, 237, 293
Video depositions, 184
Vocational rehabilitation, 155–156
Voluntary intoxication, 116

W

Websites
 American College of Occupational and Environmental Medicine, 301
 Arkansas Workers' Compensation Commission, 99
 Bureau of Labor Statistics—Work-related injuries, 210
 California Commission on Health and Safety, 68
 California Department of Health Services Prevention Services Program, 135
 California Workers' Compensation Appeals Board, 274
 Indiana Workers' Compensation Board, 274
 Industrial Commission of Arizona, 210
 IWIF, 136
 Labor Commission of Utah, 240
 Law Guru, 135
 Legal Information Institute, 23
 Louisiana Workers' Compensation Board, 99
 Minnesota Department of Labor and Industry (Temporary partial disability payments), 171
 Montana Permanent Partial Disability, 171
 Nebraska's Workers' Compensation Court, 136
 Nevada Division of Industrial Relations, 274
 New Hampshire Department of Labor, 136
 New York State Workers' Compensation Board, 23
 North Carolina Industrial Commission, 240
 Ohio Bureau of Workers' Compensation, 68
 Pennsylvania Department of Labor and Industry, 240
 Rhode Island Workers' Compensation Court, 210
 State of Florida Division of Administrative Hearings, 210
 State of South Carolina Workers' Compensation Commission, 210
 State of Wyoming Department of Employment, 274
 Texas Division of Workers' Compensation—Dispute Resolution, 210
 Texas Workers' Compensation Board, 23
 Texas Workers' Compensation Commission, 136
 Vermont Department of Labor, 171
 Vermont Department of Labor and Industry, 240
 Virginia Workers' Compensation Commission, 240
 Washington State Workers' Compensation Benefits, 171
 Wisconsin Department of Workforce Development, 210

Workers' Compensation Board of Indiana, 99
Witnesses
  cross examination, 202
  direct examination, 201–202
  refusal to testify, 202
  rule of sequestration, 202
  subpoenas, 200–201, 201 exhibit, 6–13
Workers' compensation
  basic premise of, 3
  benefits. *See* Benefits
  common-law influences on
    assumption of the risk, 26
    coworker injury, 29
    duty, 25–26
    negligence, 25–26
    product liability, 26–28
    torts, 28–29
  constitutional rights and, 5–6
  coverage
    exceptions, 6
    persons covered, 7–8
    persons not covered, 8
  definition of, 2
  exclusiveness of remedy, 5
  Florida permanent total supplemental benefits in workers' compensation cases, 1995–2006, 9 exhibit, 1–2
  history of, 4
  internet sites, 301–302
  introduction, 1–2
  number of fatal work injuries, 1992–2005, 4 exhibit, 1–1
  proof of workers' compensation coverage, 89 exhibit, 3–9
Workers' Compensation Appeals Board, 253–256, 257–258
Workers' Compensation Appellate Board, 254, 257
Workers' Compensation Board
  ALJ, as employee of, 199–200
  benefit disputes, 174
  benefits, determining amount of, 3, 10, 12–13
  components of, 251
  compromise and release, 246
  coverage, failure to provide, 79, 224
  definition of, 3
  disfigurement, 153
  documentation to be submitted to, 226–227
  duties of, 79, 150
  exclusions and, 226
  findings, changing by appellate court, 254
  fines/sanctions, 283
  general components of, 251
  grievance procedures, 292
  insurance examiners and, 161
  lump sum payments, 151
  medical benefits and, 141, 159–160, 278–279
  petition for reconsideration, 251–252
  policies/procedures, regulating, 221–222
  powers of, 222
  remand, 266
  responsibility and power of, 10, 251
  state-based insurance fund, 217
  subpoena forms, 197, 201
  Workers' Compensation Appeals Board, 254–258
  workers' compensation files, 186–187
Workers' compensation file
  adding documents to, 187
  availability of, 187
  reviewing, 186–187
Workers' compensation hearings
  arbitration hearing, 187, 189
  attorneys, compensating, 195–196
  benefit review conference (BRC), 187
  canceling, 194
  concluding, 203
  conducting
    introduction, 200
    subpoenas, 200–201
    witnesses. *See* Witnesses
  "deems the case submitted", 203
  description of (Schvaneveldt), 10, 12–13
  evidentiary rules, 197
  the flow of a Pennsylvania workers' compensation claim, 188–189 exhibit, 6–9
  hearing date, 194
  Illinois Workers' Compensation Commission 19 (b-1) arbitration decision, 192–193 exhibit, 6–11
  location of, 194
  motion for a continuance, 194
  presentations, 202 exhibit, 6–14
  recording, 203
  representation at, 194–196
  secondary (or further) hearing, 203
  settling cases, 203
  workers' compensation claim flowchart (Wisconsin), 190–191 exhibit, 6–10
Workers' compensation insurance
  "accepting a claim", definition of, 216
  funds collected, investment requirements, 218, 220–221
  insurance, introduction to, 211–212
  introduction, 213–216
  "limited policy", 216
  multiple policies, 216
  notice to employees regarding workers' compensation (Massachusetts), 215 exhibit, 7–2

obtaining, ways to, 217
   enrollment in state-based insurance program, 217
   purchasing private insurance, 218
   self-insurance, 218
policy ambiguities
   declaratory judgment (or declaratory action), 228
   documentation to be submitted, 226–227
   duty to defend, 227–228
   exclusions, 226
   font sizes, 226
   introduction, 225–226
   rule of construction, 225
posting notice (New Jersey), 214 exhibit, 7–1
requirement to provide, 216–221
standard coverage form, group self-insurance (Georgia), 219–220 exhibit, 7–3
state regulation of
   classifications, 222
      complaint of improper claims handling against an insurer (Massachusetts), 223 exhibit, 7–4
      failure to secure, 224 exhibit, 7–5
      introduction, 221
      penalties, 224
      premiums, 222
      rates, 221–222
      refusal to pay benefits, 222–224
      verifying coverage, 224
worker health chartbook 2004, 238 exhibit, 7–6
Workers' Compensation Medicare Set-aside Arrangement (WCMSA), 54
Workers' compensation system
   Administrative Law Judge (ALJ)
      communicating with, 199
      ex parte meeting, 199
      powers of, 198
      request a different judge, 199
      role of, 198, 199–200
   benefit disputes, 174
   carrier's response (Michigan), 183 exhibit, 6–6
   claim petition for workers' compensation (Pennsylvania), 178–179 exhibit, 6–4
   defendant's answer to claim petition under Pennsylvania Workers' Compensation Act, 181–182 exhibit, 6–5
   discovery. *See* Discovery
   fatal occupational injuries (Illinois), 175 exhibit, 6–1
   filing a claim
      employers contest of compensability (Texas), 176 exhibit, 6–2
      introduction, 174
      request for a hearing, 176
      filing forms, 178
   hearings. *See* Workers' compensation hearings
   introduction, 173
   national health spending in millions, 299 exhibit, 9–4
   notice of hearing, 177
   proposals to improve
      claims handlers, new/better training programs for, 283
      disability ratings, training physicians in, 282–283
      evidence-based medicine, 282
      fraud protection, better, 292–293
      generic drug initiatives, 281
      grievance procedures, streamlined, 292
      medical fee schedules, 281–282
      primary treating physician's permanent and stationary report (California), 284–291 exhibit, 9–2
      sanctions and fines, revised, 281, 283
   statutes of limitation, 177
   time bars to filing for benefits (Florida), 177 exhibit, 6–3
   Utah Rule R602-2, 186 exhibit, 6–8

CPSIA information can be obtained
at www.ICGtesting.com
Printed in the USA
FFOW01n2122211216
30634FF